Religion at the European Parliament and in European Multi-level Governance

T0316384

This book presents the findings of the first ever survey of the religious preferences of Members of the European Parliament (MEPs). An international research team interviewed a large sample of MEPs, with the purpose of investigating their beliefs and how these beliefs have an impact on their role as MEPs.

The findings of this survey are offered in order to discuss, in a non-normative way, some key political and intellectual debates. Is Europe secularised? Is the European Union a Christian club? What is the influence of religious lobbying in Brussels? What are the dynamics of value politics? Contributions also compare MEPs with national MPs and citizens to measure whether the findings are specific to the supranational arena and European multi-level governance. External cases, such as the USA and Israel, are also presented to define whether there is a European exceptionalism regarding the role of religion in the political arena.

This book was originally published as a special issue of *Religion, State & Society*.

François Foret is Professor of Political Science and Jean Monnet Chair at the Université Libre de Bruxelles (ULB), Belgium. He is also Director for Political Research at the Institute for European Studies at ULB and a researcher at the Centre d'Etude de la Vie Politique (CEVIPOL). He is Senior Associate Fellow at the Von Hugel Institute, St Edmund's College, University of Cambridge, UK.

Religion at the European Parliament and in European Multi-level Governance

Edited by
François Foret

LONDON AND NEW YORK

First published 2015
by Routledge

2 Park Square, Milton Park, Abingdon, Oxon OX14 4RN
711 Third Avenue, New York, NY 10017, USA

Routledge is an imprint of the Taylor & Francis Group, an informa business

First issued in paperback 2017

British Library Cataloguing in Publication Data
A catalogue record for this book is available from the British Library

ISBN: 978-1-138-90117-9 (hbk)
ISBN: 978-1-138-08290-8 (pbk)

Typeset in Times
by Out of House Publishing

Publisher's Note
The publisher accepts responsibility for any inconsistencies that may have arisen
during the conversion of this book from journal articles to book chapters,
namely the possible inclusion of journal terminology.

Disclaimer
Every effort has been made to contact copyright holders for their permission to
reprint material in this book. The publishers would be grateful to hear from
any copyright holder who is not here acknowledged and will undertake
to rectify any errors or omissions in future editions of this book.

Contents

CONTENTS

Citation Information

The chapters in this book were originally published in *Religion, State & Society*, volume 42, issues 2–3 (June–September 2014). When citing this material, please use the original page numbering for each article, as follows:

Please direct any queries you may have about the citations to
clsuk.permissions@cengage.com

Notes on Contributors

Stefano Braghiroli is a post-doctoral researcher at the Institute of Government and Politics at the University of Tartu, Estonia. His main research interests include party politics in the European Parliament, EU–Russia relations, electoral politics in Central and Eastern Europe and Turkey, and e-politics.

Didier Caluwaerts is a post-doctoral researcher in Political Science at the Vrije Universiteit Brussel, Belgium. His research interests include deliberative and participatory democracy, social and public sector innovation, and cooperative governance.

Pieter-Jan De Vlieger obtained his PhD in Political Science at the Vrije Universiteit Brussel, Belgium, in 2012. His PhD was entitled "Lobbying in the Service of God and Church: the Adaptation of Church Representations to the European Union's Interest Group System". He is currently working at the Strategic Policy Unit of the Department of Education and Training of the Flemish administration.

Silvia Erzeel is a research officer at the Political Science Centre for Comparative Politics at the Université Catholique de Louvain, Belgium. Her research interests include comparative politics and elections, political representation and political parties.

François Foret is Professor of Political Science and Jean Monnet Chair at the Université Libre de Bruxelles (ULB), Belgium. He is also Director for Political Research at the Institute for European Studies at ULB and a researcher at the Centre d'Etude de la Vie Politique (CEVIPOL). He is Senior Associate Fellow at the Von Hugel Institute, St Edmund's College, University of Cambridge, UK.

Gloria García-Romeral is a post-doctoral researcher in the Department of Sociology at the Universitat Autònoma de Barcelona, Spain. Her research interests include religion and politics, religious pluralism and secularisation.

Magdalena Góra is a researcher at the Institute of European Studies at Jagiellonian University, Kraków, Poland. Her research interests include European foreign policy, the enlargement of the European Union, European integration, and Polish–Jewish and Polish–Israeli relations.

Mar Griera is an Assistant Professor in the Sociology Department of the Universitat Autònoma de Barcelona, Spain. Her research interests lie at the intersection of religion, spirituality, identity, politics and memory.

NOTES ON CONTRIBUTORS

James L. Guth is Professor of Political Science at Furman University, Greenville, SC, USA. A specialist in American politics, his recent work has assessed the impact of religion on the electoral process and on public policy in the Clinton, Bush and Obama administrations.

Anne Jenichen is a researcher at the Jean Monnet Centre for European Studies at the University of Bremen, Germany. Her research interests include EU foreign policies, multilevel governance, and the relationship between religion and politics.

Henrike Müller is a researcher at the Jean Monnet Centre for European Studies at the University of Bremen, Germany. She teaches on Europeanisation, gender studies and the relationship between religion and democracy.

Julia Mourão Permoser is Assistant Professor at the research platform Religion and Transformation in Contemporary European Society, University of Vienna, Austria. Her research focuses on migration, citizenship, belonging and religion. She is also particularly interested in the European Union as a political construct where politics takes place beyond the nation.

Giulia Sandri is Assistant Professor of Political Science at the Catholic University of Lille, France. Her main research interests are party politics, primary elections, political behaviour, and quality of democracy, ethno-regional parties and regional elections.

Martin Steven is a Lecturer in Politics and International Relations at Lancaster University, UK. His research interests lie in the area of comparative politics and government, with a particular focus on the United Kingdom as well as the wider European Union, examining the behaviour of political parties and interest groups in the public policy process.

Sharon Weinblum is a post-doctoral fellow at St. Anne's College, University of Oxford, UK. She is interested in competing conceptions of the border and sovereignty, and discourses on, and policies of asylum and migration, with a particular focus on the case of Israel.

Katarzyna Zielińska is an Associate Professor of Sociology at Jagiellonian University, Kraków, Poland.

INTRODUCTION

'Religion at the European Parliament': purposes, scope and limits of a survey on the religious beliefs of MEPs

François Foret

Institute for European Studies - CEVIPOL, Université Libre de Bruxelles (ULB), Brussels, Belgium

The project 'Religion at the European Parliament' (RelEP) is an attempt to provide data on the religious profile of the European Parliament (EP). Looking at what members of the European Parliament (MEPs) believe and what they do as a result of these beliefs, the research analyses the place of religion in European politics and its influence on political elites, political socialisation, decision-making and coalition-framing. Three main incentives motivated the RelEP project.

First, it is a contribution to the understanding of the new visibility of religion on the agenda of the European Union (EU). Evidence of the secularisation of European societies coexists with the recognition of the greater political and public salience of religious issues. This apparent paradox has to be documented. After a long absence, religion has become a hot topic in international scholarship since the beginning of the twenty-first century. However, the focus has been more on international relations or public policy than on politics. RelEP is a first attempt to map the religious composition of the EP, in contrast with the abundant literature detailing religion in parliamentary politics in the USA over decades.

Second, religion speaks about something beyond religion. As a social universe rooted in tradition, in the depths of individual and collective identity and intertwined with the state and national culture, it is a very sensitive barometer of the extent and modalities of Europeanisation.

Third, the RelEP survey includes a comparison between member-states but also between the supranational and the national levels. By comparing the way MEPs and national members of Parliament (MPs) handle religion, something can be said on the autonomy and specificity of the EU as a proper political order. Asking whether or not what happens in Brussels reflects what happens in national societies invites us to search for any bias possibly inherent in channels of European policy-making and representation.

The structure of this publication is as follows. This present contribution briefly places the RelEP project in the 'state of the art' on religion in European politics. It describes the purposes and means of the survey, the constraints and opportunities met by the research process, the main conceptual questions underlying the questionnaire and the composition of the sample. The second contribution presents an overview of the main findings. Case studies follow on member-states which have been particularly the focus of the analysis. To complete the reflection, contributions on two non-European and radically different countries, the USA and Israel, offer a critical distance to assess the specificity of the EU.

RelEP in context: contribution to scholarship and internal dynamic of the project

The purpose of RelEP is to fill a blank in the knowledge of the cultural profile of European political elites on the one hand, and on the specificity of interactions between religion and politics at the supranational level on the other hand. The organisation of the research reflects this purpose and complies with the constraints of a normative object such as religion, calling for a flexible and adaptative approach.

An attempt to fill a gap in the existing scholarship

God is again in the focus of social sciences. Major theorists of the expected extinction of religion by modernity have reversed their diagnosis and speak now of desecularisation all over the world (Berger 1999). Europe remains the exception (Berger, Davie, and Fokas 2008), with a steady decline of beliefs and practices. Religion does not disappear but mutates into a memory, a ritual provider or ethos (Davie 2002). Faith is less and less regulated by institutions and absolute truth, and more and more an individual relativistic choice. Its political effects persist, but mainly as a diffuse influence or symbolic material (Capelle-Pogacean, Michel, and Pace 2008; Willaime 2004).

If spiritual evolutions are well documented by sociologists of religion, linking European integration and religion is not easy for political scientists. Europe is frequently considered more as a civilisational and geographical entity than as a political system (Huntington 1993; Jenkins 2007). As a discipline rooted originally mainly in international relations and political economy with a realist mainstream, European studies has for long been little receptive of such ideational factors as religion, apart from historical or normative approaches (Habermas 2010; Weiler 2003; Weigel 2005) offering inputs in the debate on the Christian heritage of Europe but saying little on its contemporary effects.

For a long time, religion was not among the 'usual suspects' in European studies, given the interest-driven and functionalist mainstream view in this field. This has changed in the last decade, with a wave of new research by established or new scholars acknowledging the salience of the religious question. The religious issue has become totally congruent with the 'identity-turn' recently taken by scholarship on European integration: religion is being rediscovered as a part of collective culture and memory likely to frame policy preferences. The 'normalisation' of the EU, which is more and more seen as a polity to be compared to other polities of the past and the present, takes us back to one of the oldest questions of political science: relationships between spiritual and secular powers. To fight the deficit of legitimacy of the EU, many voices call for a politicisation of the bloc in order to organise and solve conflicts in European arenas. If politicisation means searching for controversial issues able to polarise collective preferences and to mobilise coalitions in democratic debates, religion is a likely candidate.

For empirical reasons regarding the difficulty of accessing data and the reluctance of actors to express their beliefs, the focus is frequently on relatively 'open sources': on relationships between denominational lobbies and the European Commission (EC) (Massignon 2007; Leustean 2012; Mudrov 2011; De Vlieger 2012), on impacts of religion on the legitimisation of the EU (Foret 2009), on how European law may relate to religion (McCrea 2011), and on how national church–state arrangements evolve in the context of European integration (Madeley and Enyedi 2003; Robbers 1997; Foret and Itçaina 2011; Leustean and Madeley 2009). The resilience and perhaps even the resurgence of the divide between sacred and secular forces in attitudes towards Europe, voting and party structuring in European elections are suggested (Nelsen, Guth, and Highsmith 2011;

Broughton and ten Napel 2000; Minkenberg 2009, 2010; Van der Brug, Hobolt, and de Vreese 2009; Hobolt et al. 2011; Chenaux 2007; Kaiser 2007; Fontaine 2009). The actual effects of religion in Brussels politics and policies are far less documented.

Much remains to be known on this potential role. Research tends to focus on philosophical and/or legal aspects, or on phenomena relatively accessible, such as lobbying. To collect and objectify data regarding religious impact on practices and decisions of politicians is more challenging. That is the purpose of RelEP.

The empirical study

Why the European Parliament?

The European Parliament is the largest sample of European political elites. Its election by universal suffrage in 27 (at the time of the survey) national spaces makes it a good reflection of the cultural and religious diversity of European societies. As an assembly expressing popular sovereignty, it is the most political arena of the EU where the full range of ideological visions can be expressed and where dissent is the most likely to emerge. In European decision-making, the EP is frequently the place where conflicts occur. Its very representative nature predisposes it to be the privileged forum for the interference of religion in politics.

An empirical survey was carried out between 2010 and 2013, leading to the completion of a questionnaire by 167 MEPs. The purpose was to study the role of religion in the activities of MEPs in order to understand to what extent and how religion becomes political. Religion (or secondarily philosophical world view) was considered at three levels: first, as a personal inspiration likely to intervene in the decision of the representative; second, as a vector of socialisation building bridges or digging gaps between established belongings (party, national and denominational), through participation in working groups or interactions with religious interest groups; third, as a political issue to be dealt with which questions the usual rationalisation of the European policy process.

A questionnaire distributed to all MEPs was used as the common analytical framework for all teams in charge of their respective national cases. This questionnaire was supplemented by two other sources. First, relevant case studies were carried out on religiously loaded policy issues discussed at the EP. These policy case studies are complementary to the findings offered by the survey and go further down the path opened by some thematic questions (especially on the Christian heritage of Europe, Turkey and bioethics). National teams may have chosen to deepen such and such a policy issue according to the relevance of the topic regarding their respective MEPs. Second, data were gathered to compare the way MEPs relate to religion to what we know of national representatives. The purpose was to assess whether there is a specificity in the level of secularisation of European legislators and, subsequently, whether it shows a secularising effect of the EU selection and decision-making process. As the quantity and quality of data on national political elites and religion are very different from one country to another, results may vary significantly.

An attempt was also made to discuss European specificities by confrontation to non-European cases. Specialists on the USA and Israel were invited to offer an insight of religion in parliamentary politics in these countries while using as much as possible the same thematic framework followed by the RelEP team. The purpose is to describe interactions between religion and politics in other modern democratic societies and to observe similarities and differences with the EU. The USA is also particularly interesting as the American literature on religion and politics is highly developed and works as a source of inspiration of the RelEP project on many points. Of course, Israel and the USA are very specific models regarding the strength of American civil religion and religiosity and the constitutive nature of Judaism for the Israeli state. To a certain extent, they appear as 'most different cases' for the EU, according to a common practice in comparative politics to confront opposite realities. Israel and the USA can be seen as kinds of control variables highlighting possible features inherent in European multi-level governance based on compromise and hybridisation, but also similar patterns at work in all parliaments and societies despite radically different contexts.

A flexible methodology required by a difficult object

Regarding the methodology, the choice was twofold: on the one hand, to use a questionnaire with closed questions in order to facilitate the commensurability and the aggregation of answers; on the other hand, to 'open' the questions when possible during the face-to-face interviews by inviting MEPs to develop and clarify their statements. This dual approach offered a way to produce a global and systematic image of the sample, while leaving room for adaptation in order to integrate variations and unexpected directions.

Similarly, the gathering of data relied on several options. Face-to-face interviews, phone interviews and online surveys were combined to maximise the number of respondents. Face-to-face interviews have the advantage of allowing in-depth interactions and the collection of extensive information. They also provide the opportunity to grasp the emotional and normative dimension of a topic such as religion and to adopt an empathic approach to an individual's incentives. That is the reason why, when possible, face-to-face interviews were preferred, especially for MEPs particularly involved with religious issues. Conversely, a survey via the internet also has many points in its favour. It is the option most often used by large-scale research projects on MEPs[1] for several reasons which are also valid for RelEP. It is cost-efficient and flexible, an important factor when the questionnaire is used in nine languages as in our research. It allows the questionnaire to be adapted to the interviewees (for example, to ask MEPs which denomination they belong to only if they say that they do in fact belong to one). It is a way of reducing the possibility of errors in collecting and coding data and of increasing the ease of aggregating them, a factor of some importance when several national teams are at work. It reinforces anonymity, a crucial dimension on sensitive issues like religion. It neutralises the effect of the interviewer, always a possible interference when a normative choice is at stake. It gives more time to the respondent. An internet-based approach may be well adapted for elite surveys which target a busy, mobile and geographically dispersed public, difficult to reach physically but used to new technologies.

Interviews were conducted and questionnaires implemented in most cases in the mother tongue of the MEP by a native speaker. National teams of researchers managed the interactions with their representatives. This is important for two reasons. First, the linguistic abilities of MEPs should not be overestimated, and a significant proportion of them are not fluent or even literate in English. Second, religion is an intimate part of collective and individual identity and it is better to tackle it within the cultural universe specific to each language. The work by national teams is also justified in the exploitation of data. The results have to be interpreted not only globally but also on a state-by-state basis, as national affiliation remains the most discriminatory variable. Besides, this enables one to put the data into national contexts, focusing in particular on two elements: the general relevance of religion in the national debate on Europe; and the comparison with the place of religion in domestic political life and in the visions of national elites of each country.

The choice to work preferably in the national language of the MEP and with a researcher highly familiar with the national debate on religion and politics comes with a cost. It would be very expensive and time-consuming to mobilise a team per member state.[2] An online survey was diffused to all MEPs in two waves with little spontaneous feedback. Most answers were gathered by direct contact through the work of national teams or of research fellows hired in Brussels. To maximise efficiency, the choice was made to focus efforts on larger member-states with the biggest delegations at the EP. The availability and willingness of MEPs to answer was another major constraint in the constitution of the sample. The case studies developed by contributors are the result of such choices and constraints.

Breaking down the sample: MEPs in their diversity

An interview-based research study of a public as difficult to access as MEPs and on a topic as controversial as religion is empirically challenging. The questionnaire was applied to 167 out of 736 MEPs, that is 22.69% of the representatives elected in 2009, the year of reference taken for all indicators. This percentage is comparable to that of many large surveys carried out on the EP or other assemblies. For example, the landmark analysis by Benson and Williams, *Religion on Capitol Hill*, relied on a study of 80 members of Congress out of 535 (about 15 per cent) (Benson and Williams 1982). When possible, findings by RelEP were compared to data produced by other surveys (Hix, Scully, and Farrell 2011; the PartiRep network) and no visible discrepancies were observed. Answers by MEPs were also compared with answers to the same questions taken from the European Values Study by ordinary citizens. The purpose of the RelEP survey was to reconcile realities in the field (the presence or absence of opportunities to have interviews) with the concern to avoid any major bias likely to distort the data. At the end of the research process, the result can be said to be satisfying. Several variables are discussed to identify the sample of MEPs and what this may mean for the findings on the religious preferences of MEPs: their nationality, gender and age, political group at the EP, national political party, seniority at the EP, and memberships of thematic committees.

Distribution by country

The survey was submitted to representatives from 27 member-states (Croatia being not yet integrated). MEPs from 16 member-states responded. In this global sample, there is an expected prevalence of larger countries (France, Germany, Italy, Romania, the UK, Poland, Spain). Several member-states are not included because of refusals or silence from their MEPs: Baltic and Scandinavian countries, Portugal, Malta, Cyprus, Slovenia, Slovakia. These countries would have offered interesting case studies, especially northern countries offering examples of Protestant cultures in interaction with Europe. Beyond reluctance to answer on the part of their representatives, these countries are small or medium-sized, and consequently have small delegations, a limit to the opportunity to gather data. Three quarters (72.46%) of the sample are MEPs from older member-states (before 2004), but there are also significant Polish and Romanian delegations. In the final sample, there is a majority of representatives from Catholic societies and a minority from Protestant societies. MEPs from Orthodox countries are also fairly well represented, though mostly by Romania.

In the final analysis, eight member-states are most specifically dealt with by national teams of researchers (France, Italy, Germany, Netherlands, the UK, Austria, Poland,

Table 1.   Distribution of respondents by country.

Member-state	Share of the sample (%)	Share of seats in the EP (%)	Difference (%)
France	14.97	9.78	5.19
Germany	14.97	13.45	1.52
Italy	11.38	9.78	1.59
Romania	10.18	4.48	5.70
United Kingdom	10.18	9.78	0.40
Poland	8.38	6.79	1.59
Belgium	5.99	2.99	3.00
Czech Republic	5.39	2.99	2.40
Netherlands	4.79	3.40	1.39
Austria	4.19	2.31	1.88
Hungary	2.99	2.99	0.00
Ireland	2.40	1.63	0.76
Spain	1.80	6.79	−5.00
Greece	1.20	2.99	−1.79
Luxembourg	0.60	0.82	−0.22
Bulgaria	0.60	2.31	−1.71

Spain). The focus on these eight countries results from a mix between analytical choices and the hazards of fieldwork. For example, a contribution was scheduled on Romania but in the end the researchers in charge of this case were not able to deliver it. Efforts were mainly targeted on these eight national delegations in order to gather as many interviews as possible. Overall, the purpose was to achieve a balance: in terms of denominations (five societies with clear Catholic majorities, two with a strong historical presence of both Protestantism and Catholicism, one Anglican usually associated with Protestantism in social surveys); in terms of legal and institutional systems dealing with religion (from the nominally established church in the UK to 'laïque' France, with several intermediary cases including consociational models); in terms of very secularised (France, the Netherlands) and less secularised (Poland, Italy) societies; large and medium countries; founding member-states and latecomers in the EU.

Since RelEP constitutes the first attempt to gather data on the religious composition of the EP, and since many MEPs declined to answer, findings are to be interpreted with due caution (Table 1).

Distribution by gender

The sample is more masculine than the whole EP (72.46% as opposed to 65% in the EP elected in 2009 (see Corbett, Jacobs, and Shackleton 2011, 53)). It is difficult to infer anything from this fact. The difference between the religiosity of men and women is tending to become less salient than it used to be in European societies. There is still a gender gap, as women are likely to be more religious, but this influence on the specific cases of MEPs is probably without major significance (Table 2).

Table 2.   Distribution of respondents by gender.

Gender	Share of the sample (%)	Share at the EP (2009) (%)	Difference (%)
Female	27.54	35	−7.46
Male	72.46	65	7.46

Distribution by age

The average age of the sample is 54, the youngest MEP of the sample being 28 and the eldest 77, with 80% of representatives being over 46. The distribution across generations is comparable to that of the whole EP, and roughly speaking is not so different from that of national political elites. No significant influence is expected from this variable (Table 3).

Distribution by political affiliation

Regarding political affiliation, the representativeness of the sample is very good. The only small bias is a slight over-representation of the European People's Party (38.32% in the sample, 36.01% in the EP), and a small under-representation of the Socialists and Democrats (21.56% as opposed to 25%). Other gaps are not significant. The ideological diversity within political groups at the EP is also well represented as representatives of about 70 different national parties responded to the survey (Table 4).

Distribution by seniority at the EP

Another important variable is seniority, as the socialising influence of the EP is likely to grow with the years in office. Again, the sample is largely congruent with the whole

Table 3. Distribution of respondents by age.

Age (intervals)	Number of MEPs interviewed	Share of the sample (%)
26–30	4	2.40
31–35	4	2.40
36–40	14	8.38
41–45	9	5.39
46–50	26	15.57
51–55	27	16.17
56–60	35	20.96
61–65	27	16.17
66–70	13	7.78
71–75	7	4.19
76–80	1	0.60

Table 4. Distribution of respondents by political group.

Political group	Share of the sample (%)	Share of seats in the EP (%)	Difference (%)
Group of the European People's Party	38.32	36.00	2.32
Group of the Progressive Alliance of Socialists and Democrats	21.56	25.00	−3.44
Group of the Alliance of Liberals and Democrats for Europe	12.57	11.41	1.16
Group of the Greens/European Free Alliance	7.19	7.47	−0.29
European Conservatives and Reformists Group	7.19	7.34	−0.15
Confederal Group of the European United Left/ Nordic Green Left	5.99	4.76	1.23
Europe of Freedom and Democracy Group	3.59	4.35	−0.76
Non-Attached Members	3.59	3.67	−0.08

Table 5.   Distribution of respondents by seniority.

Number of terms in the EP	Number of MEPs	Share of the sample (%)
1	78	46.71
2	50	29.94
3	24	14.37
4	9	5.39
5	4	2.40
6	1	0.60

assembly. In both cases, roughly half of MEPs are 'first timers' (53.29% of the sample as compared with 49.6% of all MEPs). Almost a quarter of the sample (23.5%) have served three terms or more (Table 5).

Distribution by committees

The institutional diversity of the EP is also represented in the sample with regard to the number of committees to which MEPs belong. There are no possible systematic correlations between membership of a committee and interest in religious issues. Religion is too much of a low-profile issue to structure such affiliations, and MEPs have their say but are not always able to choose where they will sit (Corbett, Jacobs, and Shackleton 2011, 146). Besides, the size of the committees ranges from 24 to 76 members, which automatically makes their statistical weight very unequal. However, the working environment offered by the different committees may influence the way MEPs deal with religion. It is therefore important to have a large picture encompassing numerous policy sectors. This is the case with the sample of interviewees (Table 6).

Table 6.   Distribution of respondents by committee membership.

Committee	Number of MEPs interviewed	Share of the sample (%)
Regional Development	18	10.78
Foreign Affairs	17	10.18
Economic and Monetary Affairs	14	8.38
Civil Liberties, Justice and Home Affairs	14	8.38
Employment and Social Affairs	13	7.78
Industry, Research and Consumer Protection	11	6.59
Budgets	10	5.99
Environment, Public Health and Food Safety	10	5.99
Development	8	4.79
Internal Market and Consumer Protection	8	4.79
Agriculture and Rural Development	8	4.79
Culture and Education	7	4.19
Legal Affairs	7	4.19
International Trade	6	3.59
Transport and Tourism	5	2.99
Fisheries	4	2.40
Budgetary Control	3	1.80
Constitutional Affairs	2	1.20
Women's Rights and Gender Equality	1	0.60
Financial, Economic and Social Crisis	1	0.60

Scientific guidelines of the project

The survey had three main lines of investigation. A first line considers how to identify religion as a political factor in parliamentary politics and how to measure its effects on various political activities and affiliations (national, denominational, party). A second line concerns religion as a policy issue. As such, it has a variable salience across policy sectors. Besides, it may challenge the usual search for compromise which rules European policy-making as it sets some values as non-negotiable. Hence, the purpose is to find out whether religion is 'business as usual' in parliamentary politics or creates specific conflicts, cleavages and strategies. A third and final line investigates the way the parliamentary institution is able to frame the religious preferences of politicians on the one hand and religious issues on the other. The framing of individual preferences can be assessed by observing the effect of the longevity of legislators within the EP on how they handle religion. As regards religious issues, the socialising effect of the EP institution can be seen if the amount of time a controversy involving moral choices related to religious beliefs has been active is shown to correlate with a kind of 'agreeing how to disagree'. Either the need for compromise prevails in order to protect the functioning of the EP and politicians develop ways to comply with this constraint while making symbolic uses of religion, or religion prevails as an absolute value.

These transversal lines of investigations underlie the questionnaire used as a framework for RelEP. Questions are gathered in five thematic sets: socio-political profile of MEPs; impact of religion on their work and on the functioning of the EP; religion in the political practice and political socialisation of MEPs; religion across policy sectors; individual religious beliefs, behaviours and attitudes of MEPs. Letters between brackets refer to the place of questions in the questionnaire at the end of this introduction.

Socio-political profile of MEPs and religion

A first set of questions (A–G) gathers information on the socio-political profile of MEPs (nationality, age, political membership in terms of party and political group, seniority in the EP, participation in committees). The relatively small size of the sample is not likely to provide evidence of very significant gaps in terms of age and gender. Nationality is expected to act as the main marker. National belonging is still the most reliable prediction factor in the framing of European identity and relationship to the EU, as well as the most discriminating variable in value surveys. The hypothesis is that national political culture and compliance with the national historical model of relationship between politics and religion are major parameters defining the attitudes and behaviours of MEPs.

Questions on party membership and political groups are used to map the ideological sphere of the EP, and to see whether responses regarding religion duplicate formal political divides. On this point, the hypothesis is twofold. On the one hand, gaps between political families are reducing and blurring, as religious/philosophical loyalties are declining and individualising. On the other hand, visible polarities still remain as path dependencies: members of parties with a history of religious affiliation are likely to display more proximity to religion, and members of a party with a strong secularist/antireligious tradition are likely to be neutral or hostile towards religion. For political groups at the EP, tactical necessities of coalition-making at the European level may lead to transgressing without deleting ideological cleavages. The best example is the European People's Party. Its heritage of Christian Democracy has been diluted by successive enlargements, but still remains, and may even have been reactivated in recent years. Social Democrats and

Liberals are committed to supporting fundamental rights. This may lead to alliances with religious forces on social rights, but oppositions on ethical issues (gender, sexual preferences, reproduction). Extreme right formations may promote culturalist views rooted in hard-core Christianity to defend national identity and/or European civilisation or various versions of paganism, but also use secularism as a resource for attacks on Islam. The relationship between party and group memberships is in itself interesting: some national parties with a strong religious reference struggle to integrate stable coalitions inside the EP, religion sometimes acting as a mischief-maker.

The number of terms an MEP has been sitting in Brussels and Strasbourg provides a fundamental indication to assess the socialising capacity of the EP, and the way individual religious preferences are dealt with and expressed in the European arena. Here, literature about religion in American legislative politics tells us that the experience of an MP is crucial (Oldmixon 2005, 35 ff.). Seasoned legislators are not necessarily more secularised; in fact the House of Representatives does not seem to have the ability to alter the personal religious preferences of its members. But they are are more likely than newcomers to compromise on moral issues. The more deals you have cut in the past, the more likely you are to cut some more. A socialising effect of the institution can be acknowledged in the form of a concern to make the machine work. However, considering the turnover at the EP, this cumulative effect of successive terms is bound to be restricted.

Taking account of committees in which MEPs are active provides an opportunity to observe possible correlations between levels of religiosity and fields of action. The hypothesis is that a high level of religiosity may influence involvement in some key policy domains where the religious dimension has a specific salience, notably those related to fundamental rights, education and culture and – to a lesser extent – foreign affairs. But again, institutional and political factors matter: an MEP is not necessarily able to choose the committees he or she is a member of, or has the time to develop a real specialisation in a given field.

Impact of religion on the work of MEPs and on the functioning of the EP

A second set of questions (1–4) deals with MEPs' assessments of the impact of religion on the way the EP works. The purpose is to establish whether or not religion as a multi-dimensional variable has effects on overall functioning of the EP (1). More precisely, religion may contribute to – or hamper – the formation of various belongings and loyalties (political groups, nationality, denomination).

The cohesive or divisive effect of religion on political groups (2) has to be understood according to its impact on their ideological identity. The hypothesis here is that it has a dual impact: religion does not work as a matrix encompassing party identity totally, but nevertheless works as a polarity attracting MEPs in greater or lesser numbers depending on their political affiliation, the right being roughly speaking closer than the left to the 'religion' pole.

The second belonging/loyalty to which religion may contribute is nationality (3). All MEPs of the same nationality may be predisposed to adopt the same attitude towards religion because of the influence of the national model of church–state relations, because of a similar values profile or because of compliance with the mainstream orientation of the national electorate. Nationality may also act in favour of coalition-building inside political groups. MEPs of the same nationality in the same political family are likely to share a common ideological posture towards religion and to react similarly to religiously-loaded issues. However, MEPs of the same nationality in the same political group can belong to different national parties with different historical relationships to religion (see for example the Italians inside the EPP with more or less proximity to the former Christian Democracy).

The third belonging/loyalty upon which religion may act is of course denomination (4). Here, cleavages may occur among different faiths. Another possibility is the existence of a gap cutting across denominations between conservative and liberals; or a more general division between religious and non-religious individuals. Denominational belonging has to be balanced by level of religiosity. Sociology of religion in contemporary Europe suggests that it works as a heritage and a cultural marker but not as a specific matrix defining the substance of political decision. Denominational belonging is likely to create a path dependence influencing the attitude and behaviour of MEPs, but the level of integration into a religious system may come into play to differentiate a given MEP from others of the same or of different denominations. To give an example, a Catholic MEP may be more influenced by the logic of 'laicisation' (separation between church and state) than a Protestant MEP who may be more in tune with the logic of secularisation (dilution of religion in the social world and combination with political modernity and national identity). However, the more or less conservative positions of the two MEPs may result more from their respective levels of religiosity (deeper integration within a religious tradition, a stronger inclination towards conservatism) than from their different faiths.

Religion in the political practice and political socialisation of MEPs

A third set of questions (5–10) tackles religion in the political practice and political socialisation of MEPs. The interference of religion with politics is to be understood firstly in terms of the frequency with which an MEP takes religion into account. Secondly, the form of interference determines its potential effect, either as source of personal inspiration, as issue, as interest group or other forms to be specified. Of course, religion may act on parliamentary life in different simultaneous forms.

Another way to understand the place of religion in the EP is to compare it with the place of religion in the national political space as reflected by the experience of MEPs in domestic politics in their home country. Considering the limited capacity of European institutions to alter the personal preferences of their agents, we see that the EP is not likely to change the views of MEPs on the relationships between religion and politics, framed as these views are by the MEPs' national socialisation. A final dimension of religion in the political socialisation of MEPs refers to religious (or philosophical) lobbying. The frequency of interactions between MEPs and religious or secular interest groups[3] is said to be regular but not very frequent, depending on which problems are on the agenda and above all the commitments of MEPs on relevant issues mobilising the religious civil society. The usual patterns of lobbying suggest that these interactions flow through national and denominational channels: an Italian Catholic MEP is likely to be particularly – but of course not exclusively – targeted by organisations sharing the same nationality and faith.

Religion across policy sectors

A fourth set of questions (11–16) investigates the policy sectors and thematic debates where religion is the most salient as an issue on the European agenda. MEPs are asked whether they consider religion as an issue *per se* requiring a specific policy from the EU (12). Religion is also investigated as identity matter related to reference to the Christian heritage of Europe in treaties (13) and to Turkey (14), or more generally to the EU's relationships with the rest of the world (15). Finally, data are also collected on an internal ongoing controversy in the EP about the meetings of the president of the EP with religious leaders, an indicator of the opinion of MEPs about the institutional recognition of churches and other faith bodies as partners in European governance (16).

Individual religious beliefs, behaviours and attitudes of MEPs

The questions in the last part of the questionnaire (17–21) tackle the religious beliefs, practices and attitudes of MEPs. Questions are borrowed from international values surveys[4] to compare the religious profiles of MEPs and average Europeans. MEPs are asked whether they belong to a denomination, which one, their (non)observance, the kind of religiosity they have (belief in a personal God, a life force …), and their attitude towards indicators of cultural liberalism regarding the place of religion in society (statements on whether politicians should have religious values, on whether religious leaders should influence public affairs and on the regulation of agents performing abortion). The purpose is to measure the congruence between the beliefs of MEPs as members of a European political elite and those of European citizens. This is a way of establishing their representativeness, the extent to which they reflect the social reality of religion in their respective home countries. Subsequently, the next step is to discuss any potential discrepancy between the way European elites and societies relate to religion, and whether various uses of religion as a political resource to justify European policies and the European polity are efficient.

Guidelines for contributors

In the analysis of the eight case studies presented by the contributions, a common framework was proposed to authors, with the flexibility required to comply with national specificities and the variable relevance of indicators (concerning for example the unequal importance of religious lobbying or the salience of religion in questions asked by MEPs or in their communication). This framework was threefold.

First, contributors were asked to present briefly the articulation of politics and religion in the country in question: religion–state model; historical evolution; level of secularisation; presence or not of a Christian Democratic tradition in party politics; level of conflictuality of religious issues in domestic politics and incentives to invest such issues; legitimacy of religious lobbying regarding the pluralist/unitary vision of public interest; link between religion and support for Europe or Euroscepticism; position taken by national politicians in the debate about the Christian heritage of Europe in the 1990s–2000s.

Second, contributors were asked to develop the analysis of data produced by interviews with national MEPs on the basis of the questionnaire acting as common framework and to explain possible specificities in the light of the national model of articulation between politics and religion.

Third, it was suggested to contributors that they offer material and interpretation for comparison with, one the one hand, national (or infranational) MPs and politicians, and on the other hand, citizens of the member-state, by reference to large-scale pre-existing surveys (EVS, Eurobarometer, national opinion polls). The purpose was to measure the potential specificities linked to the function of MEP regarding other political offices and political constituency. This can also be done by looking at positions taken by national MEPs at the EP in significant controversies involving religion.

Summary

After the above short presentation of the general findings of RelEP on the basis of the whole sample, this summary suggests some keys to bridging contributions on national cases. A guiding hypothesis is that the experience of diversity at home is the best preparation for managing diversity in European politics. Pluralism, relativism and flexibility developed in national interactions between religion and politics turn politicians into naturals in the Brussels policy-game. The apprenticeship of diversity may result from various factors: from the historical necessity to reconcile several denominations in domestic politics; from a founding compromise between spiritual and temporal powers in the transition towards modernity, democracy and nation-building; from a tradition of political pluralism legitimising the contribution of private interests (including religious ones) to governance and public will. All these conditions permitting an easy shift from national conciliation to European bargaining can supplement each other. Societies like Germany and the Netherlands which are used to coexistence and compromises between different religious groups and where religion and politics go well together are good laboratories for Europe. The UK with its formal intertwinement between religious and political institutions offers a different configuration, but its openness and political liberalism (illustrated by the role of interest representation) is also a good preparation for what is in store for MEPs. Adaptation may be more difficult for countries where either the church or the state are used to enjoying a dominant position and/or compete with each other for social hegemony. Monopoly of influence or culture wars are not the right practices to comply with the constant search for allies and compromises prevailing in the EP. France has largely adapted its 'laïcité' to contemporary requirements for the management of religious realities; but there is still a symbolic resilience of past conflicts between church and state, and the articulation between religion and politics may still offer inflammable material ready for controversies. French MEPs express this heritage through a certain rigidity in the way they deal with religious issues. For opposite reasons, Polish MEPs may sometimes struggle to get along well with what they perceive as a dominant and somehow authoritarian secularism at the EP. Asserting a Catholic identity or coming to terms with secularisation seem significantly more difficult in the EP than at the national level. Italian MEPs have had more time to negotiate such an adaptation in domestic politics; nevertheless, the blueprint of Catholicism on Italian political identity is visible in the reactivation of religious civil society and in the number of Italians among the 'soldiers of God' at the EP. A last and transient category includes countries which were once perceived as bastions of conservative religion but which have experienced significant cultural changes with political effects (such as quick secularisation, influx of migrants of different faiths, progressive legislation on sexual issues). Of course, cultural changes can meet resistance and backlash. In such cases, Europeanisation is a transformative process among others, not necessarily the most salient and influential and convergent with societal evolutions. Austrian MEPs come from a country in this category; Spanish MEPs are also influenced by similar tensions between rapid transformations at home and the possible resilience of conservative forces. Such tensions may mean that religious affairs are as delicate to deal with in politics at the European level as they are in politics at the national level.

Finally, it is helpful to look at Europe from a distance in order to define what is specific to Europe and what is not. The 'different cases' in this study were chosen on purpose to highlight contrasts and similarities. Israel is a fascinating example where religion is constitutive of the very existence of the polity. It is also a territory where several denominations and religiosities coexist. In contrast to Europe, Israel shows culturalisation of religion and the potential for several narratives to take inspiration from a same source for divergent purposes. It is a reminder of the plasticity of religion and of the polysemy of all intellectual and symbolic traditions, and it is useful to keep this in mind in debates on European heritages and original influences which are frequently framed in terms of 'or' rather than 'and'. The USA is the inverted mirror of Europe: its case has inspired a rich scholarship that has contributed much to the design of RelEP methods. The contribution on American interactions between religion and politics suggests that political institutions should not be expected to alter social realities radically, but that they can constitute an environment influencing the ways of expressing and relating to religion. Rules and balances of power do not change beliefs but may dictate arrangements of politicians with these beliefs, simply because it is part of their jobs to think more in terms of additions and coalitions than of divisions. So far from emphasising an irreducible difference between religious America and secular Europe, a comparative study of religion in the House of Representatives and in the European Parliament invites us to give credit to representative democracy for the way it is able to bridge gaps of faith and belief and contain conflicts while also giving space for the expression of dissent.

Funding

The RelEP project was funded with support from the European Commission through the Jean Monnet Chair 'Social and Cultural Dimensions of European Integration', SocEUR [529183-LPP-2012-BE-AJM-CH]. This publication reflects the views only of the author, and the Commission cannot be held responsible for any use which may be made of the information contained therein. RelEP has also benefited from the support of research grants from the Université Libre de Bruxelles and the Belgian Fonds National de la Recherche Scientifique.

Notes

1. On the methodological advantages of the internet, see Farrell et al. (2006).
2. The present research was financed by a starting grant from the Université Libre de Bruxelles and material support from this institution under diverse forms; funding by the Belgian scientific agency FNRS for the final conference; support from the Jean Monnet Chair 'Social and Cultural Dimensions of European Integration – SocEUR'; and considerable resources, time and energy from all the contributors to this project. RelEP would not have been possible without this human investment.
3. The list offered to MEPs in order to identity their most frequent interlocutors is taken from the database of organisations registered at the EP and confirmed by exploratory interviews.
4. Questions are taken from European Values Study Survey 2008. (http://www.europeanvalues-study.eu/evs/surveys/survey-2008.html) and from Special Eurobarometer 225: Social values, Science & Technology (fieldwork January – February 2005, publication June 2005), 7 (http://ec.europa.eu/public_opinion/archives/ebs/ebs_225_report_en.pdf).

References

Benson, P., and D. Williams. 1982. *Religion on Capitol Hill: Myths and Realities*. New York: Harper and Row.
Berger, P., ed. 1999. *The Desecularization of the World: Resurgent Religion and World Politics*. Grand Rapids, MI: William B. Eerdmans.
Berger, P., G. Davie, and E. Fokas. 2008. *Religious America, Secular Europe? A Theme and Variations*. London: Ashgate.
Broughton, D., and H. M. ten Napel, eds. 2000. *Religion and Mass Electoral Behaviour in Europe*. London: Routledge.
Capelle-Pogacean, A., P. Michel, and E. Pace, eds. 2008. *Religion(s) et identité(s) en Europe: l'épreuve du pluriel* [Religion(s) and Identity(ies) in Europe: Testing Plurality]. Paris: Presses de Sciences Po.

Chenaux, P. 2007. *De la chrétienté à l'Europe: les catholiques et l'idée européenne au XXe siècle* [From Christendom to Europe: Catholics and the European Idea in the Twentieth Century]. Tours: CID.

Corbett, R., F. Jacobs, and M. Shackleton. 2011. *The European Parliament*. London: John Harper.

Davie, G. 2002. *Europe: The Exceptional Case: Parameters of Faith in the Modern World*. London: Darton, Longman and Todd.

De Vlieger, P.-J. 2012. "Lobbying in the Service of God and Church: The Adaptation of Church Representations to the European Union's Interest Group System." PhD diss., Vrije Universiteit Brussel.

Farrell, D., S. Hix, M. Johnston, and R. Scully. 2006. "A Survey of MEPs in the 2004–09 European Parliament." Paper presented at the annual conference of the American Political Science Association, Philadelphia.

Fontaine, P., 2009. *Voyage au cœur de l'Europe 1953–2009: histoire du Groupe Démocrate-Chrétien et du Parti Populaire Européen au parlement européen* [Journey to the Heart of Europe 1953–2009: The History of the Christian Democratic Group and the European People's Party at the European Parliament]. Brussels: Racine.

Foret, F. 2009. "Religion: A Solution or a Problem for the Legitimisation of the European Union?" *Religion, State & Society* 37 (1/2): 37–50. doi:10.1080/09637490802693213.

Foret, F., and X. Itçaina, eds. 2011. *Politics of Religion, Religious Politics: Western Europe at the Crossroads*. London: Routledge (ECPR series).

Habermas, J. 2010. *An Awareness of What is Missing: Faith and Reason in a Post-Secular Age*. New York: Polity Press.

Hix, S., R. Scully, and D. Farrell. 2011. *National or European Parliamentarians? Evidence from a New Survey of the Members of the European Parliament*. http://www.lse.ac.uk/government/research/resgroups/EPRG/pdf/Hix-Scully-Farrell.pdf.

Hobolt, S. B., W. Van der Brug, C. H. de Vreese, H. Boomgaarden, and M. C. Hinrichsen. 2011. "Religious Intolerance and Euroscepticism." *European Union Politics* 12 (3): 359–379. doi:10.1177/1465116511404620.

Huntington, S. 1993. "The Clash of Civilizations?" *Foreign Affairs* 72 (3): 22–49. doi:10.2307/20045621.

Jenkins, P. 2007. *God's Continent: Christianity, Islam and Europe's Religious Crisis*. Oxford: Oxford University Press.

Kaiser, W. 2007. *Christian Democracy and the Origins of the European Union*. Cambridge: Cambridge University Press.

Leustean, L., ed. 2012. *Representing Religion in the European Union: Does God Matter?* London: Routledge.

Leustean, L., and J. Madeley, eds. 2009. *Religion and Politics in the Construction of the European Union*. London: Routledge.

Madeley, J., and Z. Enyedi, eds. 2003. *Church and State in Contemporary Europe: The Chimera of Neutrality*. London: Frank Cass.

Massignon, B. 2007. *Des dieux et des fonctionnaires: religions et laïcités face au défi de la construction européenne* [Gods and Bureaucrats: Religions and Secularisms Challenged by Building Europe]. Presses Universitaires de Rennes: Rennes.

McCrea, R. 2011. *Religion and the Public Order of the European Union*. Oxford: Oxford University Press.

Minkenberg, M. 2009. "Religion and Euroscepticism: Cleavages, Religious Parties and Churches in EU Member States." *West European Politics* 32 (6): 1190–1211. doi:10.1080/01402380903230660.

Minkenberg, M. 2010. "Party Politics, Religion and Elections in Western Democracies." *Comparative European Politics* 8 (4): 385–414. doi:10.1057/cep.2009.5.

Mudrov, S. A. 2011. "Christian Churches as Special Participants of European Integration: The Process of EU Treaties' Reform." *Journal of Contemporary European Research* 7 (3): 1–32.

Nelsen, B., J. Guth, and B. Highsmith. 2011. "Does Religion Still Matter? Religion and Public Attitudes Toward Integration in Europe." *Politics and Religion* 4 (1): 1–26. doi:10.1017/S1755048310000507.

Oldmixon, E. A. 2005. *Uncompromising Positions: God, Sex and the US House of Representatives*. Washington, DC: Georgetown University Press.

Robbers, G., ed. 1997. *Etat et églises dans l'Union européenne* [State and Churches in the European Union]. Baden-Baden: Nomos.

Van der Brug, W., S. Hobolt, and C. H. de Vreese. 2009. "Religion and Party Choice in Europe." *West European Politics* 32 (6): 1266–1283. doi:10.1080/01402380903230694.

Weigel, G. 2005. *The Cube and the Cathedral: Europe, America, and Politics Without God*. New York: Basic Books.
Weiler, J. 2003. *Un'Europa cristiana* [A Christian Europe]. Milan: Bibliotheca Universale Rizzoli.
Willaime, J.-P. 2004. *Europe et religions: les enjeux du XXIe siècle* [Europe and Religions: What is at Stake in the Twentieth Century]. Paris: Fayard.

Appendix

CORE QUESTIONNAIRE USED FOR THE SURVEY 'RELIGION AT THE EUROPEAN PARLIAMENT' (RelEP)

Dear Ms, Mr,
Member of the European Parliament

Religion is more and more on the agenda of the European Union. The EU is alternatively described as a 'Christian club', or criticized for its materialism and atheism. Many hopes are placed in European action to promote fundamental rights and religious freedom, but there are also questions about the influence of religious or philosophical lobbies in Brussels and Strasbourg.

Little information is available on what happens at the European Parliament with religion. Most studies focus on the European Commission. That is the reason why an international team of researchers, specialists of parliamentary politics and religious issues, is conducting a major survey on the religious preferences of members of the European Parliament. The purpose is to establish a clear and objective picture of what the MEPs believe, and what they do with these beliefs.

The findings will contribute to the public debate on religion in European politics and will offer dispassionate basis for policy reflection. Your contribution by answering these questions is irreplace-able and it will take you only a few minutes.

The results of the survey will be used for scientific purpose only and will be published as global statistics. More information on the project can be found here: http://www.releur.eu

Thank you very much for your time.

The RelEP team

Questionnaire 'Religion at the European Parliament'

- A/ Name of MP
- B/ Nationality
- C/ Age
- D/ National Party
- E/ Political Group at the European Parliament

1. Group of the European People's Party (Christian Democrats)
2. Group of the Progressive Alliance of Socialists and Democrats in the European Parliament
3. Group of the Alliance of Liberals and Democrats for Europe
4. Group of the Greens/European Free Alliance
5. European Conservatives and Reformists
6. Confederal Group of the European United Left – Nordic Green Left
7. Europe of freedom and democracy Group
8. Non-attached Members

RELIGION AT THE EUROPEAN PARLIAMENT

– F/ Number of terms
2009–2014
2004–2009
1999–2004
1994–1999
1989–1994
1989–1994
1984–1989
1979–1984

– G/ Committees
  1. Foreign Affairs
  2. Development
  3. International Trade
  4. Budgets
  5. Budgetary Control
  6. Economic and Monetary Affairs
  7. Employment and Social Affairs
  8. Environment, Public Health and Food Safety
  9. Industry, Research and Energy
  10. Internal Market and Consumer Protection
  11. Transport and Tourism
  12. Regional Development
  13. Agriculture and Rural Development
  14. Fisheries
  15. Culture and Education
  16. Legal Affairs
  17. Civil Liberties, Justice and Home Affairs
  18. Constitutional Affairs
  19. Women's Rights and Gender Equality
  20. Petitions
  21. Human Rights
  22. Security and Defence
  23. Financial, Economic and Social Crisis

– **1/ According to you, does religion have an effect on the functioning of the European Parliament?**
a/ Yes
b/ No

– **2/ At the European Parliament, religion:**
a/ reinforces the identity of each political group
b/ blurs the identity of each political group
c/ has no effect on the identity of each political group

– **3/ Does religion have a different importance depending on the nationality of the European MPs?**
a/ Yes
b/ No

– 4/ Does religion create differences between MEPs who are Catholic, Protestant, Orthodox or from other religions?

a/ Yes

b/ No

– 5/ As a MEP, do you ever take religion into account?

□a/ Permanently

□b/ Often

□c/ Rarely

□d/ Never

– 6/ If religion intervenes in your activity as MEP, is it:

□ a/ as a source of personal inspiration?

□ b/ as a social and political reality?

□ c/ as an interest group?

□ d/ other

□ e/ no effect

(several responses possible, please rank them from 1–3)

– 7/ Is the place of religion in the European Parliament different from your experiences in national politics ?

a/ Yes

b/ No

c/ Don't know/Don't answer

– 8/ Has your experience at the European Parliament changed your views on the relationships between religion and politics?

a/ Yes

b/ No

– 9/ How often are you in contact with religious or philosophical interest groups?

□a/ once a week or more

□b/ once a month or more

□c/ a few times a year

□d/ a few times over the course of a term

□e/ never

□f/ don't know/ no response

– 10/ If you are in contact with religious or philosophical interest groups, could you provide some examples?

1. AEFJN – Africa–Europe Faith & Justice Network
2. ATD QUART MONDE
3. BNAIBRITH – B'nai B'rith International
4. CARITAS
5. CCME – Church's Commission for Migrants in Europe
6. CDA – Christian Democratic Appel
7. CEC KEK – Conférence des Eglises Européennes

8. CEJI – Centre Européen Juif d'Information
9. COMECE – Commission des Episcopats de la Communauté Européenne
10. CSW – Christian Solidarity Worldwide
11. EU CORD
12. EURODIACONIA – European Federation of Diaconia
13. EUROJEWCONG – European Jewish Congress
14. EUROPEANEA – European Evangelical Alliance
15. ISLAMIC RELIEF – Islamic Relief Worldwide
16. JRS – Jesuit Refugee Service
17. LAÏCITE – Centre d'Action Laïque asbl
18. LIGHT FOR THE WORLD
19. OCIPE – Office Catholique d'Information et d'initiative Pour l'Europe
20. SPUC – The society for the Protection of Unborn Children
21. SKM – Slovenska Katolicka Misia
22. WYA – World Youth Alliance
23. YAHAD IN UNUM
24. Other (please specify)

– 11/ Which are the issues on which religion is most important at the European Parliament? (please rank the three first responses in order of importance)
☐a/ external relations
☐b/ freedom of expression
☐c/ the fight against discrimination
☐d/ social policy
☐e/ economic policy
☐f/ culture and education
☐g/ other
☐ e/ Not any

– 12/ Should the EU have a real policy towards religions?
a/ Yes
b/ No

– 13/ Should the Lisbon Treaty have made reference to Europe's Christian heritage?
a/ Yes
b/ No

– 14/ Does religion play a role in the way Turkey's candidature was received in the European Parliament?
a/ Yes
b/ No

– 15/ Does religion play a role in the external relations of the EU?
a/ Yes
b/ No

– **16/ The President of the European Parliament regularly meets with representatives of major European religion to discuss current affairs. Is it a good thing?**
a/ Yes
b/ No

– **17/ Do you belong to a religious denomination?**
a/ Yes
b/ No

– **18/ If yes, which one?**
-> a/ Catholic
-> b/ Protestant
-> c/ Orthodox
-> d/ Other Christian
-> e/ Jew
-> f/ Muslim
-> g/ Sikh
-> h/ Buddhist
-> i/ Hindu
-> j/ Atheist
-> k/ Non believer/agnostic
-> l/ Other (please precise)

– **19/ Apart from weddings, funerals and christenings, about how often do you attend religious services these days?**
-> a/ never
-> b/ once a year
-> c/ holydays only
-> d/ once a month
-> e/ once a week
-> f/ more than once a week
-> g/ no answer

– **20/ Independently whether you go to Church or not, how would you define yourself?**
-> a/ I am a religious person
-> b/ I am not a religious person
-> c/ I am a convinced atheist
-> d/ don't know
-> e/ No answer

– **21/ Which of these statements comes closest to your beliefs (one answer only)?**
-> a/ There is a personal God
-> b/ There is some sort of spirit or life force
-> c/ I don't believe there is any God, sort of spirit or life force
-> d/ don't know
-> e/ No answer

– 22/ How much do you agree and disagree with each of the following?

	Agree strongly	Agree	Neither agree nor disagree	Disagree	Disagree strongly	Don't know	No answer
a/ Politicians who do not believe in God are unfit for public office							
b/ Religious leaders should not influence how people vote in elections							
c/ It would be better for Europe if more people with strong religious beliefs held public office							
d/Religious leaders should not influence government decisions							
e/ If a nurse were asked to help perform a legal abortion, he/she should be allowed to refuse on religious grounds							

– 23/ Do you have comments on this survey?

Thank you very much!

Religion at the European Parliament: an overview

François Foret*

Institute for European Studies – CEVIPOL, Université Libre de Bruxelles (ULB), Brussels, Belgium

Introduction

The aim of RelEP is to analyse the beliefs of the members of the European Parliament (MEPs) and what they do as a consequence of these beliefs; the impact of religion on political socialisation within and between existing cleavages (national, party, denominational); the way religiously loaded issues are dealt with; how religion is (de)politicised in parliamentary activities and how it is used in various strategies to build coalitions or to gain visibility, to support or oppose European integration.

This contribution presents the main findings of the RelEP survey based on aggregated answers of the 167 MEPs who took the questionnaire. Case studies discuss the results country by country and develop a comparison between MEPs and national political elites. Thematic transversal topics are investigated in the conclusion.[1]

In a nutshell, the RelEP survey highlights the fact that religion is still very national and depends heavily on the domestic history of relationships between church and state, between the spiritual and temporal realms. At the European Parliament (EP), religion is neither a matrix framing individual or collective preferences nor a sufficient basis to mobilise. It remains a significant symbolic resource of distinction to build a political and media profile and to demarcate oneself from the competition. The most dramatic struggles concerning religion now occur more in the transnational public sphere than in the institutional space. In deliberative arenas and in decision-making processes, the occurrence of religion is discrete and elusive, but still tangible. It exists as a cultural background, a lobbying justified by the association of civil society to the definition of the public good in a participatory democracy, and the expertise attributed to religious and philosophical non-governmental organisations (NGOs) in terms of ethical affairs.

Religion as a political variable at the EP is most significant as a component of the policy process and as a secondary identity. It is not acceptable as a discourse of self-assertion and proselytism. It has to comply with the repertoires of action prevailing in Brussels: technocratic arguments relying on a knowledge of issues which suggests the 'one best way' to proceed; search for consensus in order to gather the largest coalition; respect of pluralism and relativism as all particularities have to be integrated and all normative preferences (identities, values) may have to be traded or at least downscaled. Against this background, the challenge for religious and philosophical entrepreneurs is twofold: first, to turn religious references into secular concepts capable of becoming conveyors of their values and purposes (for example, human dignity); second, to use secular principles to promote their views, sometimes by emphasising the religious roots of these concepts (for example, subsidiarity).

Summary of the specific findings

Interviews with MEPs offer evidence that religion does have an effect on the functioning of the EP. Interestingly, MEPs give more importance to it at the global level of the institution and for their counterparts than for themselves. To a extent, *religion matters mainly for others*. This is in congruence with the *individualisation* of the way to relate to faith. Religious affairs are considered as too present or absent at the EP according to the personal religiosity and personal religious belonging of a given politician.

The effects of religion are rather *conservative*: it confirms existing belongings on the basis of nationality, political groups, denomination. MEPs are confronted with a greater spiritual diversity in Brussels and Strasbourg than in their national political life, and also experience different ways of relating to it; but at the same time they do not alter their own views on religion. There is *no massive resocialisation* under the pressure of European policy-making, but there may be *adaptation* to a new context and to new ways of formulating religious claims and references.

Individually, MEPs say that they take religion into account rather infrequently. They tackle it mostly as a policy issue, secondarily as a source of personal inspiration, and thirdly through interest representation. Most frequently, then, religion arises not as a result of choice but because it is there and has to be dealt with.

The assumption that the EP is besieged by *religious lobbies* is not confirmed by RelEP data. MEPs say that their contacts with religious interest groups are limited to a few times a year or a term; that is, less frequently than similar contacts at the level of national or regional Parliaments. The structure of religious lobbying (who speaks with whom) reflects the strength of national and denominational channels and issue networks.

Religion does not arise much as a specific *policy issue*, and MEPs do not support the idea of a full religious policy for the EU. It emerges most in connection with and invoked by questions of fundamental rights, culture and social issues. In short, both as an influence and an object of public action, religion is *mediated by other matters*.

However, religion has a clear role as *a constitutive element of identity*. MEPs are almost equally divided on whether there should be reference to the Christian heritage of Europe in the treaties, and they also consider that religion has an impact in the relationships of the EU with the rest of the world, and especially with Turkey.

As far as the *personal beliefs of MEPs* are concerned, we find that they present a profile of '*cultural Christians*' largely comparable to that of the citizens they represent (with due caution because of the size of the sample and the frequent refusal to answer). A large majority claims a religious belonging, a lesser number state that they are religious persons, and an even smaller number that they are believers. The influence of their status as representatives could explain both a concern not to hurt the feelings of religious parts of the electorate, but also in some cases an outspoken atheism to assert a distinctive political identity.

MEPs display a clear *attachment to separation between religion and politics*, whatever institutional form such a separation may take. There is a consensus that there should be *no religious influence on the selection of political rulers*. Opinions are more divided regarding *whether churches should make their voices heard on political options*, as some countries with a pluralist tradition favour the free expression of all private interests in the formation of the public good and there is even less agreement on general principles when it comes to practical applications. On questions requiring *arbitration between the neutrality of institutions or rules and individual freedom of choice* (such as the right of a nurse not to perform an abortion), MEPs are polarised.

We could summarise by saying that while there is not a high potential for conflicts and cleavages on religious issues in themselves, there is a significant potential for the politicisation of religiously loaded ethical or cultural issues.

The following paragraphs detail answers by MEPs on topics investigated by the questionnaire: the impact of religion on the work of MEPs and on the functioning of the EP; religion in the political practice and political socialisation of MEPs; religion across policy sectors; individual religious beliefs, behaviours and attitudes of MEPs. As most interviews were conducted in the native language of MEPs, English translations in the quotations are ours.

Religion and the functioning of the EP: an effect perceived diversely

When MEPs are asked to assess the influence of religion (deliberately defined as a unspecified parameter)[2] on the functioning of the EP, almost a two-thirds majority (63.2%) state that religion does indeed have an effect.

Interestingly enough, MEPs who define themselves as non-religious or atheist are keener to consider that religion plays a role at the EP. Conversely, MEPs seeing themselves as religious minimise that role. This suggests that religion is more visible to those who are foreign or hostile to it, while believers may consider that its role at the EP is insufficient in view of the role it plays in their individual lives.

Perceptions of the role of religion always depend on the personal feelings and situation of an MEP. Denominational belonging also matters. Protestants (especially German and British MEPs) resent a Catholic bias in European decision-making. Orthodox (especially Romanians) think that religion is too elusive and regret that it is not taken into account enough.

The comparison of the presence of religion at the EP and in other Parliaments is made possible by another international survey, PartiRep.[3] This survey investigates members of 60 national and regional Parliaments in 15 European countries (including Israel). Its geographical scope thus largely overlaps with that of RelEP. Overall, 80.8% of regional and national MPs consider that the presence of religion in their Parliament is not at all or not very important; 19.2% think that it is fairly (16.7%) or very important. The presence of regional representatives could in some countries downscale the salience of religion, but in others (like Germany), religious issues and actors are very significant in territorial politics. As two-thirds of MEPs consider that religion has an effect at the EP but rather a weak one, the pictures in national and European assemblies are not too different. Many MEPs express their surprise at, and sometimes their disapproval of, the visibility of religion, as they are not used in their own political culture to its outspoken expression by colleagues or lobbies.

Religion confirms existing belongings

The effect of religion on the functioning of the EP is mediated partly by its role in the formation of various political belongings and loyalties: political groups; nationality; denomination.

Political groups: the resilience of ideological proximity to/distance from religion

Many MEPs (42.4%) consider that religion reinforces the identity of each political group (a slightly larger number (43.1%) think that it has no effect, while a few (14.6%) mention its possible harmful impact on political cohesion). This picture must be nuanced by the recognition that religion has different meanings according to which political group is being considered. Many MEPs believe that Christianity strengthens the unity of the European People's Party (EPP) thanks to the heritage of Christian Democracy. However, by no means all the parties composing the EPP are rooted in this ideological history despite the recent refocusing following the departure of the British Conservatives. Besides, some ultra-conservative Christians consider that the Christianity displayed by the EPP is too weak and unfocused and leaves too much room for liberal drift. As one MEP from the *Front National* states: 'There is a Christian Democratic group which, at the political level at least, instead of "Christianising" democracy, has only "democratised" Christianity; that is not the same thing at all.' For the other major groups, the effects are bound to be more peripheral. Some Socialists and Democrats think that religion blurs political belongings, maybe by dissimulating actual socio-economic cleavages in echo of a long distrust regarding the 'opiate of the people'. Within the Socialists and Democrats (S&D), some parties may have histories of antagonism against the church while others may be sympathetic with the social teaching of Christian organisations; but most are simply indifferent or non-aligned. Similarly, MEPs from the Alliance of Liberals and Democrats for Europe (ALDE) are mostly not concerned about religion. In some cases, they may be polarised: between defence of religious liberties and the fight for freedom of speech, two possible competitive causes; or between economic liberalism in alliance with economic materialistic forces on the one hand, and cultural and social liberalism where they mix with progressive religious forces against the excesses of the markets on the other. At the extremes, the situation is more contrasted: from forces promoting national, European or Western identities rooted in Christendom or pagan visions to fiercely anticlerical leftist formations.

Nationality: the weight of the past

The second belonging/loyalty to which religion may contribute is nationality. The RelEP survey asks whether religion has a different importance depending on nationality. Nationality is not an explicit basis on which to mobilise at the EP, but can be a transversal determinant: all MEPs of the same country can be predisposed to adopt the same attitude towards religion, both because of a path dependence on the historical model of church–state relations and because of a compliance with the mainstream orientation of the electorate. Nationality also interacts with party belonging. MEPs of the same nationality in the same political family are likely to share a common ideological posture towards religion and to react similarly to religiously loaded issues. However, MEPs of the same nationality inside a single political group at the EP can belong to different national parties with different historical relationships to religion (see the Italians in the EPP, for example, with more or less proximity to the former Italian party *Democrazia Cristiana* (Christian Democracy). Interferences with denominational belonging also matter. In some cases, MEPs of the same nationality can belong to different religious groups, the denominational cleavages having a political meaning. A famous example from Northern Ireland is the pastor Ian Paisley, who was an MEP from 1979 to 2004.

Almost all MEPs (82.8%) say that religion does indeed have a different importance according to nationality; this confirms the crucial importance of nationality as the main factor of discrimination in European politics, a fact extensively documented by studies both of political actors and of ordinary citizens. Like other variables, religion is constrained by the overriding rule of national belonging. A British Liberal respondent expressed this bluntly by a personal reinterpretation of a question in the survey: 'What is a "personal God"? A belief in God is usually a belief in the god of the country you were born in, so it is not personal, but a "community" God.'

Religion is often said in qualitative interviews with MEPs to create notable differences between representatives of new and old member-states, the former being more religious than the latter. This gap is confirmed to a certain extent by cross-tabulations assessing the specificity of the answers of MEPs from countries of the 2004 and 2007 enlargements. Representatives from Eastern Europe do find more than their Western counterparts that there is a big difference between the place of religion in European politics and its place in national politics. They think that religious issues are not given the same attention in Brussels as they are at home. They also differ on the symbolic way to relate to religion. They regret the lack of reference to the Christian heritage of Europe in the Lisbon Treaty, and they approve of the dialogue of the president of the EP with religious leaders. They fare significantly less on the scale of cultural liberalism.

However, this distinction between representatives of new and old member-states may profitably be examined more closely. National, political and religious belongings are intertwined. MEPs from new member-states are more on the right side of the political scale than their Western European counterparts, and thus more likely to have a greater proximity to religion and a greater conservatism on religion-related issues. This does not mean, however, that Eastern European MEPs feel less European – rather the contrary – or are less supportive of European integration. This is confirmed by a survey of MEPs conducted in 2010:

> The MEPs from the new member states in the current EP are on average more right wing than the MEPs from the old member states. However, the two groups of MEPs have statistically indistinguishable opinions on EU regulatory powers, EU powers and the powers of the EP, although MEPs from new member states have a stronger European identity than MEPs from the EU15. (Hix, Scully, and Farrell 2011, 11)

Denomination: noticeable theological differences intertwined with national specificities

Overall, MEPs deny the existence of major cleavages between different faiths. Of MEPs, 66.7% do not see differences among those who are Catholic, Protestant, Orthodox or from other religions. The 33.3% who think that there are gaps between faiths tend to be non-religious or from minority denominations. Again, a belief in the divisive effects of religion is characteristic of a personal distance from religion or of a feeling of being disrespected.

Effects of theological differences are difficult to distinguish from the influence of nationality. A British MEP is struck by the propensity of Catholics to 'go public' far more easily than at home in the UK, suggesting that the presence of colleagues of other nationalities belonging to the same denomination may have an emancipatory effect on expressing one's preference. Conversely, people of the same denominational group may voice different priority concerns according to their nationality. German Catholics will be more focused on economic issues related to religion; Italian Catholics will be particularly involved in debates on the more or less liberal way of dealing with religion in the public space. Here, the discriminating factor is not only the national political culture but also the domestic agenda, the two being naturally interconnected. German MEPs keep a vigilant eye on the fiscal status of German churches; Italian politicians cannot forget the controversy on religious signs in classrooms raging after the ruling of the European Court of Human Rights. When it comes to identifying the nationalities which are the most marked by religion, the cleavage between new and old member-states disappears: Irish and Polish MEPs are the 'usual suspects', frequently designated jointly.

Religion and political practice in the EP

Another dimension of the research tackles religion in the political practice and political socialisation of MEPs. The interplay of religion with politics is to be understood in two ways: first, in terms of the frequency with which an MEP takes religion into account; and second, in terms of the form of that interplay, which determines its potential effect: as a source of personal inspiration, or as a focus on a specific issue, or as an interest group or other manifestations.

MEPs are also asked to compare the place of religion in the EP with their experience in domestic politics in their home country. The European institutions have a limited capacity to alter the personal preferences of their agents, and the EP is not likely to change the views of MEPs on the relationships between religion and politics. A final dimension of religion in the political socialisation of MEPs refers to religious (or philosophical) lobbying. The frequency of interactions between MEPs and religious or secular interest groups[4] is a good indicator of the ability of religious civil society to maintain a sphere of social interactions that may nurture a common world view.

Various manifestations of the interplay between religion and politics in the EP

A low level of taking religion into account: two explanations

A large majority of MEPs (66.7%) say that they rarely (47.1%) or never (19.6%) take religion into account; one third of MEPs do take it into account often or permanently. This confirms religion as an at best occasional issue in the activity of an MEP. However, this contrasts with the finding that 63.2% of MEPs say that religion has an effect on the functioning of the EP. Two explanations can be proposed for this apparent discrepancy.

The first explanation is that religion is thought to work 'for the others' or as a social factor independent of the personal preferences of MEPs. This is not so remote from the view, documented by sociology, of religion as serving as vicarious memory/identity or as a commodity, a public good playing a necessary role in social life without involving an individual commitment.

The second explanation of the low level of acknowledgment of religion as an element in personal political practice is the dominant representation that political and religious affairs must be kept separated. This is a leitmotiv in off-the-record comments by MEPs. The perceived common European common principle of '*laïcité*', understood in the minimal sense of separation between the spiritual and secular fields, may prevent MEPs from testifying that they take religion into account. This is illustrated further by the fact that almost half of MEPs thinking of themselves as religious persons say that they rarely integrate religion into their practice.

Diversity of forms for the occurrence of religion

An investigation of the forms in which MEPs take religion into account shows a diverse picture. Of MEPs, 38.2% say that they tackle religion as a social and political reality, 31.2% see it in terms of personal inspiration and 19.2% see it in terms of an interest group. Other occasions on which religion may arise as an issue include actions by other MEPs or contacts by religious individuals with their MEPs as their representatives. This picture consolidates the idea that religion may willy-nilly be an issue on the plate of an MEP independently of his or her opinion on the subject. Religion has to be dealt with if a policy or political matter calls for a decision to be made. At the same time, religion is also salient as personal inspiration, in congruence with its contemporary role as a reservoir of meaning and a set of values offered – often in free use – to believers or non-believers. Finally, religion is also noticeable through interest representation. However, this is the least prevalent form of influence, and this fact qualifies the representation of the EP as besieged by religious lobbies, as it is sometimes depicted in the press of countries with a vision of the public good as the monopoly of the state, such as France.

The different ways MEPs relate to religion may also simply result from their hetero-geneous conceptions of their mandate. Indeed, MEPs play their roles in diverse ways according to their level of commitment, their political loyalty and other factors (Navarro 2009). The MEP acting as a protester against the way the EU works has more chance and incentives to mobilise religion as a protest resource. The MEP depicting himself as an animator bringing his intellectual contribution to the conceptualisation of European policies also has opportunities to find potential inspiration in religion. The MEP claiming to be a specialist knowing everything about the institutional cogs of decision-making has little chance to rely on spiritual matters. Nor do the MEPs whose core business is to act as go-between between their electors, organised interests and European institutions, except if religious motivations frame the agenda of their constituency.

When religion acts as a source of personal inspiration, it is not with a high frequency but rather at critical junctures, when a representative has to make difficult choices implying deep value judgments. Then, more often than not, what comes into play is not religion as a doctrine to comply with, but the moral teaching underlying it and offering keys to making up one's mind. As a Czech member of the EPP says: 'Religion has a minimal influence contrary to moral values which come from it. I am influenced by religion but not blindly, only on issues in rupture with fundamental Catholic teachings (cloning ...).'

European socialisation of MEPs and religion: a transformative experience?

What is new in Brussels and Strasbourg? Diversity and pluralism

There are distinct ways of relating to religion at the national and European levels.

Almost half of MEPs (45.4%) consider that the place of religion at the EP is different from their experience of it in national politics. The proportion that disagree is 31.6% and a significant number (23%) do not know, either because they may have no experience in national politics or have not encountered the religious issue enough at the EP to be able to form an opinion. A discriminatory factor to explain the view of MEPs is their national model of articulation between politics and religion. Those from countries with denomina-tional diversity and a tradition of cooperation between religious and political powers are less likely to be surprised by what they see in Brussels and Strasbourg. MEPs who do think that religion plays a different role at the EP than in national politics tend more than averagely to consider that religion has an influence in the functioning of the EP. They also tend to be non-religious or atheists. What is surprising in Brussels, then, is the impact of religion, not its discretion (except for some MEPs of new member-states who regret the secularism of the EU).

There is a consensus (84.7%) among MEPs that their experience at the EP has not changed their view on the link between religion and politics. The absence of impact of socialisation at the EP is not surprising as it is congruent with the general inability of European institutions to alter in-depth the preferences of their agents (Ban 2013; Kassim et al. 2013; Scully 2005). Among the rare examples of MEPs who have changed their views once in Brussels, there are two opposite and extreme profiles: some are struck less by the strong influence of religion than by the activism of devout colleagues, and are thus led to a greater vigilance to protect secularism; by contrast, others become 'fighters for God', finding in their confrontation with European materialism new reasons to fight for their beliefs and fresh energy to do so. This phenomenon of 'reawakening' on both sides is however very limited in our sample of MEPs.

One common explanation for the limited potential for re-socialisation in Brussels is the significant turnover between one EP term and the next. Roughly speaking, half or more of MEPs do not come back to the EP after an election. European elections are still seen as second-order elections, with second-order candidates selected more for national purposes than for their European expertise.

However, regarding religion, lesser forms of socialisation than alteration of preferences can be observed. A kind of apprenticeship for a new MEP might be to learn how to disagree and to express his or her own beliefs in a pluralistic and rational way in order to build multicultural coalitions. A way for a religious MEP or party to comply with the rules coming with the Brussels territory is to have two agendas: on the one hand, to keep one's strong political stances for symbolic issues upon which there are no direct European competencies and for media arenas; and on the other hand, to cut deals and to abstain from blocking the functioning of the assembly. This behaviour is frequently the one chosen by political-religious entrepreneurs in American parliamentary politics.

Religious lobbying

The MEPs and the lobbies: not so frequent interactions

Representation of religious interests in European arenas has developed since the 1990s. Interactions between religious (or secular) organisations and MEPs are relatively common, although not particularly intense. For the majority of MEPs, it is a matter of a few times a year (34.9%) or a few times a term (22.4%). Only a significant minority (21%) are in touch with religious actors on a very regular basis, once a month or more. A sizable group (15.8%) has no contact at all, being either disinvested in their mandate, or avoided by religious actors because of their reputation as hostile or indifferent, or simply representatives of tiny nations which slip through the net.

It comes as no surprise that MEPs who are the most assiduous interlocutors with religious groups are those who are the more convinced of the influence of religion on the EP and those who say that they are religious persons. There is no evidence that exposure to religious lobbying leads to transformation of the views of a given MEP. Those who say that they have frequent contacts with faith organisations do not change their conceptions of the relations between religion and politics (probably also because they are committed to religion and hold firm ideas on its status). This is a limitation of the possible effect of socialisation of MEPs through lobbying. At the same time, density of exchanges with religious lobbies demarcates party boundaries: politicians from the EPP are clearly the keenest interlocutors with religious civil society.

The reaction to religious lobbying depends heavily on the level of legitimacy given by MEPs to lobbying in general, and this last element is heavily dependent upon national political culture. Politicians used to a pluralist system of interest representation, where different sectoral elites mix freely and can contribute to the formation of the common will, differ from those coming from more monolithic traditions which aim to produce collective preferences under the supervision of the state and/or of political parties. As one British MEP says, 'Everybody can influence politics like lobbyists, religion included'; French MEPs are keen to disagree on both points, lobbying in general and religious lobbying in particular. Another concern is about the representativeness of lobbying, questioning the social constituency of European civil society. Some MEPs resent religious interest representation as a channel for extremists more than for balanced and rational spiritual inputs. One British MEPs comments: 'The only time I have contact with faith groups is by extremists telling scary stories, that the EU is going to ban abortion, etc. The EU does not have such power, but that does not stop self-interested organisations.'

Again, to assess the specificity of MEPs in their relationships with religious lobbies, findings of another survey on national and regional Parliaments are instrumental. According to the PartiRep research, 25.4% of representatives at national and infra-national levels have contacts with churches or religious organisations (philosophical organisations are not included) at least once a month (as compared with 21% of MEPs), 46.1% of local and national MPs have interactions with religious lobbies at least once a year (compared with 34.9% of MEPs (22.4% of MEPs have contacts a few times over a year)), 28.5% of regional and national politicians have (almost) no contact with religious interest groups (compared with 15.8% of MEPs who do not speak to religious groups). To sum up, European representatives seem slightly less assiduous in interacting with religious groups than their national and regional counterparts, even if fewer of them totally ignore such groups. This could be a sign that the EP is an open arena where politicians are confronted with a religious diversity they are not used to encountering in national spaces, but that they do not rub shoulders with religious lobbies so frequently.

Varieties of lobbies and channels of contact

In order to identify which organisations MEPs are in touch with, a list of religious NGOs or NGOs with a religious dimension taken in spring 2010 from the register of the EP where NGOs enlist on a voluntary basis was submitted to interviewees.[5] Other structures were mentioned spontaneously by MEPs. It is difficult to categorise these organisations, as the first striking element is the diversity of their natures, scopes, resources and purposes. This heterogeneity is constitutive of a pluralistic and atomistic setting of representation of religious interests, as an analysis of the dialogue between religious civil society and the EC can confirm (Foret 2009, 27–50). Their main features can however be highlighted.

The domination of Catholicism is obvious. COMECE, the commission of the Catholic national episcopates, is by far the most frequently quoted organisation dedicated entirely to religious lobbying (22.2%). The second major organisation, CEC-KEK (the Conference of European Churches), associating notably Protestants and Orthodox, is far behind COMECE (8.1%). The low profile of Protestantism is slightly counterbalanced by a flotilla of small entities which are mentioned a few times or once, which reflects the de-institutionalised nature of this denomination. A relative surprise may be the visibility of Jewish organisations (EUROJEWCONG – European Jewish Congress; CEJI (*Centre Européen Juif d'Information*)). These organisations may have a rather low public profile and a tiny social constituency but are well-connected and efficient in their strategy of relationships with European institutions in general and MEPs in particular. Orthodox Christians and above all Muslims are almost invisible, in contrast with their demographic weight in European populations. The humanists do not feature too badly considering the huge asymmetry of resources they have compared to the Catholic Church.

The second major feature is the prevalence of organisations whose main purpose is not directly the diffusion of a religious message but rather to work in the name of spiritual ideals to achieve charitable purposes. The NGO which is the most frequent interlocutor of MEPs is Caritas, an international network of Catholic charities with national branches and forms of presence in almost 200 countries worldwide. *ATD Quart Monde*, a movement founded by a Catholic priest but bringing together people of different denominational and philosophical backgrounds, also scores highly. Other structures dedicated to 'good causes', like CCME (the Churches' Commission for Migrants in Europe) or Islamic Relief Worldwide, also feature quite frequently. This salience of charities with an underlying religious dimension is a reminder that in the functionalist and highly rationalised European decision-making process and in the multicultural political arena it is easier to mobilise to defend human rights with the language of expertise than to do proselytising with an argumentation rooted in values.

It is also worth noting that national and even local organisations are mentioned spontaneously several times by MEPs. Of course, these entities are generally quoted only a few times or just once as they have relationships with a smaller number of MEPs, with limitations linked to the nationality or territory of those MEPs. Nevertheless, these national/local organisations have for the same reasons very intimate and close interactions with 'their' MEPs, they have a possible electoral weight for the re-election of those MEPs and may enjoy a greater influence than big pan-European federations.

Salience of religion according to policy sectors and topics

Policy sectors

Analysed as an issue set on the European agenda through the declarations of MEPs, religion has an unequal importance according to policy sectors. It is at its highest importance in fields related to fundamental rights: against discrimination and promoting freedom of expression. It is also prominent in social policy as this refers frequently to problems such as human dignity or gender equality, and encompasses also relief to the poor and various forms of solidarity and welfare which are not explicitly framed in terms of human rights but lead to them through the discourse of religious duty to assist fellow human beings. Culture and education is another important sector. This may overlap to some extent with freedom of expression as the question of the place of religion in the arts or sciences may arise; more broadly, it concerns the place of religion in society and the definition and transmission of collective identities. The last significant sector is international relations. Here, incentives are the influence of religion on the relationships of Europe with the rest of the world, solidarity with Christian minorities worldwide and above all risks associated with religious extremisms, mostly Islamic.

Looking for trouble

Independently from the competencies of the EP, the salience of religion could be explained in some cases by its potential for 'scandalisation'. Since the introduction of universal suffrage in 1979, the EP has met its limits by its inability to offer an attractive political drama able to catch the headlines. Political action at the EP is considered too complicated, not bipolarised enough (majority/opposition; left/right) in order to create a gladiatorial-style of debate with winners and losers, and not animated by notorious spokespersons with a real 'human interest' (Abélès 1992). Besides, the EP is a victim of the structure of national public opinion as far as Europe is concerned: where there is a clear consensus on European integration, one does not speak of Europe as there is nothing to say; where there is dissensus on European integration, one does not speak of Europe as it would be counterproductive to create divides on what is a secondary issue (Morgan 1999, 91). Religion may be a way to raise interest and to polarise both political actors and media without harming decision-making as it is mainly out of the realm of the EU. Religious topics may thus be a symbolic resource to fuel controversy and to build a high public profile relatively easily. The Buttiglione affair in 2004 is a good example of such an instrumental function of religion. That occurred in the field of fundamental rights; but it can also occur in such fields as external relations (the protection of a Christian minority for example) or education (the threat of creationism for example). In short, religion may become suddenly relevant in any policy sector provided that it has a potential for scandalisation.

An EU policy on religion?

For MEPs, religion is not an autonomous policy issue justifying a specific European process of public action. 72% oppose the idea that the EU should develop a real policy towards religion. They comply with the rule of subsidiarity leaving religion in the hands of the member-states. Another survey (Hix, Scully, and Farrell 2011, 20) nevertheless shows that MEPs support the extension of European competencies in the matter of fundamental rights, including religion. Of the MEPs questioned by Hix and his colleagues, 61% consider that there should be a lot more (30.8%) or a little more (30.2%) EU-wide regulation on discrimination on the grounds of gender, race, religion, age, disability and sexual orientation (25% are happy with the curent level of regulation and 13.9% would like to see a little less or a lot less). This confirms that MEPs see religion as an object among many others to be dealt with in the extensive action of the EU for a progressive agenda.

Religion as identity resource

Divisions on the Christian heritage of Europe

Identity, culture and memory policies are fields where religion is very salient. Since the 2000s there has been an (ongoing) debate on the mention of the Christian heritage of Europe in the preambles to the defunct European Constitution and to the Lisbon Treaty. Member-states were unable to reach a consensus so silence finally prevailed. Campaigns in favour of the recognition of the Christian heritage continue in a subdued way. This is more than a quarrel about memory. Emphasising what Europe owes to Christianity is a way to enable churches to have a say in the contemporary debates on the finalities and modalities of European integration. MEPs are almost equally divided as far as the reference to the Christian heritage in treaties is concerned. A small majority (50.3%) support the status quo by rejecting such a reference. The promoters of the Christian heritage also overwhelmingly advocate the need for the EU to have a specific religious policy. A commitment in favour of religion as symbolic resource is thus coupled with a commitment to tackle religion directly as a European issue. The Christian heritage is supported mostly by Catholics. MEPs of other denominations are far less keen. Minority denominations may be put off by the propensity to assimilate 'Christian heritage' to 'Roman Catholic legacy', a reproach frequently heard in Brussels about the way religion should be considered in the history of Europe.

Religion constitutive of 'Europeanness' in the relationship with Turkey and the world

Cultural identity is always the most asserted in situations of confrontation with otherness. The application of Turkey, a large Muslim country, to enter the EU is the most telling example. A very large majority of MEPs (77.2%) say that religion has indeed framed the way the Turkish candidature has been dealt with in the EU, although it is not an official parameter. For some MEPs, the problem may be not that Turkey is a Muslim country but how it protects religious liberties. However, in many of the qualitative interviews, the cultural argument is recurrent. The influence attributed to religion in the Turkey issue – an influence greater than on external relations in general – is a sign that religion has an increasing salience as soon as the limits and the nature of the European political community are at stake and the question of defining what is means to be European arises.

MEPs are also divided – but to a lesser extent – when it comes to estimating whether or not religion plays a role in the external relations of the EU (57.6% yes, 42.4% no). Religion surfaces in several ways: as a core cultural element underlying relationships between civilisations; as a basis for diplomatic solidarity with minorities of the same denominations (referring to the role of the EU as the protector of Christian minorities oppressed worldwide); or, most frequently, as a cause of political violence, terrorism and war when it is expressed in extremist forms: here Islam is mainly targeted as responsible for religious excesses.

Recognition of religion as a partner of good governance

A final occurrence of religion as a policy issue is about the regular meetings of the president of the EP with representatives of major European religions to discuss current affairs. This practice has raised heated controversies, secular MEPs denouncing the principle of the meeting itself and its discretionary character, or claiming that philosophical traditions should also be associated in this consultation. In response, successive presidents of the EP and their supporters argue that such a dialogue is simply an application of Article 17 of the Lisbon Treaty, which establishes a regular, open and transparent dialogue with religious and philosophical actors. So far, the preference of the authorities has been to hold a separate meeting with secularists. According to the RelEP results, 88.4% of MEPs approve of these meetings with major religions. However, while this political dialogue enjoys large agreement, it seems invested with different meanings and with different intensity according to the religious profile of the MEP concerned. While most agree with the practice as a harmless and largely useless part of consultation with civil society, some reject it as a sign of the excessive and dangerous influence of religion, and others defend it adamantly, with great expectations.

Religious beliefs and attitudes of MEPs: not so different from those of average Europeans

A last part of the research tackles the religious beliefs, practices and attitudes of MEPs. Questions are borrowed from international values surveys that provide a standard against which to compare the religious profile of MEPs with those of the European citizens who elect them. MEPs are asked to self-define whether or not they belong to a denomination, which one, their (non-) observance, the kind of religiosity they have (belief in a personal God, a life force ...), and their attitude towards selective indicators of cultural liberalism regarding the place of religion in society. The purpose is to see if their answers reflect the mainstream social reality of religion in their respective home countries.

Two hypotheses: European democracy as the conservation of religion or with a secularist bias?

Using the results, we can test two hypotheses.

The first hypothesis is that MEPs may display a higher religiosity than the rest of the population and national rulers. This could be a result of their mode of election which leaves room for traditional religious parties despite a shrinking social constituency. Indeed, proportional electoral systems do not oblige parties to enter into coalitions before the elections and allow the expression of ideological diversity.

The second hypothesis is that, on the contrary, the EU and especially the EP present a secularist bias. This could reflect the usual critical distance of European elites from religion (Berger et al. 2008). It could be a result of the rationalisation implied by European policymaking, with the prevalence of expertise and public reason to justify decisions and the strategic necessity for compromise and coalition-building on the smallest common denominator. The EP amplifies still more this trend towards rationalisation because of the imperative to search for consensus in the absence of structuring majority/opposition cleavages (or even a clear demarcation between conservatives and progressives). Thus, strong normative (and hence divisive) resources like religion would be banned from the EP, and this would also impact on the selection of candidates.

The two hypotheses can coexist. Religion could be distanced from the actual functioning of the EP (second hypothesis) but be mobilised as a symbolic and rather harmless repertoire in order to affirm a political specificity inside the EP and offer reassurance to electorates traumatised by social changes provoked by European integration. Inside the EP, political entrepreneurs could build positions and audiences on religious issues thanks to dramatic postures while playing the game of bargaining. Outside the EP, party manifestos and campaign discourses may use religion as a cultural raw material to reassert national identity and pride to counterbalance the compliance with functional requirements of European integration. Religion may play the role of a memory ensuring the feeling of continuity and thus make Europeanisation more acceptable.

MEPs as cultural Christians, belonging without necessarily believing

It is first necessary to underline a possible bias: that MEPs with religious convictions were more motivated to answer personal questions, and that many declined because they saw their religious beliefs as part of their private sphere that should not be expressed in public. Others feared possible political uses of their answers despite promises that they would be kept anonymous. The findings thus suggest a qualified picture of the religiosity of MEPs.

Table 1.   Question: independently of whether you go to church or not, how would you define yourself?

Answer	MEPs (data RelEP, $n = 114$[7]) Percentage (number of answers)	Total population (EU13, data EVS (2005–2006))[8]
I am a religious person	62.2% (71)	62.2%
I am not a religious person	19.3% (22)	29.5%
I am a convinced atheist	18.4% (21)	8.3%

Almost three quarters (72%) of all the MEPs who agreed to answer claim that they belong to a religious denomination, but only 62.2% say that they are religious persons, and only 55% say that they believe in a personal god or some sort of spirit or life force. Many do not even answer the question on attendance at religious services, but the level of religious observance is clearly smaller. This means that MEPs are a group where belonging without believing is verified, and still more belonging without practising. This observation illustrates the notion of 'vicarious religion' formulated by Grace Davie. Religion has no personal implication, but it is considered as a kind of public utility, a useful social institution that is just there; it may well not be used, but it is kept in case of need and for the sake of memory. In this respect, MEPs are not exceptional. Most 'cultural Christians' acknowledge that Christianity is part of their personal culture but consider its implications for political decision and action with great caution. It is the same for MEPs. Those claiming a religious belonging do not necessarily have a stronger assessment of the effect of religion on the functioning of the EP than those who do not do so (actually rather the contrary: atheists think that religion is too influential). MEPs denying any religious belonging are keener to see religion as a source of divisions, especially between denominations. Conversely, representatives claiming a religious belonging emphasise religious as a factor of unity. In short, the more you belong, the more you see religion positively.

To compare MEPs of the sample with their political constituencies, we used data from international values surveys on populations of thirteen countries (the countries of the MEPs who answered questions on personal beliefs) (see Table 1). On this basis, we observe that the 62.2% of MEPs defining themselves as religious persons correspond exactly to the proportion of European citizens who give the same answer. Still, there is a difference. Among MEPs, fewer respondents say that they keep to a moderate line in order to avoid offending some electors about religion; but they may also take firm stances if they choose to build a political profile on atheism to attract public attention.

Cultural liberalism of MEPs and ethical issues

Some questions aim at measuring the level of cultural liberalism of MEPs. Indicators focus on the place of religion in the political space and in the selection of rulers and on ethical issues calling for public regulation. The underlying interrogation is whether European decision-makers may be likely to promote a strongly progressive agenda on socio-cultural issues, and whether it may influence European norms in these matters.

Overall, MEPs present a certain level of cultural liberalism and an attachment to pluralism and the right for everyone to express one's own belief. There is a large consensus (83.9%) among MEPs to say 'no' to the proposition that 'politicians who do not believe in God are unfit for public office'. Clearly, faith is not a legitimate element in the selection of rulers. This does not come as a surprise, but it illustrates a difference with other regions of the world where the personal religiosity of rulers is still a key parameter.[6] However, faith is not seen as a negative factor. 46% disagree with the proposition that it would be better for Europe if more people with strong religious beliefs held public office; but 25% agree and another 25% are 'don't knows'; this suggests a relative openness. There is massive opposition to seeing religion as a normative source of authority likely to exercise any form of constraint, but there is no rejection *a priori* of religion as a possible source of inspiration. The logic is similar concerning the political role of religious leaders. A majority of MEPs consider that religious leaders should influence neither how people vote in elections (61.1%) nor government decisions (52.4%); but on both points, around a quarter hold the opposite view. In short, MEPs show a large degree of support for a separation between politics and religion, a separation rooted in most national systems under different institutional forms. To this restricted extent, it is possible to speak of something like a European '*laïcité*'. Meanwhile, a small group is still in favour of a more active presence of religion in political decisions. More MEPs are wary about the influence of religious leaders on voting in elections than about their influence on government decision-making; indeed, as a participatory democracy, the EU offers channels of dialogue to religious and philosophical communities, and such processes materialise the possibility of legitimised religious influence.

The dominant reluctance towards any form of authoritarian presence of religion in politics cannot be assimilated to a total rejection of religion. When it comes to dealing with the practice of individual liberty to choose how to reconcile one's own beliefs with professional duties, MEPs are on a permissive side: 52.3% agree that if a nurse were asked to help perform a legal abortion, she or he should be allowed to refuse on religious grounds; 32.9% disagree. Recognition of freedom of choice, linked to the 'core business' of the EU to protect fundamental rights, secures a majority, but opinions are more widely distributed on this issue, from strong agreement to strong disagreement, than on any other issue. It is useful to compare RelEP findings with results from another survey of MEPs including one question on abortion. According to a study (Hix, Scully, and Farrell 2011, 19) based on the answer of 172 respondents, 65.7% of MEPs support the right of women to decide for themselves about abortion; 15.7% disagree or disagree strongly and 18.6% neither agree nor disagree. This means that free choice on abortion is denied or at least uncertain for one third of MEPs: that is a substantial proportion, and the 'pro-life' minority is likely to be active. Answers of MEPs on abortion are more liberal than on other issues like the decriminalisation of marijuana or the reduction of restrictions on immigration. Abortion may be considered as a fundamental right for European women more written in stone than cultural practices that may be part of youth culture or policy decisions on regulating population movement, but still not totally consensual. Overall, MEPs do not show particularly striking levels of cultural liberalism as they strongly support tougher action against criminals and are rather split when it comes to arbitrating between the defence of welfare spending and the necessity to raise taxes (Hix, Scully, and Farrell 2011, 19).

MEPs as a progressive and secular but not anti-religious elite

Some MEPs are fierce supporters of secularism, to the point that they decline to answer a questionnaire about religion, considering it as already a violation of the circumscription of religion in the private sphere. According to one Belgian MEP, 'Religion must be kept in one's private life. That is the only answer I can give you. To answer this questionnaire would be against my rules and against my vision of things. The separation between church and state is at this cost.'

Other MEPs are simply concerned about the pressure from religion, which is felt to operate more strongly at the European level than at the national level, especially in very secularised and/or secular countries. According to one Czech Social Democrat, 'The Czech Republic is a secular country; that is not the case for the EU where religion plays a more important role than it should.' Comments by MEPs show that the distinction is frequently fuzzy between secularism (separation between religion and politics or between church and state) and secularisation (loss of relevance and mutation of religion), between evolution of the state and of society.

Most MEPs, however, seem to hold a moderate position regarding religion. Most of them take little or no account of religion in their routine work. When confronted with necessary choices on fundamental issues, they express a clear preference for a mild secularism ensuring separation between religion and politics and respect for individual rights, but with possible arrangements to accommodate personal preferences. The tricky question is the extent of these arrangements: that is, the point at which disagreements arise and when political differences according to national, political and religious belongings re-emerge. The dominant view is best expressed in the words of a British Liberal: '[The EU] should have a policy respecting all, discriminating against none and insisting on separation between religion and politics'.

Conclusion: national religions, secular Europe?

Overall the RelEP findings confirm that religion remains a very national matter. The EU is not able to alter significantly the way a politician relates to religious beliefs or issues. The European context may influence how positions concerning religion are expressed to comply with the multiplicity of denominations and traditions encountered in supranational arenas; but there is no substantial change: political elites resist any major shift of competencies between the national and the European level, and they stick to the behaviours and attitudes inspired by their political culture of origin.

Religion is not an autonomous variable in European political life: it does not of itself create cleavages between believers and non-believers, among denominations or among political forces. Rather, it tends to confirm and reinforce existing divisions amongst nationalities or political groups. More accurately, religion may be seen as a flux electrifying a set of polarities around which political actors gravitate rather than as a set of closed boundaries. It does not maintain homogeneous entities, as there may be various attitudes towards religion within a single nationality or political family. It works rather as an identity marker, holding together a nation or a party by distinction to other nations or parties that deal with it differently. More than on distinct principles, differences rely on various symbolic codages to interpret and display these principles. All European political actors (at least in government) agree on the separation of politics and religion and respect for human rights, but some express their view in the language of *laïcité* and emphasise the secularist side, while others use the rhetoric of the social role of religion and support an extensive definition of its mission.

Thus religion exists in European politics mostly under its cultural and social forms, and these cultural and social forms are deeply national. The asymmetric presence and legitimacy of religious civil society according to nationalities is an illustration of the resistance of the social to Europeanisation. Because of the weakness of direct European competencies to regulate religious matters, there is no proper policy process likely to enforce a significant shift of ethos and loyalty from the nation-state to the EU. Rather, religion operates as an underlying influence on the approach by MEPs to value-loaded issues, reflecting their primary socialisation or the alignment of their electors at home. Some MEPs, especially at the extremes, may use religion as a vector of 'scandalisation', in order to create controversies likely to reinforce their political profile by contrast to the competition or to attract media attention. But in doing so, these political entrepreneurs further reinforce the tendency towards the renationalisation of European politics as conflicts develop along national lines. Most often, the purpose is to defend national religion (or secularism) against the attacks of a secularist (or devout) Europe.

At the same time, there are signs of transnationalisation of civil society religious networks which interact with MEPs to contribute to deliberation and decision-making. There are also circulations of 'good practices' or discourses about religion through the channels of European policy-making. These elements of horizontal Europeanisation should not be overlooked. Such exchanges can contribute to a convergence of practices between member-states and to new solidarities around religious or – more probably – religiously loaded causes (on ethical issues more than on regulation of religion itself). As in many other fields, progression beyond national boundaries is easier in functional than in identity matters. In short, doing things together and/or in the same way in order to deal with religion may be sometimes possible, but does not necessarily announce a common sense of European belonging related to religion. For Europe, a community of doing does not pave a deterministic way towards a community of being, except maybe to a limited extent in relationships with the rest of the world. Any temptation to follow this path would probably involve more dangers than opportunities.

Funding

The RelEp project was funded with support from the European Commission through the Jean Monnet Chair 'Social and Cultural Dimensions of European Integration', SocEUR [529183-LPP-2012-BE-AJM-CH]. This publication reflects the views only of the author, and the Commission cannot be held responsible for any use which may be made of the information contained therein. RelEP has also benefited from the support of research grants from the Université Libre de Bruxelles and the Belgian Fonds National de la Recherche Scientifique.

Notes

1. Presentation of the RelEP findings here is intentionally simple and short in order to give a general insight against which to assess the comparison between member-states and with national elites, the core subject of this publication. Other pieces published elsewhere push further the theoretical implications of these findings, for example on the cultural liberalism of MEPs and the implication for the EU's rulings on human rights (Foret 2014a); on the systematic comparison between the European Parliament and the US House of Representatives (Foret 2014b); on religion as an object of European public policy and on religion as a political influence in the framing of European polity and politics (Foret 2015).
2. The term religion may here be understood in various ways: as a personal inspiration; as a set of actors; as an issue. Other questions detail its different dimensions. Here, the purpose is to measure the way MEPs relate to this multidimensional topic, as compared with other multi-dimensional factors such as nationality or ideology.
3. More details about the research protocol of PartiRep (2007–2011, $n = 1536$) may be found here: http://www.partirep.eu/datafile/comparative-mp-survey. The author would like to thank the PartiRep team (especially Pascal Delwit, Jean-Benoît Pilet and Giulia Sandri) for making unpublished data available.
4. The list offered to MEPs in order to identity their most frequent interlocutors is taken from the database of organisations registered at the EP and confirmed by exploratory interviews.

5. The criterion was simply to include all organisations having an identifiably religious dimension in their activity, either directly (a lobby emanating from churches and aiming at promoting a religious message) or indirectly (an NGO with a religious heritage acting for causes such as development, solidarity or fundamental rights).

6. The importance of the personal religiosity of rulers is a key indicator to compare the level of cultural liberalism of societies around the world. See the use of the question by Inglehart and Norris to underline the importance of social values as a necessary bedrock for democracy. They mention 88% 'yes' in Egypt, 83% in Iran, 71% in the Philippines, and 40% in the USA. See Inglehart and Norris (2003, 79), Norris and Inglehart (2009).

7. The answers 'don't know/no answer' (37 for RelEP, 24.5% of those who answered the question) are excluded to make the data commensurable with EVS data. These answers indicate a significant self-censorship by politicians on such questions, a usual phenomenon in surveys of this kind.

8. Rates calculated from World Values Survey data available for 13 countries congruent with nationalities of MEPs represented in the RelEP sample: Bulgaria (2006), Cyprus (2006), Finland (2005), France (2006), Germany (2006), Great Britain (2006), Italy (2005), Netherlands (2006), Poland (2005), Romania (2005), Slovenia (2005), Spain (2007), Sweden (2006) (http://www.wvsevsdb.com/wvs/WVSAnalize.jsp, accessed 3 November 2012).

References

Abélès, M. 1992. *La vie quotidienne au Parlement européen* [Everyday Life at the European Parliament]. Paris: Hachette.

Ban, C. 2013. *Management and Culture in an Enlarged European Commission: From Diversity to Unity?* London: Palgrave.

Berger, P., G. Davie, and E. Fokas. 2008. *Religious America, Secular Europe? A Theme and Variations*. London: Ashgate.

Foret, F. 2014a. "Religion and Fundamental Rights in European Politics: Convergences and Divisions at the European Parliament." *Human Rights Review* 15 (1): 53–63. doi:10.1007/s12142-013-0285-z.

Foret, F. 2014b. *Democratic Representation and Religion: Differences and Convergences between the European Parliament and the US House of Representatives*. http://cadmus.eui.eu/handle/1814/31404.

Foret, F. 2015. *Religion and Politics in the European Union: The Secular Canopy*. Cambridge: Cambridge University Press. (Forthcoming).

Hix, S., R. Scully, and D. Farrell. 2011. *National or European Parliamentarians? Evidence from a New Survey of the Members of the European Parliament*. http://www.lse.ac.uk/government/research/resgroups/EPRG/pdf/Hix-Scully-Farrell.pdf.

Inglehart, R., and P. Norris. 2003. "Le véritable choc des civilisations" [The Real Clash of Civilisations]. *Le Débat* 126: 76–84. doi:10.3917/deba.126.0076.

Kassim, H., J. Peterson, M. Bauer, S. Connolly, R. Dehousse, L. Hooghe, and A. Thompson. 2013. *The European Commission of the Twenty-First Century*. Oxford: Oxford University Press.

Morgan, D. 1999. *The European Parliament, Mass Media and the Search for Power and Influence*. Aldershot: Ashgate.

Navarro, J. 2009. *Les députés européens et leur rôle: sociologie des pratiques parlementaires* [European Representatives and Their Role: A Sociology of Parliamentary Practices]. Brussels: Editions de l'Université de Bruxelles.

Norris, P., and R. Inglehart. 2009. *Cosmopolitan Communications: Cultural Diversity in a Globalized World*. Cambridge: Cambridge University Press.

Scully, R. 2005. *Becoming Europeans? Attitudes, Behaviour and Socialization in the European Parliament*. Oxford: Oxford University Press.

Part I

Smooth Transition from National Conciliation to European Bargain?

A social role for churches and cultural demarcation: how German MEPs represent religion in the European Parliament

Anne Jenichen and Henrike Müller

Centre for European Studies (CEuS), University of Bremen, Bremen, Germany

This study deals with the question of how German members of the European Parliament (MEPs) represent the German model of religion–state relations at the European level. Based on a survey and interviews with German MEPs as well as a content-analysis of German MEPs' speeches, motions and parliamentary questions during the seventh term of the European Parliament (EP), our study demonstrates that this model is represented in three dimensions. First, German MEPs reflect the close cooperation between the churches and the state in Germany, primarily on social issues, through largely church- and religion-friendly attitudes and relatively frequent contacts with religious interest-groups. Second, by referring to religious freedoms and minorities primarily outside the EU and by placing Islam in considerably more critical contexts than Christianity, German MEPs create a cultural demarcation line between Islam and Christianity through their parliamentary activities, which is similar to, though less politicised than, cultural boundaries often produced in public debates in Germany. Third, our study illustrates similar patterns of religious affiliation and subjective religiosity among German parliamentarians in both the EP and the national Parliament, which to some degree also reflect societal trends in Germany. Yet our data also suggest that European political elites are more religious than the average German population. If the presence of religion in terms of religious interest-groups and arguments is included, the EP appears to be more secularist than the German Parliament.

Introduction

Germany is the largest member-state of the European Union (EU). Germans thus constitute the largest national group within the European Parliament (EP). Germany can furthermore be considered a unique case in Europe in terms of how religion and the state as well as the political sphere are linked with each other. The close cooperation of the state with the Protestant and Catholic Churches, particularly on issues of providing social welfare, and the presence of two major Christian faiths, render Germany a case that is worth studying in the context of religion and politics in the EU.

Drawing on the assumption that national models of church-state relations (in a broader sense) affect the perceptions and behaviour of parliamentarians, we examine in this study whether and how the German members of the EP (MEPs) represent the German model of publicly dealing with religion at the European level. This German model is, on the one hand, characterised by a close cooperation between church and state, primarily in the sphere of social welfare provisioning, and thus by a privileged and acknowledged role of religion in the public sphere. On the other hand, there is a continuous trend of individual and societal secularisation observable, and religion increasingly becomes politicised as a factor contributing to social conflict. It is primarily Islam which is used to mark cultural boundaries between 'us' (the – Christian or non-religious – majority society) and 'them' (allegedly primarily Muslim immigrants).

Are these trends reflected by the perceptions, attitudes and activities of German MEPs? Drawing on data obtained via the RelEP survey, semi-structured interviews with German MEPs (conducted between 2011 and 2012 in Brussels, Berlin, Hamburg and Bremen) and a qualitative content-analysis of German MEPs' speeches, motions and parliamentary questions during the seventh parliamentary term (2009–June 2013), we shall illustrate throughout the following sections how the German model is indeed mirrored in several respects. The German MEPs consider the churches and religious interest-groups to be legitimate partners in supporting social interests rather than religious interests. The analysis of parliamentary activities reveals a primarily religion-friendly attitude on the part of the German MEPs, which is facilitated by addressing religion primarily as an issue of human rights, especially freedom of religion and the rights of religious minorities, allowing a relative consensus between believers and non-believers and different denominations on issues of religion. However, the overwhelming majority of these activities refer to religious freedoms and minorities outside the EU, and place Islam in considerably more critical contexts than Christianity, disclosing a similar cultural demarcation line between 'us' (Christian Europeans) and 'them' (extremist Muslim outsiders) to that which is observable in public debates in Germany. Differences between political groups in this regard are important to consider, though, with the Group of the European People's Party (EPP) much more affirmative of Christianity and critical of Islam than, for instance, the Greens and the Left.

Our study is divided into three parts. In the first part, we describe the state–church regime, its historical development and the role of the churches in Germany, as well as the state of secularisation and religious pluralisation and the public politicisation of religion in order to delineate the German model of church–state relations. In the following part, we present our findings on German MEPs in order, first, to find out about how relevant they perceive religion to be in the workings of the EP and, primarily, to demonstrate how their activities and attitudes reflect the predefined German model. Subsequently, we ask whether their religious affiliation and religiosity mirror societal trends in Germany. In this part, we also turn to the national level in Germany and investigate religious affiliation and the religiosity of members of the German Parliament (*Bundestag*) to address this question.

Religion and politics in Germany

The current church–state regime in Germany is based on a compromise laid down in the constitution of the Weimar Republic in 1919. The compromise consisted in rejecting a state church regime (favoured by conservative and church-friendly parties), but allowing the churches a privileged status under public law, instead of strictly separating them from the state according to the French or US pattern (favoured by the parties of the left). The constitution furthermore introduced freedom of conscience and religion and the autonomy of religious communities (Cavuldak 2013, 308–314).

After the Second World War, the Federal Republic of Germany (FRG) took over the religio-political compromise of the Weimar Republic. The new constitution additionally introduced new provisions, in the end leading to a stronger integration of church and religion into the democratic state than before, including an explicit reference to God in the preamble,[1] and the introduction of religious education in state schools. State constitutions were likewise extended. The closer integration resulted from the experiences with the Nazi regime. Facing a politico-moral vacuum and economic deprivation after the war, many Germans in the western part of the country sought hope and refuge in the churches (Cavuldak 2013, 315–316). The FRG furthermore used the close cooperation with the churches to distance itself from the German Democratic Republic (GDR) and its publicly prescribed atheism. The government of the GDR actively repressed the churches for ideological as well as power political reasons, resulting in a situation for the churches characterised by scarce resources, lack of societal recognition and continually decreasing membership (Pickel 2013, 78–79; Thériault 2004, chap. 2). Despite this dichotomy of state–church relations, reunification did not seriously raise the question of the religio-political regime again. With the exception of some politicians from the Greens (formed in the 1993 merger of the West German Green Party and the East German Alliance '90) and the Party of Democratic Socialism (PDS), the successor party of the Socialist Unity Party of Germany (SED), a large political majority did not see the necessity to rearrange the regime and therefore opted for nationally adopting the western one (Cavuldak 2013, 318).

The current church–state system is characterised by separation but a considerable degree of cooperation. It can therefore be defined as a 'regime of partial establishment' (Minkenberg 2013, 58) or, citing the German canon lawyer Ulrich Strutz (1925), 'limping separation between state and church' (Cavuldak 2013, 314). Officially recognised religious communities can operate as 'corporate bodies under public law', allowing them to raise taxes from their registered members (German Constitution, art. 137.6), usually collected via the state as part of official income taxes. Further privileges connected with this status concern taxation privileges, permission to provide religious education in state schools and establish theological faculties in state universities, the right to provide pastoral care in prisons and military academies, and a voice in public bodies, such as public service broadcasting authorities or ethics committees (Cavuldak 2013, 314, 325). The two major churches, the Roman Catholic Church and the Protestant Church,[2] automatically received this status after the constitutional clause was introduced in 1919, whereas other religious communities could receive it upon application.[3] Islamic communities, though, have been unsuccessful in achieving this status so far, failing, among other reasons, because of the missing church-like institutional structure and representative bodies (Cavuldak 2013, 324). However, there are efforts by the state to improve dialogue with Islam, for example through convening 'German Islam Conferences' (2006, 2007, 2011 and 2013) (Cavuldak 2013, 324–327; Tezcan 2011; official website http://www.deutsche-islam-konferenz.de/DIK/DE/Startseite/startseite-node.html). Further regulations of religion fall into the competencies of the 16 states (*Länder*). Cooperation is furthermore regulated by concordats and contracts between the German federal state as well as some of its states with the Holy See and with officially recognised religious communities, primarily the two major churches.

An important part of the privileged role of the churches in Germany is their official inclusion into the social welfare system. The outcomes of conflicts between church and state, as well as between denominations, on the expanding role of the state in welfare provision in the late nineteenth and early twentieth centuries had a considerable impact on the formation of different types of welfare states in Europe (Manow and van Kersbergen 2009). In Germany, the peaceful resolution of this conflict yielded a compromise between religious and secular forces as well as Catholic and Protestant camps. Religion, consequently, became an institutionalised partner of social welfare provisioning.

The two welfare organisations of the churches, the Catholic Caritas (founded in 1897) and the Protestant Diakonie (founded in 1833), are the largest umbrella organisations of the German social welfare system. They are the largest actors and employers in health services and social work, including health care, elderly care, youth welfare, centres for migrants, the homeless, the disabled and rescue services. About 50% of social care is delivered through these organisations, publicly financed through a variety of insurance schemes but administered by the churches (Davie 2012, 594–595; Göçmen 2013, 11–13; Willems 2007, 317–318). Besides national welfare, the churches also run large development agencies which are important actors in German development aid. Even though the two Christian welfare associations have lost some of their privileges since the 1990s as a result of the pluralisation of the German welfare system – changes in its public financing which responded to the increasing (religious) diversity of German society – the institutionalised position of the churches in social welfare provisioning is still relatively stable (Göçmen 2013, 12–13). Facing societal secularisation processes, the German churches derive much of their legitimacy from this social role.

Levels of church membership, church attendance and individual religiosity have been decreasing in Germany since the 1970s. Both parts of Germany have been affected by individual and societal secularisation processes, though starting from very different levels. In eastern Germany, church membership decreased from 90% (1953) to 27% (1989) to about 26% (2008), one of the lowest levels of church membership in the whole of Europe. In western Germany, by contrast, despite slightly decreasing numbers over time, still almost 80% of the population is affiliated with one of the two major churches (Pickel 2013, 79–81). Yet *active* membership is in decline in the western part of Germany as well: only about 25% of the western German population regularly attends church services (Pickel 2013, 82). Only about 10% go to church at least once a week; in eastern Germany this number is even lower: 3% (Elff and Rossteutscher 2011, 113–114). The share of Catholics in this group is larger than that of Protestants as the Catholic faith puts a stronger emphasis on 'practical' worship (Pickel 2013, 82; Elff and Rossteutscher 2011, 115). In both parts of the country the numbers are shrinking. The situation regarding subjective religiosity looks similar: about 25% of the western German population and more than 50% of the eastern German population do not believe in God. In eastern Germany, about 25% define themselves as atheists (Pickel 2013, 83).

Secularisation in Germany, both eastern and western, is subject to a generational effect. Younger age cohorts less frequently attend church services, are less frequently church members and tend to be less religious than older age cohorts (Pickel 2013, 84). Secularisation processes are furthermore observable not only at the individual level but also at the societal level. Functional differentiation is highly acknowledged in the German population, in the west as much as in the east, and irrespective of confessional affiliation. Only a few citizens want a stronger influence of religious authorities, for instance, on elections or political decision-making (Pickel 2013, 86).

At the political level, however, religious-secular and denominational divisions still shape electoral behaviour in Germany: in both western and eastern Germany there is a clear correlation between support for the Christian Democratic Party (CDU) or the Christian Social Union (CSU) and regular church attendance. Catholics tend to vote for the CDU/CSU much more frequently than Protestants (Elff and Rossteutscher 2011; Liedhegener 2011). Secular people, at the other end, primarily support the Greens (in the west) and the Left (in the east) (Pappi and Shikano 2002; Liedhegener 2012).

The programmes and attitudes of the major political parties in Germany have however converged on the matter of religion. The Christian Democratic parties have increasingly

Table 1. Religious communities in Germany 1990–2010 (%).

	1990	2003	2010
Protestant	36.9	31.3	29.4
Catholic	35.4	31.3	29.4
Muslim	3.7	3.9	4.6
Other	1.6	1.7	1.8
No confession	22.4	31.8	32.5

Source: Götze, Jaeckel, and Pickel (2013, 284).

stressed their autonomy from confessional divisions and church dogmas, and have started to address non-Christian voters as well (Bösch 2013, 211, 213; Gerngroß 2010, 88ff; Liedhegener 2012, 243). Compared with other Christian Democratic parties in Western Europe, references to Christian social doctrines and religion are relatively few. It therefore has been contested how Christian both parties still are (Gerngroß 2010, 93; Liedhegener 2012). Meanwhile the Social Democrats (SPD), the Liberals (FDP) and the Greens, all three initially more critical towards religion, have become more religion-friendly, in terms of their members, office-holders, programmes and voters alike (Hering 2011; Liedhegener 2012, 252). The only exception from the convergence of the parties is the Left party (*Die Linke*), which still constitutes the secular pole in the German party system (Liedhegener 2012, 252; Pappi and Brandenburg 2010).

Germany shows an increasing trend towards religious pluralisation (Table 1). Even though the proportion of Muslims is still relatively low, resentment against Islam and Muslims in Germany is gaining currency (de Nève 2013; Götze, Jaeckel, and Pickel 2013). Increasing levels of religious plurality furthermore challenge the prevailing church–state system in Germany with its privileging of Christian and Jewish communities. Some have therefore argued that either the 'limping separation' should be extended and applied to all religions or religion separated more strictly (Cavuldak 2013, 332; Pickel 2013, 98).

Growing levels of religious pluralisation and Islamophobia have contributed to an increase in public discourses on religion (Pickel 2013, 67). Since religion is often problematised as a cause of conflict in these discourses, this politicisation does not contradict the constant loss of importance of religion at individual and societal levels; rather, both processes are mutually constitutive (Pickel 2013, 96). Most prevalent have been debates on Muslims and Islam in Germany, such as on Muslim headscarves in public institutions, on the willingness of young Muslims to integrate, or on violent Salafism. These debates often confound issues of religion and migration (Spielhaus 2013) and position a 'discrete cultural Christianity' against an 'ostentatious' Islam (Wohlrab-Sahr 2003). However, the role of religion in society has also been debated with regard to Christianity and the Christian churches, focusing, for example, on crucifixes in public institutions, on religious education in state schools, on Pope Benedict XVI speaking in the German Bundestag, on sexual and physical abuse of children by members of the clergy and other church employees, on working contracts within church and church-related welfare institutions, and on the refusal of emergency contraception in confessional hospitals.

The churches have actively participated in most of these debates, as well as in debates on moral and ethical issues such as stem cell research, prenatal diagnosis and late-term abortions, euthanasia, equal rights for same-sex relationships and family policy. They do not restrict their participation in public discourses to an exclusively sacral sphere, where the preservation and practice of religious rituals take place, but have transformed themselves into a particular sort of modern interest-group.[4] They not only publicly defend their institutional interests in keeping their privileged legal status in Germany and promote their value orientations, for example on marriage, family, sexual orientation, education or medical ethics, they also, according to their abovementioned social role, put forward moral demands, speaking up on issues such as social justice, asylum law, climate change, the environment, peace, development and human rights (Gerngroß 2010, 92; Sebaldt and Straßner 2004, 122–127; Willems 2007, 321–322). European integration has been supported by both the Catholic and the Protestant Churches in Germany (Minkenberg 2009, 1203–1206).

In sum, the model of dealing with religion in Germany, facing continuing trends of individual and societal secularisation as well as religious pluralisation and the politicisation of religion, is located between close cooperation with the churches, primarily on issues of social justice and development, on the one hand, and using religion, primarily Islam, for cultural demarcation, on the other. We now turn to the EP to explore whether and how German MEPs represent this model through their perceptions and parliamentary activities.

German members of the European Parliament and religion

Studying the German group in the EP

The 99 Germans represent the largest group of MEPs in the EP. In the seventh parliamentary term (2009–2014), the largest share of the German MEPs belonged to the European People's Party (EPP), the second-largest group to the Progressive Alliance of Socialists and Democrats (S&D). Other MEPs identified as Greens (Greens/EFA), Liberals (ALDE) and members of the Left (UEL/NGL) (Table 2).

We approached the German group in the EP using three different methods. First, 25 German MEPs filled in the RelEP questionnaire (response rate: 25.25%). The distribution

Table 2. Sample of the German case study.

	EP*	Sample	Ratio (%)
German MEPs in total	99	25	25.3
By political group			
EPP	42	11	26.2
S&D	23	6	26.1
ALDE	12	2	16.7
G/EFA	14	4	28.6
UEL/NGL	8	2	25
By sex			
Women	37	7	18.9
By year of birth			
Born in 1970s–80s	15	5	33.3
Born in 1960s	24	3	12.5
Born in 1940s–50s	60	17	28.3

Note: *Situation at time of survey and interviews (October and November 2011).

among political parties is fairly representative, with a slight bias towards the Greens, and a disproportionately low share of Liberals, female MEPs and MEPs born in the 1960s (Table 2). There might be a bias towards MEPs with stronger interests in religion (or in keeping religion out of the European political sphere) within the sample as many rejections of interview requests were based on the statement that the MEP asked would not be an expert on or interested in the issue and could therefore not provide any information on the subject. We therefore complemented the data from the survey with qualitative interviews with 20 MEPs out of the 25, who filled in the questionnaire and who were willing to be interviewed as well, and, finally, a qualitative content-analysis of all German MEPs' parliamentary activities.

The qualitative content-analysis covers all speeches in plenary, motions for resolutions and parliamentary questions of German MEPs during the seventh parliamentary term (cut-off date: 7 June 2013). The data were collected from the personal homepages of the MEPs on the website of the EP. First, we researched all activities (5324 speeches, 2334 participations in motions, 2848 participations in questions[5]) using various keywords relating to religion.[6] In a second step, we sorted out all contributions which only casually mentioned one of the keywords without really focusing on the issue of religion. We then coded the remaining material (91 speeches, 190 motions, 37 questions) using five categories: (1) status of religion in the document (primary or secondary); (2) denominations referred to; (3) territoriality (EU internal affairs: certain member-states; or EU external affairs: accession candidates, neighbouring countries, third states); (4) framing of religion (positive: for example as something to protect; or negative: for example as a factor contributing to conflict); (5) context (for example human rights, terrorism).

The impact of religion on the way the EP works

One of the first questions when reasoning about religion in the EP is about the relevance and specific impact of religion. According to the majority of our interview partners, religion has an effect on the overall functioning of the EP, though a relatively small one. In order to assess the overall effect of religion in the EP, we should differentiate between different understandings of the religious effect.

At the level of personal attitudes, beliefs and values, religion, at least for religious MEPs, is a ubiquitous force, constantly affecting parliamentary work, although this might not be expressed explicitly. Some MEPs furthermore stressed the Christian cultural tradition which arguably affects decision-making, even of non-religious MEPs.

Religious issues and arguments, by contrast, do not come up that often; only when corresponding themes are on the agenda. This uncommonness of explicitly religious issues in the EP is confirmed by our content-analysis: only 1.7% of speeches by German MEPs in the plenary, 1.6% of participations in parliamentary questions and 20% of participations in motions for resolutions included an explicit reference to religion, and in all these only 21.1% focused primarily on religion, the remainder only briefly mentioning religion, primarily freedom of religion.

The effect of religion in terms of direct influence of religious actors is perceived by the German MEPs to be rather marginal.

There are three dimensions which might affect how religion impacts the work of the EP: nationality, group membership and denominational differences.

First, national differences, according to the surveyed German MEPs, have the largest impact on the importance of religion. Slightly more than half of them (13) thought that MEPs from some countries, such as Poland, Italy, Spain and Portugal, were more inclined to use religious arguments, whereas MEPs from France and Nordic countries were reluctant to do so. The German group was often located somewhere in the middle because of its strong diversity in terms of religiosity and religious affiliation. However, other German MEPs did not see much influence of nationality, because of diversity in other national groups as well. Some of the interviewed MEPs ascribed the impact of the national dimension less to the extent of religiosity in member-states than to their traditions of church–state relations. These traditions affect how MEPs from different countries deal with the issue of religion, even if they are not part of the national majority. The historical and cultural traditions thus might have a larger impact than individual religiosity and confessional belonging.

Second, political group membership is assessed to be less effective. Most surveyed German MEPs thought that religion had no effect on group differences or even blurred them, because the political groups in the EP are represented by both religious and non-religious MEPs. There is only one exception: most surveyed MEPs agreed on the fact that religion is most important for the Christian Democrats in the EPP. The EPP in general, even though represented not only by Christian Democrats but also by other conservatives, seems to be closest to religion. For instance, it organises a range of religious events and meetings through its Group on Intercultural Dialogue and Religious Affairs.[7] As far as we know, there are no corresponding working groups within the other political groups in the EP.

Third, denominational differences are considered to be the least effective factor in the functioning of the EP. The majority of the consulted German MEPs (16) saw no impact at all. Some German MEPs, though, observed a stronger commitment of Catholic and Orthodox Christians to their church and its positions than members of other denominations. However, most MEPs also emphasised their lack of knowledge about the confessional adherence of most of the other MEPs and consequently could not perceive corresponding differences.

In the end it might be the intersection of these three dimensions, culminating in Catholicism, which has the greatest effect: MEPs from primarily Catholic countries, from the EPP as dominated by Catholics, and of the Catholic faith were, in the view of some interviewed MEPs, most prone to religious influence on the politics of the EP. However, most MEPs also stressed the diversity both within national and political groups in the EP on issues of religion as well as others, making exceptions to the rule common, and clear-cut distinctions impossible. In the end, when substantial policy issues are concerned, political divisions appear to be stronger than religious ones.

Religion in the political practice and socialisation of German MEPs

The privileged social role of the churches in Germany can also be recognised in how German MEPs interact with religious interest-groups. Although most of them consider contacts with religious interest-groups to be secondary in their work, the frequency of their contacts is comparatively high.

Half of the surveyed German MEPs frequently deal with religion in their parliamentary work. More than half of the MEPs (52%) think that religion primarily plays out as a personal source of inspiration for decision-making, especially for the German MEPs who consider themselves religious. The consulted MEPs who do not define themselves religious do not perceive any impact of religion on their work (12%) or see religion only as an external phenomenon that sometimes needs to be dealt with (20%). Contact with religion as an interest-group, trying to influence the work of MEPs, is only secondary

Table 3. Frequency of contact with religious and ethical interest-groups (%).

	At least once a week	At least once a month	Several times per year	Several times in a legislative period	(Almost) never
MEPs: How often do religious and ethical interest-groups contact you?	12	24	44	4	16
MPs from Germany*	6.4	33.9	54.6 (at least once a year)	(not included)	5.2
Average of MPs from 15 countries (Western and Eastern Europe, Israel)*	4.7	15.9	50.8	(not included)	28.5

Note: *Unpublished data from the PartiRep Comparative MP Survey (Pascal Delwit, Jean-Benoît Pilet, Giulia Sandri, ULB, Brussels) (only churches and religious organisations).

in the MEPs' perception, despite frequent contacts between some of the German MEPs and religious interest-groups.

Most of the included German MEPs have regular contacts with religious (or secularist) interest-groups. Contacts are somewhat more frequent than those of domestic German politicians, but considerably more frequent than the average for MEPs from other countries (see Foret in this publication) and for domestic parliamentarians from other countries (Table 3). The survey of German MEPs suggests a strong positive association between the religiosity of the MEP and the frequency of contacts (all MEPs who reported contacts at least once a month or once a week were religious). The political factor, in contrast, seems to be less relevant. Although the MEPs with contacts at least once a week are all members of the EEP, MEPs with contacts at least once a month or several times a year come from all parties, including the UEL/NGL. The most frequent contacts are with the German Catholic and Protestant Churches. Other contacts include: Caritas; the Commission of the [Catholic] Bishops' Conferences of the European Community (COMECE); Eurodiaconia; the Conference of European Churches (CEC); the World Youth Alliance; B'nai B'rith International; the European Jewish Congress; Laïcité; Brot für die Welt, Misereor (relief organisations of the German churches); the German Humanist Union. These contacts are of a wide variety: information, policy briefs and position papers sent by email or mail; invitations to panel discussions, conversations on certain topics, receptions, religious ceremonies; meetings with representatives of religious communities; personal contacts via telephone and lunch meetings. Religious organisations furthermore provide expertise and contacts to interesting interlocutors, and serve as forums for discussions. Most of the interviewed German MEPs have more contacts in their electoral districts in Germany than at the European level.

The German churches are regarded by many of the German MEPs as 'normal' interest groups and vital contributors to interest mediation. The contact is also often perceived as a dialogue rather than unilateral lobbying, particularly by religious MEPs. For most of the interviewed German MEPs, the commitment of the churches and non-governmental organisations with a religious background is particularly visible on substantial policy issues (such as poverty; environmental protection; genetic engineering; development cooperation; world hunger; agricultural policy; human rights; issues of social justice; the rights of refugees, migrants and minorities; fair trade; recently also the financial crisis), rather than on religious or institutional interests of the churches. This primarily altruistic, non-commercial role of the churches at the European level, resembling their social role in German politics, provides them, in the eyes of most of the consulted MEPs, with legitimacy and explains their relatively frequent contacts. It furthermore distinguishes them from other more traditional churches from Eastern Europe and from small groups of fundamentalist Christians, which in the view of two German MEPs do not possess the German tradition of social responsibility and often agitate against European values.

Given the widespread recognition among German MEPs of religious communities, primarily the churches, as legitimate partners in pursuing European values, it is not surprising that the majority of the German survey respondents across believers and non-believers as well as different religious affiliations and political groups accept the EP presidents' efforts to enter into dialogue with religious communities. Only one atheist S&D member rejected even this as an illegitimate interference of religion into the political sphere. Two non-religious Greens furthermore demanded that secularist and philosophical groups and intellectuals should also be invited.

Yet the EP does not have a socialising effect on German MEPs regarding their views on religion. Of the surveyed German MEPs 92% have not experienced any changes in these views during their service in the EP.

Policy sectors and thematic debates in which religion is most salient

German MEPs across all parties display a largely affirmative notion of religion, indirectly mirroring the cooperative, religion-friendly model in Germany. Religion is primarily framed in their parliamentary activities as something to protect, facilitated by placing it mainly in the context of protecting human rights. However, by referring to the issue as one to primarily focus on abroad, parliamentary activities also contribute to drawing a demarcation line between 'Christian Europe' and 'Muslim violators of human rights abroad'.

The content analysis reveals that the policy sector in which religion is most salient in the parliamentary activities of German MEPs is external relations. Almost 90% of all participations in speeches, motions and questions refer to EU external affairs, primarily in third countries (68%) but also in countries included in the European Neighbourhood Policy (ENP) (28%) and in accession candidates (4%). Accordingly, most of the German MEPs who are most active on religion (in terms of the number of their religion-specific parliamentary activities), or who define themselves as religious, are members of the Committee on Foreign Affairs, including its two subcommittees on Human Rights and Security and Defence. The majority of the surveyed German MEPs (72%) think that religion is an issue playing a role in EU external relations. However, as one MEP rightly points out, the competences of the EP in the EU's external relations are limited. Its politics on religion with its strong emphasis on human rights, therefore, is primarily of symbolic significance.

Human rights is an area which is particularly suitable for reconciling different views on religion. The principle can easily be deduced from Christian values of altruism, equity and human dignity, but can also be based on a non-religious humanist perspective. However, in the views of some Christian MEPs, it is primarily the joint Christian tradition which unites MEPs across political divisions even though not all of them are Christian. Accordingly, not all MEPs consider the protection of freedom of religion and of the rights of religious and secular minorities to be an issue of religion, but rather an issue of fundamental rights.

In parliamentary speeches, motions and questions, religion is most often referred to in Muslim contexts as most of the countries focused upon have Muslim majority populations, such as Pakistan, Iran, Iraq, Bahrain, Yemen and Kazakhstan, as well as Egypt, Syria and Turkey. However, German MEPs also often refer to freedom of religion and religious minorities in other countries, such as Tibet, Myanmar, Russia, Vietnam, North Korea and Belarus'.[8] A strong focus lies on the protection of Christian minorities, but minorities from other religions are also referred to, including Islam, Buddhism, Baha'i, Hinduism, Jehovah's Witnesses, Falun Dafa, Ahmadis, as well as, in some cases, the rights of converts and secular people. Jews are primarily referred to in EU internal affairs in activities against discrimination on grounds of religion, including most prominently antisemitism and Islamophobia.

The concentration on the rights of religious minorities in the parliamentary activities of the German MEPs is one reason why religion is referred to in a primarily positive way. One major exception is Islam, on which negatively framed references outweigh positive ones (by all political groups). It is often placed in the context of intolerance and extremism, as well as violence and conflict.[9] However, differences between political groups are important to mention here. When we calculate positively and negatively connoted references to Islam, we find that the German EPP and ALDE members are more critical towards Islam in their speeches, motions and questions than are the Greens and the Left; on Christianity, German EPP members are not critical at all.

Besides EU external affairs, German MEPs' views on policy sectors and thematic debates in which religion is most salient diverge. Fundamental rights are also perceived as important, including issues such as women's and reproductive rights, rights to life and the rights of sexual minorities. A field particularly often stressed by German MEPs is bioethics, such as genetic engineering, stem cell research and pre-implantation genetic diagnosis. Further fields often mentioned in the interviews include development cooperation, enlargement, environmental protection, asylum and integration, social policy, culture and education, global food protection and family policy. However, as our content analysis of parliamentary activities reveals, these are fields that German MEPs almost never frame in explicitly religious terms. Our interpretation therefore is that these policy fields are more implicitly affected by religious values (without explicit reference to them), as well as by interventions by religious interest groups, such as the churches, which, at least in Germany, are strongly involved in many of those debates.

A 'special case' in the debate about religion in EP politics is the accession of Turkey to the EU, which is not only about adding one more country to the EU but also about the identity and the borders of Europe (Minkenberg 2012, 150). Of the German respondents 68% think that religion is an important issue in the debate about Turkey's accession, but many of them perceive this impact only in a subtle way, for instance when opponents of Turkey's accession highlight cultural differences to obscure their reservations about Islam. The fact that the major German churches have been sceptical about Turkey's accession to the EU, primarily on grounds of non-respect for religious freedom and of cultural and value-based differences from the other EU members (Minkenberg 2012, 160–163), also suggests a more hidden religious factor in the EP, although religion is not explicitly referred to in debates. Of the respondents 32% think religion does not play a role at all.

Religion itself is not regarded by most of the surveyed German MEPs as an issue requiring a common approach by the EU. The case of a reference to the Christian heritage in the Treaty of Lisbon, by contrast, is clearly an issue that divides the included German

MEPs into two groups: believers in the EPP and all others. That a reference to the Christian heritage or even God was not included in the Treaty, despite extensive mobilising by EPP members and religious organisations, suggests that there is no majority in the EP for overtly religious positions.[10]

Religious affiliation and religiosity: German MEPs and MBs in comparison

One important question in the study of religion and political elites is whether political elites mirror religious trends within their societies (Oermann 2007, 151). We shall therefore now assess whether German politics at the European level is more or less secularised than at the national level, and whether parliamentarians represent the religious social structure of German society at large. To this end, we complemented our original data with a review of CVs on the personal websites of all German MEPs and an additional mini survey, asking the German MEPs only about their religious affiliation and personal faith, which eventually provided us with information on the religious affiliation of 54.5% of all German MEPs, and on the subjective religiosity of 45.5%.

According to our data, about 38.9% of German MEPs are Catholic and 38.9% Protestant, 1.9% are Muslim and 20.4% are unaffiliated with any religion. Reflecting parity between the two major Christian faiths in Germany, Christian church members are significantly overrepresented in the EP compared with the 29.4% of each of the two major denominations in Germany. People of no confession are significantly underrepresented compared with their share of 32.5% in the German population (Table 1). However, as we stated earlier, we assume a bias towards church members and religious MEPs in our sample. But even if the numbers do not allow conclusive findings about the distribution of denominations among Germans in the EP, they do mirror some trends which we also find among members of the German Bundestag (MBs) (Table 4).

Despite individual secularisation processes in German society, numbers of Christians in the German Bundestag have remained relatively stable (Oermann 2007). The over-representation might be caused by the fact that Christian church members in Germany are disproportionately often involved in civic and political engagement (Liedhegener 2011; Traunmüller 2009; Roßteutscher 2009). After reunification, Protestants were particularly overrepresented in the Bundestag as the Protestant Church was the largest church in the GDR and provided an important base for the opposition movement there. In many cases, political elites were recruited from this group, although their presence in politics has started to dwindle (Oermann 2007, 157–158). Recently the proportion of Protestants has dropped below the proportion of Catholics in the Bundestag. The majority of MBs do not specify their religion (Figure 1). We cannot say whether they have just not given any details or whether religion plays no role in their lives. This group of MBs has been

Table 4. Religious preferences of German MBs, 2010 (%).

Catholic	30.5
Protestant	28.5
Muslim	0.5
No confession	4.3
Atheist	0.3
Not specified	35.9

Source: Deutscher Bundestag (2010).

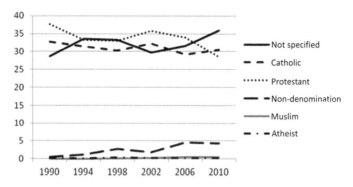

Figure 1. Denominations in the German Bundestag, 1990–2010 (%).
Source: Deutscher Bundestag (2010).

increasing over the last 20 years (Figure 1), suggesting a trend towards the privatisation of religion. Catholics, in the German Bundestag as well as in our sample of the EP, are primarily represented in the CDU/CSU (and the EPP), whereas Protestants are more evenly distributed amongst all parties. The members of the CDU/CSU in the Bundestag seem also to be more religious, as about 6% do not specify their religious preferences, whereas in the other parties the figure is considerably higher. Most of the MBs without religious preferences can be found, as expected, in the Left and the Green parties (Figure 2).

A similar distribution can be found among the German MEPs in the EP. All included MEPs from the EPP (as well as the ALDE) also define themselves as religious (with two exceptions who did not want to provide information on this question). The majority of them attend church more than once a year. Other groups, such as the S&D, the Greens and the Left, are more mixed with respect to the presence of both religious and non-religious MEPs. Although the total numbers included in the survey are small, they do suggest that the EPP among German MEPs is the most religious group and the S&D and the Left are the least religious: the five convinced atheists from our (extended) sample (11.1%) are members of these two groups.

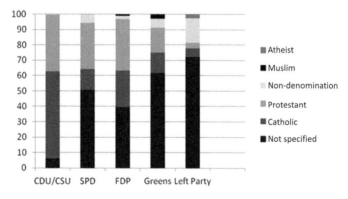

Figure 2. Religious preferences in the German Bundestag by party, 2010 (%).
Source: Deutscher Bundestag (2010).

Of German MEPs who responded to our surveys 66.7% define themselves as religious. In the German Bundestag, about 60% of the MBs do so (Deutscher Bundestag 2010). Both numbers correspond relatively well with the number of believers in German society, where about two thirds believe in a God (Pickel 2013, 83). As in society at large, the proportion of believers in the German Bundestag has decreased: from about 70% in 1990 to 60% in 2010 (Deutscher Bundestag 2010).

Our data thus suggest relatively similar patterns of religious affiliation and religiosity in the EP and the German Bundestag. This to some degree also represents societal trends in Germany. However, German political elites appear to be more Christian and religious than the German average population. If we compare the presence of religion in terms of religious interest-groups and arguments, though, the Bundestag seems to be more religious than the EP. According to Mariano Barbato (forthcoming), the German Bundestag is a 'post-secular location' which admits religious communities and respects religious argumentation. The specific arrangement is contested, but there is not a strict separation of religious discourse from the presence of a secular institution. However, explicit references to religion are not integrated into the day-to-day work of the Bundestag but confined to particular debates. If these debates relate to questions of conscience, parliamentary groups lift party discipline and allow the MBs to vote freely. In such debates, for example on pre-implantation diagnostics, MBs also exchange explicitly religious arguments and argue about different images of God and religious beliefs (Barbato, forthcoming). Other issues on which party discipline has been lifted include topics such as the living will, late-term abortions, genetic engineering, the foreign assignment of German armed forces and the fight against terrorism.

Many MBs, furthermore, traditionally maintain close contacts with the German [Catholic] Bishops' Conference and the EKD (*Evangelische Kirche in Deutschland*). Each parliamentary group has its own representative for churches and religious communities; they are often also members of prominent religious institutions such as the *Synode der Evangelischen Kirche in Deutschland* and the *Zentralkomitee der deutschen Katholiken* (Deutscher Bundestag 2012).

These considerations correspond well with the views of many of the consulted German MEPs: 60% of them think that the place of religion in the EP and in European politics differs from the position in Germany. Most think that religion is less salient in European than in German politics. One piece of evidence, often referred to in the interviews, is the fact that the German Bundestag offers many more structures for religious contemplation, spiritual exchange and religious networking than the EP. There is a (multireligious) prayer room within the Bundestag, in which religious communities organise religious services; there is a weekly 'prayer breakfast' in parliamentary premises near the building of the Bundestag; and the cross-party group 'Christians in Parliament' (*Christen im Parlament*), is regularly represented at the *Kirchentag* with its own stand (Deutscher Bundestag 2012). MEPs, by contrast, have to organise regular religious services and 'prayer breakfasts' outside the EP.

German MEPs, regardless of whether religious or not, explain the lesser presence of religious and ethical themes, debates and voices in the EP by the larger religious and cultural diversity in the EP and a considerable participation of states with strict separation between church and state, making religion too conflictual an issue to integrate in the day-to-day work of the EP. The MEPs noticing a stronger role of religion in the EP than in Germany ascribe this to European struggles to find a common identity and more explicit expressions of religious beliefs by MEPs from other countries, particularly from the south of Europe.

Conclusions

As demonstrated in the previous sections of this study, the influence of the German model of publicly dealing with religion is, to a certain extent, mirrored in the perceptions, attitudes and activities of German MEPs. The churches are largely recognised as important mediators of social interests. Religion is affirmatively referred to in speeches, motions and questions, primarily as a matter of human rights of religious minorities, facilitating a relative consensus across believers and non-believers as well as different denominations, because all MEPs, irrespective of individual religiosity or religious affiliation, can agree on this fundamental European value. The explicit referencing of religion, because of its focus on Christian minorities in Muslim countries outside the EU, as well as negative connotations of Islam, however, also contributes to symbolically drawing boundaries between a Christian or secular Europe and Islam as an 'external other'.

The EP certainly is less 'post-secular' than the German Bundestag. Explicitly religious arguments and issues are largely absent from the EP. Because of the great diversity of the EP, religion appears to be too conflictual an issue to be brought up explicitly and frequently. Leaving religion as a subject and explicit pattern of argumentation out of the EP is the smallest common denominator allowing efficient day-to-day work. However, as our study has demonstrated, this does not necessarily mean that the level of religiosity in the EP is particularly low, that religious values do not affect individual decisions and that religious interest-groups are not received well. Hence religion does affect the workings of the EP, but in a rather subtle way. The question of whether and how this might be changing and with what consequences will have to be answered by future research.

Notes

1. 'Aware of its responsibility to God and the people, inspirited by the willingness to serve peace in the world as an equal member of a united Europe, the German nation, by virtue of its constitutional power, has given itself this constitution' (our translation).
2. The Protestant Church consists of different units, called *Landeskirchen*, which together form the *Evangelische Kirche in Deutschland* (EKD).
3. The condition for receiving this status is the guarantee of continuity proven by a statute and a certain number of community members. Religious communities not operating under public law receive a civil law status as a private registered association (German Constitution, art. 137.5).
4. The classification of the churches as organised interests, however, is contested (Willems 2007, 318–321).
5. As the research presented here uses the MEP as level of analysis and since most motions and questions are issued by a group of MEPs, these numbers do not represent the number of motions and questions but exceed it.
6. We thank Johanna Voß for her assistance in this research.
7. The phrase 'religious affairs' was dropped in 2012. However, the group still works primarily on issues of religion (http://www.eppgroup.eu/intercultural-dialogue).
8. We name here only countries that were referred to at least 10 times. A complete list can be obtained from the authors.
9. Given the limited scope of this study, we can focus here only on major trends and do not report about alternative views on issues reflected in our content analysis.
10. This assumption corresponds to the impression of some of the interviewed MEPs. Another piece of anecdotal evidence from our interviews for this assumption is the failed attempt of an Italian MEP to establish an intergroup on Christian family values.

References

Barbato, M. Forthcoming. "Postsäkulares Parlament: der Deutsche Bundestag als postsäkularer Ort" [Postsecular Parliament: The German Bundestag as Postsecular Location]. In *Religionspolitik in der Bundesrepublik Deutschland* [Religious Politics in the Federal Republic of Germany], edited by G. Pickel and A. Liedhegener. Wiesbaden: Springer VS.

Bösch, F. 2013. "Christlich-Demokratische Union Deutschlands (CDU)" [The Christian-Democratic Union of Germany]. In *Handbuch der deutschen Parteien* [Handbook of German Parties], edited by F. Decker and V. Neu, 203–218. Wiesbaden: Springer Fachmedien.

Cavuldak, A. 2013. "Die Legitimität der hinkenden Trennung von Staat und Kirche in der Bundesrepublik Deutschland" [The Legitimacy of the Limping Separation of State and Church in the Federal Republic of Germany]. In *Religion und Politik im vereinigten Deutschland: was bleibt von der Rückkehr des Religiösen?* [Religion and Politics in United Germany: What's Left of the Return of the Religious?], edited by G. Pickel and O. Hidalgo, 307–335. Wiesbaden: VS Verlag für Sozialwissenschaften.

Davie, G. 2012. "A European Perspective on Religion and Welfare: Contrasts and Commonalities." *Social Policy and Society* 11 (4): 589–599. doi:10.1017/S1474746412000267.

de Nève, D. 2013. "Islamophobie in Deutschland und Europa" [Islamophobia in Germany and Europe]. In *Religion und Politik im vereinigten Deutschland: was bleibt von der Rückkehr des Religiösen?* [Religion and Politics in United Germany: What's Left of the Return of the Religious?], edited by G. Pickel and O. Hidalgo, 195–220. Wiesbaden: VS Verlag für Sozialwissenschaften.

Deutscher Bundestag. 2010. *Amtliches Handbuch des deutschen Bundestages* [Official Handbook of the German Bundestag]. Rheinbreitbach: Neue Darmstädter Verlagsanstalt.

Deutscher Bundestag. 2012. *Die Abgeordneten und ihr Glaube* [The Representatives and their Faith]. https://www.btg-bestellservice.de/pdf/20057000.pdf.

Elff, M., and S. Rossteutscher. 2011. "Stability or Decline? Class, Religion and the Vote in Germany." *German Politics* 20 (1): 107–127. doi:10.1080/09644008.2011.554109.

Gerngroß, M. 2010. "(K)eine Bindung auf ewig: die CSU und die Kirchen" [(No) Tie in Perpetuity: The CSU and the Churches]. In *Die CSU: Strukturwandel, Modernisierung und Herausforderungen einer Volkspartei* [The CSU: Structural Change, Modernisation and Challenges of a Catch-All Party], edited by G. Hopp, M. Sebaldt, and B. Zeitler, 77–98. Wiesbaden: VS Verlag für Sozialwissenschaften.

Göçmen, İ. 2013. "The Role of Faith-Based Organizations in Social Welfare Systems: A Comparison of France, Germany, Sweden, and the United Kingdom." *Nonprofit and Voluntary Sector Quarterly* Apr. 3. doi:10.1177/0899764013482046.

Götze, C., Y. Jaeckel, and G. Pickel. 2013. "Religiöse Pluralisierung als Konfliktfaktor? Wirkungen religiösen Sozialkapitals auf die Integrationsbereitschaft in Deutschland" [Religious Pluralisation as Factor of Conflict? Effects of Religious Social Capital on the Willingness to Integrate in Germany]. In *Religion und Politik im vereinigten Deutschland: was bleibt von der Rückkehr des Religiösen?* [Religion and Politics in United Germany: What's Left of the Return of the Religious?], edited by G. Pickel and O. Hidalgo, 271–304. Wiesbaden: VS Verlag für Sozialwissenschaften.

Hering, R. 2011. "SPD und Kirchen in Deutschland" [The SPD and the Churches in Germany]. *Neue Gesellschaft: Frankfurter Hefte* 4: 43–46.

Liedhegener, A. 2011. "'Linkage' im Wandel: Parteien, Religion und Zivilgesellschaft in der Bundesrepublik Deutschland" [Changing Linkage: Parties, Religion and Civil Society in the Federal Republic of Germany]. In *Religion zwischen Zivilgesellschaft und politischem System: Befunde – Positionen – Perspektiven* [Religion between Civil Society and Political System: Findings – Positions – Perspectives], edited by A. Liedhegener and I.-J. Werkner, 232–256. Wiesbaden: VS Verlag für Sozialwissenschaften.

Liedhegener, A. 2012. "'Da capo' im Wahlkampf 2009? Die Unionsparteien und die Debatte um das 'C'" [Da Capo in the Electoral Campaign of 2009? The Christian Democratic Parties and the Debate about the "C"]. In *Sphärendynamik II: Religion in postsäkularen Gesellschaften* [Sphere Dynamics II: Religion in Postsecular Societies], edited by G. Pfleiderer and A. Heit, 241–258. Baden-Baden: Nomos.

Manow, P., and K. van Kersbergen. 2009. "Religion and the Western Welfare State: The Theoretical Context." In *Religion, Class Coalitions, and Welfare States,* edited by K. van Keersbergen and P. Manow, 1–38. Cambridge: Cambridge University Press.

Minkenberg, M. 2012. "Christian Identity? European Churches and the Issue of Turkey's EU Membership." *Comparative European Politics* 10 (2): 149–179. doi:10.1057/cep.2011.24.

Minkenberg, M. 2013. "Religion und Politik in Europa: alte Fragen und neue Herausforderungen" [Religion and Politics in Europe: Old Questions and New Challenges]. In *Europa-Studien: eine Einführung* [European Studies: An Introduction], edited by T. Bcichelt, C. Bozena, G.C. Rowe and H.-J. Wagner, 53–71. 2nd ed. Wiesbaden: VS Verlag für Sozialwissenschaften.

Oermann, N.O. 2007. "The Importance of Religious Affiliation Among Political Elites: A Comparison of Germany and the United States." In *Religion and Politics in the United States and Germany,* edited by D. Pruin, R. Schieder, and J. Zachhuber, 149–173. Münster: LIT.

Pappi, F.U., and J. Brandenburg. 2010. "Sozialstrukturelle Interessenlagen und Parteipräferenz in Deutschland: Stabilität und Wandel seit 1980" [Sociostructural Ranges of Interests and Party Preferences in Germany: Stability and Change Since 1980]. *Kölner Zeitschrift für Soziologie und Sozialpsychologie* 62 (3): 459–483. doi:10.1007/s11577-010-0111-4.

Pappi, F.U., and S. Shikano. 2002. "Die politisierte Sozialstruktur als mittelfristig stabile Basis einer deutschen Normalwahl" [The Politicised Social Structure as a Stable Basis for a German Normal Vote]. *Kölner Zeitschrift für Soziologie und Sozialpsychologie* 54 (3): 444–475. doi:10.1007/s11577-002-0070-5.

Pickel, G. 2013. "Die Situation der Religion in Deutschland: Rückkehr des Religiösen oder voranschreitende Säkularisierung?" [The Situation of Religion in Germany: Return of the Religious or Progressing Secularisation?]. In *Religion und Politik im vereinigten Deutschland: was bleibt von der Rückkehr des Religiösen?* [Religion and Politics in United Germany: What's Left of the Return of the Religious?], edited by G. Pickel and O. Hidalgo, 65–101. Wiesbaden: VS Verlag für Sozialwissenschaften.

Roßteutscher, S. 2009. *Religion, Zivilgesellschaft, Demokratie: eine international vergleichende Studie zur Natur religiöser Märkte und der demokratischen Rolle religiöser Zivilgesellschaften* [Religion, Civil Society, Democracy: A Comparative International Study of the Nature of Religious Markets and the Democratic Role of Religious Civil Societies]. Baden-Baden: Nomos.

Sebaldt, M., and A. Straßner. 2004. *Verbände in der Bundesrepublik Deutschland: eine Einführung* [Associations in the Federal Republic of Germany: An Introduction]. Wiesbaden: VS Verlag für Sozialwissenschaften.

Spielhaus, R. 2013. "Vom Migranten zum Muslim und wieder zurück: Die Vermengung von Integrations- und Islamthemen in Medien, Politik und Forschung" [From Migrant to Muslim and Back Again: Mixing Issues of Integration and Islam in the Media, in Politics and Research]. In *Islam und die deutsche Gesellschaft* [Islam and German Society], edited by D. Halm and H. Meyer, 169–194. Wiesbaden: VS Verlag für Sozialwissenschaften.

Tezcan, L. 2011. "Repräsentationsprobleme und Loyalitätskonflikte bei der Deutschen Islam Konferenz" [Problems of Representation and Conflicts of Loyalty at the German Islam Conference]. In *Politik und Islam* [Politics and Islam], edited by H. Meyer and K. Schubert, 113–132. Wiesbaden: VS Verlag für Sozialwissenschaften.

Thériault, B. 2004. *"Conservative Revolutionaries": Protestant and Catholic Churches in Germany After Radical Political Change in the 1990s*. New York/Oxford: Berghahn Books.

Traunmüller, R. 2009. "Religion und Sozialintegration: eine empirische Analyse der religiösen Grundlagen sozialen Kapitals" [Religion and Social Integration: An Empirical Analysis of the Religious Foundations of Social Capital]. *Berliner Journal für Soziologie* 19 (3): 435–468. doi:10.1007/s11609-009-0100-5.

Willems, U. 2007. "Kirchen" [Churches]. In *Interessenverbände in Deutschland* [Interest Groups in Germany], edited by T. von Winter and U. Willems, 316–340. Wiesbaden: VS Verlag für Sozialwissenschaften.

Wohlrab-Sahr, M. 2003. "Politik und Religion: 'diskretes' Kulturchristentum als Fluchtpunkt europäischer Gegenbewegungen gegen einen 'ostentativen' Islam" [Politics and Religion: Discreet Christian Culture as Focus of European Counter-Movements against an Ostentatious Islam]. In *Der Begriff des Politischen* [The Notion of Politics], edited by A. Nassehi and M. Schroer, 357–381. Baden-Baden: Nomos.

'A nation of vicars and merchants': religiosity and Dutch MEPs

Didier Caluwaerts[a], Pieter-Jan De Vlieger[a] and Silvia Erzeel[b]

[a]Department of Political Science, Vrije Universiteit Brussel, Brussels, Belgium; [b]Institut de Sciences Politiques Louvain-Europe, Université Catholique de Louvain, Louvain-La-Neuve, Belgium

Religion is a major driving force in the Dutch political system and as European integration has progressed, it is often argued that these national practices affect how national representatives act in the European Parliament (EP). Our aim in this study is to determine to what extent the religious divide impacts upon the work of Dutch MEPs in the European political arena. On the basis of the RelEP survey and interviews, we argue that religious or secular views are very salient to Dutch MEPs, but that their impact is largely indirect. Moreover, we find that Dutch MEPs actively use the EP and its committee system in an attempt to redefine the relationship between church and state in the Netherlands. And finally, we argue that the European arena offers new opportunities for mobilisation among those promoting secularist interests.

Introduction

The elections of September 2012 were a bombshell for the Christian Democratic party in The Netherlands. The *Christen-Democratisch Appel* (CDA) lost another 8 seats in the elections for the Second Chamber and became only the fifth party in Parliament. In 2006 it had had 41 seats in Parliament and was comfortably head of the coalition government. In 2014 it now retains a meagre 13 seats. The total for all Christian parties is equally at a historic low with a mere 21 seats out of a total 150.

Despite this apparent decline in the electoral appeal of the Christian parties, religion is still a major driving force in the Dutch political system (Kennedy and Zwemer 2010). Debates about a clear division of labour between church and state have always been prominent in the Dutch political landscape, and recent debates about gay marriage, euthanasia, Sunday trading and – above all – religious pluralism as a consequence of immigration have strongly rekindled them.

As European integration progressed, it was often argued that these national practices and discussions affect how national representatives act in the European Parliament (EP). Members of the European Parliament (MEPs) are, after all, socialised in their national sphere, and there could be important path dependencies: cleavages at the national level could influence the behaviour of MEPs at the European level. This is particularly so for the denominational divide, which was found to impact strongly on partisan politics in the EP (Jansen 2000, 104; Silvestri 2009), and which is one of the main driving forces of conflict between and within member states.

In this study our aim is therefore to determine to what extent the religious divide impacts upon the work of Dutch MEPs work in the European political arena. Central questions are: (1) how does religion affect how Dutch MEPs act?; and (2) do the religious cleavages that characterise the Netherlands translate into political and policy conflicts at the European level? We argue that religious or secular views offer strong cues to Dutch MEPs in their parliamentary work, but that the impact of religion is largely indirect. Religion offers moral perspectives on a political issue, but rarely influences the behaviour of MEPs in a direct manner. Moreover, we argue that Dutch MEPs actively use the EP and its committee system in an attempt to redefine the relationship between church and state in the Netherlands. Finally we argue that religious mobilisation takes place primarily among those promoting secularist interests rather than among those advocating a religious agenda.

In order to substantiate these arguments, we have used two main sources of data. First we administered the RelEP survey to the Dutch MEPs to determine the relative weight that they give to religion in the work they do, how religion affects their functioning, and how closely they are related to lobby groups on this issue. Then we conducted a number of interviews with a diverse set of the key Dutch MEPs on this issue in order to further elaborate the survey data.

Before developing these arguments in our study we first discuss the historically close relationship between religion and politics in the Netherlands. In order to understand the context in which Dutch MEPs are socialised, we go into detail about the history of religious conflict and the consociational political system it created, and about how the religious cleavage runs through the current Dutch party system. Then we turn to the European level and analyse how salient the religious cleavage is to the work of the Dutch MEPs, and how religiosity affects the MEPs' representational tasks. We also examine how religious and party lines intersect, and how closely related the Dutch MEPs are to denominational lobby groups.

Religion and politics in the Netherlands

In this section we introduce some relevant aspects of Dutch politico-religious life. The behaviour and thinking of Dutch MEPs is, at least partially, a consequence of the local setting in which they were brought up. It is therefore important to analyse some relevant traits of Dutch society, its levels of religiosity and secularisation and the stance of the political parties on the relation between church and state.

Pillarisation, consociation and secularisation

The twentieth-century Netherlands is often described as a pillarised country. These pillars were – and to some extent still are – comprehensive institutional frameworks in which members are socialised on the basis of their own (religious or secular) ideology. The political party stood at the centre of the pillar and articulated the members' religious or secular preferences in the political arena. The party was, however, flanked by a wide network of auxiliary organisations, which served as socialisation and mobilising structures. Chief among these were schools, trade unions, leisure time associations, youth clubs, media outlets and health care funds (Lijphart 1968).

The deep religious divide in Dutch society and the culture of self-containment which accompanied it gave rise to four such pillars: Catholic; Orthodox-Protestant; Socialist; and a 'liberal' pillar which included all those who were not in any of the other pillars

(Knippenberg 2007). The political reality was that none of these pillar parties had a stable majority in the Parliament: forming a government always necessitated a coalition of at least two parties and an attitude of religious accommodation on the part of the elites. This type of political system is described by Lijphart (1968) as a consociational democracy. In essence this means that all political parties prefer making compromises and sharing power to marginalising the other pillars and opening up the possibility of civil conflict. Such a politics of religious accommodation required a specific set of institutions (Lijphart 1969). The divergent interests of the various pillars could be accommodated through a combination of (1) executive power-sharing in grand coalitions which regularly included more parties than were needed to have a majority, (2) a high degree of autonomy for the organisational functioning of the pillars, (3) proportionality with regard to representation in political bodies or allocation of public resources, and (4) a system of minority vetoes (Andeweg 2008; Andeweg and Irwin 2002). This consociational politics turned 'a democracy with a [deeply] fragmented political culture into a stable democracy' (Lijphart 1969, 216) and Hillebrand and Irwin (1999) even observe that if one of the main political parties (the CDA (*Christen-Democratisch Appel*), the VVD (*Volkspartij voor Vrijheid en Democratie*) or the PvdA (*Partij van de Arbeid*)) pursued conflict and polarisation as a vote-seeking strategy, it would be the two other parties which formed the government. Thus religious depolarisation proved to be a winning strategy for parties wanting to become a member of government (Adams, de Vries, and Leiter 2012).

The Dutch consociational system led to an explicit institutional acknowledgment of the religious diversity in the Netherlands and for a long time the pattern of self-containment within pillars and religious accommodation between pillars was rooted in a religiously divided society. It was not until the 'cultural revolution' of the 1960s – mainstreaming processes of individualisation and secularisation – that Dutch society started to depolarise (Girwin 2000; Knippenberg 1998).

Secularisation has been extremely rapid in the Netherlands: it is estimated that 60% of all Dutch citizens are nowadays non-denominational. Thus the label 'Protestant domination with a significant Catholic minority' (Van der Wusten and Knippenberg 2001) no longer adequately represents the wider societal reality in the Netherlands; but politics remains divided along religious lines (Engeli, Green-Pedersen, and Larsen 2013). Secularisation has nevertheless had an interesting consequence for the perception of the public role of religion: the aspiration of Christians towards a role for religion in the public domain became stronger instead of weaker with the rise of secularisation (Achterberg et al. 2009). This indicates that a public role for religion is increasingly considered to be important as the number of Christians declines.

Thus the deep secularisation of Dutch society has not been paralleled by a secularisation of politics. It has rather led to an increased emphasis on the importance of religion on the part of Christians, the idea being that individual religiosity matters more as the core of Christian voters declines (van der Brug, Hobolt, and de Vreese 2009). This compensatory strategy has become even more salient with the rise of new parties, such as D66 (*Democraten 66*), which were created outside the traditional pillared structures and in opposition to it.

A religiously divided party system

Because religious diversity was strongly institutionalised during the pillarisation, the secular-religious cleavage is still considerably vibrant in Dutch party politics to this very day. The case of the biggest Christian Democratic party, the CDA, is telling in this regard. The CDA is typically viewed as among the most 'principled' of all Christian Democratic parties (Hanley 1994), with a strong Biblical emphasis in its programme (Duncan 2007). The party continuously underlined its Christian inspiration and, as an office-seeking party, retranslated its fundamental Christian values into a politically useful ideology, becoming more conservative and anti-permissive with respect to the private sphere (van Kersbergen 2008). Nevertheless, when in government the CDA passed a large number of contentious issues (such as divorce, abortion) into liberal legislation (Andeweg and Irwin 2002; Outshoorn 2001) and it also had a policy of tolerating – while still controlling – practices such as prostitution, homosexuality, abortion and divorce (van Kersbergen 2008). This politics of religious toleration and of striking political bargains with its coalition partners shows that the CDA, as one of the main governing parties, was able to set aside its own views in the interest of pacifying religious conflict and maintaining the country's political stability (Lijphart 1969).

Besides the CDA, there are two other Christian parties in the Netherlands: the *ChristenUnie* (CU) and the *Staatkundig Gereformeerde Partij* (SGP). These two parties cater for the so-called Dutch 'Bible Belt' and they are systematically represented in Parliament because of the extremely proportional Dutch electoral system. The CU bases its policies on the Bible but it is considered centre-left ('Christian social'). It is conservative in ethical and family matters, but less radical than the SGP. The latter aims to defend the principles of Scripture at the political level and opposes gender equality, the decriminalisation of homosexuality and the legalisation of divorce, abortion and euthanasia.

At the other extreme of the fault line, D66 promotes the secular values of freedom of religion (including the choice not to believe), tolerance, human equality, self-determination and emancipation. Even though the party is not antireligious *per se*, it is in most discussions very critical of religious actors since, it claims, they limit the freedom of choice of individuals. In this it concurs with a party on the secular side of the religious cleavage, the conservative-liberal *Volkspartij voor Vrijheid en Democratie* (VVD). The VVD also refers to the right to self-determination as a fundamental principle, especially in ethical matters, and its manifesto clearly advocates the separation of church and state as an important party principle.

The other parties do not tackle religion head on. The extreme right *Partij voor de Vrijheid* (PVV) is the most outspoken as the main trademark of Geert Wilders is his fight against the 'Islamisation' of society and 'unbridled' immigration. His party programme calls for a reference in the Dutch Constitution to the Judeo-Christian and humanist tradition as the dominant culture in Holland, replacing the current article, which bans among other things religious discrimination.

Neither the Social-Democrat PvdA, the *Socialistische Partij* (SP) nor the Green *GroenLinks* (GL) speak directly about religion. The PvdA emphasises civility and links liberty, solidarity and responsibility closely together. The SP emphasises similar secular values such as human dignity, solidarity and equality but is mainly preoccupied with economic issues. The GL respects freedom of religion, but the focus of the party is on emancipation and breaking free from all (societal) constraints an individual has to deal with. Ethically speaking the party defends the individual right to self-determination.

Dutch exceptionalism?

Because of the continued salience of religion in the Dutch party system, the Netherlands seems to occupy an exceptional position in Western Europe (Kennedy and Zwemer 2010). It is therefore useful to compare the views on religion of Dutch national MPs with those of

Table 1.   The salience of religion and frequency of contacts with religious groups.

	How important is it to you to promote the views and interests of a church or religious group?[1]	How frequently are you in contact with churches or religious organisations?[2]
NET	3.68	3.89
BEL	2.95	4.13
GER	4.79	2.88
FRA	2.72	4.07
UK	4.36	2.64

Note: [1]Scale ranges from '1' (not at all important) to '7' (very important).
[2]Scale ranges from '1' (at least once a week) to '5' (no contact).
Source: Partirep MP survey.

MPs of some other Western European countries. On the basis of data from the Partirep MP survey (Deschouwer and Depauw 2014), we looked at how much importance MPs attach to religion and how much contact they have with religious groups.

The results in Table 1 show that religion is salient to the MPs from the Netherlands and that they are in contact with religious organisations, but at first sight religion is not more salient than among MPs in the other countries. The Dutch MPs have an average score that is largely comparable with the scores of other Western European MPs. However, additional analyses have shown that the variance in the Netherlands is much greater. They might have comparable mean scores, but there is a much wider gap between those who find religion important and those who do not. This indicates that there is a much stronger religious polarisation among Dutch MPs than among MPs in other countries and it also shows that religious or secular cues are exceptionally salient in Dutch politics.

When we take a closer look at the Dutch national context and disaggregate the results by party, we see this level of polarisation in more detail (Table 2). The two confessional parties, the CDA and the CU, consider religion to be very important, whereas the pursuit of a religious agenda matters very little to parties such as the GL and the VVD. This confirms that religion is still a major political cue in the Dutch political party system and that there is enduring disagreement among the parties over the extent to which religious interests should be pursued in Dutch politics.

The question that inevitably follows is whether the religious polarisation among political parties is rooted in a wider societal reality. In order to do this, we analyse data on the religious denomination, self-declared religiosity and church attendance of Dutch citizens from the European Social Survey (ESS 2010).

Table 2.   Religion among members of the Dutch House of Representatives (*Tweede Kamer*).

	How important is it to you to promote the views and interests of a church or religious group? (Scale ranges from 1 to 10)
CU	6.33
CDA	5.19
SP	3.25
PvdA	2.67
VVD	2.55
GL	2.00

Source: Partirep MP survey.

Table 3. Religiosity among citizens in Europe.

	Do you belong to a particular religion or denomination? (%)	How religious are you? (Mean on scale 0–10)[1]	How often do you attend religious services? (Mean on scale 1–6)[2]
NET	40.6	4.75	2.1
BEL	41.9	4.54	1.94
GER	55.5	3.92	2.2
FRA	48.6	3.62	2.03
UK	45.3	3.98	2.1

Note: [1]: Scale from 'not at all religious' (score 1) to 'very religious' (score 10).
[2]: Scale from 'never' (score 1), 'less often' (score 2), 'holidays only' (score 3), 'once a month' (score 4), 'once a week' (score 5), to 'more than once a week' (score 6).
Source: ESS round 5 (2010).

Table 3 indicates that the religiosity of Dutch citizens is not particularly high. Only 40% of Dutch citizens belong to a particular religion, which gives them the lowest score out of five European countries. This confirms the wide secularisation of Dutch society. Moreover, Dutch citizens attend religious services only sporadically, which sharply contrasts with the much more frequent church attendance of their MEPs (Table 1). Their self-declared religiosity is slightly higher than in other European countries, but it still remains lower than the halfway mark. Moreover, it has to be taken into account that while some areas of the Netherlands are highly secularised, other areas – such as the aptly named Dutch Bible Belt, which runs from the south-west to the north-east of the country – retain high levels of religiosity. These findings once again confirm that religion remains strongly institutionalised as a political fault line, even though the societal basis for the conflict has largely vanished. Dutch MEPs, despite their own strong religiosity, thus seem to encounter social constituencies that do not (or no longer) identify themselves on the basis of religion.

From the national to the European level

The Netherlands has evolved from a deeply pillarised society to a more open society, but – as the previous tables have shown – one in which the consequences of the pillars remain visible on the political scene. Religious parties are relatively successful and there is an open religious competition with their secular counterparts. Parliamentary debates also regularly follow the religious–secular cleavage and cleavage patterns are deeply entrenched in politics.

Because Dutch politicians at the European level are socialised in this religiously divided party system, we can expect them to represent their parties' religious views in the European arena. We therefore expect that the national setting will, to some extent, be exported to the European level, with a Dutch religious–secular divide clearly visible in EP debates, especially because the Dutch proportional electoral system for the European elections allows for the representation of all religious or secular groups.

The Dutch delegation to the EP comprises 26 members, who belong to seven parliamentary party groups: the Alliance of Liberals and Democrats for Europe (6 VVD and D66 members), the European People's Party (5 CDA), the Progressive Alliance of Socialists and Democrats (3 PvdA), the Greens/European Free Alliance (3 GL), the Confederal Group of the European United Left (2 SP), the European Conservatives and

Reformists Group (1 CU), and the Europe of Freedom and Democracy Group (1 SGP). Five members are non-attached (4 PVV and 1 independent).

As far as committee assignments are concerned, we find that Dutch MEPs often (choose to) sit on similar parliamentary committees, especially the committees on Foreign Affairs, Budget Control, Economic and Monetary Affairs, Environment, Public Health and Food Safety, and Civil Liberties, Justice and Home Affairs, each of which includes six or seven Dutch members. Also notable is the fact that a significant number of Dutch MEPs (5) are members or substitutes of the Committee on Women's Rights and Gender Equality. This is interesting since Dutch MEPs display a rather low presence in other committees focusing on 'soft' policy issues, such as Culture and Education or Employment and Social Affairs.

Dutch MEPs, religiosity and role of religion

Similarly to the method in the other country cases in this collection, we analyse the attitudes and behaviour of Dutch MEPs on the basis of the results of the RelEP survey and on in-depth interviews. The response rate for the group of Dutch MEPs is relatively high: 10 MEPs filled in (part of) the online questionnaire and four were interviewed face-to-face. We were thus able to survey 54% (14 out of 26) of the Dutch MEPs; but there were some items of non-response. One part of the data focused on MEPs' individual religious beliefs, practices and attitudes. Another part focused on the role of religion in the political practice, activities and networks of the MEPs. In this section, we discuss the findings for the individual religious preferences of the MEPs; in the following section we discuss religion in the political behaviour of MEPs.

Religiosity among Dutch MEPs and citizens

The individual religious preferences of MEPs were measured by asking whether they self-identified as religious, whether they belonged to a particular denomination, how often they went to church and what kind of religiosity they had. A large majority of Dutch MEPs in our survey dataset (7 out of 9 respondents) refer to themselves as religious, indicating that they believe either in a personal God (3) or in some sort of spirit or life force (4) (Table 4). Only three respondents say they are atheists. All those who consider themselves believers belong to a Christian denomination, either Catholic or Protestant.

Interestingly, the party differences with regard to the religious self-identification of MEPs are less clear than at the national level. Whereas religious MPs are primarily found in the CDA and CU, MEPs who consider themselves religious belong to a variety of parties, including the confessional parties the CDA and the CU but also the VVD, the PVV, the SP and the GL. The two self-declared atheists belong to the D66 and the PVV. Religious MEPs can thus be found in each party, but secular MEPs mainly in explicitly

Table 4. Beliefs of the Dutch MEPs (absolute numbers).

Which of the following statements corresponds best to your own convictions? (Absolute *N*)	
There is a personal God	3
There is a certain spirit or life force	4
I do not believe there is a God, nor a spirit of life force	2
Total	9

secular parties. The same pattern can be found with regard to church attendance. All the MEPs who say they believe in a personal God or a spirit attend religious ceremonies at least once a month and we find that the MEPs who report frequent attendance are members not only of the confessional parties but also of the SP, the VVD and the PVV.

The strong religious party divides at the national level thus seem to be more blurred at the European level, which might indicate that there has been little or no socialisation effect from the national to the European level. However, the survey shows that the majority of Dutch MEPs serve a first term in the EP and most of them are also newcomers to public office in general. They entered the EP without having occupied any elective function on the national level. This indicates that the Dutch MEPs tend to follow Scarrow's (1997) 'European career model': they are first and foremost committed to European politics (also on the long term). This lack of a thorough party political socialisation in the Dutch national arena could explain why the religious dividing lines are more vague at the European level.

This finding, that religiosity is not by definition party-related, is evident not only from the survey. The MEPs also emphasised this point in the interviews. For instance, Lucas Hartong of the extreme-right PVV says that although people are often surprised that some Christians are politically active in the PVV they should not be so: 'I am a strong proponent of the separation of church and state, I have that in common with the Liberals. … But that does not mean that I cannot personally give voice to my religious opinions in my work.' In the case of Hartong, it also helps that his religious views merge rather well with the socially conservative stance of the PVV on issues such as abortion and euthanasia. And Dennis de Jong of the socialist party the SP acknowledges that 'many people might find it surprising that someone from the SP engages with these [religious] issues, but we believe that it fits well with what the SP stands for in terms of humanitarian and human dignity'.

Religion in the work of Dutch MEPs: salient but indirect

Dutch MEPs might present a religious or secular profile, but this does not necessarily mean that religion actually influences their work. They might consider religion a private issue which should not interfere with their public lives. To find out whether religion drives their representational work, we asked them to indicate whether they ever take religion into account in their functioning as a MEP.

Despite the salience of the religious differences among Dutch MEPs, fewer than half of them say in the survey that they 'permanently' or 'often' take religious concerns into account in their parliamentary work. Most say they do so 'rarely' or 'never'. Nevertheless, the Dutch MEPs were far more eloquent in the in-depth interviews about the relevance of religion to their parliamentary work. The interviewees explicitly state that religion plays a strong role in their parliamentary activities. For instance, Corien Wortmann-Kool of the CDA says that she does not literally 'translate [the Bible] into politics, but I, we, Christian Democrats, the EPP members, do find it important to conduct politics founded in values that originate from the Christian faith'. This is even the case for MEPs who belong to parties that traditionally carry a secularist label. Lucas Hartong (PVV) says that he 'sees it as [his] task to translate [his] Christian beliefs into political behaviour on a daily basis' and Dennis de Jong (SP) says: 'Yes, religion has an influence on me. And not only as a personal inspiration, which can always be the case. Also professionally … depending on the issue, when you come into contact with religious organisations.'

The historically close relationship between religious beliefs and political activity on the Dutch national political scene is thus also present at the EU level. In part, this can be explained by electoral and strategic motivations, because religion is still perceived as a salient cue in the voters' electoral behaviour. Dennis de Jong (SP) frames it as follows: 'It is interesting for us to rid a part of the religious electorate, which would rather vote Christian Democratic, of the impression that we have a taboo on religion. ... Those [voters] we do not want to miss out on.' Moreover, given the presence of a strong public support basis for religious claims in the Dutch 'Bible Belt', a religious focus among MEPs might be a rewarding electoral strategy.

At a more abstract level, these findings suggest that religious conflict from the national level thus remains salient in the EP and that there are strong historical path dependencies. Despite its salience, however, the role of the religious–secular divide is mostly indirect. All but one of the surveyed MEPs agree that religion intervenes in their activities as MEP primarily 'as a source of personal inspiration'. So many Dutch MEPs acknowledge the role of religion, but are wary of saying that religious or secular convictions directly influence the specific decisions they make in the EP. 'If we were to deny the existence of religion', contends one MEP, 'we would deny an important aspect of society. However, to base our policies on a specific religious book ... I am not in favour of that.'

Most of the Dutch MEPs rather claim that religious convictions and attitudes offer certain perspectives on the policy issues under consideration, but that their behaviour is not directly affected by religious considerations. Religion in this context thus functions more as an ethical cue than as direct imperative. Corien Wortmann-Kool (CDA) aptly describes the situation when she says that Christian values are 'the beacons in my political position-taking'. They let her define her moral perspective on policy issues, without directly steering her towards one policy alternative or the other.

The fact that the role of religion is mostly inspired by Dutch MEPs' personal affinity rather than by their strong desire to directly include religion in the political process is also evident when we consider their attitudes towards religion and politics (Table 5). On the basis of the results of the survey, we find that the majority of Dutch MEPs disagree (strongly) with the idea that 'politicians who do not believe in God are unfit for public office' and that 'it would be better for Europe if more people with strong religious beliefs held public office'. They also agree with the idea that 'religious people should not influence how people vote in elections'. The only item that triggers some difference of opinion is that 'religious leaders should not influence government decisions'. However,

Table 5. Attitudes towards the relation between religion and politics (absolute numbers).

	Agree strongly	Agree	Neither agree/ disagree	Disagree	Disagree strongly
Politicians who do not believe in God are unfit for public office				2	5
Religious leaders should not influence how people vote in elections	2	2	4		
It would be better for Europe if more people with strong religious beliefs held public office		1	2	4	1
Religious leaders should not influence government decisions	2	1	3	1	1

once again these differences do not map onto party ideological differences among the Dutch MEPs.

Dutch MEPs and religious lobby groups: mutual rapprochement?

Religion thus plays an important yet indirect role in the representational work of Dutch MEPs. As a logical corollary, we would expect them to have close contacts with religious organisations. Interestingly, however, only two Dutch MEPs in the survey indicate that religion intervenes 'as an interest group' in their activities. Members of secular parties, such as the PVV, claim not to be in contact with religious groups because these groups 'have traditionally had contact with the CDA, CU and SGP' (interview with Hartong). However, when asked about her contacts with Christian lobby groups (for example COMECE (the Commission of the [Catholic] Bishops' Conferences of the European Community) or CEC (the Conference of European Churches), Corien Wortman-Kool, from the Christian Democratic CDA, also denies the existence of such ties.

The group of Dutch MEPs having frequent contacts with religious or philosophical interest groups thus does not coincide with the group of MEPs from confessional parties. This is somewhat surprising. After all, the Netherlands is a consociational democracy with a corporatist interest group system, which implies that there should be contacts between political elites and religious interest groups; but these contacts seem to be absent at the European level.

However, the data indicate that contacts are present where we least expect them. The ties with interest groups are most strongly established among MEPs advocating the separation of church and state. For instance, Sophie in't Veld (D66) claims to be in contact at least weekly with one of the following groups: the European Humanist Federation, the Acht-Mei-Beweging, Churches on the Move and Catholics for a Free Choice.

Counterintuitively, these findings suggest that lobbying takes place primarily among those promoting secularist interests, instead of among those advocating a religious agenda, and that this is not only the result of the fact that they are targeted by these organisations. These MEPs themselves actively seek contact with lobby groups because of the resources they can offer in terms of expertise and policy information. For instance Dennis de Jong (SP) states that when it comes to policy issues such as poverty and asylum he 'would not have access to that kind of information' without talking to religious lobby groups.

A possible explanation for these findings is that the Dutch corporatist system is very closed. There are well-established contacts between lobby groups and the previously pillarised parties, but parties such as D66, which reacted against pillarisation, were excluded from the corporatist structures in the Netherlands. At the European level, which is considered to be more open and pluralist (Schmidt 2006), seeking contacts with interest groups in order to mobilise has been much easier. Therefore the fact that there are close contacts between secular MEPs and lobby groups might indicate that the EU level opened new windows of opportunity for mobilisation on the part of the secular MEPs.

Religious and party lines: crosscutting cleavages

As we have hinted before, it is interesting to notice that the importance of religion in the work of the Dutch MEPs does not follow clear party lines. The denominational divide might run straight through the Dutch party landscape, but the salience of religion in the work of the Dutch MEPs crosscuts with party lines. In this sense, those MEPs who are most strongly using religious or secularist cues in their parliamentary work are also the ones from whom we expected it least.

The MEPs from parties with the strongest denominational profile are thus not necessarily the ones that appear to be most active in pursuing a religious agenda in their activities. The interviews rather show that there is a strong mobilisation on the secular side and that this often meets resistance and causes agitation among more religiously inspired MEPs. As one ecumenically minded MEP explains: 'It is actually unbelievable how often this Parliament votes about "reproductive health", "abortion", "gay marriage". ... It is disproportional. These issues are even dragged into resolutions that do not directly affect them. ... And there is also a bit of provocation involved and that I find particularly bothersome.' Our general finding is therefore that parties with strong historical and ideological ties to religion deliver MEPs who only infrequently use religion as a guiding principle, whereas up-front secular parties and MEPs opposing any influence of religion on politics seem to mobilise much more strongly to pursue a secularist agenda.

Policy entrepreneurs and committee memberships

A final question is whether certain committee memberships are more conducive to pursuing a religious or a secular agenda. Since MEPs can formulate a preference as to which committees they would like to join in the EP, we can theoretically expect that MEPs with strong religious or secular commitments may want to target specific policy domains of the EU, such as human rights, ethical issues, education and culture. These issues lend themselves ideally to the incorporation of religious perspectives. Membership of certain committees in the EP could thus be instrumental in the promotion of religious interests or a specific denominational agenda.

Sophie in't Veld is a case in point, confirming the fact that the committee memberships of some MEPs are functional in the pursuit of a secular agenda. She is a member of D66, a party that strongly advocates the freedom not to believe. She describes herself as a convinced atheist and has the reputation of being a political entrepreneur at the European level when it comes to defining the relation between church and state. In the survey she indicated clearly that she does not take religious considerations into account in her parliamentary activities, and she even founded and presides over the Working Group on Separation of Religion and Politics, which was initially aimed at revoking the candidacy of Rocco Buttiglione as the European commissioner for human rights but has developed into a much broader platform on religion and politics at European and national level. Sophie in't Veld is also a member of the Committee on Women's Rights and Gender Equality, and on the EU–Turkey delegation, and she is vice-president of the Committee on Civil Liberties, Justice and Home Affairs. All these memberships deal with ethical issues and lend themselves extremely well to a fight between different views of the role that religion should play in the EP.

However, the pursuit of a religiously inspired agenda should not be limited to committees relating explicitly to ethical issues. Most policy domains at the European level are considered open to a religious interpretation. When asked to indicate for which issues religion is most important in the EP (external relations, freedom of expression, the fight against discrimination, social policy, economic policy or culture and education), Dutch MEPs were unable to give a clear ranking. Each and every one of these policy areas, it appears, lends itself to the integration of a religious perspective.

A case in point is Dennis De Jong (SP). He is a member of the Special Committee on Organised Crime, Corruption and Money Laundering, and of the Committee on the Internal Market and Consumer Protection. Even though these committees do not have a clear religious or ethical undertone, he still sees religion as an important facet of his work. According to him, these policy domains are about 'fighting poverty within Europe and how that relates to the economic governance'. And poverty, he adds, has an important religious dimension: 'religious organisations have an important role in [fighting poverty] and see it as one of their main tasks. Diaconia is of course aimed at that. So it is logical that you end up with them on an issue such as poverty.' Religion is thus seen as a transversal principle that can be used to inform every policy domain, and not only in the usually suspected committees of the EP.

Conclusion

This study started from the assumption that national political contexts might impact upon the work of the MEPs. In particular, we posited that the deep conflicts that characterise the political system of the Netherlands affect the weight given by the Dutch MEPs to religion in their activities in the European political arena. Both the survey and the interviews confirmed these assumptions: Dutch MEPs consider religion to be an important cue in their parliamentary activities, and the demarcation between church and state remains a salient issue at the European level. In this sense the pacification of religious conflict in the Netherlands has not reduced religious diversity. It rather seems that the consociational system has institutionalised denominational diversity and leads to an artificial protraction of religious or secularist identities as lines of political conflict, even when the underlying society is secularising.

However, it is important to stress that our findings are more nuanced than simply the assertion that religion guides Dutch MEPs. First of all, we found that the impact of religiosity is largely indirect. The denominational conflicts rarely influence the behaviour of MEPs directly. Rather, they serve as a general framework within which the Dutch MEPs can do a religious or secularist reading of specific policy issues. Second, we assumed that some parliamentary committees would lend themselves better to a religious interpretation of the representational role of MEPs. This is only partly so: the interviews showed that every possible policy domain contains facets of religion, making it a potentially transversal aspect of every European policy domain.

The high salience of religion for the Dutch MEPs shows that the effect of the European level on transforming the opinions and identities of MEPs remains fairly limited. It is to a large extent the national level and the conflicts that rule this national level that shape the individual behaviour of MEPs. The path dependencies resulting from religious polarisation at the national level remain the primary source of inspiration for MEPs in the Dutch context.

What our results do suggest is that the European context creates new opportunities for the pursuit of interests that might have been blocked out by the closed nature of the Dutch corporatist system. After all, we find that the salience of religion is much higher among those promoting a secularist agenda. Very few of the usual suspects (MEPs from Christian Democratic parties) claim to promote a religious agenda, whereas those MEPs advocating a stricter separation between church and state are much more active political entrepreneurs of their secular agenda. This is an interesting finding which hints at the fact that secularist MEPs might see windows of opportunity in the open pluralist system of the EU. The strong mobilisation on the secular side might also be a consequence of the enlargement.

With the enlargement the number of (outspoken) Christian MEPs has considerably increased. Voices advocating a secularist agenda might therefore feel increasingly marginalised and mobilise more strongly as a reaction.

In conclusion, it can be observed that the historical representation of the Netherlands as a 'nation of vicars and merchants' (Knippenberg 1998, 209) even holds some truth at the European level. However, the definition of what Knippenberg calls a 'vicar' should in our modern age be widened to include those who represent atheism.

References

Achterberg, P., D. Houtman, S. Aupers, W. de Koster, P. Mascini, and J. van der Waal. 2009. "A Christian Cancellation of the Secularist Truce? Waning Christian Religiosity and Waxing Religious Deprivatization in the West." *Journal for the Scientific Study of Religion* 48: 687–701. doi:10.1111/j.1468-5906.2009.01473.x.

Adams, J., C. de Vries, and D. Leiter. 2012. "Subconstituency Reactions to Elite Depolarization in the Netherlands: An Analysis of the Dutch Public's Policy Beliefs and Partisan Loyalties, 1986–98." *British Journal of Political Science* 42: 81–105. doi:10.1017/S0007123411000214.

Andeweg, R. B. 2008. "Coalition Politics in the Netherlands: From Accommodation to Politicization." *Acta Politica* 43: 254–277. doi:10.1057/ap.2008.8.

Andeweg, R. B., and G. A. Irwin. 2002. *Government and Politics of the Netherlands*. Houndmills, Basingstoke: Palgrave Macmillan.

Deschouwer, K., and S. Depauw, eds. 2014. *Representing the People: A Survey Among Members of Statewide and Substate Parliaments*. Oxford: Oxford University Press.

Duncan, F. 2007. "'Lately, Things Just don't Seem the Same': External Shocks, Party Change and the Adaptation of the Dutch Christian Democrats during 'Purple Hague' 1994–8." *Party Politics* 13: 69–87. doi:10.1177/1354068806071264.

Engeli, I., C. Green-Pedersen, and L. T. Larsen. 2013. "The Puzzle of Permissiveness: Understanding Policy Processes Concerning Morality Issues." *Journal of European Public Policy* 20: 335–352. doi:10.1080/13501763.2013.761500.

ESS. 2010. ESS Round 5: European Social Survey Round 5 Data (2010). Data file edition 3.0. Norwegian Social Science Data Services, Norway – Data Archive and distributor of ESS data. http://www.europeansocialsurvey.org/data/conditions_of_use.html.

Girwin, B. 2000. "The Political Culture of Secularization: European Trends and Comparative Perspectives." In *Religion and Mass Electoral Behaviour in Europe*, edited by D. Broughton and H. -M. ten Napel, 7–27. London: Routledge.

Hanley, D., ed. 1994. *Christian Democracy in Europe: A Comparative Perspective*. London: Pinter.

Hillebrand, R., and G. A. Irwin. 1999. "Changing Strategies: The Dilemma of the Dutch Labour Party." In *Policy, Office or Votes? How Political Parties in Europe Make Hard Decisions*, edited by W. C. Müller and K. Strøm, 112–140. Cambridge: Cambridge University Press.

Jansen, T. 2000. "Europe and Religions: The Dialogue Between the European Commission and Churches or Religious Communities." *Social Compass* 47: 103–112. doi:10.1177/003776800047001011.

Kennedy, J. C., and J. P. Zwemer. 2010. "Religion in the Modern Netherlands and the Problems of Pluralism." *Bijdragen en mededelingen betreffende de geschiedenis der Nederlanden* 125: 237–268.

Knippenberg, H. 1998. "Secularization in the Netherlands in its Historical and Geographical Dimensions." *GeoJournal* 45: 209–220. doi:10.1023/A:1006973011455.

Knippenberg, H. 2007. "The Changing Relationship between State and Church/Religion in the Netherlands." *GeoJournal* 67: 317–330. doi:10.1007/s10708-007-9060-5.

Lijphart, A. 1968. *The Politics of Accommodation: Pluralism and Democracy in the Netherlands.* Berkeley: University of California Press.

Lijphart, A. 1969. "Consociational Democracy." *World Politics* 21: 207–225. doi:10.2307/2009820.

Outshoorn, J. 2001. "Policy-Making on Abortion: Arenas, Actors, and Arguments in the Netherlands." In *Abortion, Politics, Women's Movements, and the Democratic State*, edited by D. Stetson, 205–228. Oxford: Oxford University Press.

Scarrow, S. E. 1997. "Political Career Paths and the European Parliament." *Legislative Studies Quarterly* 22: 253–263. doi:10.2307/440385.

Schmidt, V. 2006. *Democracy in Europe: The EU and National Polities.* Oxford: Oxford University Press.

Silvestri, S. 2009. "Islam and Religion in the EU Political System." *West European Politics* 32: 1212–1239. doi:10.1080/01402380903230678.

van der Brug, W., S. Hobolt, and C. de Vreese. 2009. "Religion and Party Choice in Europe." *West European Politics* 32: 1266–1283. doi:10.1080/01402380903230694.

van der Wusten, H., and H. Knippenberg. 2001. "The Ethnic Dimension in Twentieth-Century European Politics: A Recursive Model." In *The Territorial Factor: Political Geography in a Globalizing World*, edited by R. Hillebrand and G. A. Irwin, 259–279. Amsterdam: Amsterdam University Press.

van Kersbergen, K. 2008. "The Christian Democratic Phoenix and Modern Unsecular Politics." *Party Politics* 14: 259–279. doi:10.1177/1354068807088446.

Consulting and compromising: the (non-)religious policy preferences of British MEPs

Martin Steven

Department of Politics, Philosophy and Religion, Faculty of Arts and Social Sciences, Lancaster University, Lancaster, UK

The UK provides an important case study when analysing the influence of religious attitudes and values on political behaviour in the European Union. Our research shows British members of the European Parliament (MEPs) to be relatively at ease working with the different faith-based organisations (FBOs) which seek to influence the European policy process – and much more so than many of their colleagues from other member-states. This can potentially be explained by the more 'pluralist' political culture which is prevalent in the UK, and can also be related to the comparatively high rates of non-church attendance among the British sample which facilitates their even-handedness towards different groups. This, in turn, produces a resistance to allowing religious factors to disproportionately influence European policymaking.

Introduction

The European Parliament (EP) is the arena of the European Union (EU) which focuses most on issues related to human rights, political culture and national identity. While other parts of the European Quarter of Brussels are preoccupied with trade agreements, tariffs and agricultural quotas, those who operate within the Espace Léopold, as well as in the main plenary hemisphere in Strasbourg, have always sought to interpret their remit in a way that represents the concerns of ordinary European citizens and wider European civil society. The EU promotes a narrative of cohesion, convergence and unity which explicitly encompasses democratic beliefs and values; meanwhile, the EP seeks to democratically represent the interests of all sections of society, including both religious and non-religious citizens (EP n.d.).

In many ways, the EU has repeatedly displayed a determination to remain formally secular, mimicking a classic French-style *laïcité* in both its treaties and directives (see Foret and Riva 2010). Yet this frequently made comparison arguably presents only a partial picture – in fact, the way different religious interest groups in Brussels are forced to compete on an even 'playing field' also has distinct overtones of the American version of church and state separation. It was the Treaty of Amsterdam in 1997 which first truly articulated the importance of protecting fundamental rights and promoting non-discrimination in relation to religion (EU n.d.). Some commentators question the success of the EU in finding the right balance between promoting religious freedoms and protecting freedom from religion (see Foret and Itçaina 2011). Indeed the logic of the EU's now longstanding policy of 'privatising' religion has become even more strained since the European Commission (EC) and the EP started to legislate increasingly in areas of social policy and human rights, complementing their traditional interest in trade and economic affairs.

So while religion may help to define Europe, it plays a much more ambiguous role in the EU. Despite the fact that Christianity has its institutional home in Europe, contributing substantially in the process to what constitutes the core of European identity, the role of churches and faith-based organisations in European integration and wider multi-level governance appears to be highly complex. Pinning down the precise influence of religion on the government and politics of Europe seems challenging. Nevertheless the UK provides an important case study when analysing the influence of religious attitudes on political behaviour and public policy. While the UK may not formally separate church and state – with Anglican bishops even sitting and voting in the upper house of Parliament – the wider policy environment unquestionably embraces the democratic spirit of equality of opportunity, applied regardless of race, religion, gender or sexuality. Members of Parliament (MPs) operate under strict codes of conduct, which cover even the way they meet constituents: for example, it is against the rules for MPs to try to help a voter who does not live in their constituency (HC 2012). Detailed regulations also cover the way individual donations are made to party organisations and election campaigns (El C n.d.). The entire political system – while far from perfect – is nevertheless designed to aid access and transparency in relation to the business of government.

Since the socio-economic reforms initiated by Margaret Thatcher's governments from 1979 onwards, Britain has developed a 'pluralist' political culture comparable with those of other parts of the 'Anglosphere' such as the USA, where elected representatives are comfortable consulting with interest groups on an equal and open basis (Dahl 1961). This can be contrasted with the more 'corporatist' system that has traditionally operated across much of Western Europe, including large economies such as Germany, where governments establish formal social partnerships with a select few business organisations and trade unions which then play a central role in public policymaking (Heeg 2012). Meanwhile accompanying 'ever closer union' in Europe a sophisticated system of interest group politics now fully operational in Brussels has developed. This system can be likened to the longer established equivalent in Washington DC: public affairs functioning as a profession, replacing the politics of class, region or religion (Mahoney 2008).

Given what has been implied about aspects of the lobbying environment operating in the European Quarter of Brussels, we should expect members of the European Parliament (MEPs) from the UK to be relatively at ease working with the different religious and non-religious representations seeking to influence different parts of the European policy process. Our research shows that this is indeed the case, and more so than it is with many of their counterparts from other member-states. We can also attempt to relate this to the comparatively high rates of agnosticism and atheism among the British sample, and also to the way that they believe public policy should be formulated – for example, in reference to foreign policy and the accession of Turkey as an EU member-state.

The survey questionnaire and the British MEP sample

The main instrument used for collecting data about the religious preferences of the British MEPs was a survey questionnaire, controlled centrally by the Institute for European Studies at the Université Libre de Bruxelles (ULB). This allows wider comparisons to be made with the other member-states included in the 'Religion at the European Parliament' (RelEP) project (http://www.releur.eu/): Austria, France, Germany, The Netherlands, Poland and Spain. The survey was divided up into a number of different sections based around a range of themes connected to religious issues and European government affairs, including the individual work of MEPs, the wider work of the EP and ultimately the activities of the EU as a whole. Christianity plays a historically important part in the civic life of European nations, so how do MEPs approach the influence and power of the church? How sensitive is the EP to religious issues and matters of faith? Religion – via Christianity – can be said to be core to European identity, uniting different nationalities when language can sometimes divide them. Yet how does the EU approach religion, especially its most democratic and representative arm, the EP?

We start by examining the profiles of the British MEPs. Sixteen out of a total 73 (22%) responded to the survey questionnaire. This type of response rate is typical of an elite survey of this nature, but still large enough to allow us to draw wider conclusions about what British MEPs think about religious issues, especially when there is unanimity or near unanimity of responses, as there frequently is with many of the questions involved. Taken as a whole with the responses from other member-states (which also generated a similar response rate – 167 out of 736 MEPs, or 23%), we are able to track certain patterns of attitudes and behaviour. Fortunately, the 16 respondents from the UK represent a range of different party groupings, terms served and committee specialisation.

Five Liberal Democrats, four Conservatives, three Labour members, three UK Independence Party members and one Scottish Nationalist participated in the survey. This meant that the largest parliamentary group represented was the Alliance of Liberals and Democrats for Europe (ALDE). The obvious point to make in addition to the above is the total absence of MEPs from the European People's Party (EPP) in the UK section of the survey sample. Perhaps the most visible formal link of all between religion and politics in the EU can be found in the chamber of the EP via the work of the EPP, the political movement that brings together MEPs who are Christian Democrats, and which, prior to the 2014 elections, constituted the largest elected group with 270 members. The EPP seeks to promote values and policies which have a religious origin, albeit not as centrally as it once did (Duncan 2013). Yet in Britain, the centre-right party, the Conservative Party, has no ideological links at all with Christian Democracy, and their MEPs even sit in an entirely different party group in the EP chamber, that of the European Conservatives and Reformists (ECR). This move came about as a result of increasing Euroscepticism in the party, and a growing unease at being part of the group that formally describes itself as 'Europe's Driving Force' (EPP n.d.).

We can also link this absence of Christian Democracy in Britain with the more pluralist interest group culture already mentioned. After all, the corporatist consensus across much of Western Europe in countries such as Germany, The Netherlands and Austria is ultimately a Christian Democratic one with its origins in the implementation of various components of the European Social Model (ESM) – a middle-way in policymaking which argues that economic growth should not come at the expense of social cohesion. In comparison, the UK adheres to a much more Anglo-American political economy model which restricts state interference in the free market and, as a consequence, promotes a more fluid and open system of organised interests (including, as in our case, faith-based ones).

Nine out of 16 members (56%) were elected in the 1999–2004 term with the next biggest intake (four or 25%) coming in 2004–2009. Only one (6%) was elected for the first time only in 2009, while two (13%) were first elected back in 1994. Two of the respondents have since resigned as MEPs, while one has changed political party. A range

Table 1. Number of terms served at the European Parliament.

Number of terms	Percentage of sample (UK only)	Percentage of sample (EU)
1	6	47
2	25	30
3	56	14
4	13	5
5	0	2
6	0	1
7	0	1

of parliamentary committees are represented by the respondents – in total, 13 out of 23– with two vice-chairs included in the sample. As we can see from Table 1, this means that the British sample included a relatively experienced group of parliamentarians compared with the EU-wide sample involving all the member-states.

These data collectively allow us to draw some conclusions about the wider religious views of British MEPs. It is unlikely that their basic responses to the questions would be dramatically different on the majority of issues, as there is often agreement among the respondents. Clearly, a larger response rate would have produced more detail and explanations, but for our purposes we can still evaluate the underlying values and attitudes on display and make a valid contribution to the literature on politics and religion, EU politics, interest groups and electoral and partisan politics. While previous research has focused on the way faith-based groups lobby the EC in Brussels (Leustean 2012), the survey questionnaire also allows us to *quantify* and *measure* political influence. The policy analysis approach mentioned before is understandable: the role of interest groups in EU government is arguably more prominent than the role of parties and elections. Even since the EP has been handed more powers, the EC has remained the EU's central political institution and 'engine of integration'. As scholars have attempted to untangle the place of religion in the EU, they have looked first to the role of the Conference of European Churches (CEC), for example, as well to treaties and constitutional reforms (Leustean and Madeley 2009). Yet the arena of the EP ought not to be ignored, especially given its overtly representative democratic remit. In an era when the democratic deficit of Europe is frequently highlighted (Cheneval and Schimmelfennig 2013), and with the Eurozone crisis raising many questions about the legitimacy of the political structure of the EU, such questions are especially timely.

An open door policy: the influence of religious interest groups

Are religious interests represented effectively by British MEPs? Freedom of religion is one of the core principles actively promoted by the EU in its neighbourhood policy (ENP), and embraced especially enthusiastically by democratically elected MEPs – yet is freedom of religion protected within the borders of the EU by those same elected party politicians? One of the most damaging criticisms levelled at the EU is that it has failed to create a functioning public sphere with a European civic society (Dür and Mateo 2012). Interest groups may well lobby at a European level but rarely exclusively: rather, they maintain one eye on their own national policy environments. While churches can hardly be said to 'democratise' the EU, their capacity for creating healthy social capital and community engagement is often the envy of many political parties and politicians (Putnam 2000). Linked to that, their ability to stimulate public debate and mobilise public opinion about moral and ethical questions is also considerable. So how do our politicians respond?

Taken together, Tables 2, 3 and 4 reveal an important trend in the responses of British MEPs. First, in Table 2, we see that they are probably more comfortable using the terminology of 'political realities' than the language of 'personal inspiration' when it comes to discussing the impact of religion upon their work activities. These responses are interesting as they show the British politicians acknowledging religion primarily when they are forced to engage with it as part of a professional relationship – 32% (6) as a social and political reality combined with 21% (4) as an interest group. However, 21% (4) of British MEPs are willing to openly admit that they mix religion and politics as a consequence of their own personal belief system – slightly less than the European average (31%). This also reinforces the argument that British MEPs – who are broadly in line with other European MEPs here – are quite happy to engage with different religious and non-religious groups, on the understanding that they have a legitimate right to representation and to participate fully in the political process.

A related survey question, meanwhile, asked the MEPs to consider the differences in behaviour within the context of multilevel governance (Table 3). Is the place of religion in the EP comparable with their experiences in national politics and government? We can

Table 2.   Religion and MEP activities.

Type of intervention (several responses possible, ranked 1–3)	Percentage of sample (UK only)	Percentage of sample (EU)
As a source of personal inspiration	21	31
As a social and political reality	32	38
As an interest group	21	19
Other	16	7
No effect	11	4

Table 3.   Experiences in national politics.

Different from national politics?	Percentage of sample (UK only)	Percentage of sample (EU)
Yes	19	53
No	38	33
Did not answer	43	14

Table 4.   Contact with religious or philosophical interest groups.

Frequency of contact	Percentage of sample (UK only)	Percentage of sample (EU)
Once a week or more	19	4
Once a month or more	6	12
A few times a year	13	30
A few times over the course of a term	38	22
Never	13	14
Did not answer	12	17

note the difference between the responses of the British MEPs and the EU-wide average: 38% (6) of UK respondents state there is no difference, compared with 19% (3) who say that there is a difference. Even taking into account the relatively high 'did not answer' rate here, this can be still considered a departure from the way their other European colleagues have answered: 53% state there is a difference between the national and EU contexts. While we cannot say for sure what has caused that differentiation we can speculate that it is linked to British MEPs feeling more comfortable in the policy and lobbying environment of Brussels.

Table 4 focuses specifically on that lobbying environment: the survey asked how often the MEPs were in contact with religious or philosophical interest groups. While the responses from the British MEPs are broadly in line with those of the European average, with both showing healthy levels of contact with religious and philosophical groups, a closer inspection does suggest that the UK MEPs are in contact slightly more with such organisations. 19% (3) state that they are in contact once a week or more, for example, compared with only 4% of the European sample. 38% (6) state that they are in contact a few times over the course of a parliamentary term, compared with only 22% of MEPs on average. Also, only 13% of respondents state that they have never been lobbied by such groups. We can therefore say that most of the British MEPs have been lobbied by religious or faith-based organisations (FBOs) at some point.

While the individual tables so far do not necessarily reveal a hugely marked difference between the UK and EU respondents, they do potentially imply that the UK MEPs are generally comfortable working within this type of pluralist policy environment functioning within the EP. Additional qualitative comments from the survey and interviews also reveal that British MEPs appear to approach this from a member-state perspective: that is, if they have a constituent who is active in a group then this will potentially help with gaining access: this appears to be the key rationale that lies behind meetings being set up, according to the MEPs.

Overall then, we see that while British MEPs are consulted regularly by faith-based organisations and churches, and often from their local constituencies, they are also clearly able to function independently. Religious representatives are certainly listened to respectfully, but beyond that there is no admission from MEPs that they are given undue influence. Religious and faith-based groups are not given special privileges or access to the corridors of power in Brussels or Strasbourg beyond what one might reasonably expect, but they are given their rightful place as part of a wider network of lobbies, interest groups and organisations.

'We don't do God': belonging but not believing?

On the occasion of his 50th birthday in May 2003, the then British prime minister Tony Blair gave a suitably glamorous interview to the American magazine *Vanity Fair*. The wide-ranging topics which were discussed included both the political and the personal, but when the interviewer David Margolick asked Mr Blair about his Christianity, the prime minister's powerful director of strategy and communications Alastair Campbell stepped in immediately: 'Is he on God? We don't do God. I'm sorry. We don't do God' (Brown 2003). Clearly, many elected British politicians do indeed 'do God' – the existence of influential internal party groupings such as the Conservative Christian Fellowship (CCF) and the Christian Socialist Movement (CSM) are testimony to that. Nevertheless, Mr Campbell's comments do neatly sum up the culture which is probably most prevalent among the British whereby generally politicians try to keep their religious views to themselves out of a fear of being perceived to be slightly odd. This has little to do with church attendance levels but instead is part of a government system where neither American-style personality politics nor Western European Christian Democracy have much resonance. Or as Pulzer would have it (1967, 98): 'class is the basis of British party politics; all else is embellishment and detail'.

The findings of the survey are very unambiguous at this point: compared with the European-wide sample as a whole, British MEPs are not particularly religious at all. We see the beginnings of this diverging pattern in Table 5 below, with a slightly higher percentage of non- or low church attendance compared with the European sample. However it should also be stated that the British respondents were broadly in line with the wider European sample in the sense that very few of them seemed prepared to answer what they must consider to be an essentially personal question.

Table 6, in contrast, does begin to add much more detail to the figures. Here we can see that only 19% (3) state that they are religious people while 25% (4) say that they are not believers and another 25% (4) state that they are 'convinced atheists'. We can discern a real divergence between the number of European respondents who define themselves as being religious and the number of British respondents: 47% of the EU aggregate total state that they are religious. We can also conversely note the reverse picture when we look at the number of non-religious and convinced atheists: only 15% and 14% respectively.

Meanwhile Table 7 also highlights disparities between the British respondents and the European sample taken as a whole. Many more British MEPs say they do not believe in God than their European MEP colleagues (44% (7) compared with 15%) and conversely fewer say that they do believe in the existence of a personal God (25% (4) compared with 32%) or some sort of spirit or life force (6% – just one MEP – compared with 18% of all European respondents).

Table 5.   Church attendance.

How often do you attend church?	Percentage of the sample (UK only)	Percentage of the sample (EU)
Never	6	3
Once a year	0	1
Holy days only	19	10
Once a month	0	16
Once a week	13	18
More than once a week	6	2
Did not answer	56	49

Table 6.   Religious identity.

How would you define yourself?	Percentage of the sample (UK only)	Percentage of the sample (EU)
I am a religious person	19	47
I am not a religious person	25	15
I am convinced atheist	25	14
Did not answer	31	25

Table 7. Personal beliefs.

What do you believe?	Percentage of the sample(UK only)	Percentage of the sample (EU)
There is a personal God	25	32
There is some sort of spirit or life force	6	18
I don't believe there is any God, spirit or life force	44	15
Did not answer	25	36

The 'pluralist' culture referred to earlier has no direct connection with low church attendances in the UK – after all, the USA has high attendance rates in comparison and is the home of pluralist politics (see Hertzke 2009). However, what we can perhaps suggest is that the UK's 'secularism' reinforces the pluralist policy arena which we have identified. Clearly, low levels of religiosity do not produce pluralism but they do possibly strengthen aspects of it, making it easier for policymakers to be even–handed in their dealings with different groups. After all, whenever aspects of America's separation of church and state do come under threat in relation to the constitution – for example, the provision of school prayer – the source tends to be faith-based organisations (see Wilcox and Robinson 2010). Furthermore, in general, these responses reflect patterns of religious behaviour and social attitudes in wider British society. When the MEPs were asked in a separate question whether they belonged to a religious denomination, 40% (6) stated that they did, against 44% (7) who stated that they did not. As we shall see in the next section, while people are often happy to identify broadly as Christians, their attendance at church and institutional or practical attachment to religion is much less consistent. We now turn to look at this in more detail, in order to provide background and context for the patterns of responses which we are detecting among the MEPs.

Representing the people: the national context

In our analysis so far, we have identified two key ways in which UK MEPs differ from the average EU MEP. First, they seem more willing and open to dealing with all types of religious interest group and are not challenged by that prospect, perhaps as a result of being used to a similar culture in London as well as local British politics. Second, they are themselves more atheistic and non-religious with especially low levels of church attendance. In fact Britain has long provided scholars interested in the interface between politics and religion with a distinctive case (see Steven 2010). Uniquely among advanced industrial western democracies, the UK has an unwritten constitution with no bill of rights, senior clergy sitting in the upper house of Parliament in London, and as has already been noted in the introduction, no confessional parties such as the Christian Democrats.

The decline in British church attendance since the 1960s is well documented; however, in general it is a somewhat complicated and multi-layered picture. The eminent British sociologist of religion Grace Davie has charted a growing trend of 'believing without belonging' (1994): in other words, people still feel some of spiritual force but no longer feel the need to comply with the social convention of attending their local church on a Sunday morning. There is also a third dimension which is perhaps of most interest to political scientists: whether or not people self-identify as 'Christian', 'Muslim' or 'Jewish'. Here again, when looking at the British context, there is evidence of decline in strength of religious identification, but equally, as we shall now discuss, the figures are not totally conclusive.

In the most recent government census (2011), 33.2 million people (59.3%) in England and Wales still described themselves as 'Christian' (ONS 2011). The previous census in 2001 was the first time that the question 'what is your religion?' had been asked in Great Britain (excluding Northern Ireland): then 71.7% had answered 'Christian'. There is an estimated Muslim population of around 4.8%. Clearly this shows a drop in the number of people identifying as Christian but it also reveals nearly 60% of respondents still identifying as such. Meanwhile, as Figure 1 below shows, there is still a large (albeit falling) number of people who do go to their local parish church on a Sunday morning. Indeed in many urban areas – especially ethnically diverse parts of London – Protestant Evangelical churches are even growing in popularity (Micklethwait and Wooldridge 2009, 136; Brierley Consultancy 2013). Linked to this is the fact that while there has been a decline since the 1960s in the number of Britons who believe in God, a substantial number also still do so.

Finally it is worth noting that the Church of England remains the established state church with the queen as its head. 26 of its senior prelates sit and vote in the British Parliament at Westminster in London. Even in the government's latest plans to reform the upper chamber, the House of Lords, to make it more democratic, the draft bill guarantees

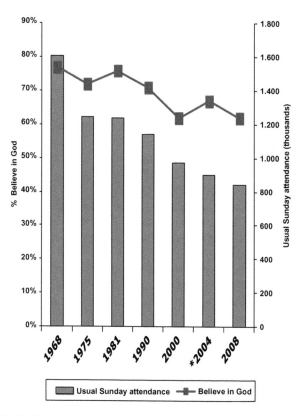

Figure 1. Belief in God and usual Sunday church attendance.

Source: Archbishops' Council, 2006: Gallup/ORB/ICM; see Barley (2006).

the continued presence of the bishops or 'lords spiritual' (CO 2012). So politicians, including MEPs, are respectful of the place of Christianity in the development of British democracy without necessarily feeling any compulsion to be under its control. We can also make comparisons with the behaviour of national MPs. Tables 8 and 9 show the responses of MPs who participated in the PARTIREP survey (http://www.partirep.eu/datafile/comparative-mp-survey) organised by a team of Belgian political scientists (2007–2011). In Table 8, we see that large numbers of British MPs regard promoting the views of religious interest groups as being important. For example, 22.2% regard it as being very important - the most popular response and one not replicated by any of the other member-states apart from Germany. Last, we see in Table 9 that British MPs were out in front in terms of the number of times they met with religious groups. For example, 12.1% of them met with representatives of religious groups once a week - significantly more frequently than MEPs from any of the other member-states apart from Hungary. Meanwhile, only 2.2% stated that they had (almost) no contact, and this response was easily the lowest amongst all EU member-states.

The sample of British MEPs appears to be very similar to the equivalent one for British MPs in their attitudes towards the way religious groups ought to be accommodated. In turn, these attitudes are representative of the wider British population: fewer people may attend church than in previous years, but there remains evidence of widespread religiosity as well as respect for aspects of religion being prominent in public life. In the 2010 British Social Attitudes Survey, 50% of respondents stated that 'all religious groups should have equal rights' compared with only 24% who disagreed with that sentiment. As the survey authors put it, 'religion has personal and social benefits, but faith should not be taken too far' (Voas and Ling 2010).

'Render unto Caesar ...': directives and policies

So far, we have argued that British MEPs are more at ease than many of their European colleagues with the concept of regularly meeting with religious interest groups as a result of the pluralist political culture prevalent in the UK. We have also seen how that is reinforced by trends in wider British society which is relatively secularised in many respects. This final section focuses as a case study on aspects of the work of the wider EU to emphasise the distinctive way in which British MEPs approach these types of affairs. Once again we see similar secularist patterns emerging: more specifically, we note that the MEPs are not comfortable at all with the idea that Europe's Christian heritage should be highlighted in the Lisbon Treaty, nor do they have any desire for the EU to have a 'real policy' towards religions.

As Table 10 indicates, there appears to be no real appetite on the part of British MEPs for the EP, the EC or any of the other European actors in Brussels to develop a strategy for engaging more with religions such as Christianity or Islam either institutionally or collectively. Ten (63%) state that they do not think the EU should have a 'real policy' towards religion, compared with only 31% (5) who do. In fact, this is actually in line with the aggregate European figures showing 72% in agreement that the EU should not try to develop such a policy.

Thus far, the views of the British MEPs are consistent with those of their European colleagues: there should be a separation between church and state when it comes to public policy formulation. But a more pronounced contrast comes when we look at the idea of enshrining the status of Europe's Christian heritage in the Lisbon Treaty of 2007, the de facto constitution of the EU. As Table 11 shows, while 41% of Europe's MEPs state that

Table 8. Importance of promoting the views and interests of a church or religious group by country (national and regional MPs).

Degree of importance	Country (%)															Total (Av.) (%)
	AUT	BEL	FRA	GER	HUN	IRE	ISR	ITA	NET	NOR	POL	POR	SPA	SWI	UNK	
1 (no imp)	15.4	25.0	31.4	3.8	9.3	8.7	5.7	7.2	20.8	19.4	12.2	8.1	14.8	22.7	11.1	13.6
2	10.6	21.9	19.6	10.0	9.3	17.4	8.6	12.0	9.4	22.2	12.2	15.1	12.7	23.7	7.4	13.4
3	16.0	18.8	15.7	10.5	13.4	17.4	14.3	18.1	9.4	16.7	19.5	14.0	10.5	12.4	16.0	13.9
4	23.9	16.4	21.6	15.5	14.4	17.4	20.0	25.3	22.6	19.4	39.0	24.4	15.3	14.4	19.8	19.2
5	10.6	6.2	3.9	20.9	21.6	8.7	25.7	15.7	18.9	13.9	12.2	18.6	12.2	13.4	16.0	14.7
6	13.8	7.8	3.9	17.2	14.4	21.7	5.7	8.4	9.4	5.6	2.4	4.7	14.0	10.3	7.4	11.4
7 (very imp)	9.6	3.9	3.9	22.2	17.5	8.7	20.0	13.3	9.4	2.8	2.4	15.1	20.5	3.1	22.2	13.8
Total (N)	188	128	51	239	97	23	35	83	53	36	41	86	229	97	81	1467

Table 9. Frequency of contact with churches or religious organisations by country (national and regional MPs).

Frequency	Country (%)															Total (Av.) (%)
	AUT	BEL	FRA	GER	HUN	IRE	ISR	ITA	NET	NOR	POL	POR	SPA	SWI	UNK	
At least once a week	4.1	1.5	0.0	6.4	15.5	0.0	6.2	5.2	1.9	2.7	8.5	1.0	2.2	2.0	12.1	4.7
At least once a month	16.4	6.1	4.8	33.9	24.7	10.3	25.0	9.3	7.4	10.8	17.0	9.4	6.6	6.9	30.8	15.9
At least every three months	27.7	17.6	17.5	32.7	20.6	17.2	18.8	23.7	25.9	18.9	10.6	21.9	15.8	17.6	39.6	23.3
At least once a year	29.7	26.0	42.9	21.9	23.7	48.3	6.2	43.3	33.3	35.1	36.2	27.1	23.7	29.4	15.4	27.5
(Almost) no contact	22.1	48.9	34.9	5.2	15.5	24.1	43.3	18.6	31.5	32.4	27.7	40.6	51.8	44.1	2.2	28.5
Total (N)	195	131	63	251	97	29	32	97	54	37	47	96	228	102	91	1550

Table 10.   EU policy towards religions.

Should the EU have a real policy towards religions?	Percentage of the sample (UK only)	Percentage of the sample (EU)
Yes	31	28
No	63	72
Did not answer	6	0

Table 11.   Lisbon Treaty and Europe's Christian heritage.

Should the Lisbon Treaty have made reference to Europe's Christian heritage?	Percentage of the sample (UK only)	Percentage of the sample (EU)
Yes	19	41
No	75	48
Did not answer	6	10

this would have been desirable, only 19% (3) of British MEPs feel the same way. Moreover 75% (12) say they do not think this would have been a good idea compared with 48% of the European average. The views expressed by Pope Benedict XVI and also Chancellor Angela Merkel that Europe's religious heritage should be acknowledged (Traynor 2007) would not find much popularity within the UK context where the whole concept of the 'roots' of Europe is probably much less central. The contrast here with the rest of Europe is very pronounced indeed.

Finally, Table 12 below focuses on a key dimension: MEPs were asked whether they felt religion had a role to play in the way Turkey's candidature for accession to the EU was received. Twelve (75%) replied that 'yes', religion was relevant – and this is back in line with the wider European average of 69%. While we do not know if the MEPs feel that this is a good or a bad thing, it is a striking finding nonetheless. European integration is indeed a Christian project in this respect. Yet this is not the formal explanation for why Turkey has not yet acceded to the EU. According to various actors, geography rather than religion is the most salient factor; but this seems a somewhat partial interpretation (EC 2013) and one that many MEPs do not support. Indeed Britain has long been an outlier in relation to Turkish accession with governments of different political persuasions, Conservative and Labour, continuously being Turkey's biggest cheerleader when it comes to EU membership (BBC 2013).

Finally, we see the MEPs putting their values into action: the average MEP does not think the EU should seek to develop a formal policy in relation to religion or religions in Europe. Yet despite this, the perception among all MEPs – regardless of nationality – is

Table 12.   Religion and Turkey's accession to the EU.

Does religion play a role in the way Turkey's candidature was received in the EP?	Percentage of the sample (UK only)	Percentage of the sample (EU)
Yes	75	69
No	6	20
Did not answer	19	11

that aspects of European enlargement policy are heavily influenced by religious factors, contrary to the official EU position. Moreover, perhaps unsurprisingly, the British MEPs are prepared to take this neutral stance a step further than most of their European colleagues and express their satisfaction that no mention was made in the Lisbon Treaty of Europe's Christian heritage.

Conclusion

Analysing the survey responses of MEPs collectively, especially those from the UK, provides us with some interesting patterns of political behaviour. First, we can state that religious organisations are able to successfully exert influence on the EP and that religion therefore still very much has some sort of institutional political power. Equally, however, there are no hidden agendas: MEPs are understandably not prepared to admit to being under the control of religious organisations or faith-based groups. Second, we can note a substantial departure from the European average with regard to the British MEPs' personal beliefs: while a clear majority of MEPs state that they do believe in God, British MEPs are considerably more agnostic. Indeed, they appear to be even more atheistic than the wider population in the UK, although there is still evidence that they identify with a religious denomination. Nevertheless the UK is now one of Europe's least religious member-states (EC 2010), so these findings are not unreasonable placed against that backdrop – and arguably reinforce pluralistic behaviour in the process. Third, we can conclude that the EU is perhaps at its most religious when it is looking beyond its boundaries – for example, in relation to enlargement policy. The MEPs – both British and from other member-states – are clear that the reason for the delay in allowing Turkey to join the EU is heavily linked to religious factors despite what the EC would officially contend. Meanwhile the British MEPs go further, arguing that it was correct that the Lisbon Treaty made no reference to Europe's Christian heritage.

'Multiple modernities' (Eisenstadt 2000) can be said to summarise the British MEPs' approach to the politics of religion – a Europe for all with different groups, religious and non-religious, coexisting alongside each other. The scholarly literature from social scientists has shifted quite significantly since the orthodoxy of the 1960s which proclaimed that religion was no longer of interest – and in many ways it is Eisenstadt's theory which has gradually come to personify that gear-change, arguing that in modern advanced industrial democracies like the UK, different sets of values need not be mutually exclusive. Eisenstadt (2000, 1) criticises scholars who 'assumed, even only implicitly, that the cultural program of modernity as it developed in modern Europe and the basic institutional constellations that emerged there would ultimately take over in all modernizing and modern societies'. So according to the survey responses of the British MEPs, the EU should neither deny its Christian roots nor trumpet them as central to its existence. The status of religious lobbies within the EU can be said to be broadly respected, but no more and no less than that of other groups, organisations or interests. Freedom of religion is protected and supported certainly, but not if it impacts upon the freedoms of other European citizens.

There is evidence throughout the survey responses and interviews of the European politicians showing considerable sensitivity to the views and values of their constituents. British MEPs appear very adept at seeking to place themselves in the mainstream of public opinion, which itself reflects generational shifts in societal behaviour. Church populations in the UK are falling – they remain significant but they do not have the institutional power that they once had, and it remains to be seen whether they will again in the future. Our MEPs tread a moderate line, respecting religion while not necessarily practising religion themselves. Europe is the historic home of Christianity but it now leads the world in levels of atheism and is the only continent where church attendances are not rising (Norris and Inglehart 2004). MEPs from the UK appear highly professional at attempting to reconcile these two competing spheres through a pluralistic process of political consultations and compromises.

References

Barley, L. 2006. *Churchgoing Today.* London: Church of England.

BBC. 2013. "Turkey Protests: Erdogan Rejects EU Criticism." *BBC News Europe.* Jun. 8. http://www.bbc.co.uk/news/world-europe-22817460.

Brierley Consultancy. 2013. *London's Churches are Growing!* http://brierleyconsultancy.com/images/londonchurches.pdf

Brown, C. 2003. "Campbell Interrupted Blair as He Spoke of His Faith: 'We Don't Do God'." *The Telegraph,* May 4. http://www.telegraph.co.uk/news/uknews/1429109/Campbell-interrupted-Blair-as-he-spoke-of-his-faith-We-dont-do-God.html.

Cheneval, F., and F. Schimmelfennig. 2013. "The Case for Demoicracy in the European Union." *JCMS: Journal of Common Market Studies* 51 (2): 334–350. doi:10.1111/j.1468-5965.2012.02262.x.

CO (Cabinet Office). 2012. *House of Lords Reform Bill.* http://www.publications.parliament.uk/pa/bills/cbill/2012-2013/0052/13052.pdf

Dahl, R. 1961. *Who Governs? Democracy and Power in an American City.* New Haven, CT: Yale University Press.

Davie, G. 1994. *Religion in Britain Since 1945: Believing Without Belonging.* Oxford: Blackwell.

Duncan, F. 2013. "Preaching to the Converted: Christian Democratic Voting in Six West European Countries." *Party Politics* 19 (5): 1–14.

Dür, A., and G. Mateo. 2012. "Who Lobbies the European Union? National Interest Groups in a Multilevel Polity." *Journal of European Public Policy* 19 (7): 969–987. doi:10.1080/13501763.2012.672103.

EC (European Commission). 2010. *Biotechnology Report (Special Eurobarometer 73.1).* http://ec.europa.eu/public_opinion/archives/ebs/ebs_341_en.pdf

EC (European Commission). 2013. *Enlargement: Turkey.* http://ec.europa.eu/enlargement/countries/detailed-country-information/turkey/index_en.htm

Eisenstadt, S. 2000. "Multiple Modernities." *Daedalus* 129 (1): 1–29.

El C (Electoral Commission). n.d. *Guidance for Political Parties.* Accessed September 14, 2013. http://www.electoralcommission.org.uk/i-am-a/party-or-campaigner/guidance-for-political-parties

EP (European Parliament). n.d. *Human Rights and Democracy.* Accessed September 14, 2013. http://www.europarl.europa.eu/aboutparliament/en/0039c6d1f9/Human-rights.html

EPP (European People's Party). n.d. *EPP Group in the European Parliament.* Accessed September 14, 2013. http://www.eppgroup.eu/home/en/default.asp

EU (European Union). n.d. *Summaries of EU Legislation.* Accessed September 14, 2013. http://europa.eu/legislation_summaries/institutional_affairs/treaties/amsterdam_treaty/a10000_en.htm

Foret, F., and X. Itçaina, eds. 2011. *Politics of Religion in Western Europe: Modernities in Conflict.* London: Routledge.

Foret, F., and V. Riva. 2010. "Religion between Nation and Europe: The French and Belgian "No" to the Christian Heritage of Europe." *West European Politics* 33 (4): 791–809. doi:10.1080/01402381003794621.

HC (House of Commons). 2012. *The Code of Conduct Together with the Guide to the Rules Relating to the Conduct of Members*. London: HMSO.

Heeg, S. 2012. "The Erosion of Corporatism: The Rescaling of Industrial Relations in Germany." *European Urban and Regional Studies* 20 (3): 1–15.

Hertzke, A. 2009. "Religious Interest Groups in American Politics." In *The Oxford Handbook of Religion and American Politics*, edited by C. Smidt, A. Kellstedt, and J. Guth, 299–329. New York: Oxford University Press.

Leustean, L., ed. 2012. *Representing Religion in the European Union: Does God Matter?* London: Routledge.

Leustean, L., and J. Madeley, eds. 2009. *Religion, Politics and Law in the European Union*. London: Routledge.

Mahoney, C. 2008. *Brussels Versus the Beltway: Advocacy in the United States and the European Union*. Washington, DC: Georgetown University Press.

Micklethwait, J., and A. Wooldridge. 2009. *God is Back: How the Global Rise of Faith is Changing the World*. London: Allen Lane.

Norris, P., and R. Inglehart. 2004. *Sacred and Secular: Religion and Politics Worldwide*. Cambridge: Cambridge University Press.

ONS (Office for National Statistics). 2011. *Religion in England and Wales 2011*. http://www.ons.gov.uk/ons/rel/census/2011-census/key-statistics-for-local-authorities-in-england-and-wales/rpt-religion.html

Pulzer, P. 1967. *Political Representation and Elections in Britain*. London: Allen and Unwin.

Putnam, R. 2000. *Bowling Alone: The Collapse and Revival of American Community*. New York: Simon and Schuster.

Steven, M. 2010. *Christianity and Party Politics: Keeping the Faith*. London/New York: Routledge.

Traynor, I. 2007. "As the EU Turns 50, Pope Says It's on Path to Oblivion." *The Guardian*, March 26. http://www.guardian.co.uk/world/2007/mar/26/eu.catholicism.

Voas, D., and R. Ling. 2010. "Religion in Britain and the United States." In *British Social Attitudes: The 26th Report*, edited by A. Park, J. Curtice, K. Thomson, M. Phillips, E. Clery, and S. Butt, 65–86. London: Sage.

Wilcox, C., and C. Robinson. 2010. *Onward Christian Soldiers: The Religious Right in American Politics*. Boulder, CO: Westview.

Part II

Master at Home, Embattled in Brussels?

French MEPs and religion: Europeanising 'laïcité'?

François Foret[a,b]

[a]Institute for European Studies - CEVIPOL, Université Libre de Bruxelles (ULB), Brussels, Belgium; [b]Jean Monnet Chair (Social and Cultural Dimensions of European Integration, SocEUR), IEE ULB, Brussels, Belgium

What French members of the European Parliament (MEPs) believe and what they do as a result of these beliefs can be understood in comparison with what we know about MEPs from other member-states on the one hand, and about French national members of Parliament (MPs) and citizens on the other hand. French MEPs do not diverge much from MEPs of other nationalities in the way they deal with religion at the policy level. Significant French specificities remain regarding religion as a cultural and memory reference. The heritage of 'laïcité' leads to an emphasis on the separation between religion and politics and may be reactivated as a symbolic material to reassert French national identity in confrontation with other political traditions. Religious issues do not make for consensus and are still used as markers of ideological and party boundaries, between right and left and within each side, as they are a relatively costless resource to build a distinctive political profile. Beyond these distinctions, a 'French way' of handling religion is commonly acknowledged and 'laïcité' works as an encompassing and resilient framework. The European Parliament (EP) may offer a structure of opportunities and constraints to reformulate slightly the national narrative about religion, but it does not alter the beliefs and practices of French MEPs, who appear largely similar to French MPs and citizens to the extent that they are largely secularised and consider religion as a secondary purpose submitted to political rules and individual choice.

Introduction: contemporary French 'laïcité' in the European context

French 'laïcité' has a historical specificity inherited from the historical path of relationships between church and state in France. However, French exceptionalism is probably weaker than is often claimed, notably by French politicians and scholars celebrating the emancipatory mission of the Republic. 'Laïcité' is an original regime, but it implements principles which are also applied under different institutional forms in other European countries. Conversely, the same term can refer to different realities (Foret and Riva 2010). In French 'laïcité', the state regulates and arbitrates and is the key reference for a pluralism of integration. This overarching conception promotes the neutrality of the public space and a direct relationship between the citizen and public authorities. There is thus little room in this configuration for intermediary bodies, including churches. This is a model very different from the Belgian 'laïcité'. In Belgium, the state guarantees a pluralism of juxtaposition where various particular identities coexist. Secularism is a philosophical vision of the world in competition with confessional visions (Martin 1994).

These two countries, however, do not appear to be those whose national models have most influenced or are the most compatible with the treatment of the religious in the institutions of the European Union (EU). The German philosophy of recognising confessional organisations both as co-contributors to the public good and as public policy actors is often seen as the most convincing 'blueprint' for EU practice (Willaime 2004, 108–109). Still, the normative neutrality demonstrated in European institutions is assimilated in many cultures to a derivative of French *laïcité*.

France opposed the mention of the Christian heritage of Europe in the defunct European Constitution and in the Lisbon Treaty in order to protect this encompassing neutrality of its public space. The French political world as almost unanimous in supporting this position, apart from alternative voices heard only peripherally, mainly in formations not likely to become government forces in the near future, or emanating from 'free riders' speaking from an intellectual and historical rather than political standpoint. This shows the influence of the national model structuring the relations between politics and religion, a model deeply rooted in the collective mind. The promotion of a '*laïcité positive*' re-enhancing the place of religion by Nicolas Sarkozy as minister of the interior, president or simple politician has not altered the basics of the French debate. Sarkozy had to face strong reactions from defenders of secularism, but also reluctance on the part of religious actors to change the status quo. The controversy over 'national identity' and the focusing on Islam contributed to complicating the relationships between the leader of the Union for a Popular Movement (*Union pour un Mouvement Populaire* (UMP)) and religious forces who were concerned about a 'restricted *laïcité*' instrumentalised by politicians (de Gaulmyn 2012). Finally, the strategic and identity use of religion by Sarkozy appear as a reflection of the contemporary secondary status of religion in the usual path dependence of the French historical context, where religious references as such are formally kept away from the official discourse but have been largely instrumentalised as cultural resources at the service of political purposes. (Portier 2008).

Another significant feature of the French model is the relative weakness of Christian Democracy. In the nineteenth century France was to become a pioneer in the elaboration of Christian Democracy, as a reaction against the Revolution which had attempted to eradicate religion by force (Maier 1992). Catholics were marginalised by the Republican victory in 1880, and their massive influx into French politics following the Second World War represents a significant turnaround, linked to their role in the resistance. But the fledgling Popular Republican Movement (*Mouvement Républicain Populaire* (MRP)) never managed to gain a solid foothold in the political scene. The Fifth Republic has meant a reduction in the traditional hostility between the Republican and Catholic traditions (Girvin 2000). Secularisation also played its role in neutralising the conflict between the political and the religious spheres. As an illustration we may take François Bayrou, president of the Union for French Democracy (*Union pour la Démocratie Française* (UDF)) and then of the Democratic Movement (*Mouvement Démocrate* (MoDem)), who is heir to the Christian Democrat tradition and a practising Catholic, and who campaigned for a *laïque* European Constitution, without reference to the Christian roots of Europe.

On the specific issue of European integration, French Christian Democrats have been notably reticent, undermining the myth that there is a 'Vatican Europe' unanimously supported by Catholic politicians (Kaiser 2007). They were deeply divided about the proposed European Defence Community in 1954 because of a resilient hostility against Germany. Progressively, they rallied to the European cause because of the communist threat and in order to counterbalance the international alliance of socialist parties, but this conversion has never excluded certain Gallican throwbacks (Chenaux 2007, 75–81,

88–89). Eurosceptic forces rooted in the tradition of the Catholic conservative right have repeatedly used European elections to access political and media recognition. As far as the Catholic Church in France is concerned, its line has always been very cautious. Since the condemnation of *Action Française* in 1926 and the abandonment of any attempt at unified political action, but also because of the vision of French Catholics regarding Europe (Airiau 2007), the French episcopate has frequently kept a low profile, focusing rather on public policy matters.

In very recent times, France has again offered the ambivalent picture both of a political practice not so different from that of other European countries and of a mobilisation of religion as a symbolic resource to reignite old passions and deal with identity anxieties. Members of the French Parliament (MPs) are telling examples of conflicting purposes regarding religion, as they oscillate between the representation of their electors for which it is not a priority and the possible temptation to instrumentalise religion in order to provoke debate or attract media attention to themselves in a political system centred on the executive. Today, all political forces converge to celebrate a '*laïcité*' coming to terms with evolving social realities, but they may have different appreciations of the term. Jean-Pierre Barbier of the conservative UMP, founder of a working group on 'Republic and religions' which held its first session in May 2013, states the paradox:

> [There is] a disappearance of religious awareness and simultaneously an increase of claims linked to the visibility of religion. There are many discourses about '*laïcité*', there is legislation to limit the presence of religious signs. But saying to people that '*laïcité*' must ignore religion is no longer possible. The question is to know whether we want a *laïque* Republic or a *laïque* society. We need to face the place of religions in society and question the role of the state to organise this place better. (le Bars 2013: my translation)

M. Barbier and his UMP colleagues are divided about a proposal by the UMP for a text aiming at regulating the expression of religious affiliations at work, a sign that positions on the religious issue do not strictly coincide with party lines (Le Bars 2013). The controversy over gay marriage was another example of how French MPs are divided between two concerns. On the one hand, they wanted a debate to take place in Parliament rather than on the street, invoking their function as representatives to voice the general will. On the other hand, they showed their reluctance to interact – or at least their little interest in interacting – with religious leaders invited to the National Assembly to explain the positions of their churches. MPs questioned the legitimacy of 'lobbies', the term being used in a pejorative sense.[1] A third example of the residual conflictual dimension of religion in French politics can be found in new public arenas such as social networks. A continually updated analysis of the Twitter accounts of parties and politicians (Elus.20) shows that extreme right formations (especially *Bloc Identitaire* and to a lesser extent *Front National*) prevail in the use of religious topics and that many references to religions are made under the pressure of external events (crises involving Islam above all). Religion has little presence as an issue in itself, and is mainly in the hands of peripheral political entrepreneurs, despite its strong visibility owing to the fact that it questions the roots of the national narrative.

The RelEP survey

The sample and method of the survey

Twenty-two out of 72[2] French members of the European Parliament (MEPs) answered the questionnaire (30.5%). This is not a representative sample allowing a precise measure of

Table 1. Composition of the sample of French MEPs.

Political group	Number of MEPs in the sample ($n = 22$)	Number of MEPs in the French delegation ($n = 72$)[3]
European People's Party	8 (36.4%)	28 (39%)
Socialists and Democrats	4 (18.2%)	13 (18%)
Greens/European Free Alliance	3 (13.6%)	16 (22.2%)
European United Left – Nordic Green Left	3 (13.6%)	5 (6.9%)
Alliance of Liberals and Democrats	2 (9%)	6 (8.3%)
Europe of Freedom and Democracy	1 (4.5%)	1 (1.4%)
Non-attached	1 (4.5%)	3 (4%)

the effects of different political/national/denominational belongings and personal characteristics, but it may give a fair enough picture of the general attitudes of the group towards religion. The distribution of the interviewed MEPs among political groups is a good reflection of the composition of the French delegation (Table 1).

Overall, more right-wing than left-wing MEPs responded. MEPs declined to take the questionnaire for various reasons: too busy a schedule; refusal to answer surveys on principle; specific reluctance to deal with the topic of the study. Among the Greens especially, some considered that religion was a private matter and must not be debated as a public issue. Conversely, some left-wingers were very keen to state their secularist views. Fifteen of our interviewees were 'freshmen' serving their first term from 2009 onwards, a proportion slightly larger than that in the French delegation as a whole. They were members of committees (Transport and Tourism, Budgets, Economic and Monetary Affairs, Development, Industry, Research and Energy, Agriculture and Rural Development) which are not particularly relevant to religion-related debates. This last point must not be over-interpreted as it depends heavily on personal contacts and channels activated to gather interviews.

Religion and the functioning of the EP

MEPs were asked to assess the influence of religion (deliberately defined as a global unspecified parameter) on the functioning of the European Parliament (EP). A narrow majority of the French MEPs who responded to the question (52.4% (11))[4] acknowledge the impact of religion. The contrast is worth noting with MEPs of all nationalities, of whom 63.2% say that religion plays an important role in the EP. As French MEPs tend to be rather secularised and reluctant to speak of religion as a public issue, this figure may be partly interpreted as linked to the strong national tradition of separation between spiritual and political affairs and the relegation of religion to the private sphere.

A majority of respondent French MEPs (56.25% (9)) consider that religion reinforces the identity of each political group, significantly more than the percentage of respondent MEPs as a whole (42.4%). This may be because religious identity is more discriminatory in the French political field than in that of other countries. There has been a strong historical polarisation as a result of the difficult relationship between church and state, and religious identity is more associated with the political right. Religion may play as an identity marker for some MEPs who take inspiration in the heritage of Christian Democracy, a label more salient in European than in national politics, and in the European People's Party (EPP) than in the UMP. It may thus be easier to view oneself as a French Christian Democrat in an enlarged multinational family in Brussels than in Paris. However, seen from the extreme right of the political spectrum, the 'Christian Democratic' label is suspicious. For one French MEP of the National Front (*Front National*), it means a betrayal of its religious origins to comply with the requirements of the political game: 'There is a "Christian-Democratic group" at the EP which, at least at the political level, has only "democratised" Christianity instead of Christianising democracy. That is not the same thing at all.' In other cases, religion may reinforce political cohesion as a scapegoat. Denunciation of Islam is clearly a factor of unity. Religion – or opposition to religion – may also work as a bridge between political cleavages. French MEPs of different political groups who want to see a clear separation between religious and political affairs are associated with the European Parliament Platform for Secularism in Politics, the secular network active within the EP.

There is almost unanimous agreement among the respondents (95.2% (20)) that nationality has a great influence on the importance of religion for an MEP (compared with 'only' 82.8% for all MEPs); but most respondent French MEPs also suspect that religion has more importance for other nationalities than for them. French MEPs are all the more likely to be of this view as the national '*laïcité*' is a leitmotif – invested with different meanings – in the discourse of political leaders and a reference of which all actors compete to enforce the dominant interpretation in public controversies about religion. Differences between denominations are not considered to be a major factor by 60% (14) of respondent French MEPs, slightly less than the percentage of all MEPs (66.7%). However, denominational and national belongings mixed together can produce stronger discriminatory effects. One French MEP views for example Italian Catholics as particularly 'showy' in the public display of their beliefs and in the political uses they make of them.

Religion, political practice and socialisation

French MEPs are quite heterogeneous in the way and frequency they take religion into account. Fifteen (71.4%) respondents do so never or rarely (56.7% of all MEPs); so French MEPs are less in touch with religion, and this is particularly visible at the extremes: no MP takes religion into account permanently, and more French MEPs ignore religion totally. French MEPs show a particularly high discrepancy between agreeing that religion has a significant role in the EP as a whole but saying that it has none at the individual level: while acknowledging religion as a socio-political object they are deeply attached to the separation of politics and religion and apply this vision in their personal practice. Twelve (80%) French MEPs who acknowledge the relevance of religion in their activity say that it is relevant as a social and political reality. Willy-nilly, religion imposes itself as an issue independently from what the MEP believes. Religion as personal inspiration and religion as representation of interests comes far behind. MEPs drawing their personal motivation from their beliefs all belong either to the EPP or to the extreme right. Those mentioning religion as lobbies can be divided into two groups. The first group includes nonbelievers who see religious interest groups as a threat. The second group includes active believers who take religion into account in several ways, lobbying being only one of them and not the most important. It is worth noting that there is very little mention of the role of religious interest groups as a possible resource of expertise useful for preparing decisions.

Despite their reluctance, most respondent French MEPs have contacts with religious or philosophical lobbies with almost the same frequency as MEPs of other nationalities do. This means that they do their job by complying with common rules. There is nevertheless a noticeable difference. None claims to be in touch with religious civil society at a very high intensity. There is no firm believer playing the 'soldier of God' and cultivating intimate relationships with religious lobbies to gain public recognition, as can be found in other nationalities. In view of French secularisation and laicisation, such a strategy would be politically unproductive.

French MEPs can also be compared with their counterparts of other nationalities by looking at the list of organisations with which they interact most frequently. The more usual interlocutors are of two kinds: charities with a more or less obvious religious dimension (ATD Quart Monde, Caritas, the Churches' Commission for Migrants in Europe (CCME)); and large federations of religious interests like COMECE (the Commission of the [Catholic] Bishops' Conferences of the European Community) or KEK-CEC (the Conference of European Churches). The general hegemony of Catholic forces at the EP is verified: this comes as no surprise in view of the demography of France. Another interesting finding concerning French MEPs is the relative weakness of their contacts with national and local religious organisations from France. Unlike MEPs from other countries, they do not export a privileged connection with territorial congregations to the supranational level. It is also intriguing to note that secular and humanist organisations are not mentioned. This is an invitation to refine the understanding of 'laïcité' as an encompassing vision of separation between church and stage (French style) and not as a philosophical secularist world view in competition with denominational world views (Belgian style).

Nine (64.3%) respondent French MEPs consider that the place of religion at the EP differs from their experience of it in national politics. This is significantly more than the average for all MEPs (45.4%). Again, the strict French separation between politics and religion is deeply challenged by the presence of religious lobbies in the corridors of the EU, by colleagues of other nationalities openly displaying their personal beliefs (and above all by priests elected as MEPs, which is quite a traumatic phenomenon for some French MEPs) and by the salience of religion as an international issue. French MEPs may be shocked by the significance of religion in Brussels and Strasbourg but they stick to their national model as other nationalities do. Seventeen (85%) of French respondents think that their experience at the EP has not changed anything in the way they relate politics to religion. As the French MEPs interviewed are largely newcomers in their first term, they are all the more unlikely to have already 'gone native'; but there is no reason to believe that they will do so in the future.

Salience of religion according to policy sectors and topics

The status of religion as a political factor for MEPs can be understood in the light of the policy fields where they see its role as the most important. The fight against discrimination and freedom of expression are the domains most frequently quoted, followed by social policy, economic policy and external relations. These domains are evidently overlapping, as some MEPs would classify the right of individuals to wear religious symbols at work as part of the fight against discrimination while others would put it in social policy. Answers from French MEPs are not very different from those of all MEPs. Small discrepancies in classification may be explained by the influence of the national cultural matrix. It is probably more natural for a German MEP than for a French MEP to think of religion as a social issue as in Germany the churches are important actors in the social sectors and are financed by the state to fulfil missions of public interest. Overall, however, differences remain limited.

This picture reflects the reality of the competencies of the EU, which has to deal with religion essentially through the prism of the defence of fundamental rights but has no direct competencies in the regulation of spiritual affairs. French MEPs can rally to this vision, which does not contradict too much the national dominant view of religion. The devil is however in the details. The interpretation of fundamental rights is different depending on whether the priority is to protect freedom of religion or to protect freedom from religion. Like their colleagues of other nationalities, French MEPs are keen to tackle religion in civilisational terms in foreign affairs, as a cultural key to deciphering international conflicts and relationships between geopolitical areas. They tend to use formulae such as 'clash of civilisations' and 'Islamisation of Europe'.

More than two thirds of respondent French MEPs reject the idea of a specific European policy for religion. Their rejection may be based on a preference for national sovereignty on the issue of the relationship between spiritual and political powers, which has a strong resonance in the French history of state-building. It may also be based on the concern to keep European institutions away from religious affairs in order to protect '*laïcité*', this time at the supranational level.

Moving now from religion as a policy issue to religion as an identity resource, we find that French MEPs are more opposed than MEPs in general to the idea that the Lisbon Treaty should have made reference to the Christian heritage of Europe (65% (13) of respondents compared with 50.3%). This is congruent with the position of France which during the constitutional process led the 'no' side together with Belgium. It is notable that those opposed to such a reference include believers, nonbelievers and atheists. Several explanations are offered. Most MEPs see such a reference as a divisive factor in a multicultural Europe which should be avoided out of political pragmatism. Others see it as an attack on the principle of separation between church and state and of the neutrality of public institutions. Others simply do not see the usefulness of such a reference.

A large majority of French MEPs (95% (19) of respondents) believe that religion plays a role in the way Turkey's candidature is being received in the EP, a much larger figure than the already very large consensus (77.2%) of all respondent MEPs on this point. Here French MEPs reflect the position of their national authorities who have often expressed concern about the European future of Turkey and doubts – to say the least – about Turkey's 'Europeanness'. The views of French MEPs on this subject also corroborate the idea, mentioned above, that French MEPs think that religion is more of an incentive for MEPs of other nationalities than it is for them. A French MEP may say that Islam does not have an impact on his/her totally secular view regarding Turkey, but that it does for a Polish/Italian/German colleague.

When the nature of the European polity is less directly at stake than in the Turkish candidature, the role of religion in the external relations of the EU is a more divisive subject among MEPs. French MEPs are almost equally divided between 'yes' and 'no' on the question whether religion has an influence on European relations with the rest of the world. Their national diplomatic tradition has not prepared them to see religious organisations play the go-between in crises abroad or to see religion as in itself a component of foreign affairs. This invisibility of the religious factor in French diplomacy may explain the fact that most French MEPs are not aware of its potential role in external relations.

Moving to a final aspect of the analysis of religion as a policy issue, we find that 75% (15) of respondent French MEPs, compared with 88.4% of all respondent MEPs, support the political dialogue which has been established as a routine between the president of the

European Parliament and religious leaders by Article 17 of the Lisbon Treaty. This is both a qualification and a slight confirmation of the exceptionalism of French '*laïcité*'. In Paris, such meetings between the highest public authorities and religious elites have also been institutionalised (by a socialist prime minister, Lionel Jospin, in 2002) Nevertheless, some MEPs continue to express reluctance, in the name of a traditional strict separation between politics and religion.

Individual religious preferences of MEPs

Fifteen (71.4%) French respondents say that they belong to a religious denomination: almost exactly the same proportion as that of all respondent MEPs (72%). Moreover, some MEPs saying that they have no religious affiliation may nevertheless say that they believe in a personal god or in something else. This illustrates the fact that that 'religion à la carte' is a reality among MEPs as well as in European societies. However, the reverse is also true: more French MEPs claim that they belong to a religious denomination than define themselves as religious persons. These are cultural Christians inscribing themselves in a lineage and acknowledging a cultural heritage in the sense of Hervieu-Léger (1993). This does not mean that religion has a significant influence on their political behaviour; but MEPs declaring a religious affiliation tend to have a more positive view of religion as a factor for unity within political groups and do not think that it creates a gap between nationalities. On the contrary, it is those who claim no religious affiliation who insist on the discriminatory effect of religion.

As far as claimed religious belonging is concerned, 86.6% (13) of respondent French MEPs are self-defined Catholics, as compared with 59.6% of the whole sample of MEPs and 46% of the French population (Bréchon 2008). The discrepancy between French MEPs and their electors may be explained by the fact that many of the French MEPs declined to answer the question, and those who did so are more religious than average, thus over-representing the majority denomination in France. Other denominations are totally invisible, the rest of the French MEPs opting for silence on their religious preferences. A small surprise may be that only one French MEP (4.5%) declares himself a convinced atheist (against 13.9% among all MEPs and 14% in the French population) (Bréchon 2008). Several explanations are possible. Politicians have to display consensual profiles in order to avoid alienating their electors, so they may be less prone to take divisive stances. In some cases, however, it may be instrumental to insist on normative choices to distinguish themselves from competitors and attract media attention and support of civil society. To be an embattled atheist may be a good strategy in countries where the secular pillar has historically been confronted with a strong religious faction (for example Belgium, which provides several MEPs acting as spokespersons for the secularist cause). This strategic choice is less relevant in France where the public space is supposed to be secular and where all private beliefs – including philosophical convictions – should be in the private sphere. Therefore, to be an outspoken atheist in the French political system is less rewarding.

Another interesting feature concerns religious observance. French MEPs have a far higher level of participation in religious services, whatever their religious belonging may be. 56% of the French population say that they never attend religious services apart from weddings, funerals and christenings, as opposed to 4.5% (1, the atheist) of respondent French MEPs (and 5.5% of all MEPs). This is a phenomenon well documented by American scholarship: for politicians, religious circles and ceremonies are opportunities to meet their electors or actors in civil society: it is part of the job to contribute to religious events, even in a mere professional capacity.

In addition to the analysis of the personal beliefs of MEPs, a last set of questions aimed at testing their attitudes on religious issues and their level of cultural liberalism. These questions were borrowed from international values surveys in order to compare MEPs and ordinary citizens.

A large majority of French respondent MEPs (86.4% (19)) disagree, and most of them very strongly (77.3% (17)), with the idea that politicians who do not believe in God are unfit for public office. Both these percentages are higher than the percentage for all MEPs taken together. The view that religious beliefs can certainly not be a condition for access to power or viewed as an indicator of public morality does not come as a surprise in view of what sociology of religion says about the European population; at the same time it reminds us of the difference between Europe (and especially France) and the USA. However, this does not mean that believers should be excluded from public office: almost a quarter of French respondents (22.7% (5)) support the view that 'It would be better for Europe if more people with strong religious beliefs held public office'.

Regarding the political role of religion, 50.1% (11) of respondent French MEPs consider that religious leaders should not influence government decisions. Even more of them, and more virulently, are of the opinion that religious leaders should not influence how people vote in elections (63.6% (14)). On these two points, they score very similarly to other MEPs. The interpretation could be that they are not very much in favour of religious lobbying allowing churches to intervene in decision-making, but that they are yet more opposed to direct pressure on citizens. Some may agree with the possibility for religious organisations to be heard in a deliberative setting (this is frequently the position of those who support the proposal that religious leaders should be allowed to influence decision-making), although pluralism in the political space is an option not yet naturalised in French political tradition; but for most respondents an authoritarian stance by churches is inconceivable. The key principle is the respect for individual free choice.

This taboo against anything that might endanger the freedom of conscience of the individual is confirmed by responses to other questions, and may even call into question a firm attitude on separation between the private and public spheres. Ten (45.4%) respondent French MEPs disagree (31.8% (7) strongly) with the proposition that if a nurse were asked to help perform a legal abortion, she or he should be allowed to refuse on religious grounds, but 36.4% (8) agree. Here we can see the resilient effect of '*laïcité*', as 52.3% of all respondent MEPs support the nurse's right to conscientious objection. French MEPs are sensitive to individual rights but are still reluctant to endorse religiously-based exceptions.

Finally, French MEPs as a political elite are less radical than ordinary French citizens. For example, 76% of the French population are opposed to religious leaders exercising influence on government decisions, as compared with 50.1% of respondent French MEPs, and 83% of the French population agree, most of them (65%) very strongly, that religious leaders should not influence how people vote in elections, as compared with 63.6% of respondent French MEPs.[5] A partial explanation may be that our sample is more right-wing than the French population. The relatively moderate position of the MEPs may also be due to contact with other cultures; however, even if socialisation with MEPs of other nationalities may have an impact on the intensity of the positions of French MEPs it is not likely to alter these positions fundamentally. MEPs themselves underline the absence of transformative effects of their experience at the EP. They may not be totally aware of their learning curves in Brussels/Strasbourg which lead them to moderate their positions, but they are not going to revise their principles.

It comes as no surprise to find that French MEPs with personal religious beliefs are more in favour of allowing religious leaders to intervene in politics, in decision-making and in the formation of the choice of voters, and more inclined to say that it is good to have political leaders with faith and to support freedom of choice for nurses in respect of their religious convictions. However, these believers share the same opposition as non-believers to the idea that religion should be a prerequisite for access to power.

Political adherence is also a factor. Right-wing French MEPs – and still more extreme right-wing ones – are less attached to a strict '*laïcité*' and more in favour of an active political role for religious leaders than their left-wing counterparts, but some left-wing or left-leaning MEPs may support pluralism (including the right for religious actors to be heard) and individual free choice (including conscientious objection for an individual facing the obligation to perform an act in contradiction with his or her beliefs). These effects of religious and political adherence are similar to those which are observed in mass surveys of the French population. Here there are no structural discrepancies between electors and elected.

Comparing French MEPs with French MPs

So far, the comparison has mainly been made between French MEPs and MEPs of other nationalities on the one hand, and with French citizens on the other hand. It is also interesting to compare French MEPs in Brussels with members of the French Parliament (MPs). Information is scarce on the religious beliefs and the political uses of religion by national MPs. Recent major surveys on French MPs (Rouban 2011; Keslassy 2012; Costa and Kerrouche 2007) say nothing about their religious profile, even when cultural or social features are dealt with to show the enlargement of the recruitment of MPs to 'visible minorities'. Religion is still an invisible factor. However, a qualitative survey (Rambour 2008) carried out on a sample of 80 MPs and senators during the term 2002–2007 offers some indications. Five elements are particularly valuable.

The first element is the fact that religion is an unexpected topic, and seen as one of doubtful legitimacy. Reactions of national MPs include surprise, irony, hesitation or rejection. It is worth noticing that in two cases, the presence of religion in the survey is attributed to Europe. One seasoned MP (PS, atheist) says 'Yeah, that is biased questions! ... Barroso made this, didn't he? ... Oh yes, the Poles!' Another young MP (UMP, agnostic) has the same reaction: 'You were asked by the Poles ...' (Rambour 2008, 7–8). Once MPs take the subject in, they are ready enough to speak about it and to give details, but the first reaction is clearly not one of engagement. It is important to make it clear that in this survey questions on religion were hidden among many questions on more 'classic' topics, which made it easier to ask them. This was not the case with the RelEP survey. However, the findings of the Rambour survey are totally congruent with the reluctance of French MEPs to answer questions on religion revealed by the RelEP survey.

A second element is the potentiality of interactions between political and religious activities when they are based on a common territoriality. Secular France cannot be compared with religious America where the churches are centres of community life and places-to-be for people holding public offices. Nevertheless, several cases show that religion matters in social life. One provincial MP (UMP) says: 'I am a Catholic, with a low practice ... . But my political activities help me to become a churchgoer, when you see the amount of masses organized by associations of war veterans and so on ... Hum ... Finally, I quite often attend religious services. That's it.' In this case, political activity leads to religious activity. In another case, that of an MP (UMP) from eastern France, it is religious observance that provokes political encounters: 'Yes, I am a Catholic ... Deeply. And I have often attended ... but it is a detail of some importance. The Chancellor Kohl lives in the neighborhood [of Strasbourg] ... and we have often met at mass, on Sunday, in the cathedral.' A last example suggests that the necessity to take part in public celebrations in their capacities as representatives to meet their constituents has a significant importance in the religious observance of MPs, as emphasised by a UMP senator: 'Hum ... "Light" ... "Light" Christian ... [she laughs] ... Especially Catholic. But I mainly have an ecumenical behavior. I often attend official worships' (Rambour 2008, 8). The intertwinement of politics, religion and territoriality is obvious in French politics where the local matters very much. MEPs are far from having the same local roots, even if their territorial implantation tends to be reinforced by the new mode of election in regional constituencies. This lack of territoriality may weaken the potential for political socialisation by religion and for religious socialisation by politics. On the lines of the model of the USA and what happens in Washington, religious networks can be a way for MEPs to find a home away from home in Brussels; but this may concern only those who want to practise their religion; and in any case French MEPs in Belgium are not far from their own geographical base.

A third element concerns the cohesive or divisive effect of religion on political belonging. The survey of French MPs confirms that religion is strongly associated with the right. However, it also qualifies the idea that religion always works as a factor of unity for the right. The left is indeed predominantly secular; but the right includes politicians from across the spectrum: very religious, moderately religious and not at all religious. So while religion provides a common background for many right-wing MEPs it may also create discrepancies in terms of intensity of relationship to religion (Rambour 2008, 14). Similarly, religion can function as a factor of both unity and disunity at the EP. Some French MEPs may feel at ease in the EPP because of its Christian Democratic identity; others may not for the same reason. These findings invite us to qualify the equation religion = right = unity.

A fourth element illustrates further the complexity of cleavages created by religion when it is combined with other factors. The attitudes of MPs towards the candidature of Turkey provide a good example. French MPs for whom religion is important (either because they are religious or because they regard religion as a threat) tend to consider that religion is indeed a problem for the integration of Turkey. Those who are opposed to religion fear attacks against secularism; believers at a certain level of religious observance fear for Christianity. Indifferent nonbelievers and mild believers care less. Thus politicians at different places in the political spectrum can show the same reaction for opposite reasons. This shows two things: that religion may have strong underlying effects, on nonreligious as well as on religious individuals; and that these effects are impossible to subsume into a coherent pattern, and still less to be used for mobilisation on a coherent and durable basis. This is all the more true at the EP, where the religious diversity is far greater, as is the number of other parameters that religion interacts with.

A fifth element is the salience of religion in dealing with the issue of identity, whether French or European. It seems that the role of religion is similar in defining what national and supranational belonging mean. 20% of interviewed French MPs consider that being Christian is a very or fairly important element in being truly French, 31% consider that it is not very important but that it can have a cultural significance, and 46.25% consider that it is not important at all. 22.5% consider that being Christian is a very or fairly important element in being truly European, 32.5% consider that it is not very important and 42.5% consider that it is not important at all. The statistical gap between the two sets of results is not significant in view of the size of the sample (Rambour 2008, 13). This score may be compared with the 35% of French MEPs who support the idea that the Lisbon Treaty should have made reference to Europe's Christian heritage, thus acknowledging the identity dimension of religion in a proportion far smaller than other nationalities. These results confirm that the identity dimension of religion is not obvious to French MPs and MEPs who are framed by the civil religion of '*laïcité*', but that they nevertheless do not totally ignore its role.

Another survey (PartiRep),[6] scrutinising national and regional MPs, offers further data. French MPs were more reluctant than those of other nationalities to answer questions about religion. Of those who did so 98.2% support the proposition that religion is not very or not at all important in their work, a far higher figure than that for MPs from the total sample of 15 countries (80.8%). French local and national MPs are also far less likely to have frequent contacts with churches or religious organisations (4.8% at least once a month as against 20.6% for the whole sample); and, conversely, more likely to have no contact at all (34.9% as against 28.5% for all countries). These findings confirm that French secularisation – understood as the low social salience of religion – is a reality at the political level. French secularism – understood as the separation between religion and politics – is therefore a significant factor, although it reduces rather than excludes interactions.

French MEPs negotiating the national model at the EP: Europeanising '*laïcité*'?

Against the French background of relations between religion and politics on the one hand, and between nation and Europe on the other, findings from the survey on French MEPs do not come as a surprise. The limited ability of the EP to resocialise its members, and above all to change their personal preferences in terms of values and attitudes, explains why the religious preferences of MEPs – French and of other nationalities – are not likely to evolve. Besides, the depth and the stability of the national support for the model of '*laïcité*' suggest that opinions of French MEPs are likely to be perennial. It does not mean that there is a consensus, but rather an agreement 'made in France' on a modus vivendi or at least a way of disagreeing about religion. The first part of the agreement concerns the secondary dimension of religion. It is an issue which cannot frame political cleavages, party-building and coalition-making. The second part of the agreement is on its symbolic value. Religion does have a role as a symbolic resource to fuel political strategies of differentiation in a narrow political space (for example inside the parties of the right, or between the right and the extreme right. It is also a memory and an identity-marker, as expressed by the greater proximity of the right to religion. It has no major effect on most political choices, apart from on ethical matters, a field where the EU has limited competences and where European actors are not really willing to make frontal choices likely to create problematic tensions. It has an influence (in competition with many other factors) on the level of political liberalism (for example the freedom of choice of an individual to arbitrate between one's religious convictions and one's professional duties). Finally, it is a trace marking the discourse to define oneself when confronted with cultural otherness.

Among French MEPs, as in French society, religion works as a magnetic pole exercising a diffuse influence rather than as a deterministic belonging: it does not prescribe anything in an authoritarian way; it is not heteronomous as religion is less and less transcendent and more and more cultural; it is little systematised and more and more flexible and subjective, the same religious references nourishing radically different value systems; it has no pretention to govern other social spheres, including politics (Donegani 2007, 89–92).

In other words, French MEPs are not so different from French citizens, once one takes into account an elitist bias tending to attenuate the intensity of attitudes as a result of the necessity to compromise as a politician having to deal with social and cultural diversity among one's constituents and with the different models defended by MEPs of other nationalities. French MEPs are not so different from their counterparts in other countries. They reflect trends at work in all European societies, these trends being simply framed by each national model of relations between politics and religion. Religion is neither a transformative nor a divisive force in itself. Rather, it serves as a political resource to reformulate – in a euphemised way – old struggles and demarcations (between parties or between nations) and to nurture individual political entrepreneurships. The restricted impact and range of the religious reference means that it is mainly an element of symbolic politics, a discursive repertoire offering raw material to decorate bigger narratives without being able any more to structure a narrative on its own.

To a certain extent, as was observed in national political spaces during the debate on the Christian heritage of Europe, European integration reactivates latent debates. MEPs are led to come back to the roots of national belonging to reassert their identity as French representatives, French Christian democrats or socialists, French Catholics or atheists. Confrontation with the difference of other nationalities infuses new vigour into faded meanings. It relativises battles of the past (we are not so different among ourselves, French people with the same heritage, regarding other communities); but our internal differences are also highlighted by the way other people deal with the same issues to produce similar or dissimilar patterns. Religion could be described as a symbolic arena with a variable geometry where reassuring fratricides (Anderson 1983) take place. Struggles are struggles because there is an opposition between different world views. But these struggles are reassuring as they are the continuation of past battles in new clothes. As such, they are a sign of identity continuity in a changing world, and the promise of future similar battles. Old enemies are part of the family, so conflicts are constitutive of a sense of closeness by habit. This family has shifting boundaries according to the moment or to the issue: A MEP may disagree about '*laïcité*' as a French socialist with a French member of the UMP; as a French republican with a Polish or Irish supporter of an active role for the Catholic Church in politics; as a Christian European attached to the separation between church and state with a Turkish politician marked by another heritage. Brotherhood is a situational bond in politics, and religion is only a small part of this bond.

Funding

The RelEP project was funded with support from the European Commission through the Jean Monnet Chair 'Social and Cultural Dimensions of European Integration', SocEUR [529183-LPP-2012-BE-AJM-CH]. This publication reflects the views only of the author, and the Commission cannot be held responsible for any use which may be made of the information contained therein. RelEP has also benefited from the support of research grants from the Université Libre de Bruxelles and the Belgian Fonds National de la Recherche Scientifique.

Notes

1. For different accounts of the hearings of religious leaders at the National Assembly, all concluding to different extents that the process was unsatisfying and controversial, see Guénois (2012), Lesegretain (2012).

2. Two more MEPs were designated by the National Assembly after the European elections of 2009 in application of the Lisbon Treaty. The design and schedule of the survey on the French delegation did not allow for their integration.
3. This was the total number of French MEPs at the time the survey was administered: see note 2.
4. All the percentages are calculated on the basis of the number of MEPs who answered each question (referred to in the text as 'respondents'). The number of respondents (indicated between brackets) does not always correspond to the whole sample and may vary according to the question. The rate of those who 'do not answer' is analysed when it is significant.
5. Data on the French MPs are taken from Rambour (2008, 9).
6. More details about the research protocol of PartiRep (2007–2011, $n = 1536$) may be found here: http://www.partirep.eu/datafile/comparative-mp-survey. The author would like to thank the Partirep team (especially Pascal Delwit, Jean-Benoît Pilet and Giulia Sandri) for making unpublished data available.

References

Airiau, P. 2007. "Disputatio dei: l'action politique des catholiques français partisans de l'héritage chrétien" [Disputatio Dei: Political Action by French Catholic Champions of the Christian Heritage]. In *La Constitution européenne: élites, mobilisations, votes* [The European Constitution: Elites, Mobilisations, Votes], edited by A. Cohen and A. Vauchez, 197–208. Bruxelles: Editions de l'Université de Bruxelles.

Anderson, B. 1983. *Imagined Communities: Reflections on the Origins and Spread of Nationalism*. London: Verso Editions/NLB.

Bréchon, P. 2008. "La religiosité des Européens: diversité et tendances communes" [The Religiosity of Europeans: Diversity and Common Tendencies]. Special issue: "Dieu loin de Bruxelles: l'européanisation informelle du religieux" [God Far From Brussels: The Informal Europeanisation of the Religious], edited by F. Foret and X. Itçaina. *Politique européenne* 24: 21–41.

Chenaux, P. 2007. *De la chrétienté à l'Europe: les catholiques et l'idée européenne au XXe siècle* [From Christendom to Europe: Catholics and the European Idea in the Twentieth Century]. Tours: CID Editions.

Costa, O., and E. Kerrouche. 2007. *Qui sont les députés français? Enquête sur des élites inconnues* [Who Are the French Deputies? An Enquiry into the Unknown Elites]. Paris: Presses de Sciences Po.

de Gaulmyn, I. 2012. "Nicolas Sarkozy, de la laïcité positive à la laïcité restrictive" [Nicolas Sarkozy: from Positive *Laïcité* to Restrictive *Laïcité*]. *La Croix*, February 15.

Donegani, J.-M. 2007. "Religion et politique" [Religion and Politics]." In *La politique en France et en Europe* [Politics in France and Europe], edited by P. Perrineau and L. Rouban, 61–94. Paris: Presses de Sciences Po.

Elus 2.0. "Religions ... les élus en parlent sur le Web!" [Religions ... Elected Representatives Talk about them on the Web!] *Elus 2.0.* Accessed May 20. http://www.elus20.fr/actualites-web-facebook-twitter/religions/

Foret, F., and V. Riva. 2010. "Religion between Nation and Europe: The French and Belgian 'No' to the Christian Heritage of Europe." *West European Politics* 33 (4): 791–809. doi:10.1080/01402381003794621

Girvin, B. 2000. "The Political Culture of Secularisation: European Trends and Comparative Perspectives." In *Religion and Mass Electoral Behaviour in Europe*, edited by D. Broughton and H. M. ten Napel, 7–27. London: Routledge.

Guénois, J.-M. 2012. "Mariage gay: les religions entendues à la sauvette" [Gay Marriage: Religions Hastily Consulted]. *Le Figaro*, November 29.

Hervieu-Léger, D. 1993. *La religion pour mémoire* [Religion as a Chain of Memory]. Paris: Éditions du Cerf.

Kaiser, W. 2007. *Christian Democracy and the Origins of the European Union*. Cambridge: Cambridge University Press.

Keslassy, E. 2012. *Une Assemblée nationale plus représentative? Sexe, âge, catégories socio-professionnelles et pluralité visible* [A More Representative National Assembly? Sex, Age, Socio-Professional Categories and Visible Plurality] (*Les Notes de l'Institut Diderot* Autumn). http://www.institutdiderot.fr/?p=4219.

le Bars, S. 2013. "La religion une nouvelle fois au menu des députés" [Religion Once More on the MPs' Menu]. *Le Monde*, May 29.

Lesegretain, C. 2012. "Les responsables religieux auditionnés à l'Assemblée sur le 'mariage pour tous'" [Religious Officials Questioned at the Assembly about 'Marriage for All']. *La Croix*, November 11.

Maier, H. 1992. *L'Église et la démocratie: une histoire de l'Europe politique* [The Church and Democracy: A History of Political Europe]. Paris: Criterion.

Martin, J. P. 1994. "Laïcité française, laïcité belge: regards croisés" [French *Laïcité*, Belgian *Laïcité*: Complementary Perspectives]." In *Pluralisme religieux et laïcités dans l'Union Européenne* [Religious Pluralism and *Laïcités* in the European Union], edited by A. Dierkens, 71–83. Bruxelles: Editions de l'Université de Bruxelles.

Portier, P. 2008. "Retour sur la 'laïcité positive' de Nicolas Sarkozy" [The 'Positive *Laïcité*' of Nicolas Sarkozy Revisited]. *Esprit* 344: 196–198. doi:10.3917/espri.0805.0196

Rambour, M. 2008. "Religion and Europe in the French Parliamentary Arena: First Results of a Qualitative Survey." Paper presented at the workshop "Religion in Europe, Religion and Europe" (organised by F. Foret and X. Itçaina), ECPR conference, Rennes, April 11–16. 22 pp.

Rouban, L. 2011. *Sociologie politique des députés de la Ve République, 1958–2007* [The Political Sociology of the Deputies of the Fifth Republic, 1958–2007] (*Les Cahiers du CEVIPOF* 55). Paris: CEVIPOF – Centre de recherche politiques de Sciences Po. http://www.cevipof.com/fichier/p_publication/829/publication_pdf_cahier_55.3_jp.pdf.

Willaime, J.-P. 2004. *Europe et religions: les enjeux du XXIe siècle* [Europe and Religions: What is at Stake in the Twentieth Century]. Paris: Fayard.

Defenders of faith? Victims of secularisation? Polish politicians and religion in the European Parliament

Magdalena Góra[a] and Katarzyna Zielińska[b]

[a]Institute of European Studies, Jagiellonian University, Ul. Gołębia 24, 31-131 Kraków, Poland;
[b]Institute of Sociology, Jagiellonian University, Ul. Gołębia 24, 31-131 Kraków, Poland

Recent years have shown a growing academic interest in the role and function of religion in the EU. This resulted from ongoing discussions on the symbolic deficit of the European project and politicised debate on the Christian roots of European identity, as well as from the enlargement of 2004, which brought into the EU new member-states with different traditions of church–state relations and distinctive forms of religious governance. Our study contributes to this scholarship by focusing on the role of religion in the context of the European Parliament (EP) as exercised by Polish members. The first part provides some background information on the relationship between religion and politics in the Polish domestic context. This is followed by presentation of the research findings from a survey conducted among Polish members of the European Parliament (MEPs) and from a qualitative content analysis of the arguments used by them in plenary sessions. In conclusion, we argue that religion is an important resource in the hands of right-wing politicians for justifying various claims in the EP. Furthermore, we also maintain that the national context and the national understanding of the functions of religion influence the way it is presented and used at the European level.

Introduction[1]

The new EU member-states – among them Poland – have introduced a new perspective in terms of who they are and what their experience and understanding of Europe is. One of the concurrent themes of the pre-enlargement debate in the West was about who these 'barbarians at the gates' were, and how they would influence the EU. In this context Polish society was frequently perceived through a combination of its high religiosity and homogeneous Catholic denomination, unusual characteristics for Western Europe. Questions arose regarding the extent to which the EU enlargement and accepting such a society into the EU would change the EU itself. Similarly, in Poland questions were frequently asked as to the impact of Europeanisation. The debate at the level of both political and intellectual elites focused to a great extent on axiological issues. It touched upon the role of religion in the contemporary modern state and European integration, but it also revealed uncertainty expressed in particular by circles associated with Catholicism on the outcome of the impact of (presumably) secular Europe on (presumably) Catholic Poland.

The aim of our study is to map the role of religion in the context of the European Parliament (EP) as exercised by Polish MEPs. We argue that religion is an important resource in the hands of right-wing politicians for justifying various claims in the EP. Furthermore, we also maintain that the national context and the national understanding of the functions of religion influence the way it is presented and used at the European level. In order to provide a broader picture, we start by analysing the role of religion in the Polish context, with special attention to the interconnection of religion and Europe in domestic politics and discourse. In the second part we present the results of the RelEP survey of Polish MEPs devoted to uncovering their personal beliefs and attitudes towards the role of religion in the European polity. In the third part we present an analysis of the religious arguments used by Polish MEPs in plenary debates in the EP.

Religious, national and political encounters

Poland, as one of the most religiously homogeneous and most religious countries in Europe, constitutes an interesting case for studying the intersections between religion and politics. Data show that 91% of the population say that they belong to the Roman Catholic Church (RCC), 83.5% say that they believe in God and 51% participate in religious practices at least once a week (EVS 2008). Although these trends are quite stable over time, the younger generation of Roman Catholics seems to be becoming more selective in their acceptance of religious dogmas and dictates. For example, research shows that among young people aged 18–24 who are regular churchgoers, about 75% accept premarital sex, more than 50% do not perceive divorce as wrong, and 20% accept abortion (Boguszewski 2009, 7–9). This suggests that, as in the case of other European societies, we can observe processes of religious individualisation; but they are progressing at a much slower pace.

The RCC is the largest and most influential religious organisation in Poland. Its significant position in society and in politics needs to be understood in the light of Polish history. During troublesome times (the partitions, communism), the RCC stood on the side of the nation and against the enemies, sustaining national identity (Casanova 1994, 92–93; Zubrzycki 2006, 36–39). In the communist era the RCC actively assisted the democratic opposition and was involved in the struggles for human rights, civil society and democracy (Borowik 2002, 241). All these elements contributed to an interweaving of the national, religious and political identities of Poles. However, after 1989 the strong position of the RCC triggered tensions and heated debates in the newly established independent state on church–state relations and the role of the Christian tradition in the newly re-established democracy, as well as in the construction of collective identity.

The RCC entered the post-1989 democratic era in Poland as one of the country's most trustworthy and respected institutions, and Catholicism was perceived as a potential 'sacred canopy' unifying the entire society. Acting in the name of the nation and in cooperation with right-wing politicians, it attempted to impose Christian values and norms on society, such as the introduction of a strict anti-abortion law, the enforcement of legal protection of Christian values in the mass media and the reintroduction of religious education in state schools (see Eberts 1998). The involvement of the RCC in the first political campaigns and its active support for parties conforming to Catholic tenets proved to be particularly controversial, and triggered widespread criticism. The disapproval came not only from liberal political and intellectual elites, but also from Catholic intellectual circles as well as the wider population (Borowik 2002, 242).

Criticism of the political engagement of the RCC and debates on the role and place of religion in the new democracy were particularly visible in the process of the drafting of the new Polish Constitution (1997) (Korbonski 2000, 138). After fierce discussions, state–church relations were defined as based on the principle of respect of autonomy and the mutual independence of each in its own sphere, as well as on the principle of cooperation for the individual and the common good (article 25.2). The reality, however, shows that church–state relations in Poland fit the model of 'positive accommodation' or 'positive neutrality', according to which the state is obliged to actively support (traditional) religion and to offer a space for religion to flourish in the polity (Robbers 2012, 180). Similar models can be found in other European countries, for example Germany or the Netherlands (Stepan 2010).

Controversies over the political engagement of the RCC resulted in a sharp drop in trust towards this institution in the mid-1990s and a revision in its strategies of political involvement. The impact of the RCC on political and social life became less direct and limited to the influence mediated through the right-wing political parties representing its stances and interests (Korbonski 2000).

The Polish political system in the 1990s was marked by great dynamism and changes. The main line of division was drawn between post-Solidarity and post-Communist political formations. Parties declaring a Christian identity and often closely cooperating with the representatives of the RCC belonged exclusively to the former, constituting the centre and the right wing of the political spectrum. Their initial success in 1991 was quickly followed by frequent changes of governments as a result of internal disputes. As a consequence, as soon as 1993 the post-Communist left won and ruled the country for a full term in office. The second half of the 1990s was marked by a new mobilisation of the post-Solidarity camp. In 1997 a new alliance of centre-right parties, Solidarity Electoral Action (*Akcja Wyborcza Solidarność*) (AWS), which openly invoked the Christian Democratic tradition and was supported by the RCC (both by the hierarchy and by the Catholic mass media, Radio Maryja in particular), won the election and formed a ruling majority in the Sejm (Wenzel 1998). Inner conflicts within the AWS triggered a split and reconstruction of the right side of the political spectrum. As a result, in 2001 two major new centre-right parties were created. Civic Platform (*Platforma Obywatelska*) (PO) combined Freedom Union (*Unia Wolności*) (UW) and moderate conservatives from the AWS. Law and Justice (*Prawo i Sprawiedliwość*) (PiS) held a much more revisionist position toward the existing political system, calling for respect for conservative values and displaying a self-declared commitment to Christian tradition. At the same time, two other more radical and populist parties gained growing support: the League of Polish Families (*Liga Polskich Rodzin*) (LPR) and Self Defence of the Republic of Poland (*Samoobrona RP*) (SRP). The former represented radical right-wing and conservative views, its political programme referring to pre-war right-wing fascist organisations and ultra-conservative circles. The SRP could be characterised as a populist and agrarian–nationalistic formation much less interested in axiological and religious topics. Meanwhile the Polish People's Party (*Polskie Stronnictwo Ludowe*) (PSL), present on the political scene from the 1990s and forming ruling coalitions with both right- and left-wing election-winners, tended to pronounce support for Christian values in line with its conservative constituency.

To sum up, the Polish domestic political landscape has now been dominated for over a decade by centre-right and right-wing parties referring indirectly to the Christian Democratic tradition (Hanley et al. 2008, 414–417). Despite the self-proclaimed links of these parties to Christian tradition, some scholars doubt their belonging to Christian

Democracy. The profile of the existing parties only loosely passes the test of 'family resemblance' to Christian Democracy (society seen as an organic whole, importance of family, 'social capitalism', emphasis on transnationalism and reconciliation in external relations, Christian values as principles for governance, but with government remaining in the hands of the laity) (Bale and Szczerbiak 2008, 482–483). The domination of the centre-right and right-wing parties on the political scene and the conflicts between them distinguish politics in Poland from Western European politics, where the main division lies between right-wing and left-wing parties.

Religion and integration of Poland with the EU

The debate on Poland's future EU membership focused primarily on economic aspects. The aspiration for EU membership was supported with unprecedented unanimity among the major political forces in Poland; however, the closer it came to actual membership, the more strongly some of the disagreements surfaced. The most contentious aspects were related to the axiological dimension of the process of European integration, and it was in this area, rather than in that of economic arguments, that the greatest polarisation of debate occurred (Góra and Mach 2010).

The main bone of contention was the role of Christian traditions, both in the Polish state after enlargement and in the European polity. The discussions focused in particular on social issues (education, gender equality, reproductive rights, rights for gays and lesbians), the role of the RCC in European integration and the construction of European identity. Various standpoints can be identified.

First, the liberal groups presented European integration as beneficial and strengthening the democratic nature of the political system in Poland. They also perceived Europe as representing a liberal and post-Enlightenment tradition promoting values leading to the increased separation of religion and state.

Second, more conservative groups – even though still pro-European – stressed the need for a more cautious approach to the integration process. They argued that Polish sovereignty and the Polish national identity, interwoven with Christianity, needed to be protected and respected. Western liberal traditions were seen as possible threats to the status of the Christian values central to Polish identity (Góra and Mach 2010, 230–231). The position of this group was strengthened by Pope John Paul II, who stressed on various occasions that Poles should reinforce the conservative, Christian Democratic stream in European politics and ultimately allow Europe to 'breathe with two lungs': the Western and the Eastern (Delong 2011, 47). His unequivocal support for European integration was also expressed in his speech to the Polish Parliament on 11 June 1999.[2]

Third, there was also a faction opposing European integration, occupying a marginal position in the political debate of the 1990s, but gaining substantial support closer to the enlargement (Góra and Mach 2010, 230–231). These ultra-conservative parties and groups perceived EU membership as an act of betrayal leading to yet another instance of dominance and surrender of sovereignty, freedom and the fundamental Christian values on which Polish national identity was built. They perceived secularised western societies as a source of decay and a threat to Polish religiosity.

The salience of religion in the debate on European integration became particularly visible during the work of the European Convention on the Draft Treaty establishing a Constitution for Europe (TCE) (Foret and Itçaina 2011). The shape of the preamble to the TCE and the inclusion or exclusion of references to Christianity were a contentious matter that came to divide European publics. In Poland, most of the elite circles unequivocally supported the inclusion of references to God and Christian traditions as reflecting the Christian foundations of the European identity and polity.

The role of religion in the EU and axiological aspects of integration were thus an important issue for Polish society and elites. These areas of interest remained visible in the contributions of Polish MEPs to the debates in the sixth and seventh terms of the EP.

The newcomers in the European Parliament

Poland's first representation to the EP, elected in 2004, was characterised by a much more right-wing and conservative political orientation than for its western counterparts, reflecting an increasing domination of centre-right and right-wing parties on the country's political scene since the 2000s and a stabilisation of its party system (Gwiazda 2009). In addition to the domestic dynamics, it is likely that the composition of MEPs resulted from the low turnout in the elections in the new acceding countries. In Poland the turnout was 20.87% – the second-lowest in the entire EU. The low turnout led to the victory of parties that had a much more mobilised and disciplined electorate, and hence the right-wing and populist parties gained significant support. Moreover, the elections were organised a year after the referendum on EU membership, which probably also had an impact on voters' behaviour, being a counter-reaction to the massive campaigns and also to the social mobilisation before the referendum.

The first Polish delegation to the EP thus turned out to be composed mostly of representatives of parties which defined themselves as conservative and aligned with the Christian Democratic tradition and which strongly emphasised the axiological dimension (and in some instances religion) in their political programmes (36 MEPs out of 54 in the sixth EP). This is further confirmed by scholars assessing the impact of the enlargement on the functioning of the EP. They have claimed that the results of the 2004 elections strengthened the conservative voice in the EP and allowed it to express its view on many issues in the supranational arena (see for example De Clerck-Sachsse and Kaczyński 2009). In both the sixth and the seventh EPs the majority of MEPs from Poland joined centre-right and right-wing party groups in the EP (see Table 1). It is also important to note that the ongoing process of consolidation of the parties at national level was reflected in the activities of MEPs. LPR, PSL and SRP MEPs frequently changed their party affiliation and consequently their party groups in the EP. This process, clearly visible in the sixth term, was to some extent continued in the seventh EP, with some further defections from PiS (see Table 1).

Methodology and data collection

In approaching the topic of religion in the EP, we applied two separate but connected research strategies.

First, we used the data results from the RelEP survey among the Polish representation to the EP.[3] The survey was completed by 30% of the Polish representation (15 out of 51), a sample in which MEPs from PO were overrepresented (66% of the sample, 10 MEPs). Additionally, we received answers from three MEPs representing PiS and one each from the PSL and SLD.[4] Men were also overrepresented in the sample: 73% of the sample (11 out of the 15). The minority female MEPs all belonged to PO. This disproportion, however, reflects the structure of the whole Polish representation in the EP, in which women comprise only 21% (11 out of 51 MEPs). Two MEPs refused to answer the questionnaire, claiming that religion is a private matter and there is no place for it in the EP. This indicates a potential limitation of our research: possibly only those who consider

Table 1. Party affiliation of Polish MEPs and results of EP elections 2004 and 2009.

Party	Score (%)		No. of seats		Affiliation[5]	
	2004	2009	2004	2009	2004	2009
PO	24	44.43	15	25	European People's Party–European Democrats Group (EPP–ED)	Group of the European People's Party (Christian Democrats) (EPP)
LPR (Libertas 09)	16	1.14	10	0	Independence/ Democracy Group (IND/DEM)	–
PiS	13	27.4	7	15	Union for Europe of Nations Group (UEN)	European Conservatives and Reformists Group (ECR)/Europe of Freedom and Democracy Group (EFD)[6]
SRP	11	1.46	6	0	Union for Europe of Nations Group (UEN)	–
Democratic Left Alliance – Labour Union (Sojusz Lewicy Demokratycznej – Unia Pracy – SLD-UP)	10	12.34	5	7	Party of European Socialists (PES)	Group of the Progressive Alliance of Socialists and Democrats (S&D)
PSL	6.5	7.01	4	3	EPP–ED	EPP
Freedom Union (Unia Wolności – UW)	7.4	2.44	4	0	Alliance of Liberals and Democrats for Europe Party (ALDE)	–
Polish Social Democracy (Socjaldemokracja Polska – SdPL)	5.3		3	0	PES	–

Source: EP official website http://www.europarl.europe.eu

religion to be a significant feature of politics decided to take part in the survey. This could also explain the overrepresentation of members of right-wing parties in our sample.

Second, we analysed the contributions of Polish MEPs to the plenary debates in the EP during the whole of the sixth term and the first half of the seventh term (until the end of 2011). This qualitative content analysis allowed us to map the functions and use of religion by the Polish MEPs. The aim of these data was to overcome limitations related to the rather small size of our sample and its uneven representation of the political spectrum.

The religious orientations of Polish MEPs

Our data allow us to analyse the religious preferences of the MEPs. Not surprisingly, the sample is dominated by Catholics (only one of the MEPs is a Protestant, and one did not answer the question). It also seems that the group is quite religious: most of them declare a belief in a personal God (73.3% (11)) and only one says that he/she is an atheist (two others did not respond to this question). Most of them are also quite regular churchgoers: 40% (6) say that they attend church every week and 26.6% (4) once a month. The religious profile of the MEPs reflects well the religiosity patterns of the Polish population as briefly introduced in the first part of this paper.

Religion in the European Parliament in the view of the Polish MEPs

Perceptions of the impact or religion on the work of the EP and of MEPs

The first part of the RelEP survey attempted to assess the perceptions of the impact of religion on the work of the EP. Most of the Polish MEPs who took part in the survey see religion as an important element in the functioning of the EP (66.6% of the sample (10 MEPs)); 9 of these see it as a salient identity marker for political groups. The rest of the sample either reject the proposition that religion is important for the identity of each political group (26.6% (4)) or see it as blurring the identity of political groups (13.33% (2)). MEPs from PO, the party that dominated the sample, see religion as important for the identity of political groups. It is worth noting that they belong to the EPP–ED group, which defines itself in Christian Democratic terms.

Almost all the MEPs (86.6% (13)) agree that religion has a different significance depending on the nationality of a politician. However, at the same time, the same number, and also almost the same respondents, do not consider religion as creating dividing lines between MEPs representing different religions in the EP.

Most of the respondents say that they frequently take religion into consideration in their work in the EP (53.3% (8)); 40% (6) say that they rarely do so; and only one says that he/she permanently does so. Religion is usually used as a source of personal inspiration and as a social and political reality: 66.6% (10) chose both these answers, of whom 13.3% (2) also say that religion influences their work through lobbying groups.

Nonetheless, the Polish MEPs rarely come into contact with the religious lobbying institutions operating at the Brussels level. Although 53% of MEPs from our sample (8) have had an encounter with a religious lobbying group, these have happened very sporadically. Only two MEPs say that they have more regular contacts with lobbying organisations, once or more per month or once or more per year. In the light of the denominational composition of our sample, it is not surprising that the Commission of the [Catholic] Bishops' Conferences of the European Community (COMECE) and Caritas are the most frequently cited organisations. Interesting enough, those two MEPs who said that they had more frequent contacts with such organisations had also had contacts with Jewish organisations (see Table 2). These data suggest that despite declarations on the influence of religion in the work of most of the MEPs from the sample, it does not take the form of closer cooperation with the religious organisations representing various religions in Brussels, but seems rather to be an outcome of personal religious involvement.

The majority of the MEPs who took part in the survey (66.6% (10) see a difference between the roles religion plays in politics at the national and the European levels. On the basis of the discourse on Poland's accession to the EU at the domestic level, we could assume that the European level is perceived by Polish politicians as more secular or religiously indifferent than the national level. According to the collected responses, most of the MEPs (66.6% (10)) stress that their experience in the EP has had no impact on their previous views regarding the relationship between religion and politics.

Table 2. Polish MEPs' contacts with religious lobbying organisations.

Name of organisation	Number of MEPs having contact with this organisation
BNAIBRITH – B'nai B'rith International	1
Caritas	5
CDA Christian Democratic Appeal	1
CEC KEK – Conférence des Eglises Européennes	1
CEJI – Centre Européen Juif d'Information	1
COMECE – Commission of the Bishops' Conferences of the European Community	7
EU CORD	1
EURODIACONIA – European Federation of Diaconia	2
EUROJEWCONG – European Jewish Congress	2
LIGHT FOR THE WORLD	1
SKM – Slovenska Katolicka Misia	1
WYA – World Youth Alliance	2
YAHAD IN UNUM	1
Others – Conference of European Rabbis	1

Most of our respondents (66.6% (10)) reject the proposition that there is a need for a real/direct policy on the part of the EU towards religious organisations. Again, this could be understood as an expression of the different understanding of the location of religion in the national and supranational contexts. Traditionally, religion is regulated at the national level. This is expressed in a variety of traditions of church–state relations and distinctive forms of religious governance resulting from differences in the religious composition, tradition and history of each country. The EU, in contrast, often viewed by the Polish politicians as a regulatory power focused mostly on market issues, is perceived as a secular institutional order.

However, all participants in the survey agreed that meetings with the representatives of various religions organised by the president of the EP are a positive initiative. On the one hand, acceptance of this practice could be understood as proof of acknowledgment of the privileged position of religious organisations in the European polity and as implementing Article 17 of the Lisbon Treaty by the EP. On the other hand, such unequivocal support for the practice may stem from the national experience. Contacts between religious authorities and politicians happen frequently in the Polish context. Catholic bishops often attempt to influence the decisions of politicians by means such as issuing communiqués or addressing letters to them. Contact between politicians and religious authorities in Poland is also institutionalised in the form of the Joint Commission of Representatives of the Government and of the Conference of the Polish Episcopate (*Komisja Wspólna Przedstawicieli Rządu i Konferencji Episkopatu Polski*). Similar commissions between the government and some of the minority churches also function in Poland, but their activities are much less visible.

Nonetheless, almost all the MEPs (with one exception) who took part in the research agree that the Lisbon Treaty should have made reference to religion. This suggests that in their view European identity is strongly linked with Christianity. This is a continuation of the positions in the debate in Poland on inclusion of religion in the preamble to the TCE, as mentioned earlier. This standpoint is also confirmed in the analysis of the plenary debates. On various occasions the Polish MEPs have stressed the Christian heritage of the

EU, often demanding that this legacy should find explicit expression in EU political documents and decisions. These arguments resemble the claims made by the right-wing parties at the level of the national Polish Parliament. The linking of Polish history and Christian tradition as well as the predominantly Catholic composition of the society serve as justifications for including its legacy and values in the process of lawmaking.

Religion and particular policy fields

The survey also aimed to answer the general question of the perception of the role of religion at the supranational European level. Asked to identify the policy fields in which religion is most important, the Polish MEPs who took part in the research indicate freedom of expression, the fight against discrimination and social policy (see Table 3). Culture and education are also chosen as important, but to a much lesser degree. These data suggest the traditional location of religion in 'social issues', closer to the private sphere. However, they can also be interpreted in the light of José Casanova's deprivatisation thesis: religion can intervene in the public sphere to protect modern freedoms and rights (Casanova 1994). The perception of the role of religion in education offers an interesting contrast to the national level. As various debates in the Polish Parliament indicate, the importance of shaping education according to religious (Catholic) values and norms is highly stressed by the rightist and centre-right parties.

Interestingly enough, external relations are rarely seen as the most important field for the presence of religion. Some 60% (9) of the MEPs in our sample say that religion is not important in external relations. However, some contradictions to this view can be seen in the almost unanimous agreement in our sample that religion plays an important role in the perception of Turkey's membership (93.3% (14)). Similarly, in the analysis of the plenary debates we find that the Polish MEPs often express the view that the EU should make its external relations conditional on respect for religious freedom. Most often, such statements are made in the context of the Muslim countries where the rights of Christian minorities are violated.

How far should religion influence politics?

Questions regarding the place of religion in society provide an interesting perspective. The MEPs who took part in the survey seem not to support the intervention of religious leaders, either in the political decisions of individuals or in government decision-making.

Table 3. Which are the issues in which religion is most important in the European Parliament? (Rank the three first responses in order of importance) (frequency and percentage).

	1 (most important)	2	3
Social policy	3/20%	4/26.6%	3/20%
External relations	1/6.6%	1/6.6%	2/13.3%
Freedom of expression	7/46.6%	4/26.6%	
Fight against discrimination	4/26.6%	4/26.6%	2/13.3%
Economic policy		1/6.6%	
Culture and education			5/33.3%
No answer		1/6.6%	

Table 4. Attitudes towards the relationship between religion and politics (frequency and percentage; the data for the entire population are presented in the lower line*).

	Agree strongly	Agree	Neither agree nor disagree	Disagree	Disagree strongly	No answer
Politicians who do not believe in God are unfit for public office	– 3%	2/13.3% 12.8%	– 28.0%	2/13.3% 39.0%	10/66.6% 16.7%	2/13.3% –
Religious leaders should not influence how people vote in elections	7/46.6% 38.2%	3/20% 38.8%	1/6.6% 15.8%	2/13.3% 5.5%	1/6.6% 1.7%	1/6.6% –
It would be better for Poland if more people with strong religious beliefs held public office	– 6.2%	– 19.7%	11/73.3% 42.1%	2/13.3% 21.6%	1/6.6% 10.4%	1/6.6% –
Religious leaders should not influence government decisions	6/6.6% 29.0%	1/6.6% 41.0%	2/13.3% 19.5%	3/20% 39.0%	– 1.4%	3/20% –
If a doctor were asked to help perform a legal abortion, s/he should be allowed to refuse on religious grounds**	8/53.3%	3/20%	1/6.6%	1/6.6%	–	1/6.6%

Notes: *Data for entire population indicate percentage of valid cases.
**This question was not asked in EVS 2008.
Sources: RelEP and EVS 2008.

Similarly, the majority do not see belief in God as a necessary condition for holding public office. At the same time, most of them neither agree nor disagree with the question regarding the potential impact of more religious people holding public office in Europe. In the case of the right to conscientious objection based on religion with respect to legal abortion, the majority of respondents (73.3% (11)) agree or strongly agree with a law to this effect. These answers suggest that the MEPs accept a division between the religious and political spheres, seeing religious identity as irrelevant in the public sphere. At the same time, most of them accept the relevance of religious identity in other contexts (for example the professional context). A comparison between the results on the place of religion in society provided by our research with the results provided by the last wave of the European Values Study (EVS) of 2008 in Poland shows similar trends in various opinions (see Table 4).

The Polish perspective on religion and Europe in the EP debates

The following analysis is based on the contributions by Polish MEPs in the plenary debates of the sixth and seventh EPs in which references to religion occur. Our analysis confirms the findings from previous studies that the axiological aspects of European integration are important for Polish MEPs (Gierycz 2010). However, it also needs to be stressed that religion arises relatively infrequently as a topic in the plenary debates (Szczepanik 2013). The analysis also allows us to identify contrasting images of the nexus between religion and Europe, which we discuss in detail in the following subsections. Many Polish MEPs, like leading participants in the national pre-accession debate, continue to identify Europe with Christian values and tradition. This is revealed particularly strongly in the context of both internal and external significant Others, such as Muslim immigrants in Europe and Turkey respectively.

Defining and defending Christian Europe

A need to protect Christian values is expressed frequently in debates about the future institutional shape of the EU after the rejection of the TCE. In particular, discussions about the Reform Treaty (Lisbon Treaty (LT)) and the role of the Charter of Fundamental Rights (CFR) have triggered justifications connected to religious beliefs, especially by politicians from the parties which previously strongly opposed the CFR. Reference to God, or at least to the Christian roots of the EU project, has been strongly demanded by some Polish MEPs in the context of preparation of the LT.

Christianity is also used as an identity marker drawing a clear line between Europeans and the Other, and serves the purpose of defining what Europe is and who belongs to it. Some of the contributions by MEPs suggest that Christianity, perceived as a foundation of European identity, the source of common values and principles and European solidarity, could serve as a basis for a definition of Europe. Islam, by contrast, is often referred to as threatening, alien to European values and destructive for European civilisation based on Christian values. This has been specifically evident in the debates on further EU enlargement and the European Neighbourhood Policy (ENP), but also occasionally in discussions on social issues in the European context. Orientalistic discourse can be identified in those discussions stressing Islam as both internal Others (immigrants, though in many instances in fact European citizens) and external Others (Turkey). On the one hand, some MEPs perceive the Muslim population of Europe as not fitting the European model, destroying its values and culture. Some of them have called for change in the immigration policy of the EU and demanded that the influx of immigrants be halted, specifically referring to Muslims who are perceived as a threat to a Europe based on Christian values. On the other hand, in the discussions on Turkish membership many Polish MEPs have frequently used religion to stress the 'Otherness' of Turkey vis-à-vis Europe. In this respect, Turkey has been seen as a Muslim country, and as such posing an existential threat to an EU based on Christian values. At best, Turkey has been presented as different, and those putting this view forward have demanded the development of a new set of tools for Turkey to become involved with the EU, but not necessarily as a member. Our findings coincide with those of another analysis of the debates on Turkish membership (Müftüler-Bac 2011).

The visions of European identity constructed *vis-à-vis* Islam as presented by some of the Polish MEPs fit with recent transformations in the narratives on European identity expressed by various politicians at the European level (Casanova 2004). However, the stance of the Polish MEPs in this context is particularly interesting, as the function of the significant Other for construction of the European identity project has only recently shifted towards Turkey and Islam in Europe. Before 1989, the division between the European 'Us' and 'Others' related to the communist hammer and sickle rather than to Islam's star and crescent (Challand 2009, 68; Stråth 2002). By eagerly othering Turkey and Islam, the newcomers exhibit the zealotry of their pursuit to reclaim their identity and reconfirm their belonging to the imagined community in question, and religion plays an important and useful part here. Nonetheless, it is also important to note that Islam is an imagined Other for Polish MEPs, and that the Polish encounters with Islam occur mostly at the supranational level, as there is no significant Muslim minority in Poland. However, the threat of Islam has been an integral part of the Polish national identity constructed as the 'antemurale' of Christianity against – among others – the Ottoman threat (Tazbir 2004).

Christianity as a foundation for European identity and a condition for belonging to European civilisation and therefore to the EU has also been invoked by Polish MEPs in debates about EU involvement in and future membership prospects for the Western Balkan and Eastern European countries. In this context, religion has been used as a justification for Poland's geopolitical strategies as regards its eastern neighbourhood. Countries dominated by the Christian faith – regardless of the denomination of Christianity – seem to be treated as fitting the EU. They are presented as truly European, belonging to civilisation, sharing its fate and history.

The religious arguments as discussed above have often been used to demarcate the territorial boundaries of Europe, which for these political actors overlap with Christianity. Yet religious arguments can also refer to non-territorial identification of religious community transcending the territorial boundaries. Demands for stronger solidarity with persecuted Christians around the world are a good example of such a construction. Particular attention has been paid by MEPs to the persecution of Christian communities in Muslim countries, particularly Pakistan and Iraq, and recently also during the turbulent events of the Arab Spring in Tunisia and Egypt.

Challenging European secularism?

Some Polish MEPs continue to see Europe as dominated by secular tradition and the enforcement of secularising policies. They perceive the EU as endangering the survival of Christian values in Europe, and therefore as a threat to Polish values based on Christianity. The contributions of these MEPs at the plenary sessions have stressed the Christian heritage and foundations of European civilisation and the European project, and some of them have also continued to express their fear of the secularism of the EU. Such perceptions seem to be activated in the context of conflicts over the acceptance of religious identity in the public sphere and of the Polish identity as rooted in Catholic tradition.

Further in this vein, some of the MEPs have expressed the opinion that Christians in Europe are in the minority, not accorded respect and denied rights and recognition. One of the first and most prominent debates revealing this kind of argumentation was connected with the appointment of the European Commission and controversy over the Italian candidate for commissioner, Rocco Buttiglione. The rejection of Buttiglione's candidacy was perceived by some Polish MEPs as discrimination against the Catholic world view and beliefs and as an attack on Christian values in general.

Similarly, the criticism expressed towards the Polish government, especially regarding homophobia and racism,[7] has been perceived as based on denied recognition of the Catholic values on which the country is built. This goes hand in hand with the accusation that European politics and elites are secular and prejudiced towards faith per se. Some of the Polish MEPs have stressed the need to protect the Christian identity of Europe and Poland *vis-à-vis* secularist notions lacking sensitivity and respect for religious freedom. In other words, they demand that religious (Christian) identities be fully recognised in the secularist context of the EU. Clearly, religion is used here as a cultural operating system through which groups may express their particularities. Such a demand for recognition also often runs parallel with the strategy of victimisation by the alleged opponents. There is a sense of exclusion of Christians, who feel discriminated against and marginalised. Interestingly, in order to receive the required recognition of their conservative religious position they recall fundamental European values such as tolerance, recognition of minority rights and ultimately protection of diversity of world views. Although this may be a strategic move, it seems to lead to structural outcomes of accepting a certain common set of European values.

Perception of the EU as a secular hegemony can also be recognised in the contributions by Polish MEPs to the discussions on gender equality and lesbian, gay, bisexual and transgender (LGBT) rights.

Gender equality and the underlying notion of the rights of women as individuals are among the fundamental values of the EU. This view often clashes with the definition of a woman as a 'womb of the nation' responsible for the preservation of the community, which is predominant at the Polish national level and has been represented by some of the Polish MEPs. In their contributions to the discussions, they have presented gender roles as natural and polarised, viewing women as protectors of the community and family. Their argument has been that gender equality policies should therefore respond to the needs stemming from these different roles and sustain the 'natural' difference between men and women by making it easier to realise the fulfilment of their 'natural' callings. Christianity is often used as a legitimisation of these traditional visions of gender roles. Some MEPs have even demanded that Poland, with its distinctive vision of the role of women, should be exempt from the imposed and foreign European principles of gender equality. Furthermore, they have attempted to upload their vision of gender relations at the European level as a basis for gender equality policies.

Claims for recognition of cultural difference and of moralities based on religious outlooks have also been used by some of the MEPs in debates on the rights of LGBT people in the EU. The debates on the resolution condemning homophobia in Poland illustrate this point well. The criticism expressed towards the Polish government was perceived by some of the MEPs as based on a denial of recognition of the Catholic values on which the country is built. The demand for respect for difference and the particularity of other cultures and societies based on different morality was thus again justified by European values – tolerance, democracy and respect for diversity.

Similarly, the promotion of European understanding of gender equality and LGBT rights outside the EU is perceived as a sign of its cultural hegemony and an attempt to impose its cultural secular values on other countries. Some Polish MEPs have claimed that the European secular standpoint on gender equality or LGBT rights should not be imposed on other societies, as this means forcing solutions that are alien to their (religious) traditions and culture.

At the same time, we can also find a few voices among the Polish MEPs evaluating European secularism positively. From this perspective the EU is viewed as a useful resource or a model for increasing religious tolerance, a clearer separation of church and state and enhancement of women's reproductive rights and LGBT rights in the Polish national context.

Conclusions

Our aim in this study has been to provide a survey of answers to the questions of the role of religion in the EP as presented by Polish MEPs.

The data collected from the RelEP survey suggest that for most of these MEPs religious identity plays an important role in both their private life (attachment to religious practices and tenets) and their work. They recognise the role of religion in the EP, but also see the difference between the EU and national levels. The comparison of data from the survey with some data on the wider Polish population shows similarities regarding religious involvement. Yet the results also suggest that they share the core concepts as to the relations between state and religion with other European politicians and accept the limited presence of religion in the public sphere.

The analysis of the contributions by Polish MEPs to the plenary debates confirms that the use of religion is to some extent instrumental. Furthermore, the way religion is activated and used in the EP shows close connections to the national context and domestic constituency. It seems that religion is an important identity marker for many of the MEPs. It helps to define who they are as Europeans and where Europe ends. This reveals a strong connection between the ways Poles define their national identity through religion and how they project a similar nexus on Europe. Being Polish for many almost automatically invokes religious denomination, and they use similar mechanisms for defining Europe. They therefore reproduce well-known mechanisms of identity construction at the European level. The EU is in their perception associated with Christian identity and traditions which are expected to be preserved, protected and promoted. A feeling of cultural superiority may also be extracted from the contributions drawing on such a vision, especially in the context of Islam. Furthermore, the Polish MEPs perceive the EU as a 'secular club'. When the EU is associated with secularism, it is accused of cultural imperialism lacking respect for diversity, tolerance or freedom of religion.

Locating our findings within the existing scholarship allows for some comparison. On the one hand, it seems that the frequent use of religion by the MEPs in the EP confirms the observation that the new member-states are putting religion back on the agenda. As Katzenstein (2006, 2) stresses, the enlargement infused 'renewed religious vitality into Europe's political and social life, thus chipping away at its exceptional secularism'. On the other hand, it seems to fit the broader tendencies. Juxtaposing the Polish MEPs with MEPs from other predominantly Catholic countries researched within the RelEP project indicates some resemblances in terms of perception of Islam as the significant (threatening) Other (the Austrian case) and in defining Europe through Christian tradition by right-wing MEPs (the Spanish case). Secondly, comparing the findings from the EP with the data on national political elites also shows some similarities. Research on the national Parliaments in various European countries suggests that Catholic politicians consider the EU as a potential challenge to their religious values rather than an institutional framework representing the 'Christian occident' (Best 2012, 226).

Notes

1. This study is based on a combination of data collected within two projects: Religion at the European Parliament (RelEP) and RECON Reconstituting Democracy in Europe (FP6-028698), the EC's Sixth Framework Programme for Research.
2. The full version of the speech is available at http://orka2.sejm.gov.pl/Debata3.nsf/9a905bcb5531f478c125745f0037938e/9ef3f7bc739bfe88c125749d0048a5e8?OpenDocument
3. The survey was conducted between June 2010 and May 2012.
4. Party affiliations as of the time when the survey was taken.
5. These are affiliations as declared immediately after the elections. In the course of the term in office numerous MEPs changed affiliation to both party and party group.
6. There were defections from PiS to the newly formed parties Poland Comes First (*Polska Jest Najważniejsza*) (PJN) (three MEPs) in 2010 and United Poland (*Solidarna Polska*) (SP) (four MEPs) in 2011. the PJN remained in the ECR, while the SP joined the EFD.
7. Debates on 'Increase in racist and homophobic violence in Europe' 14 June 2006 (http://www.europarl.europa.eu/sides/getDoc.do?type=CRE&reference=20060614&secondRef=ITEM-009&language=EN&ring=P6-RC-2006-0330) and on 'Homophobia in Europe', 25 April 2007 (http://www.europarl.europa.eu/sides/getDoc.do?type=CRE&reference=20070425&secondRef=ITEM-017&language=EN&ring=P6-RC-2007-0167).

References

Bale, T., and A. Szczerbiak. 2008. "Why Is There No Christian Democracy in Poland – And Why Should We Care?" *Party Politics* 14 (4): 479–500. doi:10.1177/1354068808090256.

Best, H. 2012. "Elite Foundations of European Integration: A Causal Analysis." In *The Europe of Elites: A Study into the Europeanness of Europe's Political and Economic Elites*, edited by H. Best, G. Lengyel, and L. Verzichelli, 208–233. Oxford: Oxford University Press.

Boguszewski, R. 2009. *Moralność Polaków po dwudziestu latach przemian* [The Morality of Poles after Twenty Years of Transformation]. Warsaw: CBOS.

Borowik, I. 2002. "The Roman Catholic Church in the Process of Democratic Transformation: The Case of Poland." *Social Compass* 49 (2): 239–252. doi:10.1177/0037768602049002008.

Casanova, J. 1994. *Public Religions in the Modern World*. Chicago: University of Chicago Press.

Casanova, J. 2004. "Religion, European Secular Identities, and European Integration." *Eurozine*. http://www.eurozine.com/articles/2004-07-29-casanova-en.html.

Challand, B. 2009. "From Hammer and Sickle to Star and Crescent: The Question of Religion for European Identity and a Political Europe." In *Religion, Politics and Law in the European Union*, edited by L. Leustean and J. T. S. Madeley, 59–74. London: Routledge.

De Clerck-Sachsse, J., and P. M. Kaczyński. 2009. *The European Parliament – More Powerful, Less Legitimate? An Outlook for the 7th Term* (*CEPS Working Document* 314/May). http://www.ceps.eu/files/book/1846.pdf.

Delong, M. 2011. "The Approach of Pope John Paul II to European Integration." *Politics and Society* 8: 845–852.

Eberts, M. W. 1998. "The Roman Catholic Church and Democracy in Poland." *Europe-Asia Studies* 50 (5): 817–842. doi:10.1080/09668139808412567.

EVS. 2008. *European Values Study 2008: Integrated Dataset (EVS 2008)*. GESIS Data Archive, Cologne (ZA4800 Data file Version 3.0.0.) http://info1.gesis.org/dbksearch/sdesc2.asp?no=4800&db=e&doi=10.4232/1.11004.

Foret, F., and X. Itçaina. 2011. "Introduction: Western European Modernities and Religion." In *Politics of Religion in Western Europe: Modernities in Conflict?*, edited by F. Foret and X. Itçaina, 3–22. London: Routledge.

Gierycz, M. 2010. *Rola polskich posłów do Parlamentu Europejskiego VI kadencji w kształtowaniu jego polityki w obszarze aksjologii praw człowieka* [The Role of the Polish MEPs in the 6th Term of the European Parliament in Shaping Policies in the Field of Axiology of Human Rights]. http://www.pe2004-2009.europeistyka.uw.edu.pl/dzialy/wyniki-badan/.

Góra, M., and Z. Mach. 2010. "Between Old Fears and New Challenges: The Polish Debate on Europe." In *European Stories*, edited by J. Lacroix and K. Nicolaïdis, 221–240. Oxford: Oxford University Press.

Gwiazda, A. 2009. "Poland's Quasi-Institutionalized Party System: The Importance of Elites and Institutions." *Perspectives on European Politics and Society* 10 (3): 350–376. doi:10.1080/15705850903105769.

Hanley, S., A. Szczerbiak, T. Haughton, and B. Fowler. 2008. "Sticking Together: Explaining Comparative Centre-Right Party Success in Post-Communist Central and Eastern Europe." *Party Politics* 14 (4): 407–434. doi:10.1177/1354068808090253.

Katzenstein, P. J. 2006. "Multiple Modernities as Limits to Secular Europeanization?" In *Religion in an Expanding Europe*, edited by T. A. Byrnes and P. J. Katzenstein, 1–33. Cambridge: Cambridge University Press.

Korbonski, A. 2000. "Poland Ten Years After: The Church." *Communist and Post-Communist Studies* 33 (1): 123–146. doi:10.1016/S0967-067X(99)00028-8.

Müftüler-Bac, M. 2011. *The European Union and Turkey: Democracy, Multiculturalism and European Identity* (*RECON Online Working Paper* 2011/20). http://www.reconproject.eu/main. php/_publicationPreview?publicweb=1&publid=1240.

Robbers, G. 2012. "Challenges in the Constitution Making Process: Problems of Participation and Protecting Diversity in the Interplay Between Rule of Law and Democracy." *Hacettepe Hukuk Fakültesi Dergis (Hacettepe Law Review)* 2 (2): 178–180. www.hukukdergi.hacettepe.edu.tr/ dergi/C2S2hakemsiz2.pdf.

Stepan, A. 2010. "The Multiple Secularisms of Modern Democratic and Non-Democratic Regimes." Paper presented at the annual meeting of the American Political Science Association. http:// papers.ssrn.com/sol3/papers.cfm?abstract_id=1643701.

Stråth, B. 2002. "A European Identity." *European Journal of Social Theory* 5 (4): 387–401.

Szczepanik, M. 2013. *Polacy w Parlamencie Europejskim: podsumowanie pierwszej połowy 7 kadencji* [Poles in the European Parliament: Summary of the First Half of the 7th Term]. Warsaw: The Institute of Public Affairs. http://www.isp.org.pl/uploads/filemanager/ PolacywPEPodsumowaniepoowykadencji-komunikatprasowyISP.pdf

Tazbir, J. 2004. *Polska Przedmurzem Europy* [Poland as the Bulwark of Europe]. Warsaw: Twój Styl.

Wenzel, M. 1998. "Solidarity and Akcja Wyborcza 'Solidarnosc': An Attempt at Reviving the Legend." *Communist and Post-Communist Studies* 31 (2): 139–156. doi:10.1016/S0967-067X (98)00007-5.

Zubrzycki, G. 2006. *The Crosses of Auschwitz: Nationalism and Religion in Post-Communist Poland*. Chicago: University of Chicago Press.

Religion at the European Parliament: the Italian case

Stefano Braghiroli[a] and Giulia Sandri[b]

[a]Institute of Government and Politics, University of Tartu, Estonia;
[b]European School of Social and Political Sciences, Université Catholique de Lille, France

Italy is a predominantly Catholic country that developed historically on the basis of a strong, dominant religion and weak state institutions. Yet, openly clerical parties, direct advocates of the interests of the Catholic Church, have nowadays virtually disappeared and the relevance of the religious cleavage is decreasing, in favour of a more indirect support for these interests, mainly among moderate and conservative forces. Although the overall level of secularisation in Italy has increased, the degree of religiosity of Italian society remains one of the highest of the 27 member-states of the European Union (EU) and polarisation over religious issues in domestic politics remains high, particularly regarding moral values and family matters. In our study we explore the role of religion within the Italian political sphere with regard to the functioning of political representation, by taking into account the sub-national, national and European levels of government. We focus on the attitudes and behaviours of Italian political elites at the EU level. We hypothesise a strong influence of religion on the articulation between national and European politics. Our findings consistently show that the degree of religiosity of the Italian delegation to the European Parliament (EP) is high. However, the impact of such a high degree of religiosity among the members of the EP (MEPs) on their political activities appears less direct than one might predict, while the degree of political secularism is higher among Italian MEPs than among their national or regional counterparts. When we discuss a case study, namely the accession of Turkey to the EU, our data show that the religious attitudes of Italian MEPs play a crucial role in their stance on Turkish accession. The picture that emerges is thus nuanced. Religion significantly impacts on Italian MEPs' ideological, political and moral attitudes, but plays a smaller role in their activities; while their left-right collocation emerges as the most relevant predictor, despite a number of exceptions.

Religion and multi-level politics: the Italian case

According to international surveys such as the European Values Study, more than four fifths of Italian citizens declare themselves to be Catholic although fewer than one fifth regularly attend religious services (mass) (Giordan and Swatos 2011; see also, for example, US 2009; Eurispes 2009, 1104–1113, 2010). Nevertheless, it is difficult to estimate the degree of religiosity and the denominational convictions of Italian citizens on the basis of contextually grounded data because the national census does not include questions on religious affiliation but only on practices. Even so, Italy is a predominantly Catholic country that developed historically on the basis of a strong, dominant religion and weak state institutions (Jemolo [1948] 1961; Ferrari 2011). While the Catholic Church and more specifically the Italian Conference of Bishops still play an important role in Italian politics and seem to exert a relevant influence over the public sphere, the role and size of religious political parties (Christian Democrats) has significantly weakened from the First (1948–1993) to the Second Republic (1994–2013) because of fewer religious voters (Biorcio, Giorgi, and Grasso 2008). The Catholic Church is intertwined with Italian history and nowadays the relationship between religion and politics in Italy appears complex, sometimes incoherent and rapidly evolving. The question of the role of religion within the political sphere in Italy raises important issues with regard to the functioning of political representation, especially when all the different levels of government in Europe – subnational, national and European – are taken into account.

Since the unification of the Italian nation-state, Italian institutions have been strongly affected by Catholicism (Jemolo [1948] 1961; Ignazi 2008). In the postwar period the Catholic religion has remained a crucial feature of Italian national identity and social structure. Even today Catholicism maintains its form of civic religion within Italian society (Bellah 1980; Segatti and Brunelli 2010). In terms of church–state model, the historical elements strongly affected the relationship between religion and the Italian state (Jemolo [1948] 1961; Garelli 2007). The constitution of 1948, on the one hand, quotes the Lateran Treaties, which were signed by the state with the Catholic Church during the fascist era (1929) in order to pacify the growing opposition of the Church to the formation of the Italian nation-state since 1870. On the other hand, in its article 7, the constitution asserts the separation between state and church and refers specifically to the Catholic religion. The relations between the state and the Catholic Church are nowadays regulated by the Agreement of Villa Madama, which updated the Lateran Treaties in 1984.

The overall level of secularisation in Italy has increased during the last decades, but the level of religiosity of Italian society remains one of the highest of the 27 member-states of the European Union (EU) (Inglehart and Norris 2004). The frequency of religious practice shows a general pattern of slightly decreasing religious participation. However, religion as a value and as an element of cultural and political identity remains crucial in contemporary Italian society (Garelli, Guizzardi, and Pace 2003; Giorgi 2013). With regard to the level of political secularism, Diamanti and Ceccarini (2007) define the Catholics in Italy as an influential political minority. The denominational belonging is not as strong a determinant of social cohesion and political and voting behaviours as was in the 1950s–1970s, but the overall level of secularisation in Italy remains lower than in other European countries and the Catholic religion is highly politicised. After 1948, the high level of political involvement of Italian Catholics generated a wide network of cultural and political Catholic associations which contributed to encapsulating the citizens into segmented party and social networks, which led to the growing relevance of the religious pillar during the 1950s and the 1960s (Biorcio, Giorgi, and Grasso 2008). The Christian Democracy party (*Democrazia Cristiana*) (DC) that dominated political life during the First Republic (1949–1993) was the privileged partner of the church hierarchy and translated political issues into the political arena.

Given the strength and stability over time (at least before the 1990s) of the party representing denominational interests, the DC, Italy appears to be consistent with the hypothesis that in countries where there are strong parties speaking for religion there will also be weak religious lobbies. Nevertheless, some of the cultural and political Catholic associations that have flourished since the 1950s could be categorised as lobbies because of their widespread political presence and degree of influence on public decision-making (Giorgi 2013). The most relevant one is *Comunione e Liberazione*, which was created as a youth movement linked to the Catholic Church in 1969 and which has nowadays developed into a fully fledged international confessional movement tightly intertwined with local political life in Italy: for instance, the previous governor of the northern region of Lombardy (from 1995 to 2013), Roberto Formigoni, is an high-ranked member of the organisation.

Moreover, the secularisation process affected Italian territory according to a hetero-geneous pattern, generating the emergence of two distinct political subcultures, charac-terised by both territorial concentration and strong religious (or anti-religious) traits. During the First Republic, the extremely limited alternation in office, with the DC always in government, led to the emergence of territorially concentrated subcultures, namely the communist (the non-religious one) in the regions dominated by the Communist Party of Italy (*Partito Comunista Italiano*) (PCI) (the 'red belt': mainly Tuscany, Emilia-Romagna and Umbria) and the Catholic one in the regions dominated by the DC (the 'white belt': mainly Abruzzo, Basilicata and Veneto). The change of the national electoral system in 1993, together with the collapse of the traditional parties, sanctioned the beginning of the Second Republic (Morlino and Tarchi 1996). Similar patterns of partisan identity and voting behaviour are still relevant today concerning either local, national or European elections (Cotta and Verzichelli 2007). Since the collapse of the old DC its electoral base has split among various parties. Every political party but the extreme left, and especially the centre-left Democratic Party (*Partito Democratico*) (PD) and the centre-right The People of Freedom (*Il Popolo della Libertà*) (PdL), try to attract the vote of Catholics. Today, however, the relation between religiosity and voting behaviour in Italy is less clear (Diamanti and Ceccarini 2007; Ballarino et al. 2010).

Thus, the level of conflictuality of religious issues in domestic politics remains quite high nowadays, particularly regarding moral values and family matters. Since the early 2000s, the level of political polarisation between parties, religious associations and civil society groups on issues such as the potential adoption of marriage equality laws or laws regulating *in vitro* fertilisation has grown significantly and the public debate on these issues has become increasingly heated. The level of conflictuality in the debate on euthanasia in 2009, for instance, reached unprecedented levels with the case of Eluana Englaro (Italy and the Right to Die: Death in Udine 2009). This phenomenon could be partially explained by the fact that most Italian parties have significant incentives to invest such issues, which are considered electorally appealing in a time of high electoral mobility and issue voting.

The study of the attitudes and behaviour of Italian political elites is not equally developed, but is indeed relevant for a better understanding of the dynamics of political representation in multi-level settings. In fact, a strong link has recently emerged between religion and Euroscepticism in Italy: the parties positioned on the religious side of the church–state cleavage have moved from being strongly pro-European (DC) in the past to being either weakly (PdL) or strongly (Northern League (*Lega Nord*) (LN)), opposed to European political integration nowadays. Thus, the possible influence of religion on the articulation between national and European politics appears very salient, with the two main centre-left and centre-right parties equally competing to attract the vote of Catholics in both national and European elections. For instance, Italy offers some embattled Catholics elected within both national and European assemblies, as there are numerous Italians among religious activists. But it seems also possible to find Italians among atheists in a mission at both levels. For instance, in the EP, but also in the national Parliament, the battles of the leader of the Radical Party Marco Pannella for euthanasia and gay rights are well known. This could confirm that, when religion is conflictual in domestic politics, it is rewarding to invest the issue at the EP.

Concerning the European level, the literature shows that, in the absence of ideological glue or nationally-oriented pressures, MEPs tend to behave and take their decisions in the light of their perceptional world view at the expense of the collective voting coherence of the EP (Hix 2002). The often chaotic intertwining of the perceptional universe of beliefs, individual preferences, national interest and partisanship of MEPs can be clearly exemplified by a number of 'traumatic events' directly or indirectly related to religion such as the Buttiglione affair.

In October 2004, the Italian candidate commissioner Rocco Buttiglione – a centre-right hardliner Catholic and affiliated to the European People's Party (EPP) – declared during his hearing before the Committee on Civil Liberties, Justice and Home Affairs of the EP that 'the family exists in order to allow women to have children and to have the protection of a male who takes care of them' and reiterated his homophobic views in front of the plenary (EU Panel Opposes Justice Nominee 2004). The Party of European Socialists (PES), the Alliance of Liberals and Democrats for Europe (ALDE) and the Greens/European Free Alliance (Greens/EFA) expressed reservations regarding Buttiglione's ability to take positive political action in the area of citizens' rights, particularly with regard to combating discrimination, and on 11 October the committee voted not to endorse the nomination. Although Italian Catholic politicians and church leaders rallied to defend Buttiglione's views, the Italian government (then led by Silvio Berlusconi), increasingly put under pressure by the president nominate José Manuel Barroso and by the EPP itself, announced on 30 October that it had withdrawn Buttiglione's nomination.

Similar tones were raised when the Polish candidate to the presidency of the EP, Jerzy Buzek, was selected by the plenum of the EPP rather than the Italian candidate, Mario Mauro, well known for his conservative religious views. Many in the EPP believed that the conservative views of Mauro would have eclipsed the votes of the European liberals (and of the Socialists and Democrats (S&D)), necessary to secure the election of a centre-right president. A few days before Mauro's exclusion a prominent member of the European liberals, Sophie in 't Veld, said that Mauro saw his mission as the defence of Christianity, and that while he had the right to his opinion, she would like the EU 'to stand up to discrimination, intolerance and racist and homophobic violence' (EU Elections: Christian Barroso under Fire 2009).

In an environment characterised by multiple and competing loyalties, the role cognition, beliefs and perceptions of MEPs (Bale and Taggart 2006; Pasquinucci and Verzichelli 2004) affect their behaviour, thereby implying direct repercussions in terms of perceived costs and benefits related to their voting choices. In this respect, it is worth considering that the parliamentary behaviour of MEPs generally reflects a varying balance of functional/interest-based and identitarian factors.

The data

The Italian delegation to the EP comprises 72 members (plus one observer) belonging to five of the seven main political groups at the EP level and affiliated to 11 different parties at the national level.

At the time of writing the affiliation of Italian MEPs in the EP was as follows: 33 EPP; 22 S&D; nine Europe of Freedom and Democracy (EFD); five ALDE; two European Conservatives and Reformists (ECR). No Italian MEPs belong to the Greens/EFA or the European United Left (GUE/NGL) and the number of non-attached Italian members has recently risen to two after Mario Borghezio (LN) was expelled from the EFD because of racism and xenophobia allegations. Two vice-presidents of the EP (Gianni Pittella (PD) and Roberta Angelilli (PdL)), and five presidents of EP committees (Regional Development (REGI), Constitutional Affairs (AFCO), Petitions (PETI), Industry,

Table 1.   Italian MEPs and the RelEP survey.

Party	Number of MEPs	Percentage of MEPs	Number of respondents	Percentage of respondents
PdL	20	27.7	7	36.8
PD	20	27.7	7	36.8
UdC	5	6.9	1	5.2
LN	8	11.1	2	10.8
IdV	4	5.5	1	5.2
Indep.	2	2.7	1	5.2
Other	13	18.4	0	0
Total	72	100	19	100

Research and Energy (ITRE), and Organised Crime, Corruption and Money Laundering (CRIM)) are Italians.

In terms of national party affiliation, most of the Italian MEPs come from Berlusconi's party PdL, the main centre-right party (20 MEPs) and the PD, the main centre-left party (also 20 MEPs). The affiliations of the other MEPs are: LN, a right-wing populist and regionalist party, formerly junior partner in several government coalitions with the PdL (eight MEPs); the Union of the Centre (*Unione di Centro*) (UdC), one of the minuscule heirs of the old Christian Democracy (five MEPs); Italy of Values (*Italia dei Valori*) (IdV), a small left-wing populist party (four MEPs); some small rightist parties (Brothers of Italy (*Fratelli d'Italia*), Future and Freedom (*Futuro e Libertà*), The Right (*La Destra*)) (four MEPs). Two MEPs are independents and the rest are members of small, often non-parliamentary parties.

The data discussed in this section are from the RelEP elite survey and also those from an original dataset developed in 2010 by the international research group PartiRep (www.http://partirep.eu/).

The composition of the Italian delegation to the EP and the response rate to the RelEP survey by political party is shown in Table 1. The overall response rate to the survey is relatively low (26.4%). The members of the two main parties – the PdL and the PD – are clearly overrepresented in our sample, but the distribution of MEPs affiliated to the other Italian parties in the sample broadly corresponds to that in the whole Italian delegation at the EP.

The response to the PartiRep elite survey is shown in Table 2. A sample of 150 members of Parliament (MPs) within both upper (Senate) and lower (Chamber of

Table 2.   Italian MPs and the PartiRep survey.

	National MPs	Regional MPs	Total
Government	29	45	74
Opposition	38	38	76
Total	67	83	150
Centre-left	35	44	79
Centre and regionalists	2	13	15
Centre-right	30	26	56
Total	67	83	150

Note: Centre-right: PdL, LN, The Right; Centre-left: PD, small radical left parties; Centre and regionalists: UdC, UDEUR Populars (*Popolari* UDEUR), ethno-regionalist parties from Valle d'Aosta and The Movement for Autonomies (*Movimento per le Autonomie*) (MpA).

Deputies) houses were surveyed and also a sample of MPs from 6 different regional Parliaments (out of a total of 20): Calabria, Campania, Lazio, Lombardia, Toscana and Valle d'Aosta. The response rate was overall quite low (11.5%), but the sample population was generally well distributed geographically and in terms of territorial level of government. Of the 150 interviews, 45 were with members of the Chamber of Deputies (out of a total of 630 MPs), 22 with members of the Senate (out of a total of 315 Senators) and 83 with members of regional Parliaments (out of a total of 364 regional MPs). Respondents divide equally between members of the government and of opposition parties. As in the case of the interviewed Italian MEPs, in terms of party affiliation, MPs from the PdL and PD are quite overrepresented in our sample (102 interviews in total). As noted above, the total sample comprised 150 interviews, but the number of interviews integrated in the Italian dataset dropped to 99 after weighting according to gender, age and territorial distribution. In the next section we shall display the results from the elaborations on the PartiRep dataset after the weighting and thus the total N will drop to 99 regional (57) and national (42) Italian MPs.

Italian MEPs and Religion

In this section, we develop the analysis of data produced by interviews with MEPs following the order of the questionnaire in order to explore both the degree of political secularisation of Italian MEPs and the relationship between religion and politics. Given that the question wording and the choice of variables and indicators of the two different surveys (RelEP and PartiRep) is not exactly the same, a direct comparison between three territorial levels (regional, national and European) of political representation cannot be developed. Nevertheless, the exploration of the attitudes and behaviour of Italian regional and national MPs allows a better understanding of the articulation between the national and European arenas concerning political secularisation.

Personal religious beliefs and practices

In terms of general religious beliefs, preferences and practices, it is worth noting that – unsurprisingly – out of 19 MEPs surveyed only four declare that they do not belong to a religious denomination and only two say they are not 'religious persons' (while more than 26% of the interviewed MEPs, namely five individuals, refused to answer to the latter question or did not know). Among those 12 (63.2%) Italian MEPs who declare themselves to be religious and among those 13 (68.4%) who say they belong to a religious denomination, the majority (10 (52.6%) are Catholics, of course, but one (5.3%) is a Protestant and two (10.5%) belong to other Christian churches. These results are not surprising given the distribution of the general Italian population in terms of religious belonging. Of the 19 MEPs, almost one third (six) attend religious services once a week and three (15.8%) once a month while one (5.3%) does not attend religious functions (see Figure 1). Nevertheless, it is worth noting that six of the surveyed MEPs (almost 32%) declined to answer this question.

Here a comparison with the general Italian public seems revealing (see Figure 2). If we compare the frequency of responses for the two extreme categories ('never' and 'once a week/more than once a week') between MEPs and the general public, it emerges that the former appear to attend religious functions much more often than the latter. While only 5.3% (one) of the MEPs define themselves as non-practising the percentage grows to 18 among the general public. Similarly, while 36.84 % (7) of the MEPs attend religious

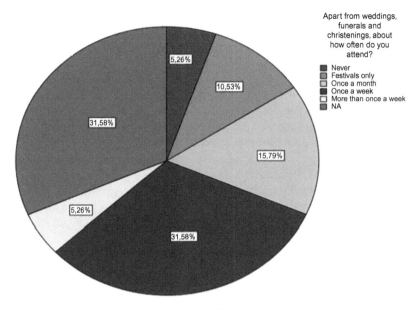

Figure 1.   MEPs' religious practices (Italian sample).

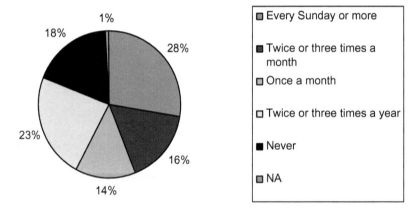

Figure 2.   Religious practices among the general public.

Source: IStat (Italian National Institute of Statistics), http://dati.istat.it/Index.aspx, accessed June 28 2014.

functions once a week or more than once a week the percentage falls to 28 among the general public. The data thus suggest that, in the Italian case, the European parliamentary elite appears less secular than the general population.

If we compare the Italians' attendance at religious functions with the distribution in the full RelEP sample a few relevant points emerge and are worth mentioning (see Figure 3). The first point concerns those Italian MEPs who declined to answer this specific question, comprising one of two most frequent responses in the Italian sample (32% (six MEPs)). Interestingly, the whole RelEP sample of interviewed MEPs shows them even more reluctant, with almost half of the interviewees (49%) declining to answer

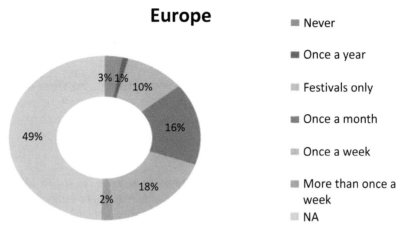

Figure 3.   MEPs' religious practices (RelEP sample).

this question. When it comes to the frequency of religious practices, the Italian MEPs confirm themselves far above the average (32% as compared with 20% for the categories 'once a week/more than once a week'). However, the percentages of those never attending religious services appear comparable (5% as compared with 3%).

Impact of religion on the work of MEPs at the EP

As far as impact of religion on parliamentary work is concerned, the overall evaluation of the current situation in terms of relationship between religion and politics at the EP seems to split the Italian MEPs evenly into two groups: 47.4% (nine) of the respondents perceive a relevant effect of religion, while 42.1% (eight) do not. The Italian delegation appears divided on religious issues, as could be expected. Among the 19 interviewees, 31.6% (six) of the MEPs think that religion reinforces the identity of each political group, while 42.1% (eight) of them think that it has no effect whatsoever on the identity of the groups, and 15.8% (three) think, on the contrary, that religion blurs the political identity of the groups.

Moreover, 78.9% (15) of the interviewed Italian MEPs think that this differential in the degree of influence of religion on the EP is due to the nationality of the elected representative, which is not surprising given the specificities of Italian political culture. The strong perception by Italian MEPs of national specificities (and particularly their own) concerning the role of religion in politics also emerges when they are asked about their personal experiences: 21.1% (four) of the 19 interviewed MEPs think that the place of religion in the EP is different from their experience in national politics (while 47.4% do not think so and 21% do not know). Therefore, given their cultural and political back-ground, Italian MEPs are well aware of the issues raised at European level by the interaction between religion and politics. Moreover, the RelEP survey data show that their overall degree of secularisation is higher than might be expected on the basis of the literature on the Italian case (Ignazi 2008; Ballarino et al. 2010). As far as self-reported political behaviours are concerned, when asked whether they take religion into account in their work as MEPs the great majority of the respondents say that they do so only on an irregular basis (see Table 3).

Table 3.   Frequency of 'taking religion into account as a MEP'.

Frequency of contact with religious or philosophical interest groups	Percentage
Permanently	10.5
Often	21.1
Rarely	57.9
Did not answer	10.5
Total (N)	19

Unsurprisingly, the denominational adherence of the interviewed Italian MEPs seems to play a significant role with respect to the extent to which they take religion into account in their work. However, the limited variance in this sample does not allow statistically significant considerations, given that only four out of 19 MEPs say that they do not belong to a specific religious denomination. If we compare those 'belonging to some religious denomination' to those who do not, the percentage of those who permanently or often take religion into account in their European political activity grows from 31.6 (five) to 38.5 (seven) (see Figure 4).

The variation in terms of party affiliation with regard to this variable is not surprising. More specifically, among conservative MEPs (PdL and LN) a majority (50% (10)) of the respondents stress the role of religion in their political activity while most of the leftist-progressive ones (57% (11) of the respondents affiliated to PD and all those affiliated to IdV) do not take religion into account. Berlusconi's PdL and LN discourses have often framed the role of religion within society as part of their values and political identity, especially in terms of bioethical and social/family issues. For instance, the LN's MEP Mario Borghezio (who has been in the EP since 2001), a member of the Committee on Civil Liberties, Justice and Home Affairs (LIBE), has organised several pilgrimages of

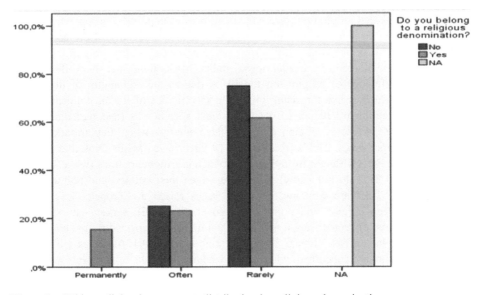

Figure 4.   Taking religion into account: distribution by religious denomination.

Table 4. Responses to the question 'If religion intervenes in your activity as MEP, is it...?' (first choice, out of three possible).

Impact of religion	%
Of no effect?	5.3
As a source of personal inspiration?	36.8
As a social and political reality?	42.1
As an interest group ?	5.3
NA	10.5
Total – first choice (N)	19

MEPs to Fatima and other sacred sites and is known for his anti-Islamic stances. By contrast, given that centrist and particularly Christian Democratic parties such as the UdC traditionally translate religious issue into the political sphere, it is striking that the only UdC MEP interviewed said that he took religion into account only on an irregular basis.

In terms of impact of religion on policy-making, 73.7% (14) of the 19 interviewed MEPs support the idea that the EU should have a real policy towards religions. Unsurprisingly, the majority of Italian MEPs (52.6% (10)) believe that the Lisbon Treaty should have made reference to Europe's Christian heritage, although the proportion of undecided is rather relevant (10.5%). Furthermore, when the interviewees were asked to detail the way they take religion into account in their political activity at the EP, fewer than 37% (seven) of the respondents said that they saw it as a source of personal inspiration (see Table 4).

What is the impact of religious or philosophical interest groups on the practices and parliamentary activities of Italian MEPs? As far as their interaction with denominational groups or organisations is concerned, only 26.4% (five) of the 19 interviewed MEPs said that they were in contact with such groups on a regular basis (once a week or more and once a month or more) (Table 5). Given that almost 32% of the Italian respondents take religion into account on a regular basis in their activity at the EP (permanently or often: see Table 4) but only 5.3% (one) acknowledge the influence of religious interest groups (see Table 5), we can easily assume that this is not the result of the effective lobbying work conducted by religious organisations at the European level. With regard to the political behaviour of MEPs, if we look at the explanatory potential of denominational adherence we see that interactions with religious organisations are somewhat more frequent (once a week/month) among religious

Table 5. Frequency of contact with religious or philosophical interest groups (%).

Frequency	(%)
Never	21.1
Once a week or more	5.3
Once a month or more	21.1
A few times a year	31.6
A few times over the course of a term	10.5
DK-NA	10.5
Total (N)	19

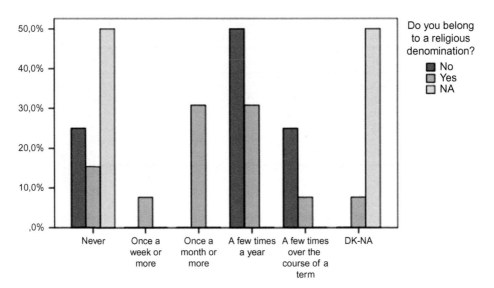

Figure 5. Frequency of contact with religious organisations: distribution by religious denomination.

MEPs than among those who do not belong to a specific denomination (Figure 5). However, if we look at political attitudes towards religion and politics (Table 6), the picture that emerges is more nuanced, in the sense that the overall level of secularisation of Italian MEPs seems to follow less 'traditional' trends with regard to Italian politics. As expected, religion (and particularly Catholicism) plays an important role especially with regard to family, civil rights and bioethical issues (Bellah 1980; Mancina 2006). The data show that the overall degree of political secularism is relatively high among the interviewed Italian MEPs, the majority of whom (73.7% (14)) disagree or strongly disagree with the idea that politicians who do not believe in God are unfit for office and generally oppose the idea that religious leaders should influence voting behaviour (see Table 6). However, a significant proportion of respondents

Table 6. Attitudes towards the relationship between religion and politics (%).

	Agree strongly	Agree	Neither	Disagree	Disagree strongly	NA	Total (N)
Politicians who do not believe in God are unfit for public office	0	0	5.3	31.6	42.1	21.1	19
Religious leaders should not influence how people vote in elections	21.1	31.6	0	26.3	5.3	15.8	19
It would be better for Europe if more people with strong religious beliefs held public office	10.5	15.8	21.1	31.6	5.3	15.8	19
Religious leaders should not influence government decisions	26.3	26.3	21.1	10.5	5.3	10.5	19
If a nurse were asked to help perform a legal abortion, she should be allowed to refuse on religious grounds	15.8	26.3	10.5	26.3	10.5	10.5	19

think that there should be more 'religious-oriented' political leaders in Europe (26.3% (five) agree or strongly agree). It is worth mentioning that none of the interviewees belonging to the Berlusconi coalition deny the necessity of leaders with strong religious beliefs. This attitude seems to be at the origin of the strong criticisms among the conservative ranks following the substitution of Buttiglione and the exclusion of Mauro, perceived as clear evidence of a soulless Europe. Besides, 42% (eight) of the respondents display conservative positions in terms of political attitudes with regard to ethical issues by supporting the right of nurses to conscientious objection. The majority of respondents thus appear to be less liberal, but also less influenced by religious issues on this specific issue.

If we look now at attitudes with regard to the role of religion in the political sphere in Italy at the level of national and regional elected representatives, we can obtain a more complete overview of the patterns of political secularisation of Italian political elites.

The PartiRep elite survey data show that the distribution of opinions of national and regional MPs on the relevance of promoting the interests of religious groups are generally closer to those of less secularised MPs such as those in Poland rather than those in ideal-typical lay states such as France (see Table 7). When asked 'how important is it to you, personally, to promote the views and interests of a church or religious group', in fact only 13.3% of the Italian respondents considered it very important on a scale from 1 (of no importance) to 7 (very important). However, the great majority of the interviewed Italian regional and national MPs (76%) do not consider it important that 'the various groups corresponding with religious divisions within society are present in Parliament in proportion to their number in the population' (see Table 8).

The only variable on which it is possible to develop a cross-level comparison is the one concerning the elected representatives' personal practices, and in particular the frequency of contacts with religious groups or organisations (see Table 9). The frequency of contacts between such groups and Italian national and regional MPs is slightly higher than at the EP level: if the exactly same proportion of surveyed representatives state that they have contacts with religious groups at least once a week (5.3% both at national/ subnational and at European level), by contrast 43.3% of national/subnational MPs say they interact with religious groups at least once a year while 31.6% (six) of Italian MEPs do so a few times a year and 10.5% (two) a few times over the course of a term. However, the proportion of those interacting with religious groups at least once a month rises to 21.1% (four) at the EP level, while in national and regional Parliaments it is only 9.3% of the respondents.

As a significant proportion (37.4%) of surveyed MPs consider it rather important to promote the interests of religious groups as part of their personal practices and parliamentary work (positions 5 to 7 on a 1–7 scale, see Table 7), it is worth looking at the explanatory potential of the level of territorial government and at their own ideological positioning (Figure 6). The differences in terms of territorial level of government are quite strong, showing a significant proportion (almost 70%) of regional MPs supporting the views and interests of religious groups in their activities. This seems to suggest a persistence of the impact of regional political subcultures, and in particular of the non-secular 'Christian Democratic' subculture.

Also the impact of ideology seems relevant (see Figure 6).[1] Unsurprisingly, most right-wing (74.5%) and moderate/centrist (75.3%) regional and national MPs consider it rather important to promote the interests of religious groups as part of their parliamentary work, as opposed to only 42% of left-wing ones. This confirms the variation in terms of party affiliation with regard to the role of religion in political activity that we observe at the EP level (see above).

Table 7. Importance of promoting the views and interests of a church or religious group by country (national and regional MPs).

Degree of importance	Country (%)															Total (%)
	AUT	BEL	FRA	GER	HUN	IRE	ISR	ITA	NET	NOR	POL	POR	SPA	SWI	UNK	
1 (no imp)	15.4	25.0	31.4	3.8	9.3	8.7	5.7	7.2	20.8	19.4	12.2	8.1	14.8	22.7	11.1	13.6
2	10.6	21.9	19.6	10.0	9.3	17.4	8.6	12.0	9.4	22.2	12.2	15.1	12.7	23.7	7.4	13.4
3	16.0	18.8	15.7	10.5	13.4	17.4	14.3	18.1	9.4	16.7	19.5	14.0	10.5	12.4	16.0	13.9
4	23.9	16.4	21.6	15.5	14.4	17.4	20.0	25.3	22.6	19.4	39.0	24.4	15.3	14.4	19.8	19.2
5	10.6	6.2	3.9	20.9	21.6	8.7	25.7	15.7	18.9	13.9	12.2	18.6	12.2	13.4	16.0	14.7
6	13.8	7.8	3.9	17.2	14.4	21.7	5.7	8.4	9.4	5.6	2.4	4.7	14.0	10.3	7.4	11.4
7 (very imp)	9.6	3.9	3.9	22.2	17.5	8.7	20.0	13.3	9.4	2.8	2.4	15.1	20.5	3.1	22.2	13.8
Total (N)	188	128	51	239	97	23	35	83	53	36	41	86	229	97	81	1467

Table 8. Presence in Parliament of religious groups by country (national and regional MPs).

Degree of importance	Country (%)															Total (%)
	AUT	BEL	FRA	GER	HUN	IRE	ISR	ITA	NET	NOR	POL	POR	SPA	SWI	UNK	
Not important	43.5	45.7	55.6	19.7	47.9	23.3	22.6	20.8	15.4	50.0	34.8	40.8	39.4	40.2	31.0	35.6
Not very important	40.0	41.9	42.6	53.3	45.8	43.3	22.6	55.2	44.2	35.0	43.5	45.9	46.8	45.1	39.1	45.2
Fairly important	13.5	11.6	1.9	23.8	5.2	30.0	48.4	24.0	36.5	5.0	21.7	10.2	10.8	13.7	26.4	16.7
Very important	3.0	0.8	0.0	3.3	1.0	3.3	6.5	0.0	3.8	10.0	0.0	3.1	3.0	1.0	3.4	2.5
Total (N)	200	129	54	244	96	30	31	96	52	40	46	98	231	102	87	1536

Table 9. Frequency of contact with churches or religious organisations by country (national and regional MPs).

								Country (%)								
Frequency	AUT	BEL	FRA	GER	HUN	IRE	ISR	ITA	NET	NOR	POL	POR	SPA	SWI	UNK	Total (%)
At least once a week	4.1	1.5	0.0	6.4	15.5%	0.0	6.2%	5.2	1.9	2.7	8.5	1.0	2.2	2.0	12.1	4.7
At least once a month	16.4	6.1	4.8	33.9	24.7%	10.3	25.0%	9.3	7.4	10.8	17.0	9.4	6.6	6.9	30.8	15.9
At least every three months	27.7	17.6	17.5	32.7	20.6%	17.2	18.8%	23.7	25.9	18.9	10.6	21.9	15.8	17.6	39.6	23.3
At least once a year	29.7	26.0	42.9	21.9	23.7%	48.3	6.2%	43.3	33.3	35.1	36.2	27.1	23.7	29.4	15.4	27.5
(Almost) no contact	22.1	48.9	34.9	5.2	15.5%	24.1	43.8%	18.6	31.5	32.4	27.7	40.6	51.8	44.1	2.2	28.5
Total (N)	195	131	63	251	97	29	32	97	54	37	47	96	228	102	91	1550

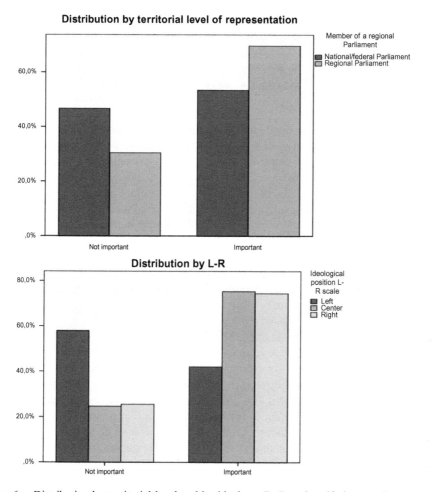

Figure 6.   Distribution by territorial level and by ideology (L–R scale self-placement).

In sum, religion does indeed seem to play a role in the political attitudes and the activity of Italian MEPs, but their overall degree of political secularisation is higher than expected. The majority of the Italian MEPs display high levels of religiosity, but they do not take religion into account in their parliamentary work on a regular basis; it plays an important role mainly with regard to bioethical issues. The presence of interest groups at the EP level is clear and Italian MEPs interact with religious organisations quite frequently. Although religion is not perceived to generate tensions between denominations, it is considered to have a different impact according to nationality. In conclusion, Italian MEPs seem to confirm the patterns of interactions between religion and politics present at national level in Italy, although the overall degree of secularisation is slightly higher than expected.

The case of Turkey's EU bid through the lens of religion

In this section we discuss a case study of particular relevance for the Italian MEPs: the accession of Turkey to the EU. The issue of Turkey's EU ambitions has become increasingly divisive along left–right ideological lines in the EP as well as in Italian politics, while identitarian and/or functional opposition towards Turkish membership has increasingly characterised the Italian right and centre-right (mostly the LN and the PdL).

When the European Council decided to start accession negotiations with Turkey in December 2004, the decision was supported by the EP, with 359 votes in favour and 181 against. Of the Italian MEPs, 42 (66%) supported the EP resolution, 12 (19%) opposed it and 10 (16%) abstained. Despite the promising start of the negotiations, within a few months the EU's commitment lost momentum. At the same time, the functional use of the 'Turkey discourse' gained ground among mainstream parties both at the national and EP level as a practical short cut to convey popular concerns about immigration, unemployment, multiculturalism and Islam (McLaren 2007). The growing scepticism is reflected by the new Negotiating Framework endorsed by the EP in 2006 which defines the negotiations as 'an open-ended process, the outcome of which cannot be guaranteed beforehand'.

In the Italian case, clear examples of the functional opposition side are represented by those – especially among the conservative ranks of the Berlusconi coalition – raising concern about the shift of EU structural funds to Turkey or about the massive influence that Turkey as a member would have within the European institutions. However, the opposition of the Northern League to Turkish membership denotes a clear identitarian nature as Turkey is defined as an 'external other' and as a cultural exogenous threat to the Christian identity of Europe and its civilisation. Thus when it comes to understanding Turkey and the specific role played by the religious feelings of MEPs, the views expressed by individual MEPs appear diversified. The excerpts from the debate on some of the most recent progress reports on Turkey adopted by the European Commission could serve as an example (see Appendix). The quotations in the Appendix show that the positions of the Italian MEPs on Turkish membership range from support to open Turkophobia and that the political use of Turkey's religious distinctiveness ranges from functional to identitarian. While some praise Turkey's role as a bridge between Europe and the Islamic world or as a model for other Muslim countries, others stress the risk of an Islamic threat, the non-European and non-Christian nature of Turkey, and the ongoing discrimination against religious minorities, thereby reflecting widespread concerns among the European public.

Empirical analyses prove that the religious feelings of MEPs and their vision of Islam play a very relevant role in determining their support or opposition towards Turkish membership of the EU (Redmond 2007). Braghiroli (2012) demonstrates that perception of Islam emerges as one of the most relevant explanatory factors. MEPs who believe that Islam and democracy are compatible are more likely to support Turkish EU membership. The acceptability of Turkish membership seems therefore largely conditioned by the religious distinctiveness of the country.

The same study (Braghiroli 2012) highlights the impressive perceptional gap between 'Christian' and 'non-Christian' or 'non-believer' MEPs. Among the former (Italians or others), the percentage of supporters of Turkish membership is very small, while it is significantly larger among the latter. A number of analyses confirm that being Christian represents a very powerful identitarian shortcut widening the cleavage between Christian Europe and Islamic Turkey. In the RelEP elite survey 19 Italian MEPs were asked whether they thought that 'religion plays a role in the way Turkey's candidature was received in the European Parliament'. It is worth stressing that this question was not about whether MEPs were in favour of Turkish membership, but about the perceived impact of religion in MEPs' attitudes towards this. Significantly, 53% (10) of the interviewed MEPs think that religious considerations play a role in the EP's attitude towards Turkey's candidature, while only 37% (seven) think the opposite (Figure 7). In contrast to the case of support/opposition as far as Turkish membership is concerned, no substantial differences can be

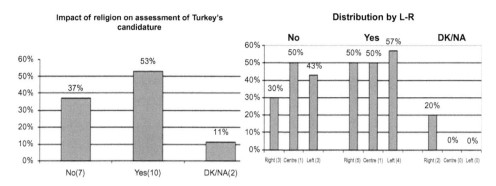

Figure 7.   Assessment of Turkey's candidature: general distribution and distribution by ideological positioning.

measured along the left–right continuum.[2] Among conservative and leftist-progressive MEPs, a majority of the respondents stress the role of religion in this specific issue, respectively 50% (five) and 57% (four) (Figure 7).

It is worth noting that the impact of religion seems to be more strongly perceived by the two non-religious MEPs, while among those who define themselves as believers 42% (five) think that religion does not play a role in this issue (Figure 8).[3] The same trend emerges if we look at the religious denominations of MEPs. If we compare those 'belonging to some religious denomination' with those who do not, the percentage of those who perceive the role of religion as relevant in the EP's voting on Turkey grows from 54% to 70% (Figure 8). Similar trends emerge if we look at MEPs' attendance at religious functions: the non-religious or less religious MEPs seem to attach a negative connotation to the perceived role of religion in this issue, and unlike their religious colleagues, seem to look at it as an improper interference.

An indirect way to highlight the same phenomenon is to look at the explanatory potential of the level of support for a reference to Europe's Christian heritage in the Lisbon Treaty (Figure 9). Among the 19 Italian respondents, a clear majority (70%) support some reference to Europe's Judeo-Christian roots. Interestingly, among the supporters 40% (four) think that religion plays a role in the way the EP treats Turkey, while 86% (six) who oppose it do not think so. So it seems that those who favour the more identitarian position in the Treaty also support a stronger role for religion in the EP's

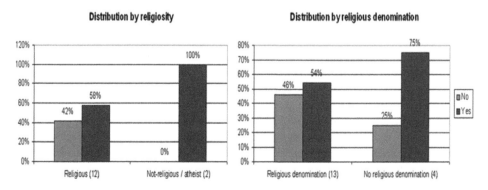

Figure 8.   Assessment of Turkey's candidature: distribution by religiosity and denomination.

**Distribution by preference concerning the religious
references in the Lisbon Treaty**

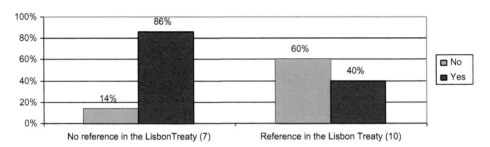

Figure 9.   Assessment of Turkey's candidature: distribution by preferences *vis-à-vis* religion in Lisbon treaty.

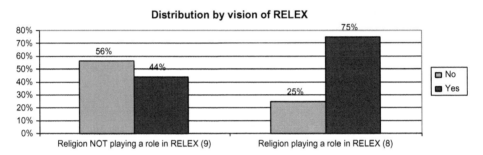

Figure 10.   Assessment of Turkey's candidature: distribution by vision of RELEX (the Directorate-General for External Relations of the European Commission).

approach to Turkey and show some disappointment with the current state of things, where religion plays – in their eyes – no role, or a very limited one.

A last indicator that seems worth mentioning concerns the perceived role of religion in the external relation of the EU, to which Turkey's accession pertains. Among those who think that the EU's external relations are affected by religious considerations, 75% (six) of the respondents say that religious considerations also play a role also in the EP's attitude towards Turkey, while among the others the percentage of those who think so falls to 56% (five) (Figure 10).

Conclusions

Religiosity remains a salient factor in contemporary Italian politics. While a number of recent studies have explored the impact of religion on the voting behaviour of the Italian public, highlighting a progressive trend towards secularisation, similar studies on the attitudes and behaviour of Italian political elites appear much more rare and dated. Our main aim in this study is to contribute to filling this gap in the EP context, exploring the impact of religion and religiosity on the attitudes and behaviours of the Italian MEPs. In this respect, our study has proved highly revealing: the picture of the Italian delegation (and of Italian political elites) that emerges is much more nuanced than it might appear at first sight.

Our analysis unsurprisingly reveals that widespread religiosity – massively Catholic – is a distinctive trait of the Italian delegation. Of 19 MEPs surveyed only two (10%) did not declare themselves as 'religious persons': one of the lowest percentages of non-believers in the sample. Also the frequency of religious attendance appears far higher than the RelEP average. Interestingly, our analysis shows that the Italian MEPs seem to attend religious functions much more often than the general public.

While the degree of religiosity of the Italian delegation seems indisputably high, the impact of MEPs' religious feelings on their political activities appears much less direct and less strong. Not only does the Italian delegation seem divided on religious issues, but our data also show that, overall, the degree of political secularism is relatively high among the interviewed Italian MEPs when compared with that of their national or regional counterparts. Clear differences in terms of secularisation can be identified along the left–right continuum, with the conservative and moderate MEPs more likely to project their religious beliefs onto their political activity. PartiRep data show that among regional and national representatives most right-wing (75%) and moderate/centrist (75%) MPs consider it important to promote the interests of religious groups as part of their parliamentary work, as opposed to only 42% of left-wing ones. This is in line with the findings based on the RelEP data on the attitudes and behaviours of Italian representatives at the European level. The persistence of a clear left–right divide emerges also when it comes to key issues that might reflect a clear identitarian nature, such as Turkey's membership of the EU and the reference to Europe's Christian heritage in the Lisbon Treaty.

The evidence from our survey data shows a resilience of the influence of religion with regard to party affiliation and particularly on the patterns of belonging to political organisations representing the two extremes of the left–right ideological spectrum. Religion still plays a crucial role in defining the (more or less) stable identity of the left (lay) and right (religious) poles. Religion still represents one of the main dimensions of political cleavages and it contributes to determining the ideological belonging of political elites and elected representatives to political families with a tradition of proximity to religion, such as the Italian centre-right.

However, religion also functions as a key but volatile ideologically charged issue that can be exploited and appropriated by various political forces, mostly the heirs of the former Christian Democracy. This element clearly emerges from our data, but can easily be observed in the relevance of, and conflictuality over, the strategic use of religious and moral issues by right-wing parties (and particularly Berlusconi's re-founded *Forza Italia*) aimed at mobilising electoral support in the 2014 EP election campaign. Beside austerity and economic policies, religious identity (in relation to immigration issues) and ethical questions (abortion) were among the most salient issues of the campaign, as a result of the communication strategy of right-wing parties.

Moreover, the level of conflictuality of religious topics in domestic politics is likely to explain the way Italian elites address religion in European arenas. For instance, if the matter is controversial, it may be used by peripheral political entrepreneurs to attract attention but avoided by mainstream actors. For instance, the debate about gay rights and same-sex marriage has recently been used by small right-wing forces (and the LN) both at national and European level in order to exploit the political momentum created in France with the '*Manif pour tous*' demonstrations.

Worth mentioning, in this respect, is the political use of the *Lautsi v Italy* case originally brought before the European Court of Human Rights in 2006, dealing with the display of crucifixes in classrooms of state schools in Italy. Following a decision of a section of the Court condemning Italy and declaring that the display of the cross represented a violation of the European Convention on Human Rights, the centre-right forces (and, in particular, Berlusconi's PdL) started a very active political campaign against the ruling (which was eventually overturned by a second ruling by the Grand Chamber of the same Court in 2011). In particular, it is worth mentioning a petition initiated by the PdL addressed to the president of the EP 'against the vulgar violation of religious rights of millions of citizens' (*Petizione populare* 2014).

In general, it seems that, despite a number of religiously based disputes that in recent years have marked the activity of the Italian delegation at the EP, the actual impact of religion on the activities of the Italian MEPs has to be contextualised within the framework of this very specific multinational, multilingual and multicultural parliamentary environment. This is also confirmed by the fact that a significant number of interviewed MEPs consider that the place of religion in the EP is different from that of their experience in national politics.

Although MEPs' contacts with religious lobby groups seem to be quite limited, if compared with those of other national delegations, the weight of religious sentiments appears strong, and in some cases they seem to have a definite impact on the voting behaviour of MEPs far beyond their natural conservative-moderate political realm. Worth mentioning in this context is the case of the vote in 2013 on the Estrela draft Report on Sexual and Reproductive Health and Rights, including sex education in state schools and abortion. In that case, five Italian MEPs affiliated to the PD – mostly close to national clerical circles – did not follow the party line of their group (S&D) to vote in favour of the report: two did not vote, two abstained and one voted against it. This seems to confirm that, in country cases such as Italy, where there are strong religious parties (or rather, where religion still plays a crucial role in determining party affiliation and in politics in general), religious lobbies in the national Parliament appear to be relatively weak. This is because, to put it simply, they are not needed by the Catholic Church to defend its own interests.

All in all, our study shows the ongoing relevance of most symbolic and ideological aspect of religion in Italian politics as well as the resilience of the Catholic Church as a political force. However, our study also shows a mutation in the forms of the influence of the Catholic Church, confirming secularisation but also showing its limits.

Notes

1. In the PartiRep survey this variable is measured on the basis of the respondents' self-placement on a 10-point left-right scale, where 0 means left and 10 means right (the variable has been recorded as a three-point scale for reasons of simplicity).
2. The latter variable is recoded on the basis of party affiliation of the interviewees and thus according to the ideological positioning of the respective party family.
3. Unfortunately, the limited variance in this sample – only two out of 19 MEPs do not declare themselves as 'religious persons' – does not allow statistically significant considerations.

References

Bale, T., and P. Taggart. 2006. *First-Timers Yes, Virgins No: The Roles and Backgrounds of New Members of the European Parliament*. SEI Working Papers 89. https://www.sussex.ac.uk/webteam/gateway/file.php?name=sei-working-paper-no-89.pdf&site=266.

Ballarino, G., M. Maraffi, H. Schadee, and C. Vezzoni. 2010. "Le fratture sociali: classe, religione, territorio" [Social Cleavages: Class, Religion, Territory]. In *Votare in Italia: 1968-2008: dall'appartenenza alla scelta* [Voting Behaviour in Italy: From Identification to Choice], edited by P. Bellucci and P. Segatti, 149–211. Bologna: Il Mulino.

Bellah, R. N. 1980. "The Five Civil Religions of Italy." In *Varieties of Civil Religion*, edited by R. N. Bellah and P. E. Hammond, 86–118. San Francisco, CA: Harper and Row.

Biorcio, R., A. Giorgi, and I. Grasso. 2008. "Class, Religion and Electoral Behaviour in Italy: An Analysis of Trends over Time." Paper presented at the first ISA Forum of Sociology, Barcelona, Spain, September 5–8.

Braghiroli, S. 2012. "Je t'aime…moi non plus! An Empirical Assessment of Euro-Parliamentarians' Voting Behaviour on Turkey and Turkish Membership." *Southeast European and Black Sea Studies* 12 (1): 1–24. doi:10.1080/14683857.2012.661219.

Cotta, M., and L. Verzichelli. 2007. *Political Institutions in Italy*. Oxford: OUP.

Diamanti, I., and L. Ceccarini. 2007. "Catholics and Politics After the Christian Democrats: The Influential Minority." *Journal of Modern Italian Studies* 12 (1): 37–59. doi:10.1080/13545710601132912.

"EU Elections: Christian Barroso under Fire." 2009. *DutchNews.nl*, May 7. http://www.dutchnews.nl/news/archives/2009/05/eu_elections_christian_barroso.php.

"EU Panel Opposes Justice Nominee." 2004. *BBC News*, October 11. http://news.bbc.co.uk/1/hi/world/europe/3734572.stm.

Eurispes. 2009. *Rapporto Italia 2009* [Italy Report 2009]. Eurispes. http://eurispes.eu/content/rapporto-italia-2009-0.

Eurispes. 2010. *Rapporto Italia 2010* [Italy Report 2010]. Eurispes. http://eurispes.eu/content/rapporto-italia-2010.

Ferrari, A. 2011. "L'esperienza cattolica nella construzione dell'ordinamento giuridico italiano: osservazioni minime a centocinquant'anni dall'unità" [The Catholic Experience in the Construction of the Italian Legal Order: Preliminary Observations for the 150th Anniversary of Italian Unity]. *Quaderni di diritto e politica ecclesiastica* 1: 255–268.

Garelli, F. 2007. "The Church and Catholicism in Contemporary Italy." *Journal of Modern Italian Studies* 12 (1): 2–7. doi:10.1080/13545710601132672.

Garelli, F., G. Guizzardi, and E. Pace. 2003. *Un singolare pluralismo: indagine sul pluralismo morale e religioso in Italia* [A Peculiar Form of Pluralism: An Inquiry into the Religious and Moral Pluralism in Italy]. Bologna: Il Mulino.

Giordan, G., and W. Swatos. 2011. *Religion, Spirituality and Everyday Practice*. Berlin: Springer.

Giorgi, A. 2013. "Ahab and the White Whale: The Contemporary Debate Around the Forms of Catholic Political Commitment in Italy." *Democratization* 20 (5): 895–916. doi:10.1080/13510347.2013.801257.

Hix, S. 2002. "Parliamentary Behavior with Two Principals: Preferences, Parties, and Voting in the European Parliament." *American Journal of Political Science* 46 (3): 688–698. doi:10.2307/3088408.

Ignazi, P. 2008. "The Persistence of Class and Religion." Paper presented at the first ISA Forum of Sociology, Barcelona, Spain, September 5–8.

Inglehart, R., and P. Norris. 2004. *Sacred and Secular: Religion and Politics Worldwide*. Cambridge: Cambridge University Press.

"Italy and the Right to Die: Death in Udine." 2009. *The Economist*, February 12. http://www.economist.com/node/13110088.

Jemolo, A. C. (1948) 1961. *Chiesa e stato in Italia negli ultimi cento anni* [Church and State in Italy in the Last Century]. Turin: Einaudi.

Mancina, C. 2006. "Laicità e politica" [Laicism and Politics]. In *Laicità: una geografia delle nostre radici* [Laicism: A Geography of Our Roots], edited by G. Boniolo, 5–7. Turin: Einaudi.

McLaren, L. M. 2007. "Explaining Opposition to Turkish Membership of the EU." *European Union Politics* 8 (2): 251–278. doi:10.1177/1465116507076432.

Morlino, L., and M. Tarchi. 1996. "The Dissatisfied Society: The Roots of Political Change in Italy." *European Journal of Political Research* 30: 41–63. doi:10.1111/j.1475-6765.1996.tb00667.x.

Pasquinucci, D., and L. Verzichelli. 2004. *Elezioni europee e classe politica sovranazionale: 1979–2004* [European Elections and Supranational Political Elites: 1979–2004]. Bologna: Il Mulino.

Petizione popolare al presidente del Parlamento Europeo: il crocifisso va rispettato [People's Petition to the President of the European Parliament: We Should Respect the Crucifix]. 2014. http://ilpopolodellaliberta.it/notizie/arc_17314.htm.

Redmond, J. 2007. "Turkey and the European Union: Troubled European or European Trouble?" *International Affairs* 83 (2): 305–317. doi:10.1111/j.1468-2346.2007.00620.x.

Segatti, P., and G. Brunelli. 2010. "Italia religiosa: da cattolica a generalmente cristiana" [Religious Italy: From Catholic to Christian in General]. *Il Regno* 10: 337–342.

US (US Department of State). 2009. *Italy: International Religious Freedom Report 2009*. http://www.state.gov/g/drl/rls/irf/2009/127317.htm.

Appendix

Contributions by Italian MEPs to the EP debate on the 2010 and 2011 reports on Turkey adopted by the European Commission.

Mara Bizzotto (EFD), in writing:
Turkey's economic potential is not a valid argument for continuing to support its entry into the EU. … Turkey not only does not share or respect the EU's ideological values, as exemplified by its relations with Cyprus, but last year expressed on several occasions its complete disinterest in continuing along the road to accession. I therefore remain firmly opposed to Turkey's entry into Europe.

Carlo Fidanza (PPE), in writing:
I voted against the motion for a resolution on Turkey cause it is calling for what I consider a forced integration of two very different regions, Europe and Turkey. As well as the profound cultural differences and the fact that Turkey does not totally belong to the European continent. […] An acceptable choice would be to create a privileged partnership without seeking integration at all costs, which, in many ways, does not make sense.

Mario Mauro (PPE), in writing:
EU dialogue and cooperation with Turkey on stability, democracy and security in the broader Middle East are strategic. Furthermore, Turkey, built on a solid secular State, could, in the context of an effective reform process, prove to be a source of inspiration for democratising Arab States in their efforts to complete their democratic transition and socio-economic reforms. I am not in favour of enlargement to include Turkey, but I agree with the fact that it is fundamental to maintain privileged relations with this actor.

Claudio Morganti (EFD), in writing:
I think it is absurd that we are still debating the progress, which is non-existent, of Turkey as regards its possible accession to the European Union. Leaving aside the numerous criteria requested that still have not been met, a fact recognised by the EU itself, the underlying issue is still, in my opinion, essentially a historical-political one. Turkey is not part of Europe from either a geographical or a historical and religious point of view.

Debora Serracchiani (S&D):
Mr President, ladies and gentlemen, I voted in favour of the resolution on Turkey because the constitutional reform that took place 12 September last was unanimously recognised as an important step forward made by Turkey in relation to Europe. Naturally, there are still many more steps to be taken and in this vein, I would express my concern over the numerous arrests of journalists. I would

like to underline that Turkey is the seventh largest commercial partner of the European Union, that the European Union is Turkey's main commercial partner.

Mario Borghezio (NI):

... today's vote has yet again shown the hypocrisy of political correctness, in that it seeks to leave out the need for a clear position statement from the demands that Europe has a duty to put to Turkey's leaders and institutions – the same people who welcomed the Pope's words and forthcoming visit with vulgar, violent language and Mafia-like threats. Europe just looks on, while their school books still teach Turkish children that the Armenian genocide is a fabrication of history. ... We no longer have a Europe of human rights, but a Europe that could not care less about human rights!

Marco Cappato (ALDE), in writing:

Mr President, on behalf of the Transnational Radical Party, I voted against the Eurlings report on Turkey, because Parliament is thereby authorising the European Union to shut itself off from the Mediterranean and the Middle East yet again. Instead of showing its willingness to speed up the process of integrating Turkey into Europe, Parliament is proposing alternative ways to bring Ankara closer to Brussels that have nothing to do with serious accession negotiations.

Luca Romagnoli (NI), in writing:

Mr President, I have voted against the 2008 progress report on Turkey. The fact is that there are too many unresolved issues for us to claim that significant progress has been made on the accession negotiations, which began almost four years ago. I refer to the situation of the Kurdish population, to capital punishment, which is still in force in Turkey, and to the cultural and religious issues that need to be addressed. Under no circumstances can these be dealt with superficially or lightly.

Part III

In Transit: From Religious Stronghold to Liberal Laboratory

Austrian MEPs: between privatisation and politicisation of religion

Julia Mourão Permoser

Research Platform Religion and Transformation in Contemporary European Society, University of Vienna, Vienna, Austria

This contribution investigates the role of religion in the work and attitudes of Austrian members of the European Parliament (MEPs). It is based on the Austrian results of a large-scale survey of MEPs, RelEP, and on the analysis of parliamentary questions. The study argues that the attitudes of Austrian MEPs to religion are characterised by two seemingly contradictory phenomena: the privatisation and the politicisation of religion. The privatisation of religion expresses itself in the MEPs' refusal to disclose information about their religiosity and in the absence from the political agenda of topics related to the role of churches and majority religions within European societies. By contrast, human rights abuses against Christian minorities abroad, the religious dimension of Turkey's candidacy to the European Union and the difficulties of integrating Islam in Europe are all highly politicised topics. In short, the religion of the Other is politicised, while the religion of the majority is privatised. In this context, it is the attribution of religious belonging to the Other which serves the symbolic function of drawing identity boundaries, whereas the Self is envisaged as secular.

Introduction

This contribution investigates the role of religion in the European Parliament (EP), focusing in particular on the work and attitudes of Austrian members of the European Parliament (MEPs). What do Austrian MEPs think about religion? What role does religion play in their daily work? Do Austrian MEPs differ from other MEPs as far as religion is concerned? The answers to these questions can tell us much about the relationship between Austrian political elites and religion, and about the influence that European integration has upon that relationship. Furthermore, it can also help us understand how the relationship between religion and politics is being (re)configured within the context of 'postsecularism' and the 'return of religion'.

For a long time, the idea prevailed that modernity and secularism were intrinsically related. The secularisation theory predicted that modernisation and economic prosperity would engender political and social secularisation. From this perspective, the European Union (EU) – a quintessentially modern organisation linked to globalisation and economic liberalisation – would be expected to fit the secularising logic, with politics being totally separated from religion. From the mid-1990s onwards, however, the consensus surrounding the secularisation thesis started to crumble. Scholars realised that religion had remained important despite modernity even in apparently secular societies like those of

Europe. According to José Casanova (1994, 2006), in the European context the connection between secularism and modernity had acquired normative character: in order to be modern, Europeans could not be religious. Secularism had become a 'knowledge regime' which prevented Europeans from acknowledging that religion had retained an important social and political role. In addition, scholars noted, a number of phenomena were contributing to a 'return of religion' to the European public sphere (Katzenstein 2006; Katzenstein and Byrnes 2006). Among other things, immigration to Europe increased the diversity of the population and worked against the trend towards the privatisation of religion. Especially the influx of large numbers of religiously observant Muslims contributed to this phenomenon, both because religion became more visible and because it became increasingly politicised (Katzenstein and Byrnes 2006; Casanova 2006). By the same token, the diversification of European societies and the need to deal with claims for accommodation of religious practices from immigrant minorities has also increased the awareness of the many ways in which religious symbols and traditions still permeate the secularised public sphere, often under the guise of culture.

Speaking of the return of religion to European public spheres and the change in consciousness that has accompanied it, Jürgen Habermas (2008) argues that European societies have become 'post-secular'. For Habermas (2008, paras 38–41), this term has both descriptive and normative connotations. Descriptively, it refers to a society that is secular in the sense of neutral between various religions and towards non-believers, but in which the 'knowledge regime of secularism' described by Casanova no longer holds. Normatively, this implies an obligation on the part of secular society to accept religious reasoning and religious actors in the public sphere. The idea is that mutual recognition requires a process of 'complementary learning' with efforts on both sides. On the one hand, religious citizens must 'appropriate the secular legitimation of constitutional principles under the premises of their own faith', and must be able to 'translate' religiously derived opinions into a language accessible to all. On the other hand, secular citizens must learn to welcome religions into the public sphere and be prepared to participate with religious citizens in the process of democratic will formation under conditions of equality.

The theoretical insights from post-secularism have helped move the empirical and analytical research agenda on the return of religion one step forward. In particular, from an empirical perspective, these new insights call for a shift in attention from the question of whether and why there is a return of religion – a research agenda still very much embedded in the old academic paradigm that considered secularism and religion as being mutually exclusive – to the questions of when, where and how the presence of religion makes itself felt in (post)secular societies. Researching religion in the context of the postsecular implies overcoming the dichotomous divide in order to, as Nilüfer Göle (2013, 365) puts it, 'understand the ways in which religions become contemporaneous of the secular modern' through interpenetrations and reconfigurations.

In this study I build upon these theoretical insights to research the attitudes of Austrian MEPs. In order to do so, I draw on data collected through a survey carried out within the framework of the RelEP project and complement it with an analysis of the parliamentary questions posed by Austrian MEPs during the seventh term of the EP (2009–2014). My study pursues both empirical and theoretical goals. Empirically, the aim is to increase knowledge of the attitudes of Austrian MEP towards religion. Theoretically, the aim is to make a contribution to the literature on the return of religion and postsecularism by identifying ways in which the religious/secular reconfigurations are manifested within the EP.

The main thesis is that, in the Austrian case, two seemingly contradictory phenomena coexist: the privatisation and the politicisation of religion. The privatisation of religion expresses itself in the refusal to disclose information about individual belief and in the absence from the political agenda of topics related to the role of churches and majority religions within European societies. By contrast, human rights abuses against Christian minorities abroad, the religious dimension of Turkey's candidacy to the EU and the difficulties of integrating Islam in Europe are all highly politicised topics. In short, the religion of the Other is politicised, while the religion of the majority is privatised. In this context, it is the attribution of religious belonging to the Other which serves the symbolic function of drawing identity boundaries, whereas the Self is envisaged as secular. Nevertheless, the strong mobilisation potential of this strategy points to an unacknowledged but lasting link between religion and culture in the Austrian national imaginary.

My study starts with a historical contextualisation of the Austrian case. The following sections present the empirical data from the survey and from the analysis of parliamentary questions. Finally, the conclusion assesses the data against the theoretical framework laid out in this introduction and summarises the main findings.

Religion and politics in Austria

Under Habsburg rule, the early, absolutist, Austro-Hungarian monarchy was a driving force behind the Counter-Reformation in the sixteenth and seventeenth centuries. Non-Catholics – especially Protestants and Jews – were either persecuted and expelled or forced to convert to Catholicism. The late eighteenth and nineteenth centuries saw the end of religious persecution, and with the establishment of a constitutional monarchy in 1867 freedom of religion was formally enshrined in the new constitution and laws were passed that established a liberal policy towards minority religions (Prainsack 2006). Of particular importance was the *Anerkennungsgesetz* (Law of Recognition) of 1874, which granted official recognition to the most important religions present within the empire, transforming them into 'quasi state churches' (Kalb et al. 2003, 73). After the start of the First World War and the end of the monarchy, Austrian history underwent a period of intense turbulence and political conflicts, including the rise of a fascistic variant of political Catholicism during the interwar period followed by state antagonism towards religion during the totalitarian regime of National Socialism. When the new Austrian democratic and republican state was created after the Second World War, the new constitution revived the Law of Recognition from the times of the monarchy and reconstructed a system of church–state relations based on cooperation.

Thus the Law of Recognition was instrumental in setting the legal premises for the establishment of the pluralistic inclusionary model of religious governance that remains in place in Austria to this day (Mourão Permoser and Rosenberger 2009). Of major importance is the fact that the Law of Recognition introduced into Austrian law the principle of the equality of treatment by the state of all officially recognised religions; the law therefore extended to all recognised religions the same level of rights enjoyed until then only by the dominant religion, in this case the Catholic Church (Kalb et al. 2003, 72). The establishment of this inclusionary model of religious governance thus reflected a desire to maintain the privileged position of the Catholic Church, while at the same time guaranteeing state neutrality by granting equal recognition to other religions as well.

Despite the existence of a model of religious governance based on legal pluralism, religion remained one of the defining elements in the political cleavage that characterised the Austrian state until 1918 and further into the interwar period (Pelinka and Rosenberger

2003, 199). This period was characterised by a highly divided society structured along three ideological camps (*Lager*), each possessing its own parties and organisational structures: the social democratic, the Christian social, and the German nationalist camps. The conflict between these three camps was as much about political ideology as it was about defining the identity of the polity. The position of each party towards religion reflected this conflation between identity and ideology. The social democrats propagated the creation of a Marxist parliamentary republic (*Austromarxism*), whereas the German nationalists were liberals who took an ethnic view of identity and aimed for Austria to become a part of Germany. Both were critical of the political and societal influence of the Catholic Church, which was identified with the monarchy and with political conservatism. The Christian social camp, by contrast, defined identity in religious terms, and defended the union between state and church in the form of 'political Catholicism' (Pelinka and Rosenberger 2003, 21).

This conflict was settled in the period following the Second World War, when structural transformation gradually led to the erosion of the *Lager* mentality, and democratic consolidation was accompanied by political secularisation, with all parties now accepting the separation between church and state and the Catholic Church refraining from direct interference in politics (Pelinka and Rosenberger 2003, 202). Since at least the 1970s, the role of religion in organising political preferences and social membership has been in decline, in line with the general European trend (Plasser and Ulram 2002, 93). Nevertheless, the history of entanglements between religion, identity and politics reviewed above produced three important legacies.

The first of these legacies is the role of religion as an element within the dominant national cultural narrative. As Olivier Roy points out, if we understand culture to be 'the production of symbolic systems, imaginative representations and institutions specific to a society', then religion can be seen as 'an integral part of a given culture' (Roy 2010, 26). Independently of the levels of religiosity in the population, in the national imaginary 'Austrian culture' is strongly associated with (largely desacralised) Catholic traditions. For example, Christmas and Easter are considered as part and parcel of Austrian culture. Both rituals have been largely desacralised and are perceived much more as cultural than as religious traditions. In the context of migration, however, the religious particularity of certain cultural traditions gets exposed, revealing asymmetrical power relations and providing material for political mobilisation.

The second legacy is the highly consensual model of religious governance based on institutional cooperation with several recognised religions (Potz 1996, 235). This model enjoys a very large degree of legitimacy among the population and the political elites. Evidence of the perceived legitimacy of the model can be seen in the results of a recent attempt to organise a petition against the legal privileges granted to religious communities. The petition did not receive support from any of the political parties represented in the national Parliament, and managed to collect only 56,600 signatures, which is equivalent to less than one per cent of the electorate (Volksbegehren gegen Kirchenprivilegien gescheitert 2013). The virtual consensus surrounding the model of religious governance means that the institutional arrangement governing church–state relations is a topic without any party political relevance. Political struggles over religion are fought in the symbolic, rather than the institutional, arena.

The third political legacy is visible in the party system and the way in which political ideology is emblematically associated with a certain attitude towards religion. Despite having gone through a process of transformation, democratisation and renewal, in terms of their ideological foundation the three biggest political parties – the Social Democratic

Party (*Sozialdemokratische Partei Österreichs* (SPÖ)), the People's Party (*Österreichische Volkspartei* (ÖVP)) and the Freedom Party (*Freiheitliche Partei Österreichs* (FPÖ)) – can be considered as the historical successors of, respectively, the social democratic, the Christian social and the German nationalist *Lager* of the late nineteenth and early twentieth centuries (Pelinka and Rosenberger 2003, 143–147). As we have seen, in previous times attitudes towards the Catholic Church were a key factor differentiating between these three camps. Today, the societal cleavage that gave origin to this differentiation has disappeared, but attitudes towards religion continue to influence the self-definition of the parties and their perception by the electorate.

The high degree of stability in the institutional relationship to religion at the level of the polity, as discussed above, stands in stark contrast to important transformations in terms of societal dynamics, politics and policy.

For one thing, migration and secularisation are contributing to the creation of a more diverse society. In comparison with other European countries, levels of religious observance, belief and belonging in Austria are still above average (Prainsack 2006; Polak and Schachinger 2011). Nevertheless, longitudinal data show a clear negative trend on all religious indicators, in particular since 1999 (Polak and Schachinger 2011, 197–202). Thus, according to the European Value Survey, the percentage of Austrians who believe in God has dropped from 82.9 in 1999 to 72.3 in 2008 (Polak and Schachinger 2011, 197). At the same time, society is becoming less homogeneous. As shown in Table 1, the number of persons who declare themselves as non-believers or as belonging to a religion other than Catholicism – particularly Islam – has been increasing steadily (Statistik Austria 2001). In addition, recent sexual scandals have contributed to eroding the social status of the Catholic Church, decreasing confidence in the institution and leading to a steep rise in withdrawals of membership (Kirchenausgänge gehen leicht zurück 2013).

Second, changes in legislation such as the adoption of a new civil partnership open to homosexuals in 2009 reflect the diminished influence of religion also in terms of policies (*Eingetragene Partnerschaft-Gesetz* 2009). Whereas moral arguments did play a role in the political debates surrounding the adoption of the new legislation, these were mostly restricted to symbolic issues, such as whether the new partnership could be celebrated in the same room as weddings or not, and whether partners adopting a double name should be allowed to use a hyphen between the names in the same way as married couples (Homo-Partnerschaft: ÖVP lehnt Kompromiss ab 2009). As in many other cases, here also it was at the level of symbols that the battle between secularists and defenders of religious morality was fought.

This relates well to the third and last point, which has to do with the growing importance of religion as a discursive element within exclusionary discourses targeted against immigrants. Anti-Muslim sentiments are expressed in politics through negative campaigning primarily by the far-right parties FPÖ and BZÖ (Alliance for the Future of

Table 1. Religious affiliation of the Austrian population (percentages).

Year	Catholic Church	Protestant Church	Jewish community	Islamic community	Other religion	Without religion	Not indicated
1971	87.4	6.0	0.1	0.3	1.4	4.3	0.6
1981	84.3	5.6	0.1	1.0	1.9	6.0	1.0
1991	78.0	5.0	0.1	2.0	2.8	8.6	3.5
2001	73.6	4.7	0.1	4.2	3.4	12.0	2.0

Source: Census (Statistik Austria 2001).

Austria (*Bündnis Zukunft Österreich*)). Despite the historically sceptical attitude of the Austrian far right towards religion, in the context of immigration and the growing pluralisation of society we observe a strategic use of religion as a tool for political mobilisation of feelings of belonging among the native population (Rosenberger and Mourão Permoser 2012, 49ff.; Rosenberger and Sauer 2008; Rosenberger and Hadj-Abdou 2010). Rejection of foreigners and assertion of religious identity become conflated in a strategy that aims to tap into the fears of socio-economically marginal sections of the population (on the strategic use of fear by the FPÖ see Geden 2006, especially 144ff.). This strategy has the potential to be highly effective, as opinion polls show that Austria is among the countries with the highest levels of xenophobia and Islamophobia in Europe. Thus, in a comparison of 16 Western European democracies using data from the European Value Survey 2008, Rosenberger and Seeber show that, of all countries surveyed, Austrians had by far the highest level of antipathy towards Muslims, immigrants and persons of other skin colour (Rosenberger and Seeber 2011, 182; see also Friesl et al. 2009). Also, the number of hate crimes against Muslims has risen steadily since 2008 (Muslime als Zielscheibe von Angriffen 2011; Bundesministerium für Inneres 2011). It is interesting to note that this increase in expressions of religious intolerance towards Islam occurs despite the fact that religious belonging and religiosity have been actually declining among the Austrian population. This indicates that while the societal importance of religious belief and observance is waning, the role of religion as a marker of identity is not. As we shall see, this trend is also reflected in our empirical findings about the role of religion in the attitudes of Austrian MEPs.

The survey

The Austrian delegation to the EP during the seventh term (2009–2014) was composed of 19 politicians from six political parties: six MEPs from the ÖVP, five from the SPÖ, two from the FPÖ, two from the Greens (*Die Grünen*), three who were elected through the party list known as *Liste Martin*,[1] and one from the BZÖ. The ÖVP, SPÖ and the Greens are members of the Christian Democratic (EPP), Social Democratic (S&D) and Green (Greens–European Free Alliance (EFA)) political groups in the EP respectively. The FPÖ and BZÖ are non-aligned. The *Liste Martin*, a populist anti-EU party without representation in the national Parliament, is also non-aligned, although one MEP elected through this list joined the liberal group (ALDE).

The response rate of Austrian MEPs to the RelEP questionnaire was 68% (13 out of 19 MEPs). This is a rather high response rate, even considering the small size of the overall population of Austrian MEPs. As can be seen in Table 2, the sample is well

Table 2. Austrian MEPs: number and sample.

National party	EP party group	No. in delegation	No. in sample	Share of delegation (%)	Share of sample (%)
ÖVP	EPP	6	5	32	38
SPÖ	S&D	5	2	26	15
Grünen	Greens	2	2	11	15
FPÖ	NA	2	2	11	15
Liste Martin	NA	3	1	16	8
BZÖ	NA	1	1	5	8

Source: Own compilation with information from EP website (www.europarl.europa.eu).

balanced, but is not statistically representative. In the following, given the low number of Austrian MEPs, their responses will be given in absolute numbers. Only seldom will the answers also be given in percentages in order to enable comparison with the general results. It should be noted that the low number of Austrian MEPs is nevertheless an important limitation. The generalisations made in this study must be qualified against this caveat.

Religion in the work of the EP and in the MEPs' own political practice

Broadly speaking, the results of our survey show that religion is a presence in the EP, but not a very strong one. This is true both for the average of all European MEPs and for the specific case of Austrian MEPs. Thus, a majority of Austrian MEPs (eight) say that religion has an effect on the functioning of the EP, in comparison with five who say that it has no effect. Nine Austrian MEPs (69%) and 82.8% of all MEPs believe that religion has a different importance depending on nationality. By contrast almost all Austrian MEPs (12) believe that religion does not create differences among denominations.

In terms of their own political practice, the results of our survey show that religion is a present but secondary issue on the agenda of most MEPs. Only three Austrian MEPs say that they 'often' take religion into account, whereas six say they take it into account regularly; and three say that they never have to do so and one refrained from answering this question. Thus, in total, 12 out of 13 Austrian MEPs say they have to take religion into account at least sometimes, which indicates the continued relevance of religion for politics even in a highly secularised environment such as the EP. Nevertheless, no Austrian MEPs say that they take religion into account 'permanently'. Even though within the Austrian delegation to the EP there is one MEP whose political persona is strongly defined by his religiosity – Ewald Stadler (BZÖ/NA) – there is no Austrian MEP running on an exclusively religious platform.

Among the Austrian MEPs for whom religion plays a role in their own political practice, most say that they take religion into account primarily as a social and political reality (33% (seven)); but the impact of religion as a source of personal inspiration is substantial as well (24% (five)) (see Figure 1).

Although a significant proportion of respondents acknowledge the influence of religious interest groups, the frequency of contacts between such interest groups and Austrian MEPs is lower than the average for European MEPs. About a third (four) of Austrian MEPs surveyed state that they have contact with religious or philosophical interest groups a few times a year or more, compared with over half (55.9%) of all MEPs. By contrast, about half (six) of Austrian MEPs surveyed say they have contact with religious or philosophical interest groups a few times over the course of a term, as opposed to only 22.4% of all MEPs. Only one Austrian MEP claims to have no contacts with religious interest groups at all, and two preferred not to answer this question.

Religion in policy-making

The impact of religion is felt differently across policy areas, with the areas most mentioned by Austrian MEPs being the fight against discrimination (10), social policy (six), freedom of expression (five) and external relations (five) followed by culture/education (three). The results for the whole EP are similar, except that Austrian MEPs stress the fight against discrimination as the key area where religion plays a role in the EP even more strongly than their counterparts.

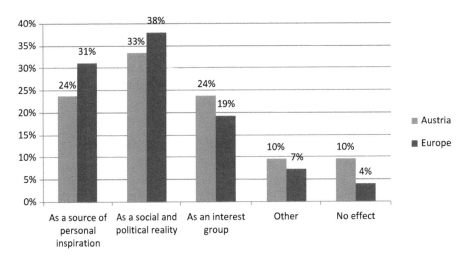

Figure 1.   If religion intervenes in your activity as an MEP, is it ...? (several responses possible). Source: Own compilation based on RelEP data.

Although MEPs are more or less evenly split as to whether religion plays a role in the EU's foreign policy (six say no, five say yes), there is nearly a consensus that it does play a role in the way that Turkey's candidacy has been received in the EP (10). These results are unsurprising given the negative attitudes towards Muslims and immigrants among the Austrian population, and they serve to highlight the importance of religion as a marker of identity, as discussed above. As Gerhards and Hans (2011) show, Austria is the EU country with the lowest support for Turkish membership in the whole EU, and one of the key variables explaining opposition to Turkish membership is perceived cultural differences and the feeling of being threatened in one's own religious values.

MEPs are almost evenly split on whether the Lisbon Treaty should have made reference to Europe's Christian heritage, with 'yes' winning in the Austrian case by six to five and 'no' winning in the European-wide case by 50.3%, even though in both cases the number of undecided is rather high. By contrast, the great majority of MEPs (69% (9) for Austria, 88.4% for Europe as a whole) approve the current practice of the president of the European Parliament of meeting regularly with representatives of major European religions to discuss current affairs.

Religious belief and preferences

The most interesting findings of RelEP for Austria refer to the questions about religious belief and preferences. Unsurprisingly, most Austrian MEPs say they are Catholic (seven). This is similar to the results for the whole of Europe. What is striking, however, is that proportionally twice as many Austrian as European MEPs of other nationalities refused to answer questions about their personal religiosity (38% (five) as opposed to 24.5%). If we concentrate on those who did answer the questions about personal religiosity, we see that only one Austrian MEP declares him/herself to be an atheist, compared with 18.4% of all European MEPs who claim to be either non-religious or atheists; and not a single Austrian MEP surveyed answers that they 'do not believe that there is any God, kind of spirit or life force', compared with 16.8% of all European MEPs.

The suspicion arises that many of those who do not believe decided not to answer. Although we cannot know for sure if those who do not declare themselves are religious or not, the contrast to the European average (in both cases about half the MEPs surveyed say that they believe in God or in a kind of spirit or life force) suggests that in the Austrian case, despite all social and political transformations, it is still politically undesirable to declare oneself as not religious. Declaring non-religiosity seems to be a taboo for Austrian politicians. Furthermore, given the high levels of consensus enjoyed by the existing cooperative model of religious governance and the low number of atheists among the population, we can surmise that it is not politically rewarding to identify oneself as an atheist.

The division of the Austrian MEPs along the lines of declared religiosity appears to be related to the ideological cleavage within the Austrian party system in a way that is reminiscent of the early twentieth century. Let us take as an example the question about the ways in which the MEP takes religion into account in his/her political practice. The percentage of Austrian MEPs who declare that they do take religion into account as a source of personal inspiration in the exercise of their mandate is relatively low in comparison with the European average (24% compared with 31.2% for the overall sample – see Figure 1). This is clearly much less than the percentage of right-wing Austrian MEPs in the EP, which totals 48% if we add together the MEPs elected through the lists of the FPÖ, BZÖ and ÖVP. So there are ideologically conservative Austrian MEPs who do not declare themselves to be inspired by religion. Nevertheless, all Austrian MEPs who say that religion is a source of personal inspiration in the exercise of their mandate are from parties which are right of centre or populist (FPÖ, BZÖ, ÖVP, Liste Martin). Not a single one of the MEPs from the Greens or the SPÖ says that religion is a source of personal inspiration for them.

Silence about one's own (non-)religiosity is therefore ideologically laden. And this ideologically-laden silence about one's own (non-)religiosity instigates a reflection about the role of religion in the definition of political identities. One possibility would be to interpret the refusal by Austrian MEPs to declare their (non-)religiosity as a strong commitment by left-wing MEPs to the narrative that modernity and the privatisation of religion are intrinsically and normatively linked. If modernity is considered to imply the banning of religion from the public sphere, a total privatisation of religion, then not declaring one's (non-)religiosity might be a way of conveying the message that one is modern and progressive. An alternative hypothesis could be that these results indicate a deep but unacknowledged link between religion and identity in Austria. In that sense, the absence of declared non-religiosity among the Austrian MEPs would be the biggest testimony to the lasting presence of religion in Austrian politics.

This interpretation is supported by the findings of the analysis of parliamentary questions to which I shall turn now. By revealing the way in which silence about one's own (non-)religiosity goes hand in hand with politicisation of the religion of the Other – in particular of Islam – this analysis enable us to better understand the link between culturally embedded religion and identity.

Parliamentary questions

In order to complement the data collected through the RelEP survey, and to gain more insight into the activities of Austrian MEPs in the EP with regard to religion, I conducted a content analysis of parliamentary questions posed by Austrian MEPs during the seventh parliamentary term (cut-off date 20 January 2013). I analysed a total of 2390 questions.

Parliamentary questions are an important political instrument for all parliamentarians. They allow MEPs to question the executive (control function) and to raise awareness about a certain issue. They are an interesting source of data in particular because they are not so strongly conditioned by party discipline, party group size or agenda-setting dynamics. In other words, they reflect the individual engagement of an MEP for a certain issue. Theoretically, parliamentary questions can also be asked about themes for which the EP has no competence, reflecting more general political concerns and controversies rather than concrete preferences on specific policy issues. However, we must take into account the fact that, as parliamentary questions are first and foremost an instrument for the legislative to control the executive, the topics of the questions are generally targeted at the actions of the European institutions that have executive function: the European Commission and the Council of the European Union. In practice they do not, therefore, address the whole palette of policy issues and topics that are potentially relevant to the relationship between religion and politics.[2] Also, non-aligned members resort to this instrument more often, because they have little access to other types of parliamentary engagement. These limitations notwithstanding, parliamentary questions are an interesting source of data for analysing the extent to which religion is visibly and explicitly brought into the legislative arena, and in what ways. They are thus a good complement to the survey, which concentrated on the more subtle and invisible ways in which religion impacts the work of MEPs.

The questions were collected from the personal webpages of the MEPs within the website of the EP. The coding was done on the basis of a content analysis of the body of the questions, not through an automatised keyword search. The aim was to select all questions related to religion. Out of the 2390 questions posed by Austrian MEPs during this term up to the cut-off date, 3.1% (75) related to religion (see Table 3). This shows that

Table 3. Parliamentary questions by Austrian MEPs during the 7th Term (2009–2014) (until the cut-off date 20 January 2013).

No.	Name	European Party group	Total questions	Religious questions	Share of total religious questions (%)
1	Angelika Werthmann	NA/ALDE	360	6	8
2	Elisabeth Köstinger	EPP	35	0	0
3	Hubert Pirker	EPP	9	0	0
4	Eva Lichtenberger	Greens	30	1	1
5	Evelyn Regner	S&D	40	2	3
6	Franz Obermayr	NA	314	25	33
7	Hannes Swoboda	S&D	19	0	0
8	Heinz K Becker	EPP	6	0	0
9	Jörg Leichtfried	S&D	56	2	3
10	Karin Kadenbach	S&D	28	0	0
11	Martin Ehrenhauser	NA	380	0	0
12	Othmar Karas	EPP	30	5	7
13	Paul Rübig	EPP	53	0	0
14	Richard Seeber	EPP	40	0	0
15	Ulrike Lunacek	Greens	84	3	4
16	Hans-Peter Martin	NA	375	3	4
17	Ewald Stadler	NA	0	0	0
18	Josef Weidenholzer	S&D	14	1	1
19	Andreas Mölzer	NA	517	27	36
	TOTAL		2390	75	100

Source: Own compilation with information from EP website (www.europarl.europa.eu).

religion is not a dominant topic among the very wide palette of topics dealt with by MEPs. Nevertheless, the analysis of the questions that do refer to religion brings a few valuable insights.

First, we see that the questions are very unevenly distributed among the MEPs, with two MEPs in particular being responsible for nearly 70% of all religion-related questions. These two MEPs are Franz Obermayr and Andreas Mölzer, both from the FPÖ. These are two of the MEPs who ask the most questions in general, but nevertheless the proportion of religious to non-religious questions asked by these MEPs is also rather high in comparison with those asked by most of their colleagues.

Second, almost all the questions about religion concern Islam in one way or another. In terms of the topics addressed, nearly 50% of the questions (36 out of 75) deal with rights violations abroad. Although this category includes violations of the rights of women, homosexuals and all types of religious minorities, the overwhelming majority of these questions are denunciations of restrictions on the freedom of religion of Christian groups in Islamic countries. And whereas most of these questions were asked by the two MEPs from the FPÖ mentioned above, one third of all questions concerning the rights of minorities abroad were asked by other MEPs. If we add to these the questions related to the threat posed by radical Islamist groups or the Islamist tendencies of foreign governments (14 out of 75) and the questions about the difficulties of incorporating Islam in Europe (7 out of 75), we find that these three categories together account for 75% of all religion-related questions asked by Austrian MEPs during the period under study.[3]

Third, no questions critically address issues related to Christianity and the role of religion within Europe. Questions relating to contentious issues within Europe that could potentially have a religious dimension, such as the negotiation or application of anti-discrimination laws, homosexual rights, women's rights and family policy, and hate crimes, are very seldom framed as having a connection to religion. Issues directly related to church–state relations – such as subsidies and privileges granted to recognised religions, or religious education in schools – are entirely absent. The issue of Christian symbols comes up only with regard to a specific, circumstantial issue, related to school calendars produced by the Commission and distributed in the member-states. These calendars did not feature any Christian holidays, including such important holidays as Christmas and Easter, and this generated great controversy. In other words, in the data analysed Christianity is made into a political topic only when it is threatened, and never in order to challenge the hegemonic position of Christian churches in Europe or to question existing institutional arrangements.

Conclusions

This study started out from the notion of postsecularism and the idea that the return of religion should not be seen as consisting in a homogeneous phenomenon, but rather in a collection of 'reconfigurations' and 'interpenetrations' between the religious and the secular. What has the study of the attitudes of Austrian MEPs shown us about these reconfigurations?

From a theoretical perspective, the main contribution of the study lies in highlighting how, in a postsecular context, the privatisation and the politicisation of religion can go hand-in-hand. The results of the RelEP survey, when combined with those of an analysis of parliamentary questions, show a strong contrast between the visibility of the religion of the Others (in this case Muslims) as a political issue on the one hand, and the invisibility of the majority religion as a political issue on the other hand.

In order to illustrate this point, it is useful to differentiate between three levels at which religion can play a role within the secular context of the EP: issues, actors, and preferences.

Our analysis shows that for Austrian MEPs religion plays a role at the level of issues, in the sense that religion is in fact a topic of political deliberation, but in the data analysed this concerns primarily the religion of the Other. There is an imbalance in the way that different religions are subject to politicisation. Pieter de Wilde defines politicisation through three elements: (i) the political salience of a given issue; (ii) the fact that a topic is contentious; (iii) the expression of demands for change (de Wilde 2007). The place of religion within the EU or in the national politics of European countries is neither salient, nor contentious, nor subject to demands for change by Austrian MEPs. Arrangements between church and state, violations of religious freedom and incompatibilities between religious demands and human rights are made into a salient political topic subject to demands for change only when they concern non-European countries and non-European religions, in particular Islam. In other words, whereas the religion of the Other is politicised, the religion of the Self is not.

Revealingly, this politicisation of the religion of the Other is carried out not primarily by those historically linked to religion, but rather by far-right populists without strong religious ties. The phenomenon can also be observed in national politics. For example, during a demonstration against an Islamic prayer house in 2009 the leader of the FPÖ, Heinz-Christian Strache, appeared holding a big wooden crucifix. Catholic authorities heavily criticised this and other appearances as a manipulation of Christian symbols for electoral purposes (Strache will Schönborn treffen 2009). Strache also decided to take the sacrament of confirmation in the run-up to the local elections (FPÖ-Chef Strache lässt sich firmen 2009). However, this symbolic rapprochement with religion has not prevented him from recently making anticlerical statements when criticising the Catholic Church for hosting a protest by asylum seekers (Schönborn rügt FPÖ-Politiker Strache wegen Zeitungsinserat 2013).

The opportunist use of religion is explained by the fact that, in the context of immigration, when traditional notions of identity come under threat, the politicisation of the religion of the Other (in this case Islam) serves the function of mobilising feelings of belonging among the majority population (see Rosenberger and Mourão Permoser 2012). But the question arises as to how this is possible in a period in which religious belief and affiliation to the dominant Catholic Church is waning. In order to understand this, it is important to take into consideration the role of culturally embedded religion in the definition of national identity. The mobilisation of belonging on the basis of the politicisation of religious difference does not target particularly faithful groups in the majority population. Rather, it is aimed at the masses, and its success is due to the existence of a largely unacknowledged link between identity and religion in the Austrian self-perception. In that sense, one can also speak of a return (or a permanence) of religion at the level of 'actors' – in terms of their identities – although this return is ideologically laden and politically sensitive (thus often repressed), with an ethicised and largely de-sacralised understanding of religion functioning as a concealed marker of distinction.

On the third dimension, we note that many MEPs argue that religion plays a role in defining the preferences of MEPs on issues of moral relevance, even though this impact does not appear in the discourse of the MEPs, as exemplified by the analysis of the parliamentary questions. One of the implications of this is that we should be wary of drawing conclusions about the impact of religion in politics from its mere visibility or invisibility. In particular with regard to political preferences, we should not take visibility of religion in public discourse for influence and invisibility for irrelevance. As political actors acting in a postsecular context translate religiously motivated positions into secular vocabulary, the influence of religion becomes less visible and more difficult to identify.

Acknowledgments

I would like to thank the participants of the conferences 'Religion in the European Parliament' (Brussels, 13–14 June 2013) and 'Rethinking Europe with or without Religion' (Vienna, 20–23 February 2013), the editor of *Religion, State & Society* and the anonymous reviewers for their helpful comments on earlier versions of this study. I would like to especially thank François Foret for his advice during the course of this research and for his helpful suggestions on earlier drafts, as well as for having invited me to participate in the RelEP project in the first place.

Notes

1. Two of the three MEPs elected through this list left the party following accusations of corruption directed at Hans-Peter Martin. Angelika Werthmann left in 2010 and eventually joined the ALDE (liberals) group at the EP. Martin Ehrenhauser left in 2011 and remained unaligned. In order to avoid confusion, in this text I shall classify all politicians according to the party through which they were elected.
2. This might explain why topics such as stem-cell research or the controversies over the Christian heritage of Europe did not come up at all, which again might help explain the absence of politicisation of Christianity. In that sense, the limitations of the data might have contributed to the findings presented in this study. Nevertheless, there are a number of areas in which the EU has competence and the EU executive is responsible for monitoring implementation of controversial policies that stand in potential conflict with the majority religion, and yet which nevertheless do not come up in the parliamentary questions (for example anti-discrimination policy). For this reason it can be argued that the data presented in this study, despite the limitations, do provide a solid indication of a trend towards a disproportionate politicisation of Islam in comparison to Christianity. (I would like to thank an anonymous reviewer for calling my attention to this point.)
3. A complete list of all religious questions and detailed information on the method used for coding can be obtained from the author on request.

References

Bundesministerium für Inneres. 2011. *Verfassungsschutzbericht 2011* [Constitutional Report 2011]. http://www.bmi.gv.at/cms/BMI_Verfassungsschutz/BVT_VSB_2011_online.pdf.

Casanova, J. 1994. *Public Religions in the Modern World*. Chicago: Chicago University Press.

Casanova, J. 2006. "Religion, European Secular Identities, and European Integration." In *Religion in an Expanding Europe*, edited by P. J. Katzenstein and T. A. Byrnes, 65–92. Cambridge: Cambridge University Press.

de Wilde, P. 2007. *Politicisation of European Integration: Bringing the Process into Focus* (*ARENA Working Papers* 18). http://www.sv.uio.no/arena/english/research/publications/arena-publications/workingpapers/working-papers2007/wp07_18.pdf.

Eingetragene Partnerschaft-Gesetz [Federal Law on Registered Partnerships]. 2009. https://www.ris.bka.gv.at/GeltendeFassung.wxe?Abfrage=Bundesnormen&Gesetzesnummer=20006586&ShowPrintPreview=True.

"FPÖ-Chef Strache lässt sich firmen" [FPÖ Leader Strache Receives the Sacrament of Confirmation]. 2009. *Österreich*, May 29. http://www.oe24.at/oesterreich/politik/FPOe-Chef-Strache-laesst-sich-firmen/540361.

Friesl, C., U. Harnachers-Zuba, and R. Polak, eds. 2009. *Die österreicher/-innen: Wertewandel 1990–2008* [The Austrians: Value Changes 1990–2008]. Vienna: Czernin.

Geden, O. 2006. *Diskursstrategien im Rechts-populismus* [Discursive Strategies in Right-Wing Populism]. Wiesbaden: Springer VS.

Gerhards, J., and S. Hans. 2011. "Why not Turkey? Attitudes Towards Turkish Membership in the EU among Citizens in 27 European Countries." *JCMS: Journal of Common Market Studies* 49 (4): 741–766. doi:10.1111/j.1468-5965.2010.02155.x.

Göle, N. 2013. "Manifestations of the Religious–Secular Divide: Self, State and the Public Sphere." In *L'europe et le legs de l'Occident* [Europe and the Legacy of the West], edited by Académie de la Latinité, 359–382. Rio de Janeiro: Educam. http://www.alati.com.br/pdf/2013/paris/18-Paris-Nilufer-Gole.pdf

Habermas, J. 2008. "Notes on a Post-Secular Society." *Signandsight*. http://www.signandsight.com/features/1714.html.

"Homo-Partnerschaft: ÖVP lehnt Kompromiss ab" [Homosexual Partnership: ÖVP Rejects Compromise]. 2009. *Die Presse*, November 14. http://diepresse.com/home/politik/innenpolitik/521709/HomoPartnerschaft_OeVP-lehnt-Kompromiss-ab.

Kalb, H., R. Potz, and B. Schinkele. 2003. *Religionsrecht* [Religious Law]. Vienna: WUV.

Katzenstein, P. J. 2006. "Multiple Modernities as Limits to Secular Europeanization?" In *Religion in an Expanding Europe*, edited by T. A. Byrnes and P. J. Katzenstein, 1–33. Cambridge: Cambridge University Press.

Katzenstein, P. J., and T. A. Byrnes. 2006. "Transnational Religion in an Expanding Europe." *Perspectives on Politics* 4 (4): 679–694.

"Kirchenausgänge gehen leicht zurück" [Church Withdrawals Slightly Decline]. 2013. *ORF*, January 8. http://oesterreich.orf.at/stories/2566195/

Mourão Permoser, J., and S. Rosenberger. 2009. "Religious Citizenship versus Policies of Migrant Integration: The Case of Austria." In *International Migration and the Governance of Religious Diversity*, edited by P. Bramadat and M. Koenig, 259–292. Montreal: McGill–Queen's University Press.

"Muslime als Zielscheibe von Angriffen" [Muslims as Targets of Attacks]. 2011. *Die Presse*, September 6. http://diepresse.com/home/panorama/integration/691255/Muslime-als-Zielscheibe-von-Angriffen.

Pelinka, A., and S. Rosenberger. 2003. *Österreichische Politik: Grundlagen, Strukturen, Trends* [Austrian Politics: Fundamentals, Structures, Trends]. Vienna: WUV.

Plasser, F., and P. Ulram. 2002. *Das österreichische Politikverständnis: von der Konsens – zur Konfliktkultur?* [The Austrian Political Consciousness: From a Culture of Consensus to a Culture of Conflict?]. Vienna: WUV.

Polak, R., and C. Schachinger. 2011. "Stabil in Veränderung: Konfessionsnahe Religiosität in Europa" [Stable in Change: Confessional Religiosity in Europe]. In *Zukunft. Werte. Europa. Die Europäische Wertestudie 1990–2010: Österreich im Vergleich* [Future. Values. Europe. The European Value Study 1990–2010: Austria in Comparison], edited by R. Polak, 191–222. Vienna: Böhlau.

Potz, R. 1996. "State and Church in Austria." In *State and Church in the European Union*, edited by G. Robbers, 229–258. Baden Baden: Nomos.

Prainsack, B. 2006. "Religion und Politik" [Religion and Politics]. In *Politik in Osterreich: das Handbuch* [Politics in Austria: Handbook], edited by H. Dachs, P. Gerlich, H. Gottweis, H. Kramer, V. Lauber, W. C. Müller, and E. Talos, 538–549. Vienna: Manz.

Rosenberger, S., and L. Hadj-Abdou. 2010. "Islam at Issue: Anti-islamic Discourse of the Far Right in Austria." In *The Far Right in Contemporary Europe*, edited by B. Jenkins, E. Godin, and A. Mammone, 149–163. New York: Palgrave Macmillan.

Rosenberger, S., and J. Mourão Permoser. 2012. "Zugehörigkeit mobilisieren, politisieren, de-politisieren: Analysen aus dem Wiener Gemeindebau" [Mobilising, Politicising and Depoliticising Belonging: Analyses from the Viennese Social Housing Complexes]. In

Living Rooms: Politik der Zugehörigkeit im Wiener Gemeindebau [Living Rooms: Politics of Belonging in Viennese Social Housing], edited by F. Bettel, J. Mourão Permoser, and S. Rosenberger, 19–74. Vienna: Springer.

Rosenberger, S., and B. Sauer. 2008. "Islam im öffentlichen Raum: Debatten und Regulationen in Europa: eine Einführung" [Islam in the Public Sphere: Debates and Regulations in Europe: An Introduction]. *Österreichische Zeitschrift für Politikwissenschaft* 4: 387–399.

Rosenberger, S., and G. Seeber. 2011. "Kritische Einstellungen: BürgerInnen zu Demokratie, Politik, Migration" [Critical Attitudes: Citizens on Democracy, Politics and Migration]. In *Zukunft. Werte. Europa. Die Europäische Wertestudie 1990–2010: Österreich im Vergleich* [Future. Values. Europe. The European Value Study 1990–2010: Austria in Comparison], edited by R. Polak, 165–189. Vienna: Böhlau.

Roy, O. 2010. *Holy Ignorance: When Religion and Culture Part Ways*. New York: Columbia University Press.

"Schönborn rügt FPÖ-Politiker Strache wegen Zeitungsinserat" [Schönborn Reprimands FPÖ Politician Strache for Newspaper Advert]. 2013. *Katholische Nachrichten*, January 17. http://www.kath.net/news/39700

Statistik Austria. 2001. *Bevölkerung 2001 nach Religionsbekenntnis und Staatsangehörigkeit* [Population in 2001 according to Religious Affiliation and Citizenship]. http://www.statistik.at/web_de/statistiken/bevoelkerung/volkszaehlungen_registerzaehlungen/bevoelkerung_nach_demographischen_merkmalen/022894.html.

"Strache will Schönborn treffen" [Strache Wants to Meet Schönborn]. 2009. *Österreich*, May 25. http://www.oe24.at/oesterreich/politik/Strache-will-Schoenborn-treffen/537105.

"Volksbegehren gegen Kirchenprivilegien gescheitert" [Petition against Church Privileges Fails]. 2013. *ORF*, April 22. http://religion.orf.at/stories/2581175/.

Politics and religion beyond state borders: the activity of Spanish MEPs on religious issues

Gloria García-Romeral and Mar Griera

ISOR- Departament de Sociologia, Universitat Autònoma de Barcelona, Edifici B 08193, Bellaterra (Barcelona), Spain

This study examines the interplay between the political and religious factors in the activity of Spanish members of the European Parliament (MEPs) in their work within the European Parliament (EP). First, we explore the impact of Spanish MEPs' religious preferences and ideological beliefs regarding religious affairs on their parliamentary activity. Second, we analyse the parliamentary activity of Spanish MEPs (parliamentary questions and motions for resolution) related to religious affairs. We argue that the rapid and profound process of secularisation in the Spanish population is also observable in the stances of MEPs towards religious affairs. Most of them perceive religious issues as belonging to only the private sphere, and do not consider that their personal religious affiliation and preferences should play any role in their political activity in the EP. The analysis also shows that religion is mainly addressed in an indirect way in the EP and is not a central concern on the agenda. We conclude that despite the fact that religion plays a minor role, the analysis of the activity of Spanish MEPs permits us to detect an affinity between ideological and religious positions. Therefore we argue that the religious cleavage that has characterised the history of Spain, despite having lost its historical strength, is still detectable in the activity of MEPs: right-wing parties are defenders of the values and interests of the Catholic Church within the EP, while left-wing parties have a more secularist agenda and use the EP as an arena to denounce the privileges and attitudes of the Catholic Church in Spain.

Introduction

Over the last decade religion has again become a contested issue in the public sphere (Casanova 2008). The secularisation thesis has been widely questioned within academia (Berger 1999; Beckford 2003) and we are witnessing a revival of religious traditions all over the world (Davie 2002). At first glance, Europe seems to be an exception to this scenario, as most data concerning individuals' religious beliefs and practices indicate that there are no clear signs of a religious revival. On the contrary, in most European countries, personal affiliations to world religions and the practice of religious rituals are declining, as is the case in Spain (Pérez-Agote 2012).

However, a closer look at this context shows that 'one of the ironies of secularisation (however the term is defined) is that it does not necessarily mean that religion becomes unproblematic ... on the contrary, religion becomes more controversial' (Beckford 1999, 55). To a certain extent the diversification of the religious sphere and the increasing importance of Islam in Europe have become fertile soil for public controversy. Likewise, the emergence and growth of far-right groups in Europe (Zúquete 2008; Hernández-Carr 2011) have contributed to problematising the new religious landscape and have led to a greater saliency for religion in the public sphere.

In this scenario it is also extremely important to recognise that it would be a 'big mistake to attribute this new attention on issues of religion solely or even mainly to the rise of Islamic fundamentalism and to threats and challenges which it poses to the West, particularly to Europe' (Casanova 2008, 71). The role played by Christianity in the current context must not be underestimated. On the one hand, it is important to recall that Europe's historical churches still have a hegemonic position in most European societies and most of them maintain close ties with governments (Bader 2007; Davie 2000). On the other hand, the reconfiguration of the Christian sphere has led, in recent years, to the participation of new Christian groups in public and political spheres. To some degree these groups are becoming increasingly important players in shaping the public, political and media perspectives toward conflictive issues such as abortion and religious education (Hennig 2012; Aguilar Fernández 2012). On this question, Julio Ferrari says

the decline of the historical churches' power to speak on behalf of the whole European society has been balanced by the development, within these same churches, of new groups and movements, such as Pentecostals and 'born again' Christians in the Protestant field and Communion and Liberation and Opus Dei in the Catholic one. All of these are motivated by a desire to give expression to their strong religious identity in all fields of human life and, consequently, they want to affirm the religious foundation of ethical, cultural and political choices. (Ferrari 2008, 105)

There are some authors who have already addressed the European dimension of this increasing salience of religion (Katzenstein 2006) through the analysis of key debate issues in the framework of the European Union (EU), such as the debate over the preamble of the EU Constitution (and its mention of Christianity) (Casanova 2006; Schlesinger and Foret 2006), or the debate over Turkey's membership of the EU (Yeğenoğlu 2006; Klausen 2005). However, in general, the role that religion plays in the 'EU political system' (Hix 1999; Hix and Hoyland 2011) has received very little attention to date (Silvestri 2009). Furthermore, there is an absolute lack of research on the interplay between member-states and the European Parliament (EP) concerning religious affairs. Most of the existing literature focuses on the impact of religious actors on the European Commission, but analysis of the role of religion in the legislative activity of members of the EP (MEPs) has been neglected.

This study aims to address this gap through a twofold approach: first by analysing the impact of the religious preferences and ideological beliefs regarding religious issues of Spanish MEPs on their parliamentary activity; and, second, by examining the activity of Spanish MEPs regarding religious affairs in the context of EP (parliamentary questions and motions for resolution). This dual approach permits us to better capture the idiosyncrasy of the interplay between political and the religious factors in the activity of MEPs in the framework of the EP, as well as to provide a more complex, nuanced and empirically grounded picture. We place a special focus on inquiring into the links between the political ideological positions and the religious positions of MEPs, with the aim of exploring the evolution and shape of this relationship.

The methodological approach was designed combining two complementary research methods. First, in order to explore the personal religious beliefs and opinions of Spanish

Table 1. Parliamentary questions and motions for resolution regarding religious affairs by Spanish MEPs and political group (from 1999 to April 2013).

Political group	MEPs	Parliamentary questions	Motions for resolution
EPP	57 (41%)	3069	1090
S&D	54 (38.8%)	2820	1031
ALDE	9 (6.5%)	1526	623
Greens/EFA	11 (7.9%)	2389	806
GUE/NGL	6 (4.3%)	1122	559
NI	2 (1.4%)	141	9
Total	139 (100%)	11,067	4118

Source: European Parliament website. Own compilation.

MEPs regarding religious issues, a survey based on the general questionnaire designed for this purpose in the framework of the RelEP project[1] was conducted. A total of 11 questionnaires were collected, which represents 20.4% of Spanish MEPs. Once all the information was collected, an analysis of descriptive statistics was developed. Second, we analysed the parliamentary activity of Spanish MEPs in plenary sessions by examining and assessing the presence and role of religion in the parliamentary questions and motions for resolution. This led to the creation of a sample of all the 11,067 parliamentary questions and 4118 parliamentary motions posed by Spanish MEPs during the 5th (1999–04), 6th (2004–09) and 7th legislatures (from 2009 to April 2013) of the EP (Table 1).[2]

Our study argues that the rapid and profound process of secularisation in the Spanish population is also observable in the stances of MEPs towards religious affairs. Religious issues are considered to belong to the private realm and MEPs state that their personal religious affiliations do not play a role in their political activity in the EP. However, the analysis also shows that religion is mainly addressed in an indirect way in the EP and is not a central concern on the agenda. We conclude that despite the fact that religion plays a minor role in the EP, the analysis of the activity of Spanish MEPs permits us to detect a clear affinity between ideological and religious positions. Therefore we argue that the religious cleavage that has characterised the history of Spain, although it has lost its historical strength, is still observable in the activity of MEPs: right-wing parties are defenders of the values and interests of the Catholic Church within the EP while left-wing parties have a more secularist agenda and use the EP as an arena to denounce the privileges and attitudes of the Catholic Church in Spain.

Our study is structured as follows: the first section discusses the general political and social role that religion has played in Spain's recent history; the second section examines the main results of the survey; and the third section is devoted to analysing the parliamentary activity of Spanish MEPs. We conclude with some final reflections.

The Catholic Church in Spain: some insights on its social, political and historical role

The Catholic Church and the fierce and bloody battles between its opponents and defenders have comprehensively marked the Spanish path towards democracy. The zenith of this complicated relationship was during the Second Republic and the subsequent Civil War (1936–39). The Second Republic was characterised by the acute confrontation between clericalist and anti-clericalist groups over all the initiatives aimed at regulating the role of the Catholic Church in the country (Piñol 1993). These disputes completely blocked the functioning of democracy. The rebellion of far right and right-wing groups commanded by Franco in 1936 put an end to the democratic period and led to the Civil War and the dictatorship. As Casanova (1994) says, the case of Spain represents an extreme version of what David Martin has termed 'the French (Latin) pattern' in which

> such revolutionary explosions become endemic, and religion as such is frequently a political issue. Coherent and massive secularism confronts coherent and massive religiosity ... one ethos confronts an alternative ethos, particularly where the elite culture of the secular Enlightenment acquires a mass component and achieves a historicised ideology, i.e. Marxism. (Martin 1978, 6)

To some extent, this was a conflict between 'moderns' and 'ancients' in which liberal and Europeanised sectors of society confronted the Catholic sectors and vice versa (Casanova 1994).

The Civil War was a zero-sum game; the country was completely divided and the Catholic Church took a clear side: it welcomed the nationalists who promised to restore Christian civilisation and once in power re-established the dominant position of the Church in the public and political spheres (Anderson 2003). The 1953 Concordat between the Spanish government and the Vatican granted legal recognition to this monopolistic position and reinforced the role of the Church as one of the most salient institutions during this period. The Concordat not only secured the hegemonic position of the Church in Spanish society, but also strengthened the power of the dictator within the Church, since it granted Franco a key role in appointing the diocesan bishops. To a certain extent the Spanish dictatorship favoured a symbiotic relationship between the political and the religious realms. Both powers went hand in hand and they mutually legitimised each other.

However, the Second Vatican Council and the modernisation of the country opened fissures in the stance of the Catholic Church towards Franco and favoured the emergence of dissident Catholic groups (Piñol 1993). This generated a reconfiguration of the Catholic scene that opened up new possibilities for democracy in Spain (Brassloff 1998).

The death of Franco in 1975 facilitated regime change in Spain. During the democratic transition the main political parties opted to 'depoliticise' issues with religious connotations, such as the debate on abortion or on the funding of religious schools (Montero, Calvo, and Martínez 2008, 44). Spanish policymakers were convinced that in order to maintain the 'consensus climate' of the democratic transition it was necessary to postpone these debates until the consolidation of democracy (Díaz-Salazar 1990). To some extent, the memory of the Civil War was still very vivid and no one was willing to jeopardise the democratic transition. Martínez-Torrón says that

> the triumph and subsequent consolidation of democracy in Spain required, as an indispensable condition, a situation of 'religious peace', which could be reached only by careful avoidance of extreme solutions. Otherwise, there was the risk that fears of a 'new Second

Republic' would condemn Spain again to a period of political stagnation. (Martínez-Torrón 2006, 788)

In a similar vein, Casanova says that 'the immediate need to defend the transition still threatened by the danger of military coup and by the terrorism of the right and the left, partly explains the willingness to compromise exhibited by most political forces' (Casanova 1994, 88). The new democratic Constitution declared Spain to be a non-confessional country and the signing of the Concordat Agreements between the Spanish government and the Vatican in 1979 set the rules for church–state cooperation under democracy. Likewise, the Religious Freedom Act (7/1980) and the Cooperation Agreements between the Spanish government and the Jewish, Protestant and Muslim communities (1992) granted freedom of thought and religion to every individual.

During the 1980s the Catholic Church did not play a consistent political role in Spain but maintained a low public profile. The relationship between the Spanish government and the Catholic Church was not always smooth, especially in the first years of the socialist (PSOE) government (Brassloff 1998), but 'religious battles' were losing their previous relevance (Griera 2012). In certain political debates the Spanish Episcopal Conference made its voice heard in defending its interests, but this was not a general pattern. It is also worth noting that some of the interventions by the Church in the public arena in that period were aimed at strengthening the democratic profile of the Church by showing its support for government decisions, such as when Spain joined the EU. The Spanish Episcopal Conference made several statements on the benefits of being part of the EU and giving support to deepening the Europeanisation process (PCEE 1985; APCEE 1993).

However, the evolution of the political debates in Spain during the 1990s, and above all since the 2000s, has been deepening the opposition between the two major parties on the basis of religion (Montero, Calvo, and Martínez 2008). In this sense, the political agenda of the so-called 'moral politics' of the Zapatero government was strongly contested in the public sphere but also in the legal arenas by Catholic groups and lobbies. According to Aguilar Fernández, in contrast with other churches under similar political circumstances the Spanish Catholic Church 'has explicitly adopted a belligerent political role in the fight against abortion and same-sex marriage' (Aguilar Fernández 2012, 685) and embarked upon a confrontational strategy in alliance with conservative Catholic groups and like-minded political parties.

This strategy of confrontation has also been apparent concerning the position of the Church towards EU affairs, as revealed by the attitude of the Episcopal Conference to the proposed European Constitution (SGCEE 2005). The Spanish Church publicly stated its disagreement on several issues addressed in the Constitution, such as the lack of explicit affirmation of Europe's Christian heritage or the Constitution's so-called 'ambiguous' position on moral issues such as abortion and stem cell research.

During the last decade, new Catholic-inspired interest groups have emerged in the public sphere, which have been developing diverse mobilisation strategies including mass public demonstrations, lawsuits and the dissemination of manifestos (Díaz-Salazar 2008). To some extent, the Catholic Church has increased its presence in the public sphere and has started to play politics in a more direct fashion. On most occasions it is not the Church itself that promotes these mobilisation strategies but new pastoral movements such as the *Camino Neocatecumenal*, the *Legionarios de Cristo* or Christian organisations focused on particular issues such as pro-life or Christian parents' associations. The victory of the People's Party (*Partido Popular*) (PP), a right-wing party, in the 2011 general elections has reduced the tension between the government and the Catholic Church, because of the affinity between the political programme of the PP and the Church's interests and values (Aguilar Fernández 2011).[3] Berretini defines the relationship of the Catholic Church with the PP as 'characterised by a tension between proximity and blackmail' (Berretini 2013, 169). Rajoy's government has revealed its affinity with the Church through certain political measures very close to the interests of the Church and Catholic lobbying groups.[4]

This increase in the profile of religious–moral issues in the public sphere in recent years has gone in parallel with the greater visibility and salience of religious minorities in Spain. The growth of Islamic and Pentecostal groups, owing to the rise of international migration flows towards Spain, has been especially notable (Martínez-Ariño et al. 2011; Díez de Velasco 2012). However, as de Busser says, Spain has shown itself to be a 'relatively tolerant country, particularly when compared to other Western European countries' (de Busser 2006, 292) regarding its attitude towards religious minorities. In a similar vein, Itçaina stresses that, in general, the Catholic Church has not displayed an attitude of distrust toward, or opposition to, religious minorities, but has adopted a 'favourable position on religious pluralism' (Itcaina 2006, 1480). However, this rise in the visibility of religion in the public sphere has not been accompanied by a general growth in religious memberships. On the contrary, religious affiliation and religious practices and belief have been declining gradually and constantly (Pérez-Agote 2012).

Spanish secularisation occurred later than the European average but, after the democratic transition and as noted by Davie, the collapse of religious practice has been stronger than anywhere else, and the same has happened with priest recruitment (Davie 2001). According to Aguilar Fernández (2012), it is important to take into account that the Catholic Church is a questioned and delegitimised institution within the Spanish context. González-Anleo (2008) says that fewer than 50% of the Spanish population place any kind of trust in the Spanish Episcopal Conference – a percentage that is below the European average. In addition, around 80% of Spaniards say that the Catholic Church should not have any influence on voting or political life. Also noteworthy is the significant number of Spaniards who affirmed that the Spanish Episcopal Conference has much more power in Spain than it deserves.

A significant point is that in general Spaniards have liberal attitudes towards contentious moral issues. Aguilar Fernández says that it is important to note that

> In a recent survey by the Sociological Research Centre, CIS (n° 2752, 2008), 60 per cent, 62.1 per cent, and 51.7 per cent of the respondents were against the Spanish Catholic Conference stance on abortion, same-sex marriage, and the adoption of children by gay couples, respectively. The prevalence of 'liberal' approaches to moral issues is most extraordinary in the face of the existence of 95.1 per cent of Spaniards above 18 who in 2002 affirmed to have had a Catholic upbringing. (Aguilar Fernández 2012, 683)

To summarise, despite the fact that the historical political cleavage between clerical and anticlerical forces has lost strength, it is still perceptible at the political level and forms an identity trait of both the left-wing and the right-wing ideological families. In addition, the Spanish population has experienced a strong and rapid secularisation process that has contributed to spreading the idea that religion has no role in politics.

The stances of Spanish MEPs towards religious issues

There are 54 Spanish MEPs in the EP, distributed along the following political lines. The European People's Party (Christian Democrats) (EPP) and the Socialists and Democrats

Table 2. Summary of responses to the RelEP survey by Spanish MEPs in the 7th Legislature (2009–14).

Political group	MEPs	RelEP responses	Explicit refusal to participate	No answer
EPP	25	3	3	19
	(46.3%)	(12%)	(12%)	(76%)
S&D	23	6	4	13
	(42.6%)	(26.1%)	(17.4%)	(56.5%)
ALDE	2	0	1	1
	(3.7%)		(50%)	(50%)
Greens/EFA	2	1	0	1
	(3.7%)	(50%)		(50%)
GUE/NGL	1	0	0	1
	(1.9%)			(1%)
NI	1	1	0	0
	(1.9%)	(100%)		
Total	54	11	8	35
	(100%)	(20.4%)	(14.8%)	(64.8%)

Source: Compiled by the authors.

(S&D) are the major parliamentary groups with 25 and 23 MEPs respectively.[5] The others are: the Alliance of Liberals and Democrats for Europe (ALDE) (2 MEPs),[6] the Greens/ European Free Alliance (Greens/EFA) (2 MEPs),[7] the European United Left/Nordic Green Left (GUE/NGL) (1 MEP),[8] and one non-attached MEP.[9] 40% (22) of Spanish MEPs in this legislative term are women.

In this section we examine the main results of the survey conducted in the framework of the RelEP project aimed at studying the religious preferences of MEPs and the impact of those preferences on their political behaviour. Table 2 summarises the responses collected.

Among the respondents, 7 out of 11 were men (64%). The average age of the MEPs who answered the survey was 57; the youngest was 37 and the oldest was 72. The majority of respondents (7) are MEPs first elected in this legislative term (2009–2014), in comparison with those who have been MEPs in two or three terms (4). To a certain degree, both the responses collected and the refusal to participate in the survey – the refusal rate was 14.8% (8 MEPs) – are indicative of the uncomfortable, ambiguous and changing relationship of Spanish policymakers towards religion. We first provide a brief analytical description of the results and then explore the reasons behind the low participation rates.

Regarding the questions about the impact of religion on the way the EP works, 7 out of the 11 respondents (63.6%) believe that religion does not have any effect at all. But there is no clear position on the role that religious affiliation plays in the configuration of European political groups: 6 MEPs (54.5%) think that religion reinforces the identity of each political group, while the remaining 5 do not think it does. Only 2 MEPs believe that religion produces differences between MEPs; 9 of the 11 respondents (81.8%) say that the significance of religion depends on the nationality of the MEP.

Regarding the role of religion in the political practice and political socialisation of MEPs, 6 of the Spanish MEPs (54.5%) say that they rarely take religion into account in the course of their duties and 4 say that they never do so. Most of the respondents do not consider religion to have any effect on their activity as an MEP. Six think that there are no differences between the role of religion in the EP and in the Spanish Parliament; 10 of the 11 respondents (90.9%) think that their experience as MEPs has not changed their perception of the relationship between religion and politics. However, a significant portion of them (45%) hold meetings with religious interest groups at least once a legislative sitting, with Caritas being one of the most frequently mentioned (by two MEPs from the EPP and one from the S&D). Only one of the respondents (from the S&D) reports meeting with an atheist lobby group a few times per year. These values are close to the frequency with which Spanish MPs hold meetings with religious interest groups. According to the results of the PartiRep research project,[10] 48.3% of Spanish MPs hold meetings with religious organisations at least once a year.

In relation to policy sectors and topics where religion is the most salient as an issue on the European agenda, the responses show that Spanish MEPs do not identify a clear sector or issue in the EP where religion plays an important role. Seven respondents (63.6%) believe that religion should not be an area of EU policy action. The same number think that religion has no influence in the external relations of the EU and that no reference to a Christian heritage should be included in the preamble of the Lisbon Treaty. At the same time, 9 of the respondents (81.8%) recognise that religion has played an important role in certain debates such as the entry of Turkey into the EU; and 8 respondents (72.7%) value positively the fact that religious leaders hold meetings with the president of the EP.

Finally, as far as the religious preferences of the MEPs are concerned, 8 of the 11 Spanish respondents (72.7%) say that they have no religious affiliation. Only 3 respondents (two from the EPP and one from the ALDE) define themselves as Catholics; 3 define themselves as 'non-religious'; while 5 (45.5%) (all from the S&D) define themselves as 'atheists'. The questions on religious practice confirm these results: 8 of the 11 respondents (72.7) say that they never go to any religious services other than weddings, funerals and religious celebrations such as Christmas. Likewise, regarding the separation between political and religious spheres, 10 of the 11 believe that religious leaders should not influence individuals' votes in an election and 7 (63.6%) think that religious leaders should not influence government decisions. At the same time, 9 (81.8%) of the respondents do not consider that it is better to have strong religious values in the exercise of public office. Virtually all the respondents (10) disagree strongly with the statement that non-religious individuals are less suitable for public office. These findings are highly consistent with the results of surveys of the broader Spanish population (Pérez-Agote 2012).

After this brief description of the survey results, it is important to analyse what has been one of the most unexpected findings: the low rate of participation and the explicit refusal to participate by many of the Spanish MEPs: 35 (64.8%) did not answer the questionnaire despite being contacted by mail and telephone several times (and in most cases we reached their assistants). Even more interesting sociologically is that 8 (14.8 %) not only did not participate but made their disagreement with the types of question raised in the survey explicit. The primary argument put forward by these MEPs was that 'religious preferences and opinions are a strictly private affair'. Initially, we assumed that they were concerned about issues of confidentiality, as Spanish legislation does not permit the collection of information on religious affiliation.[11] Aiming to increase the number of respondents, we worked to increase the anonymity of the MEPs; however, most were still reticent about filling in the questionnaire.[12]

To a certain degree, the refusal to answer questions about one's religious preferences and beliefs is consistent with the conviction that religion belongs to the private sphere, a principle that is shared by most Spaniards and that goes hand in hand with the rapid and deep secularisation process that has occurred in the country. However, we argue that we cannot understand this almost aggressive refusal to talk about one's religious beliefs and preferences without taking into account Spain's conflictive and dramatic religious past. Furthermore, this dramatic past has not been openly discussed yet. There is no shared historical narrative of the clericalist-anticlericalist division in Spain that could serve as a common framework for dealing with religious issues in current times. During the democratic transition, the strong fear of reproducing history kept religion out of the political debate. As Casanova pointed out 'only the more remote background of the collective memory of the negative experience of the civil war and of the system of exclusion which followed it may explain the fact that the politics of consensus, so characteristic of the Spanish transition, became almost an end in itself' (Casanova 1994, 88). The transition followed a politics of consensus and silence that was very useful at that moment in time but did not permit a historical and political narrative to be constructed (Colom González 2010). This lack of a common and shared narrative makes religious issues (and above all, the relationship between religion and politics) especially uncomfortable.

Spanish MEPs' parliamentary activity and religion

This second section is devoted to an examination of the parliamentary activity of Spanish MEPs in religious matters, conducted through the construction of a data-set including all the questions and motions for resolution dealing with religious affairs. The aim has been to address the following questions. What presence does religion have in the EP? What issues related to religion do Spanish MEPs raise or debate? How does an MEP's political affiliation influence the themes and content of his or her interventions regarding religious affairs? The content search was carried out manually through the examination of the personal profile of every Spanish MEP at the EP website. We analysed all the questions and motions for resolution related to religious issues. When the title of the document was not clear we searched inside using a list of keywords.[13]

The activity of Spanish MEPs on religious issues has been classified into two main areas: foreign policy and EU policy. We labelled as foreign policy those debates where MEPs have requested an assessment and/or an intervention by EU institutions on issues or events related to religion that have occurred outside the borders of the EU. This includes, for instance, interventions by MEPs that seek to defend the rights of minority groups (such as religious minorities, children, women or LGBT community members) that are in a vulnerable situation. With regard to EU policy, we include all those debates on the treatment of religious issues by member-states of the EU on issues such as religious freedom, the European Constitution and the relationship between European institutions and religious lobbying groups. Special attention has been given to Spanish issues.

The first and foremost conclusion of our analysis is that religion is present as an element but not as a central issue in political debate. The religious questions are mostly part of the context in which an MEP's speech is framed, but are usually not a central element of it. When Spanish MEPs refer to religious issues they do so in an indirect way. Examining the data in more detail, we observe that, on the one hand, as shown in Table 3, the percentage of motions for resolution that make reference to religious questions (8.4%) is greater than the percentage of parliamentary questions that do so (0.8%). This difference could be explained by the characteristics of each kind of political participation. As emerged in the analysis, many motions for resolution are related to the desire to protect human rights and defend democracy. Religious

174

Table 3. Parliamentary questions and motions for resolution related to religious issues presented by Spanish MEPs (from 1999 to April 2013).

Political group	Parliamentary questions	Religious issues questions	Motions for resolution	Religious issues motions
EPP	3069	26 (0.8%)	1090	64 (5.9%)
S&D	2820	27 (1%)	1031	107 (10.4%)
ALDE	1526	10 (0.7%)	623	78 (12.5%)
Greens/EFA	2389	18 (0.7%)	806	64 (7.9%)
GUE/NGL	1122	4 (0.4%)	559	30 (5.4%)
NI	141	0	9	2 (22.2%)
Total	11,067	85 (0.8%)	4118	345 (8.4%)

Source: European Parliament website. Own compilation.

issues are mentioned as a part of the context of these resolutions. On the other hand, as shown in Table 3, the differences between groups are not statistically significant and it would be necessary to look beyond the quantitative data in order to explore the political and ideological differences that exist on this issue. It is also worth noting that the majority of these interventions involve matters of foreign policy (Table 4): 54.3% of parliamentary questions and 81.5% of motions for resolution do so. This finding is also consistent with the results obtained by Silvestri (2009) in her study of the presence of Islam in European institutions. Silvestri points out 'the issue of Islam in Parliamentary Questions almost always came up in relation to situations that are external to the EU, and not the day-to-day engagement with faith issues and with religious communities within the EU borders' (Silvestri 2009, 1225), which is also what has been observed in this case study.

Another result that stands out from the analysis is that the political affiliation of the MEPs is an explanatory variable in understanding their position towards religious affairs. The most active groups concerning foreign policy issues are the ALDE, Greens/EFA and S&D MEPs. The concerns of liberal and left-wing MEPs in the EP regarding religious affairs are usually linked to complaints about oppression in a specific international context. Usually, religious issues are part of this context in which they are demanding the protection of human rights. A sample of such interventions are all related to the defence of human rights in Islamic societies, with a total of 21 parliamentary questions (66.6%) linked with this issue, including the rights of women and LGBT communities. The oppression of religious minorities, such as the cases of practitioners of Falun Gong and Tibetan monks in China, is also another issue raised by MEPs.

The activity of the EPP MEPs related to religious affairs in the foreign policy area follows a similar pattern. Most of the questions and motions for resolution presented by the MEPs are also related to the defence of human rights. In this regard, and in contrast to other political groups, the defence of Christian minorities has had a special relevance in

Table 4. Parliamentary questions and motions for resolution presented by Spanish MEPs by theme[1] (from 1999 to April 2013).

Political group	Parliamentary questions			Motions for resolution		
	Foreign affairs	UE affairs	Total	Foreign affairs	UE affairs	Total
EPP	9	5	14 (20%)	43	4	47 (20%)
S&D	17	8	25 (35.7)	43	7	50 (21.3%)
ALDE	7	3	10 (14.3)	49	7	56 (23.8%)
Greens/EFA	5	12	17 (24.3)	44	9	53 (22.5%)
GUE/NGL	0	4	4 (5.6)	20	7	27 (11.5%)
NI	0	0	0	1	1	2 (0.8%)
Total	38 (54.3%)	32 (45.1%)	70 (100%)	200 (85.1%)	35 (14.9%)	235 (100%)

Source: European Parliament website. Own compilation.
[1]The difference in the total numbers arises from the fact that in this Table we count only once any questions and motions for resolution that are posed by more than one Spanish MEP.

the activity of the EPP MEPs. Eight parliamentary questions are about the defence of the rights of Christian minority groups: of these six have been presented by Spanish MEPs. This is the case in debates such as 'EU reaction to attacks on Christians in third-world countries', 'Christian minorities in Egypt' and 'Reciprocity concerning religious practices between Saudi Arabia and the EU'.

The examination of the data concerning EU policy leads us to draw the following conclusion: right and centre-right Spanish MEPs show greater internal consensus and cohesion regarding religious affairs than left and centre-left MEPs. In other words, they take a common (and disciplined) position towards these issues and internal variation is less common. To illustrate the importance that the EPP as a political group gives to the defence of Europe's Christian roots it is useful to look at the debate on the display of religious and cultural symbols in public places. We refer, specifically, to the debate over the acceptance by the European Court of Human Rights of an application from an Italian-Finnish citizen who sought to remove crucifixes from schools. It generated a parliamentary question in 2009, posed by an Italian MEP and supported mainly by Italian, Polish and Spanish MEPs. The concrete text of this question emphasised the risk of this attitude towards the symbols of the Catholic faith being used some day against EU emblems (with a reference to the possible Marian iconography in the EU flag). It received the support of 14 Spanish EPP MEPs.

Another example of the debates around which the centre-right MEPs close ranks was the parliamentary question on the official EU diary for young people published and distributed in 21,000 secondary schools in 2011. It included the dates of the main

Table 5. Spanish MEPs' support for motion for a European Parliament resolution on respect for the principles of religious freedom and the secular nature of the state in the future European Constitution.

Political group	Motion code: B5-0364/2003	5th Legislature MEPs
EPP	1 (3.4%)	29
S&D	22 (91.6%)	24
ALDE	3 (75%)	4
GUE/NGL	3 (75%)	4
Greens/EFA	2 (66.6%)	3
NI	1 (100%)	1
Total	32 (49.2%)	65

Source: European Parliament website. Own compilation.

religious festivals (including Muslim, Hindu, Sikh, Jewish and other holy days) but not the Christian feast days, which were omitted. That question, presented mostly with the support of EPP and conservative MEPs, considered the omission of the Christian religious tradition as a violation of the principle of freedom of thought, opinion and religion. A total of eight Spanish MEPs from the EPP group supported this question.

In contrast, the activity of left-wing Spanish MEPs regarding internal affairs or EU policy reveals different interests. Examples of the issues in this area are the parliamentary questions posed by Greens/EFA MEPs on dialogue with churches and non-confessional organisations, seeking transparency and control over this activity; the criticism of state-ments by Catholic leaders on paedophilia (Greens/EFA and ALDE); and the condemna-tion of the 'threats posed to basic freedoms by fundamentalists following the publication of cartoons featuring Mohammed' (S&D).

The commitment among the left-wing Spanish MEPs on the defence of religious freedom and the secular nature of the state was revealed to be one of the points of consensus in debates on the future European Constitution in 2003. As shown in Table 5, 49% of Spanish MEPs gave their support to this motion for resolution. In comparison with other political groups, the S&D MEPs gave overwhelming support (91.6%) to this motion for resolution that sought to avoid the direct or indirect reference to a specific religion or faith in the future European Constitution.

Finally, it is also important to note that on some occasions the left-wing Spanish MEPs use the EP as a place to denounce the privileges of the Catholic Church in Spain. These interventions are not very frequent, but data analysis shows 11 parliamentary questions on themes such as the condemnation of homophobic and hate speech by the bishop of Tarragona (by a Greens/EFA MEP) or criticism of the inequality generated by the tax-exempt status of the Catholic Church (questions presented by a GUE/NGL MEP in 2007, 2008 and 2009).

Conclusion

Religious affairs have unexpectedly gained ground in the European public sphere in recent decades. The religious landscape has significantly changed, as the perceptions, judgments and strategies of the actors in this field have been widely transformed, which has created more room for religious issues within the political realm. This greater relevance of religion is evident in Spain but also at the European level. In this regard, as Soper and Fetzer suggest, 'religion is more significant for the politics of Western Europe than classical secularisation theory would have predicted' (Soper and Fetzer 2002, 169).

This context makes it important to closely examine the role that religion plays in the European political sphere. The main goal in our study has been to understand the complex interplay between the national and the European sphere regarding religious affairs. We have examined both the attitudes, preferences and opinions of Spanish MEPs concerning religious affairs and the presence and role of religious affairs in their activity within the EP. In addition, the links between the political and ideological positions of the MEPs and their religious preferences and activity regarding religious issues have been analysed.

Three main conclusions can be drawn from the research.

First, the process of secularisation and privatisation of religious beliefs has clearly permeated Spanish society, and is reflected in the opinions of MEPs on religious issues. Religion is considered mostly as a private affair that should not play a role in the public sphere and even less in politics. There is a general consensus, at least on a normative level, that religion and politics should be kept separate. This also becomes an explanatory factor of the high refusal rate of Spanish MEPs to participate in the RelEP survey. Moreover, we have also hypothesised that the dramatic and conflictive relation between politics and religion in Spanish history causes a sense of discomfort among MEPs when faced with issues regarding religious affairs. As Colom González (2010) argues, a coherent and shared narrative about Spain's dramatic past has not been constructed, which makes some issues 'taboo'.

Second, although religious issues seem to be a minor aspect of European legislative activity, the detailed analysis of the parliamentary activity of Spanish MEPs shows that it cannot be inferred that religion has a negligible presence in the EP. Religious affairs are mainly addressed indirectly, but there are a considerable number of political initiatives that consider issues of religion. At specific moments, disputes related to religious affairs come to the fore and the role of religion becomes more visible, which is usually when right-wing groups use religion as an identity resource. In addition, the analysis of the data has shown that religion is also present in a more discrete but persistent mode in the EP. However, since its presence is diffused through multiple and diverse policy sectors and issues, ranging from culture and education to freedom of expression and social policy, it is less visible at first sight.

Finally, it is important to state that a relationship between the religious and ideological identity of MEPs has been detected. Our analysis is consistent with what Montero, Calvo, and Martínez (2008) state about domestic politics: it is possible to draw two main profiles when dealing with religious issues. On the one hand, Spanish right-wing politicians follow a similar pattern regarding religious affairs: they are mainly concerned with the need to defend Europe's Christian heritage and they do it in a disciplined manner by closing ranks around contentious issues. On the other hand, the views of Spanish left-wing MEPs around religious issues are much more heterogeneous and it is not possible to detect a single and disciplined stance towards such issues. However, the type of questions and motions posed in the EP by left-wing MEPs show that they attribute greater importance to European secularity and that they prioritise human rights and democratic arguments over religious ones.

In short, it is important to recognise that despite the strong secularisation process experienced by Spanish society

> it is improper to confuse the real weakening of the Catholic organisation with the disappearance of its influence on social logics. ... Its political role has not disappeared as quickly as traditional indicators of religiosity would make us to believe. Its role is different from what it used to be under the former authoritarian and denominational political regime, but the church still exerts some influence on political developments. (Itcaina 2006, 1472)

The empirical analysis of the role of religion in the activity of Spanish MEPs has shown that religion is not a crucial and hot topic on the parliamentary agenda but neither is it an insignificant element. We have seen that the historical clerical–anticlerical cleavage still has influence on right-wing and left-wing political identity that can be mobilised on certain specific occasions. Religion is a resource to fuel specific debates that help to more clearly draw the boundaries between left- and right-wing groups. The greater relevance that religion is acquiring in the public sphere in Spain (Montero, Calvo, and Martínez 2008; Aguilar Fernández 2012) may foster a resurgence of controversies over religious affairs in the EP, which makes research on this topic more pertinent.

However, the research in this area is still at an early stage. Our study has drawn a general picture but it would be especially relevant to take a closer look at the interaction between politics and religion while considering variables such as intra-national differences in MEPs' positions or analysing the effect of gender and age on this issue. Likewise, a qualitative and detailed approach to some of the controversies over religious issues could provide new insights into the complex and changing relationship of religion and politics in contemporary Europe.

Notes

1. The questionnaire was adapted to the Spanish case, while keeping the same structure and overall design. To follow the Spanish data protection law it was necessary to eliminate the first question (item A), which requested the name of the interviewee. The MEPs were contacted via e-mail and telephone calls from September 2012 to May 2013.
2. The analysis took several factors into consideration, such as the MEPs' political affiliation, the committees to which they belonged and the total number of questions and motions for resolution presented during these periods. We analysed the parliamentary questions and motions for resolutions posed (between 1999 and April 2013) by the 139 Spanish MEPs in the plenary sessions at the EP. Data were accessed through the website of the EP.
3. In this vein, the Episcopal Conference published a note (SGCEE 2011) which indirectly appealed for votes for the PP in the 2011 general election (Berretini 2013).
4. These include the proposed reform of the abortion law and the recent changes to the law on education. The education reform includes the subject of (Catholic) religion as part of the general curriculum and the suppression of the 'Education for Citizenship' subject, as some elements in the Catholic Church demanded during the Zapatero government.
5. Apart from one Catalan MEP, from the Democratic Union of Catalonia (*Unió Demòcratica de Catalunya*), a Christian Democratic party, the members of the EPP group belong to the Spanish People's Party (*Partido Popular*). The socialist group, S&D, is composed entirely of MEPs from the Spanish Socialist Workers' Party (*Partido Socialista Obrero Español*) (PSOE).
6. The ALDE MEPs are two regional nationalist MEPs, from the Democratic Convergence of Catalonia (*Convergència Democràtica de Catalunya*) (CDC) and the Basque Nationalist Party (*Partido Nacionalista Vasco*) (PNV).

7. The Greens/EFA MEPs are one from the Initiative for Catalonia Greens (*Iniciativa per Catalunya/Verds*), a green left-wing Catalan party, and one from the Galician Nationalist Bloc (*Bloque Nacionalista Gallego*) (BNG), a Galician nationalist party.
8. This MEP is from the United Left party (*Izquierda Unida*) (IU).
9. This MEP is from the Union, Progress and Democracy party (*Unión, Progreso y Democracia*), a liberal party which split from the Spanish Socialist Workers' Party (*Partido Socialista Obrero Español*) (PSOE).
10. For more details on the Partirep project (2007–2011, n = 1536) see http://www.partirep.eu/datafile/comparative-mp-survey.
11. The Spanish Constitution says that 'No one may be compelled to make statements regarding his or her ideology, religion or beliefs' (article 16.2), which in practical terms has meant the impossibility of undertaking census or panel studies on religious affiliation.
12. One illustrative answer was: 'Thank you for maintaining anonymity but I do not think that I have to answer questions on issues that are part of my private life and that are not related to my work in the European Parliament' (Female, S&D).
13. The following keywords were used for the analysis: religi, secular, church, islam, imam, evang, jew, spiritual.

References

Aguilar Fernández, S. 2011. "El movimiento antiabortista en la España del siglo XXI: el protagonismo de los grupos laicos cristianos y su alianza de facto con la Iglesia católica" [The Pro-Life Movement in Spain in the XXI Century: The Role of Lay Christian Groups and their De Facto Alliance with the Catholic Church]. *Revista de estudios políticos* 154: 11–39.

Aguilar Fernández, S. 2012. "Fighting Against the Moral Agenda of Zapatero's Socialist Government (2004–2011): The Spanish Catholic Church as a Political Contender." *Politics and Religion* 5 (3): 671–694. doi:10.1017/S1755048312000351.

Anderson, J. 2003. "Catholicism and Democratic Consolidation in Spain and Poland." *West European Politics* 26 (1): 137–156. doi:10.1080/01402380412331300237.

APCEE (Asamblea Plenaria Conferencia Episcopal Española). 1993. *La construcción de Europa, un quehacer de todos: declaración LVIII* [Building Europe, a Task for Everyone: Declaration VIII]. http://www.conferenciaepiscopal.nom.es/archivodoc/servlet/DocumentFileManager?document=4768&file=00001000.PDF.

Bader, V. 2007. *Secularism or Democracy? Associational Governance of Religious Diversity.* Amsterdam: Amsterdam University Press.

Beckford, J. A. 1999. "The Management of Religious Diversity in England and Wales with Special Reference to Prison Chaplaincy." *International Journal on Multicultural Societies* 1 (2): 55–66.

Beckford, J. A. 2003. *Social Theory and Religion.* Cambridge: Cambridge University Press.

Berger, P. 1999. "The Desecularization of the World: A Global Overview." In *The Desecularization of the World: Resurgent Religion and World Politics*, edited by P. Berger, 1–18. Washington, DC: Ethics and Public Policy Center & William B. Eerdmans.

Berretini, M. 2013. "The Spanish Catholic Church From the Zapatero Era to the Rajoy Government." In *Politics and Society in Contemporary Spain: From Zapatero to Rajoy*, edited by B. N. Field and A. Botti, 161–178. New York: Palgrave Macmillan.

Brassloff, A. 1998. *Religion and Politics in Spain: The Spanish Church in Transition, 1962–96*. New York: Macmillan.

Casanova, J. 1994. *Public Religions in the Modern World*. Chicago: University of Chicago Press.

Casanova, J. 2006. "Religion, European Secular Identities, and European Integration." In *Religion in an Expanding Europe*, edited by T. A. Byrnes and P. J. Katzenstein, 65–92. New York: Cambridge University Press.

Casanova, J. 2008. "The Problem of Religion and the Anxieties of European Secular Democracy." In *Religion and Democracy in Contemporary Europe*, edited by G. Motzkin and Y. Fischer, 63–74. London: Alliance Publishing Trust.

Colom González, F. 2010. "El pasado en el presente: qué hacer con la memoria de la guerra civil" [The Past in the Present: What to Do with the Memory of the Civil War]. *Res publica* 23: 161–174.

Davie, G. 2000. *Religion in Modern Europe: A Memory Mutates*. New York: Oxford University Press.

Davie, G. 2001. "Europe: l'exception qui confirme la règle" [Europe: The Exception Which Proves the Rule]. In *Le réenchantement du monde*, edited by P. Berger, 99–128. Paris: Bayard.

Davie, G. 2002. *Europe: The Exceptional Case*. London: Darton, Longman and Todd.

de Busser, C. 2006. "Church–State Relations in Spain: Variations on a National-Catholic Theme?" *GeoJournal* 67 (4): 283–294. doi:10.1007/s10708-007-9067-y.

Díaz-Salazar, R. 1990. "Política y religión en la España contemporánea" [Politics and Religion in Contemporary Spain]. *Reis: Revista española de investigaciones sociológicas* 52: 65–84.

Díaz-Salazar, R. 2008. *España laica: ciudadanía plural y convivencia nacional* [Secular Spain: Plural Citizenship and National Coexistence]. Madrid: Espasa.

Díez de Velasco, F. 2012. *Religiones en España: historia y presente* [Religions in Spain: Past and Present]. Madrid: Ediciones AKAL.

Ferrari, S. 2008. "State Regulation of Religion in the European Democracies: The Decline of the Old Pattern." In *Religion and Democracy in Contemporary Europe*, edited by Y. Fischer and G. Motzkin, 113–124. London: Alliance Publishing Trust.

González-Anleo, J. 2008. "El postcatólico español y el pluralismo religioso (I)" [Spanish Post-Catholicism and Religious Pluralism]. *Iglesia viva: revista de pensamiento cristiano* 233: 103–112.

Griera, M. 2012. "Public Policies, Interfaith Associations and Religious Minorities: A New Policy Paradigm? Evidence from the Case of Barcelona." *Social Compass* 59 (4): 570–587. doi:10.1177/0037768612460800.

Hennig, A. 2012. *Moralpolitik und Religion: Bedingungen politisch-religiöser Kooperation in Polen, Italien und Spanien* [Moral Politics and Religion: Conditions for Politico-Religious Cooperation in Poland, Italy and Spain]. Würzburg: Ergon-Verlag.

Hernández-Carr, A. 2011. "La derecha radical populista en Europa: discurso, electorado y explicaciones" [The Populist Radical Right in Europe: Discourse, Electorate and Explanations]. *Reis: Revista española de investigaciones sociológicas* 136: 141–159.

Hix, S. 1999. *The Political System of the European Union*. London: Macmillan.

Hix, S., and B. Hoyland. 2011. *The Political System of the European Union*. London: Palgrave Macmillan.

Itçaina, X. 2006. "The Roman Catholic Church and the Immigration Issue: The Relative Secularization of Political Life in Spain." *American Behavioral Scientist* 49 (11): 1471–1488. doi:10.1177/0002764206288459.

Katzenstein, P. J. 2006. "Multiple Modernities as Limits to Secular Europeanization?" In *Religion in an Expanding Europe*, edited by T. A. Byrnes and P. J. Katzenstein, 1–33. New York: Cambridge University Press.

Klausen, J. 2005. *The Islamic Challenge: Politics and Religion in Western Europe*. Oxford: Oxford University Press.

Martin, D. 1978. *A General Theory of Secularization*. Aldershot: Gregg Revivals.

Martínez-Ariño, J., M. Griera, G. García-Romeral, and M. Forteza. 2011. "Inmigración, diversidad religiosa y centros de culto en la ciudad de Barcelona" [Immigration, Religious Diversity and Places of Worship in Barcelona]. *Migraciones* 30: 101–133.

Martínez-Torrón, J. 2006. "Religious Freedom and Democratic Change in Spain." *Brigham Young University Law Review* 3: 777–810.

Montero, J. R., K. Calvo, and Á. Martínez. 2008. "El voto religioso en España y portugal" [The Religious Vote in Spain and Portugal]. *Revista internacional de sociología* 66 (51): 19–54.

PCEE (Presidencia de la Conferencia Episcopal Española). 1985. *Carta de Gabino Díaz Merchán, presidente de la CEE, a Jean Hengen, presidente de la Comisión de Episcopados de la Comunidad Europea (COMECE), con motivo del ingreso de España en la Comunidad Económica Europea* [Letter from Gabino Díaz Merchán, President of the CEE, to Jean Hengen, President of the Commission of the Bishops' Conferences of the European Community (COMECE), About the Entry of Spain into the European Economic Community]. http://www.conferenciaepiscopal.nom.es/archivodoc/jsp/system/win_main.jsp.

Pérez-Agote, A. 2012. *Cambio religioso en España: los avatares de la secularización* [Religious Change in Spain: The Avatars of Secularisation]. Madrid: Centro de Investigaciones Sociológicas.

Piñol, J. M. 1993. *El Nacionalcatolicisme a Catalunya i la resistencia, 1926–1966* [National Catholicism in Catalonia and the Resistance, 1926–1966]. Barcelona: Edicions 62.

Schlesinger, P., and F. Foret. 2006. "Political Roof and Sacred Canopy?: Religion and the EU Constitution." *European Journal of Social Theory* 9 (1): 59–81. doi:10.1177/1368431006060463.

SGCEE (Secretaria General de la Conferencia Episcopal Española). 2005. *Nota acerca del referéndum sobre la 'Constitución para Europa'* [Note on the Referendum for the 'European Constitution']. http://www.conferenciaepiscopal.es/index.php/documentos-secretaria/1984-nota-sobre-el-referendum-de-constitucion-para-europa.html.

SGCEE (Secretaria General de la Conferencia Episcopal Española). 2011. *Nota antes las elecciones generales de 2011* [Note Before the 2011 General Elections]. http://documentosepiscopales.blogspot.com.es/2011/10/nota-ante-las-elecciones-generales-de.html.

Silvestri, S. 2009. "Islam and Religion in the EU Political System." *West European Politics* 32 (6): 1212–1239. doi:10.1080/01402380903230678.

Soper, J. C., and J. S. Fetzer. 2002. "Religion and Politics in a Secular Europe: Cutting Against the Grain." In *Religion and Politics in Comparative Perspective: The One, the Few, and the Many*, edited by T. G. Jelen and C. Wilcox, 169–191. New York: Cambridge University Press.

Yeğenoğlu, M. 2006. "The Return of the Religious." *Culture and Religion* 7 (3): 245–261. doi:10.1080/14755610601056975.

Zúquete, J. P. 2008. "The European Extreme-Right and Islam: New Directions?" *Journal of Political Ideologies* 13 (3): 321–344. doi:10.1080/13569310802377019.

Part IV

So Far, Not So Dissimilar: European 'Exceptionalism' Challenged by Other Western Cases

Religion in the Israeli Parliament: a typology

Sharon Weinblum

School of Interdisciplinary Area Studies, University of Oxford, Oxford, UK

Because religion has been a constant source of social divisions and political conflicts, the role of Judaism in Israel is very often studied through the prism of a rigid religious–secular cleavage. Without denying the contentious character of religion in the political and social arenas, I suggest in this study that a closer look at the usages of religion in Israeli politics offers a more nuanced picture of the role of Judaism in Israel. In order to uphold this thesis, I identify the main usages of Judaism in the Israeli Parliament (the Knesset) and scrutinise the extent to which these different mobilisations overlap or crosscut the secular–religious cleavage. This analysis leads to a typology of three usages of religion: religion as a source of authority, religion as a marker of identity and nation, and religion as a source of values. On this basis, I demonstrate that the role of religion in Israel and especially in the Israeli Parliament cannot be reduced to the divide between religious and secular groups. If in its first usage, the religious–secular cleavage indeed predominates, the use of religion as an identity marker does not necessarily lead to a conflict with secular members, while in its final form, religion is mobilised as a resource by members of both groups.

Listen, I'm not religious. If it's a religious state, a Jewish Iran, I will not be here. If it is the state of the Bible, I will not be here. If it is a state without democracy, I will not be here. So I mean, the rabbis should go to synagogues and should stay there, and they should not run the country. If they run the country, we lose the essence of the country.

> (Member of the Knesset Daniel Ben Simon (Labor Party),
> personal interview with author, Tel Aviv, 27 May 2010).

Introduction

In February 2012 the Israeli Supreme Court overruled the so-called Tal law, a law specifying the conditions according to which ultra-orthodox men studying in yeshivas (religious schools) could temporarily or indefinitely defer military service (Law on Deferral of Service for Yeshiva Students for whom Torah is their Profession 2002). The law was deemed unconstitutional by the court on the ground that it violated the right to equality, itself part of the right to human dignity guaranteed by Israeli legislation (High Court of Justice 6298/07, 3). One year later a new government was elected after several parties had carried on an electoral campaign largely based on the slogan 'sharing the burden', implying that young ultra-orthodox men too should give a few years of their lives to the Israel Defense Forces. In October 2012 and February 2013 several members of the movement Women of the Wall were arrested by the police after their presence at the Western Wall had sparked violent clashes with other religious groups for the reason that their way of praying contradicted the traditional orthodox norms.[1] Following these events, the government tried to appease the conflict by offering the Women of the Wall a special prayer space near the Western Wall (Maltz 2013). These events are two of the most recent issues that the Israeli secular authorities, including the government and the Supreme Court, have had to deal with since the establishment of the state. In this sense, religion can be seen as an integral part of politics while politics has, to a wide extent, introduced itself into religion.

Because these issues often generate tensions between secular and religious groups, it has been common to look at Israeli society through the prism of a religious-secular divide where both sectors would be in competition for the control of the public and political arenas (Ben-Porat 2000, 223). While this religious versus secular struggle indeed reflects an important historical cleavage in Israeli political life, I argue in this study that a closer look at the use of religion in Israeli politics offers a more nuanced picture. In order to demonstrate this, I identify the main usages of Judaism[2] in the Israeli Parliament (the Knesset) and scrutinise to what extent these different usages overlap with or cross-cut the secular–religious cleavage. This analysis leads to the elaboration of a typology of three usages of religion: religion as a source of authority, religion as a marker of identity and nation, and religion as a source of values. On this basis, the analysis shows that the use of religion in Israeli politics, and more specifically in the Knesset, cannot be reduced to a religious–secular divide: on the one hand, because the use of religion by religious members of the Knesset (MKs) does not necessarily lead to a conflict with secular MKs; on the other hand, because in some cases religion is a resource that is drawn upon by MKs from both religious and secular backgrounds. Before presenting the core of the analysis in the second part of this study, in the first part I give an account of the secular–religious divide in Israel and briefly describe the present place of religion in the state. I therefore come back to the Zionist project, the aim of which was to create a state for the Jews; I highlight the conflicts that the secular Zionist project generated with the orthodox and ultra-orthodox segments and show the influence that these conflicts have had on the contemporary shape of the state. This overview of the historical tensions and divisions allows us to understand the positions and oppositions currently at play in the Knesset.

Israel as a state of the Jews, Israel as a Jewish state

The current form of the state of Israel and the ambiguous role of religion in politics can be understood only in the light of the history of Zionism and of the various movements which coexisted and competed in Palestine before the establishment of Israel in 1948. Although there existed an important religious Zionist movement, most members of the Zionist movement of the late nineteenth century who would later dominate the life of the state were secular. According to their view influenced by the nation-state model of the epoch and based on a secular reading of the Bible (Shindler 2001, 101), the Jewish people was entitled, like any other nation, to be given a state on the land from which it had been expelled long before. This state should ideally be a secular state in which religious institutions would be separated from the state. Created by and for the Jewish people, the state of Israel that was established in 1948 became a typical nationalising state aiming at the realisation of a Jewish nation-state through various sets of policies (Weinblum

2013). Among those policies was the very symbolic Law of Return, allowing every Jewish person to immigrate to Israel and to become full citizen of the state (Law of Return 1950; Law on Citizenship 1952).[3] The ethno-cultural Jewish character of the state was also to be realised through many other aspects of life of Israelis, including the use of languages, the distribution of land[4] or the use of Jewish symbols in the public sphere (the national anthem, the flag and public holidays based on the Jewish calendar are some such symbols).

While the secular Zionist movement clearly predominated in mandatory Palestine and ruled the country after 1948, its conception of the state has not remained unchallenged. Besides the strong opposition stemming from the Palestinians, who today form 20% of the Israeli population,[5] Jewish residents of the mandatory Palestine were divided on the question of the Zionist project. On the one hand, the so-called orthodox 'national-religious' movement, although it adhered to the pre-state Zionist institutions put in place in the 1920s, rejected the idea of a secular state and promoted the creation of a state that would ultimately be ruled according to the Torah. On the other hand, completely hostile to the secular Zionist project, and as a matter of fact to Zionism altogether, was the ultra-orthodox religious sector. In contrast to the Zionist religious movement which believed that Zionism could be a tool to achieve messianic redemption, ultra-orthodox figures saw the formation of a Jewish realm through human action as a 'desecration of God and a desecration of the holiness of our land [as] an organized public rebellion against God and his Torah ...' (Mazie 2006, 24–25, 28). However, because ultra-orthodox leaders sensed that the state of Israel would ultimately become fact, they adopted a pragmatic attitude toward the Zionist movement and its institutions over time, and today only a small minority of ultra-orthodox groups does not recognise the state of Israel. As a consequence of this pragmatic stance the religious movement was able to negotiate, even before the establishment of the state of Israel, an informal agreement known today as the 'status quo', which guaranteed that religion would not be excluded from the state-to-be.[6] According to the agreement, religious courts were to be granted the right to maintain exclusive jurisdiction over matters of family status (such as marriage, burial, divorce, inheritance). It was also agreed that the sacred day of rest, Shabbat, would be publicly observed and that *kashrut* would be respected in the kitchens of public institutions. The agreement also included the preservation of the autonomy of two religious school systems (orthodox and ultra-orthodox), the exemption from military service for students at religious schools, and the allocation of public funding to religious schools and students. After 1948, the support of both religious groups given to the government – either from within or from without – allowed the preservation of the status quo at the same time as it guaranteed orthodox and ultra-orthodox segments the monopoly of control on religious affairs – hence leaving aside other streams of Judaism. Until today, this control is significantly manifested by the exclusive representation of orthodox and ultra-orthodox rabbis in the Chief Rabbinate of Israel, the institution in charge of super-vising religious courts, interpreting the respect of Shabbat, supervising the holy sites, recognising conversion and providing kosher certification. As a consequence, although rabbis from other movements such as the conservative and reform movements perform marriages and other rites, the acts they perform are not officially recognised by the state, even though, following an appeal to the Supreme Court, the state agreed in 2012 to fund the salaries of reform and conservative rabbis (High Court of Justice 8944/05).

To a large extent, the implementation of the status quo and the (ultra-)orthodox monopoly on the interpretation of religion has turned Israel into a state much more religious than secular Zionists had imagined and hoped for. The fact that Shabbat is imposed in public spaces concretely means that most shops are closed on Saturday and that there is no, or limited, public transport, while the imposition of *kashrut* and its supervision have many concrete implications for farmers, food producers and importers, restaurants, scientific research, advertisers. Furthermore, the fact that personal matters are controlled by the religious sectors (Jewish but also Muslim and Christian) practically means that there is no room for civil marriage, with the exception of civil unions for couples registered as 'without religion' (according to the recent Law for the Union of Couples without Religion 2010). Therefore mixed couples, secular couples, homosexual couples and, until 2010, 'without religion' partners wishing to marry before the state must do so outside the country and have these marriages recognised *ex post facto* by the Israeli authorities. In addition, until 1989, people who had been converted abroad by non-orthodox movements could not be registered as Jewish citizens, a rule that applied to people converted in Israel until a Supreme Court ruling in 2002 (High Court of Justice 5070/95). Not being registered as a Jew means not being recognised by the Chief Rabbinate and not being able to marry, divorce or be buried according to the Jewish ritual. Religion is thus omnipresent in the life of Israelis and its role in society has led political institutions as well as the courts to intervene, regulate and rule on these matters on many occasions.

This strong interrelation between state and religion can seem surprising considering the declared level of religiosity of the population in recent polls. In 2012, a survey revealed that 8% of Israeli Jews (who comprise 80% of the population) defined themselves as *haredim* (ultra-orthodox) or *haredi leumi* (national ultra-orthodox), 12% as orthodox, 13% as religious traditionalists, 20% as non-religious traditionalists (not strictly adhering to Jewish prescriptions), and as many as 45% as secular (Hermann et al. 2012, 177). Because of the composition of society, the privileges and the control granted to the small orthodox and ultra-orthodox sectors and their impact on policies have time and again appeared abusive, reinforcing what is sometimes depicted as a *Kulturkampf* between religious and secular groups (Katz 2008). At the same time, the work of Guy Ben-Porat and several surveys show that a great part of the Jewish population of Israel, including secular Jews, favour the idea of a Jewish state in Israel,[7] and that secular and religious practices go hand in hand for most of traditionalist and secular Israeli Jews (Ben-Porat and Feniger 2009). This study demonstrates that the same complexity is at play in the political arena. Through the scrutiny of different usages of religion in the Knesset, the analysis reveals a picture that problematises and brings nuances to the classic paradigm of a religious-secular divide.

Religion in the Israeli Parliament (the Knesset)

The Israeli Parliament, like the state of Israel, is marked by Jewish life and symbols: the calendar of the Knesset sessions – as that of other public institutions – follows the Jewish holidays, a large menorah stands in front of the Knesset gates, MKs have the choice between dairy and meat canteens and every Knesset opening and special events start with the national anthem describing the longing of the Jewish people for its land. At the level of its representatives, religion is very present as well. The Knesset epitomises to a large extent the complexity of the Israeli society. The proportional electoral system allows the representation of many different groups, from anti-Zionist to ultra-nationalist, ultra-orthodox and Zionist-religious streams. Today, the ultra-orthodox parties Shas (Sephardi) and United Torah Judaism (Ashkenazi) have 18 seats out of 120 while the Zionist-religious party Jewish Home won 11 seats in the last elections. Overall, according to Ofer Kenig,

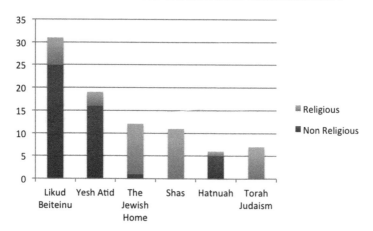

Figure 1.   Representation of religious MKs in the Parliament (source: Kenig 2013).

nearly a third of the members of the 19th Knesset are religious – either orthodox or ultra-orthodox – with 11 from Shas, 10 from Jewish Home, seven from United Torah Judaism, six from the non-religious party Likud Beiteinu (a merger of Likud and Israel Beiteinu), three from the party Yesh Atid and one from the party of Tzipi Livni (Hatnuah) (see Figure 1).[8]

On the basis of these figures, the correlation between religious belonging and political cleavage seems to hold. Most ultra-orthodox and national religious MKs indeed belong to religious parties corresponding to their groups. Moreover, as Table 1 shows, the correlation between level of religiosity and political orientation is strong: the more religious the voters are the further right they vote on a left-right axis (where left and right are self-defined by the respondents) (Hermann et al. 2012, 178).

While they confirm the importance of religion in political orientation and the strong 'pillarisation' of religious groups who are directly represented in the Knesset, these figures do not, however, tell us much about how religion is in effect used in the Knesset and how this affects the relations between political groups. This is the subject I propose to tackle in the following three subsections. On the basis of secondary sources, analysis of a wide range of debates in the Knesset and interviews conducted in 2010, I scrutinise three of the most important usages of religion in the Knesset and the different conflicts they generate: religion as a source of legal authority which overlaps the secular--religious divide; religion as the marker of a nation which allows convergences between

Table 1.   Political orientation and religiosity (source: Hermann et al. 2012, 178).

Political Orientation	Right	Centre	Left
Ultra-Orthodox	8.9	1.2	1.1
Haredi Leumi	3.8	0.8	0
Orthodox Traditional	17.1	6.0	1.1
Religious–Traditional	15.5	10.8	3.3
Non-Religious Traditional	21.6	19.6	12.0
Secular	32.4	60.4	82.5
Other/Don't know/Refuse	0.7	1.2	/
Total	100	100	100

secular and religious MKs; and religion as a source of values which is used by both secular and religious MKs and goes beyond the religious–secular divide. This typology is not the only possible way of informing oneself on the use of religion in the Knesset, but it is useful in that it permits us to grasp most manifestations of religion in the political arena as well as the political divergences and convergences which accompany them. In order to give account of each of the three usages, in the next three subsections I focus on specific political issues and debates in which these usages of religion have appeared. I illustrate the usages of religion in the debates by excerpts from speeches by MKs.

Religion as a source of legal authority

The most obvious and polarising use of religion in the Knesset takes the sacred book of the Torah as a guide to conduct in private and public life and as a primary source of law in the state of Israel. This interpretation of religion in politics emanates first and foremost from MKs who belong to religious parties, especially ultra-orthodox. Opposing them are roughly all the rest of the political spectrum, above all left-wing and Russian parties. The influence of this usage of religion in the Knesset is vast. Indeed, religion as a source of authority appears in debates that concern most policies linked to the status quo, such as regulation of personal matters, recognition of a person as Jewish, respect for *kashrut* and Shabbat. The use of religion as a code of conduct and as the superior law has influenced parliamentary life even more deeply as a result of other essential unresolved questions: the writing of a constitution and of a bill of rights and the role of the Supreme Court in the Israeli political regime.

In 1948 the Declaration of the Establishment of the State of Israel stated that a 'constitution ... shall be adopted by the Elected Constituent Assembly not later than the 1st of October 1948' (Declaration of the Establishment of the State of Israel 1948). However, in 1950, as a result of reluctance on the part of religious leaders as well as the prime minister, David Ben Gurion, a majority of the representatives decided to opt for the enactment of several basic laws instead of an overarching constitutional document (between 1950 and 2014, 12 basic laws have been passed: Lerner 2004, 238; Peleg 1998, 230). In 1992, after consecutive failed attempts to craft either a constitution (Gavison 2003; Lerner 2004) or a bill of rights, the Knesset decided to draft two separate basic laws entrenching basic rights: one protecting freedom of occupation and the other protecting human dignity and liberty (Basic Law: Freedom of Occupation 1992; Basic Law: Human Dignity and Liberty 1992). During the debate on one of the laws religious leaders clearly expressed their opposition to a hierarchically superior legal document. A member of the religious party Agudat Israel, for instance, declared that 'we, the religious Jews, have a constitution, that is the Torah Constitution. We believe that only a constitution given by divine order is significant, not a constitution made by humans ...' (MK Avraham Ravitz, Agudat Israel, debate on the Basic Law: Human Dignity and Liberty, 17 March 1992).[9] After several amendments to the laws, however, religious MKs mitigated their opposition to them and reached an agreement with the secular MKs.[10] The content of the laws clearly reflects the compromise that was struck between secular and religious groups (see Sapir 2008). First, the law on human dignity does not mention freedom of expression, equality or freedom of and from religion. Second, a reference to Israel as a 'Jewish and democratic state' was added to the laws (section 1 of the Basic Law: Human Dignity and Liberty and section 2 of the Basic Law: Freedom of Occupation). Third, at the demand of religious groups, a clause was inserted into the Basic Law: Human Dignity and Liberty providing that the 'Basic Law shall not affect the validity of any law in force prior to the commencement of the Basic Law' (section 10). Finally, only the law on freedom of occupation provides that it shall be modified by a special majority in the Knesset, which according to the constitutional doctrine accepted at the time meant that only this law was intended to enjoy a superior status (Sapir 2008, 15). In spite of this, the Supreme Court was prompt to declare that both laws did in fact have quasi-constitutional status and ruled that they could be used to overrule not only policies of the government but also laws passed by the Knesset (Barak 1992; Court of Appeal 6821/95). Two years later the law on freedom of occupation was amended in order to circumscribe this interpretation by the courts (Goldberg 1998, 225).

Ten years after this failed attempt to write an all-encompassing bill of rights, the Knesset resumed the constitutional process once more, with the intention of enacting a constitution that would be submitted to the public in a referendum. The subsequent failure of this project reflected the difficulty in reconciling (ultra-)orthodox and secular conceptions of the state. The discussions in the committee tasked with writing a draft constitution do indeed reveal divergences on most fundamental issues, such as equality, freedom of religion, the definition of the state of Israel, the place of minorities. During the presentation of the draft constitution to the Knesset, ultra-orthodox MKs expressed their fear that the document would not ultimately take their view into account in those terms:

> Being believers, we have no doubt that when the redemption will come, there will be a time where the Torah will rule the people of Israel. But until redemption, our duty is to guard the Jewish and spiritual character of a Jewish state, which is not guaranteed in the draft constitution, and therefore we will vote against it. (MK Meir Porush, Agudat Israel, vote on the Draft Constitution, 13 February 2006)

The reluctance of both ultra-orthodox and Zionist religious MKs stemmed not only from the content of the draft but also from the fear that the Supreme Court would interpret the future constitution and the rights laid down in the document in a way that contravened Jewish law. This concern was partly a consequence of a series of Supreme Court rulings on religious issues, as transpired in many declarations of religious leaders before and during the constitutional process. In 1999 an ultra-orthodox leader for instance declared that 'Even if the Ten Commandments were proposed as Basic Laws we would oppose the legislation ... because if I accept the Ten Commandments as Basic Laws ... the Supreme Court may interpret them and overturn them' (MK David Tal, Shas, 14 July 1999, in Lerner 2009, 448). Although more open to the constitutional process, Zionist religious MKs also expressed concerns, which ultimately led the National Religious Party to vote against the draft constitution. An MK of the party identified one of the reasons:

> We talk about the Jewish home. What is a Jewish home? ... We see the ruling of the Court – the Supreme Court – on Jewish homes consisting of two women, and all sorts of different things that our ancestors did not imagine, like things that once, by definition, were called an act of Sodom and Gomorrah. I do not want to call it this, I'm just saying, 'were once called this', and here today it's turned into something legal according to the rulings of the Supreme Court. What does the constitution say about it? (MK Nissan Slomiansky, National Religious Party, vote on the Draft Constitution, 13 February 2006)

The failure to enact a constitutional document and a bill of rights is probably one of the most striking and emblematic consequences of the use of religion as a source of authority in the Israeli Parliament. As already noted, this usage has been time and again the object of harsh criticisms and has generated conflicts that overlap the religious–secular divide. However, as the next section shows, other forms of religious mobilisation have allowed convergences between both camps in the Knesset and permitted common positioning in many policy areas.

Religion as the marker of a nation: the Jewish people and their sovereignty

The second way in which religion appears in the Knesset is in the form of a marker of nation. This usage of religion plunges its roots in the Biblical narrative which holds that the Jewish people has been chosen by God and conferred a land, 'Eretz Israel', over which the Jews are entitled to exert their sovereignty. While the religious version of this narrative is first and foremost mobilised by religious MKs, the conflicts generated by the interpretation of religion in national terms do not overlap the religious–secular divide. Even though debates about the very definition of who is to be defined as a Jew often generate clashes between religious and secular MKs,[11] the Biblical narrative of a Jewish people having been 'dispersed' and being granted the right to come back to their land is in fact a core tenet of the secular Zionist project itself. Ben-Porat underlines in this respect that while

> scholars make a valid analytical distinction between Judaism and Jewishness, relating the former to religion and the latter to culture, ethnicity, and a historical sense of belonging to the Jewish people [t]he two, however, overlap ... Judaism would function as the binding glue and as a source for mobilization and legitimation from which Zionism would borrow its symbols and legitimate its territorial claims through a divine promise of redemption. (Ben-Porat 2000, 230)

Indeed, many 'secularized religious symbols' (Ben-Porat 2000, 234), such as the Bible and the Holy Land, are part of the dominant national narrative (Ram 1995), as the Declaration of the Establishment of the State of Israel signed by the secular leader David Ben-Gurion illustrates:

> Eretz Israel was the birthplace of the Jewish people. Here their spiritual, religious and political identity was shaped. Here they first attained to statehood, created cultural values of national and universal significance and gave to the world the eternal Book of Books. After being forcibly exiled from their land, the people kept faith with it throughout their Dispersion and never ceased to pray and hope for their return to it and for the restoration in it of their political freedom. (Declaration of the Establishment of the State of Israel 1948)

Even when totally devoid of religious symbols, secular MKs often reproduce the story of an exiled Jewish people returning to their land. As the minister Benny Begin put it to me,

> I think that the essence of the state of Israel is described by its definition as the nation-state of the Jewish people. There is only one place on earth in which Jews have been privileged and lucky to be able to establish a sovereign independent state on their own, especially here in their ancient homeland. There is no other state for the Jews. (Minister Benny Begin, Likud, personal interview with author, Jerusalem, 28 July 2010)

Because both religious and Zionist secular groups draw on a similar story – the Biblical narrative and its secularised version – to legitimise the presence of Jews in the land of Israel, the interpretation and use of religion as a marker of nation creates more convergences between religious and secular MKs than the usage of religion investigated in the first section.

Among the various manifestations of religion as a marker of nation, two main forms can be distinguished, which produce distinctive alliances among MKs.

The first relates to the question of Jewish sovereignty over the state of Israel and to the ability of the Jews to preserve a majority so as to rule the Jewish state and preserve its 'Jewish identity'. It is this specific usage that permits the widest consensus between religious and secular MKs. This usage of religion pervades a large array of policies, including those connected to the use of Hebrew as the official language, the laws defining Israel as a Jewish state, and the policies directly linked to the question of demography: immigration and citizenship policies. The recent Knesset debates on the Law on Citizenship and Entry into Israel (Temporary Order) 2003 which prevents Palestinians from the occupied territories from residing in Israel with their spouses is a good illustration of how the religious notion of Jewish sovereignty is deployed in matters of immigration and citizenship. While this law was originally passed in 2003 in order to limit potential terror attacks by Palestinians, subsequent debates on the law (which has been was prolonged a 15 times since 2003) have largely touched upon the question of demography and seen the emergence of the Biblical narrative on various occasions. One MK from the Zionist religious party supporting the law for instance declared during the debates that

> There is no more vital law and more important law for the state of Israel . . . . It is not only a security question. This question is marginal. In fact, it is important, but it is not the core. The just and moral basis is that the people of Israel has returned to their land, and that we must ensure the demographic balance here in Eretz Israel. (MK Eliahu Gabbay, National Religious Party, debate on the Law on Citizenship and Entry into Israel, 15 January 2007)

Shared by nationalist religious MKs and by religious ultra-nationalist MKs claiming that 'Eretz Israel belongs to the Jewish people and not to the Arabs' (MK Arieh Eldad, religious MK of National Union, debate on the Law on Citizenship and Entry into Israel, 27 July 2009), the argument that 'we have the right to demographic self-defence, we must keep the Jewish majority, and all other questions are peripheral' also appeared repeatedly in the speeches of ultra-orthodox MKs (MK Nissim Zeev, Shas, debate on the Law on Citizenship and Entry into Israel, 20 July 2004). Because it can be interpreted in both religious and secular terms, this narrative of the Jewish people attempting to protect their sovereignty by ensuring a 'demographic balance' has also been used by secular MKs in the debates on the law. When asked about the rationale of the law, an MK from Kadima for instance argued that 'it's a demographic issue . . . . The Palestinians want to be able to come back to Tel Aviv, Haifa, it's not acceptable for Israel, even for people like me from the left' (MK Shlomo Molla, Kadima, personal interview with author, Tel Aviv, 16 May 2010) while an MK from the self-proclaimed secularist party Shinui declared in the plenum that there exists 'a basic right for every son of the [Jewish] majority to keep and protect the [Jewish] identity of the state' (MK Erela Golan, Shinui, debate on the Law on Citizenship and Entry into Israel, 25 July 2005). Only in the far-left and the anti-Zionist camps was this reference to the Jewish people to justify demographic policies challenged during the debates.

Beside the connection between the Jewish people, the state and demography, a second way in which religion as a marker of nation is deployed in the Knesset is by linking the Jewish people to a territory: the 'Promised Land'. It is typically in the framework of policies on the allocation of land and territorial compromises that this usage appears. The debates on the disengagement from the Gaza Strip that took place in the Knesset in

October 2004 are a good illustration of the ways religion is used in this perspective. During the debates, the Biblical promise according to which Eretz Israel would belong to the Jews was referred to on several occasions by religious MKs. Despite the fact that in rare instances, MKs from the ultra-orthodox party Shas asserted that 'human life is more important than land' (MK David Azulay, Shas, debate on the disengagement from Gaza, 26 October 2004), most Zionist and non-Zionist religious MKs, including from the party Shas,[12] opposed the disengagement on the basis of the Biblical narrative. Hence, both national-religious and ultra-orthodox claimed for instance that 'the Torah is Israel's *kushan* [certificate of registration] on his homeland. Every concession on Eretz Israel is extremely problematic in the first place' (Minister Zevulun Orlev, National Religious Party, debate on the disengagement from Gaza, 26 October 2004) or that 'Eretz Israel was given to the people of Israel by God the creator .... This is not a simple land, a simple place to live; this is the Promised Land given to the chosen people' (MK Meir Porush, United Torah Judaism, debate on the disengagement from Gaza, 26 October 2004). Similarly to the first instance of religion as a marker of nation, this specific use of religion allows convergences with secular MKs. As mentioned previously, the secularised narrative of the Promised Land acknowledges the special relationship between the Jewish people and the land of Israel. Consequently, even though most secular nationalist MKs opposing the disengagement from Gaza employed security rhetoric rather than Biblical rhetoric, some of them also invoked Eretz Israel in order to assert the non-negotiable borders of the state:

> Whoever votes today, for a plan [of disengagement from Gaza] that says somewhere that a Jewish presence in Eretz Israel is illegitimate ... must understand that in the future he will have to deal with exactly the same argument in many other places: the West Bank, the Negev and Galilee. (MK Gideon Ezra, Likud, debate on the disengagement from Gaza, 26 October 2004)

Despite the possibility of convergences between secular and religious MKs on the link between the Jews and the land, this interpretation of religion is nevertheless more contested by secular MKs than the previous instance linking the Jews to the Jewish state. Beside the very strong contestation emanating from MKs on the left and in anti-Zionist parties, the narrative of the non-negotiable Jewish land has sometimes clashed with the previous narrative of the Jewish people in the Jewish state. Recent debates in the Knesset on the need to resume talks with Palestinians offer a good example of these clashes. On one of these occasions a religious MK of the Zionist religious party opposing the resumption of the talks with the Palestinians shouted 'This is our land, this is our land' (MK Orit Struck, The Jewish Home, Knesset Committee on Foreign Affairs and Defence, 21 May 2013, quoted in Ravid 2013). In response to this the (secular) minister in charge of the peace negotiation answered 'This is our land, but the question is if this state will remain ours or not' (Minister Tzipi Livni, Knesset Committee on Foreign Affairs and Defence, quoted in Ravid 2013). Hence, even when they share the premise that Eretz Israel is the land of the Jewish people, the wish of a number of secular centrist and left-wing MKs that Jews maintain sovereignty on their state and its institutions sometimes challenges the historical or sacred link between the land of Israel and the Jews.

    Yet in contrast with the first usage of religion – as a source of authority – the use of religion as a marker of nation linking the Jewish people to the Jewish state or to its territory does not generate a reinforcement of the religious–secular divide. On the contrary, because of the similarities between religious and secular narratives on the Jewish people, this usage permits convergences between actors of both groups, who have in other contexts sometimes violently opposed one another.

The last interpretation of religion investigated in the following section reveals a usage that is more marginal but even more spread across the political arena.

Religion as a set of values

In the last usage of religion identified in the Knesset, Judaism is seen and mobilised as a set of values. In that perspective, religion is interpreted as entailing ethical principles such as respect, love and empathy that Jews should follow in their daily lives, *vis-à-vis* both Jews and non-Jews. Because of its nature, this usage of religion is most frequently observable in debates on equality and rights and on questions pertaining to both internal and external 'others'. At the level of politics, it plays a role in policies such as those relating to the Arab minority, to Palestinian residents and more recently to migrant workers or asylum seekers. This interpretation of religion can be particularly well illustrated by some of these recent discussions on the status of asylum seekers arriving from Africa: the debates on the status of asylum seekers from Darfur and the debates on the law criminalising asylum seekers who cross the borders from Egypt to Israel. As the analysis of the debates shows, the equation between Judaism and ethical principles does not only permit convergences among secular and religious MKs, but also allows secular MKs to directly and explicitly make use of it. It is in fact first in the discourse of secular MKs that this usage can be witnessed. The statement of an MK from the anti-Zionist party Hadash during the recent debates on asylum seekers is an example:

> My fellow members of Knesset ... this commandment to love the stranger who lives within your gates is as I said a commandment repeated many times in the Torah. And it is imperative that whoever sees himself loyal to the values, to the beautiful and progressive elements of the Torah of Israel, takes this as a real opportunity to show loyalty to those values. (MK Dov Khenin, second and third readings of the Law on Prevention of Infiltration, 9 January 2012)

In comparison with the former usage of religion, the Bible is here invoked not as a history book but rather as a guide to values, which include, among others, respect for strangers. In such an interpretation of religion, Judaism is seen as a set of principles which entails universalism and humanism. In earlier debates on whether or not Israel should grant the status of refugee to a few hundred Darfur asylum seekers, a Zionist MK from the left made a claim that clearly expresses this vision of Judaism:

> The refugees whose families were murdered because of their skin colour and ethnic affiliation came to us. They are seeking asylum. The idea to expel them is a delusive idea. It is an immoral act that is against the extreme values of universal culture, and especially contrary to the values of Jewish culture. (MK Ran Cohen, Meretz, debate on Darfur refugees, 17 October 2007)

The equation between Judaism and humanism was also present in the discourse of several secular right-wing MKs during these debates, for example:

> This discussion ... as I see it crosses party boundaries and ideologies, and concerns the Israeli Jewish common denominator, the human. We are talking about people who are refugees ... no matter now who kills whom, when refugees come to our borders, we are committed to care for them. We cannot under any circumstances expel them. (MK Michael Eitan, Likud, debate on Darfur refugees, 17 October 2007)

Finally, we should note that this usage of religion is present, although more rarely, in the speeches of religious MKs who believe that 'the Torah of Israel defends the human being, its liberty, its dignity and its property' (MK Yitzhak Levi, National Religious Party, debate on the Basic Law: Human Dignity and Liberty, 17 March 1992). During the debates on the fate of the refugees from Darfur an ultra-orthodox MK expressed this view of religion:

> Of course the Torah was given only to Israel, but still, everybody in the world was created in the image of God and we must act accordingly. Many laws of the Shulhan Aroch speak and derive rules on how to deal with the human race .... That is why I think we cannot ignore this moral obligation in our relationship to a man as a man. (MK Avraham Ravitz, United Torah Judaism, debate on Darfur refugees, 17 October 2007)[13]

In comparison with the two other usages of religion that we have investigated, the interpretation of religion as a set of values crosscuts the entire political spectrum. The equation between Judaism and certain universal principles is indeed found in the speeches of Jewish MKs in all political parties including secular and anti-Zionist parties. Nevertheless, this discourse remains marginal in comparison with the usages of religion as a source of authority and as a marker of nation, and sometimes even clashes with the latter usage. Discussing the issue of migrant workers' children on the verge of being expelled from Israel, on 25 July 2010 prime minister Netanyahu explicitly opposed this interpretation of Judaism in those terms: 'The issue [of migrant workers' children] touches on two things: One is humanity, and the other is a Jewish and Zionist state' (quoted in Ravid and Weiler-Polak 2010). Indeed, the analysis of the debates under scrutiny reveals that in the political arena this second aspect usually prevails over the interpretation of Judaism as humanism and universalism.

Conclusion

The theory of multiple modernity provides for the fact that the various forms of secularisation in western societies would not have fully obliterated the role of religion. Despite the decrease in religious practices, religion would have remained 'a constitutive basis of national identity and nationalism' (Spohn 2003, 267) and hence a continued dimension of modern societies. The case of Israel is certainly a good example of the multiple interpretations of religion, including by self-proclaimed secular groups. This study has underlined the fact that at least three usages of religion are at play in the Israeli Parliament.

The first usage of religion investigated is the use of religion as a source of legal authority. As I have shown, this interpretation and mobilisation of religion is mainly present among orthodox and ultra-orthodox parties. The blockage in the constitutional process and in the writing of a bill of rights reveals that this use of religion can be understood in many ways as a classic clash between 'modernity' and 'religiosity', where groups have divergent interpretations of the role of secular and religious institutions in the state. The rancour born out of the entrenched privileges granted to the religious sector reinforces this secular–religious cleavage and sometimes leads to violent clashes between the groups.

Nevertheless, the relationship between secular and religious MKs is far from being one of constant opposition. The second mobilisation of religion – as a marker of nation – allows many convergences between secular and religious groups. Because the religious narrative of the Jewish people having the (sacred) right to rule in the state of Israel (first form) and on its land (second form) also exists in a quasi-identic way in the secular discourse, its mobilisation by religious MKs in the debates generates marginal contestations among Jewish MKs. The debates on the demographic question and on territorial compromises investigated in this study reveal that the use of religion as a marker of nation leads to antagonisms that in fact crosscut the religious–secular divide: on the one hand, the justification of demographic-oriented policies opposes mostly religious and Zionist MKs to far-left and anti-Zionist MKs, and on the other hand, the narrative of Eretz Israel to justify the occupation opposes religious and (ultra)nationalist MKs to a composite group of MKs from the far left to the centre of the spectrum.

The last way in which religion is used interprets religion as a set of universal values and is the most crosscutting of all. First, like the former usage, the use of religion as a set of values allows convergences between MKs from different backgrounds and hence does not produce a clash between religious and secular MKs. The reference to the teachings of the Bible to justify openness to the 'other' and the interpretation of Judaism as a source of ethical principles is indeed largely consensual. Second, not only is the interpretation of religion as a set of values not contested by secular MKs but it is also very often used by secular MKs themselves. The debates on the fate of asylum seekers even show that this usage appears mostly in the speeches of secular (Zionist and anti-Zionist) MKs. While crosscutting the political arena, this discourse is however marginal as it often clashes with the religious and secular interpretation of Judaism as a marker of nation.

Overall, the analysis of the different usages of religion in the Israeli Parliament displays a far more complex and dynamic picture than the secular–religious divide paradigm would have suggested. Among the three usages of religion in political debates, only the first one provokes a classic religious–secular clash opposing religious and secular MKs. The second usage is much more consensual, which can be explained by the fact that Israel was established in great part by a secular movement drawing on a secularised version of the Biblical narrative. The last usage, while more rare, not only allows convergences between secular and religious MKs but also appears to be used by non-religious MKs as well as religious ones. In spite of the very specific character of Israel and of its singular state-building process, this typology of three usages to understand the role of religion in the Israeli Parliament might be useful to grasp the dynamic present in other states, including in Europe, a comparison which would in turn enrich this proposed typology.

Acknowledgments

I am grateful to the Israel Institute and to the Wiener-Anspach Foundation for their funding support.

Notes

1. The movement allows women to pray out loud and with the religious shawl and allows them to hold the rolls of the Torah, all practices usually reserved to men within orthodox and ultra-orthodox movements.
2. The use of Islam and Christianity by Members of the Knesset is not part of this project.
3. Despite the formal possibility of becoming Israeli through naturalisation outside the Law of Return, in practice the Israeli regime of citizenship is mostly a *jus sanguini* regime that gives preference to members of the Jewish diaspora over any other category of person.
4. In Israel the land is allocated to citizens by the Israel Land Authority (previously called the Israel Land Administration). This government agency officially and systematically discriminated against non-Jews in the allocation of land until a 2005 Supreme Court ruling (High Court of Justice 9010/04) prohibiting these practices. See Yiftachel (2006) on the issue of land in Israel.

5. In 2008, 83% of the Israeli Arabs were Muslim, 8% were Christian and 8% were Druze (State of Israel Central Bureau of Statistics 2009).
6. The Declaration of the Establishment of the State of Israel, the founding document of the state, reflects the compromise reached between secular and religious before the establishment of the state. The declaration states: 'Placing our trust in the Rock of Israel, we affix our signatures to this proclamation at this session of the provisional council of state, on the soil of the home-land, in the city of Tel Aviv, on this Sabbath eve, the 4th day of Iyar 5708 (14 May 1948)' (Declaration of the Establishment of the State of Israel 1948). While for secular signatories it was clear that the rock of Israel referred to the heritage of the Jewish people, religious leaders who signed the document interpreted it as synonymous with God. As Mazie points out, 'although the Rock of Israel compromise allowed groups with contradictory world views to work past their disagreements, at least for one historic moment, it did not put an end to their competing notions of what the Jewish state ought to become' (Mazie 2006, 23).
7. When asked what were more important, the Jewish or the democratic dimensions of the state, 34% of respondents said the former were more important. These respondents included 80% of the ultra-orthodox, 51% of the religious traditionalists and 43% of the secular (Hermann et al. 2012, 32). However, as emphasised above, the meaning of Jewish state varies, and it must not be understood from this that 43% of secular Jews would like a state guided by the Torah.
8. One should bear in mind that these figures take into account only MKs who are 'ostensibly' religious, namely ultra-orthodox or orthodox MKs. Religious traditionalists, who are more difficult to identify (especially in the case of women), are thus absent from the figures.
9. All similar quotations are of contributions by the named individual to debate on the named law in the Knesset. Quotations from parliamentary debates are all from the Knesset online protocols: http://www.knesset.gov.il/plenum/heb/plenum_search.aspx. The quotations have been translated from Hebrew to English by the author.
10. Most religious MKs voted against the two laws in the first reading but abstained or voted in favour of the laws in the second and third readings (Goldberg 1998; Sapir 2008).
11. In the orthodox vision, the boundaries of the Jewish people are those defined by religion, which means that a Jewish person will be considered Jewish if his/her mother is Jewish. The secular definition is often more extensive, and not consensual among secular groups them-selves. Interestingly, Israeli legislation had first endorsed the religious definition of a Jew, hence defining a Jewish person in the Law of Return as a person with a Jewish mother (or having converted). Since the amendment of the Law of Return in 1970, the definition has been expanded and a Jew is now defined as a person having a Jewish grandparent (or having converted). Nevertheless, as mentioned above, this definition has time and again conflicted with concrete practices since those who do not answer to the orthodox criteria are not recognised as Jews.
12. The ultra-orthodox MKs of Shas indeed voted against the disengagement.
13. While asserting the necessity to welcome Darfur refugees, the same MK at the same time urged the United Nations to get involved in the handling of the refugees.

References

Barak, A. 1992. "The Constitutional Revolution: Protected Human Rights." *Mishpat Umimshal: Law and Government in Israel* 1: 9–35.

Basic Law: Freedom of Occupation. 1992. http://www.knesset.gov.il/laws/special/eng/basic5_eng.htm.

Basic Law: Human Dignity and Liberty. 1992. http://www.knesset.gov.il/laws/special/eng/basic3_eng. htm.

Ben-Porat, G. 2000. "A State of Holiness: Rethinking Israeli Secularism." *Alternatives: Global, Local, Political* 25 (2): 223–245.

Ben-Porat, G., and Y. Feniger. 2009. "Live and Let Buy? Consumerism, Secularization, and Liberalism." *Comparative Politics* 41 (3): 293–31. doi:10.5129/001041509X12911362972232.

Court of Appeal 6821/95. *United Mizrahi Bank Ltd v Migdal Cooperative Village* http://elyon1. court.gov.il/verdictssearch/HebrewVerdictsSearch.aspx.

"Declaration of the Establishment of the State of Israel." 1948. Official Gazette 1, May 14.

Gavison, R. 2003. "Constitutions and Political Reconstruction? Israel's Quest for a Constitution." *International Sociology* 18 (1): 53–70. doi:10.1177/0268580903018001004.

Goldberg, G. 1998. "Religious Zionism and the Framing of a Constitution for Israel." *Israel Studies* 3 (1): 211–229. doi:10.2979/ISR.1998.3.1.211.

Hermann, T., T. Atmor, E. Heller, and Y. Lebel. 2012. *The Israeli Democracy Index 2012.* Jerusalem: The Israel Democracy Institute. http://en.idi.org.il/media/1365574/Index2012%20-%20Eng.pdf.

High Court of Justice. 5070/95. *Naamat, Working and Volunteer Women's Movement v Minister of Interior.* http://elyon1.court.gov.il/files/95/700/050/A40/95050700.a40.htm.

High Court of Justice. 6298/07. *Ressler v Knesset Israel.* http://elyon1.court.gov.il/files/07/980/062/n18/07062980.n18.htm.

High Court of Justice. 8944/05. *Kehilat Birkat Shalom v Office of the Prime Minister of Israel.* http://elyon2.court.gov.il/files/05/440/089/A07/05089440.A07.htm.

High Court of Justice. 9010/04. *The Arab Center for Alternative Planning et al. v The Israel Lands Administration et al.* http://elyon1.court.gov.il/verdictssearch/HebrewVerdictsSearch.aspx.

Katz, G. 2008. "The Israeli *Kulturkampf.*" *Israel Affairs* 14 (2): 237–254. doi:10.1080/13537120801900243.

Kenig, O. 2013. "The 2013 Knesset Election Results: A Preliminary Analysis of the Upcoming Parliament." *The Israel Democracy Institute*, January 24. http://en.idi.org.il/analysis/articles/the-2013-knesset-election-results-a-preliminary-analysis-of-the-upcoming-parliament/

Law for the Union of Couples without Religion. 2010. http://www.justice.gov.il/NR/rdonlyres/678C3A01-085A-4F60-9A59-4D13B320FB18/19486/2235.pdf.

Law of Return. 1950. http://www.knesset.gov.il/laws/special/eng/return.htm.

Law on Citizenship. 1952. http://www.nevo.co.il/law_html/Law01/011_001.htm (in Hebrew).

Law on Citizenship and Entry into Israel (Temporary Order). 2003. http://www.nevo.co.il/Law_word/law01/999_180.doc (in Hebrew).

Law on Deferral of Service for Yeshiva Students for whom Torah is their Profession. 2002. http://www.nevo.co.il/law_word/law01/999_489.doc (in Hebrew; with 2005 amendments).

Law on Prevention of Infiltration. 2012. http://www.nevo.co.il/law_word/law14/law-2332.pdf.

Lerner, H. 2004. "Democracy, Constitutionalism, and Identity: The Anomaly of the Israeli Case." *Constellations* 11 (2): 237–257. doi:10.1111/j.1351-0487.2004.00374.x.

Lerner, H. 2009. "Entrenching the Status-Quo: Religion and State in Israel's Constitutional Proposals." *Constellations* 16 (3): 445–461. doi:10.1111/j.1467-8675.2009.00552.x.

Maltz, J. 2013. "What Was Bennet's Big Rush to Announce Western Wall Plan?" *Haaretz*, August 27. http://www.haaretz.com/jewish-world/the-western-wall-project/.premium-1.543806

Mazie, S. 2006. *Israel's Higher Law.* Lanham: Lexington Books.

Peleg, I. 1998. "Israel's Constitutional Order and the Kulturkampf: The Role of Ben-Gurion." *Israel Studies* 3 (1): 230–250.

Ram, U. 1995. "Zionist Historiography and the Invention of Modern Jewish Nationhood: The Case of Ben Zion Dinur." *History and Memory* 7 (1): 91–124.

Ravid, B. 2013. "Government Rifts over Peace Process Revealed during Knesset Committee Meeting." *Haaretz*, May 21. http://www.haaretz.com/news/diplomacy-defense/government-rifts-over-peace-process-revealed-during-knesset-committee-meeting-1.525153

Ravid, B., and D. Weiler-Polak. 2010. "Netanyahu: We Want to Adopt Migrant Workers' Children, but Retain Jewish Majority." *Haaretz*, July 25. http://www.haaretz.com/news/national/netanyahu-we-want-to-adopt-migrant-workers-children-but-retain-jewish-majority-1.303923

Sapir, G. 2008. *The Israeli Constitutional Revolution: How Did it Happen?* (*Bar Ilan University Public Law Working Paper* 8 (2)). http://papers.ssrn.com/sol3/Jeljour_results.cfm?npage=2

&form_name=journalBrowse&journal_id=572261&Network=no&SortOrder=ab_title&stype=asc&lim=false&selectedOption=1.

Shindler, C. 2001. "Likud and the Search for Eretz Israel: From the Bible to the Twenty-First Century." *Israel Affairs* 8 (1–2): 91–117. doi:10.1080/13537120208719632.

Spohn, W. 2003. "Multiple Modernity, Nationalism and Religion: A Global Perspective." *Current Sociology* 51: 265–286. doi:10.1177/0011392103051003007.

State of Israel Central Bureau of Statistics. 2009. *The Arab Population in Israel.* http://www.cbs.gov.il/www/statistical/arab_pop08e.pdf.

Weinblum, S. 2013. "Nationalising Discourse Vs. Minorities' Political Demands: The Case of the Palestinian Minority in Israel." In *New Nation-States and National Minorities*, edited by J. Danero Iglesias, N. Stojanovic, and S. Weinblum, 140–167. Colchester: ECPR Press.

Yiftachel, O. 2006. *Ethnocracy: Land and Identity Politics in Israel/Palestine.* Philadelphia: University of Pennsylvania Press.

Religion in the American Congress: the case of the US House of Representatives, 1953–2003

James L. Guth

Department of Political Science, Furman University, Greenville, SC, USA

Although there has been a surge of scholarship on the role of religion in American electoral politics, there has been much less analysis of its influence over the behaviour of public officials, such as national legislators. In this study, I review the literature on religion in the Congress, noting the limitations of that research, primarily its failure to measure adequately the religious affiliations, activities and beliefs of members. I then outline an alternative approach that promises a fuller assessment, showing how both ethnoreligious affiliation and theological perspectives have influenced legislative voting since the 1950s. Ethnocultural affiliation was the most powerful influence until the 1990s, but has recently been overlain by deepening 'culture war' divisions. The study concludes with a stringent multivariate analysis that controls for important variables typically included in legislative roll call analysis, showing that many religious measures survive those controls.

Introduction: religion in US politics

Religion has always played an important role in US politics, but constitutional and historical factors make the US situation 'exceptional', or at least different from that in most European nations. The constitutional separation of church and state produced a lively religious marketplace which has created a complex mosaic of faiths, further diversifying the traditions that early immigrants brought to America. The USA was also distinguished by a fairly high level of religious practice even in the late twentieth century, seemingly resisting the secularising tides sweeping over much of Europe.

The combination of religious diversity with high religiosity has precluded development of 'religious' and 'secular' political parties. Rather, as ethnocultural theory observes, parties in the USA have always comprised opposing coalitions of ethnoreligious groups, with distinct world views, cultural preferences and negative reference groups (Swierenga 2009). In the nineteenth century, for example, the Whigs and later the Republicans represented the 'old-line' Protestant churches, such as Congregationalists, Episcopalians, Presbyterians and Methodists, while Democrats spoke for religious minorities, especially Catholics and Jews in most of the country, and Evangelical Protestants in the South. These coalitions persisted with marginal changes well into the 1930s and 1940s, supposedly the era of New Deal 'class politics'.

By the 1990s these old coalitions had been transformed by religious and political changes: old-line (now 'mainline') Protestants dwindled in number and lost their historical Republican preference, replaced by the growing ranks of Evangelicals. The ancient Catholic–Democratic alliance frayed, as many Catholics left the party (Kellstedt and Guth 2014) at the same time that newly enfranchised Black Protestants became a crucial Democratic bloc. Growing religious diversity added Latinos (Catholic and Protestant), Muslims, Hindus, Buddhists and others to the equation, usually on the Democratic side. Thus, modern American party coalitions are as religiously distinct as ever, but look very different from those of the New Deal (Campbell 2007; Kellstedt and Guth 2013).

The 'culture wars' complicated these shifting religious coalitions. Sociologist Robert Wuthnow (1988) first noted this new phenomenon, which he labelled 'religious restructuring', but the term entered common political parlance with James Davison Hunter's *Culture Wars*. Hunter perceived new battles *within* the old ethnoreligious traditions between 'orthodox' believers in 'an external, definable, and transcendent authority', and 'progressives' who replaced old religious tenets with new ones based on experience or scientific rationality (Hunter 1991, 44). The progressives were joined by the growing ranks of 'Seculars' who saw morality in a similar vein (Hansen 2011). Although there has been heated debate over the extent and depth of the culture wars, such divisions certainly animated 'moral' conflicts over abortion, feminism and gay rights, and arguably influenced attitudes on economic management, taxation, social welfare, the environment and even foreign policy, especially among party activists and elites (Green et al. 1991; Williams 1997; Layman 2001; Green and Jackson 2007).

Despite the pervasive influence of religion on US electoral politics, there has been little analysis of its role in legislative institutions (for a comprehensive review, see Oldmixon 2009). There are many reasons for this neglect. Social scientists have long assumed that the primary cleavages in American politics are economic, not cultural (Wald and Wilcox 2006) and many hold standard academic assumptions about the inevitable secularisation of modern societies, despite challenges to this model (see Norris and Inglehart 2004; Toff et al. 2011). Scholars usually favour strict separation of church and state and assume that religion does not influence legislative politics or that it should not. The strongest deterrents, however, are practical: few analysts invest the time and energy to understand the complexities of American religion (Smidt et al. 2009) and to gather systematic but sensitive religious data on legislators (Benson and Williams 1982).

The methodology

In this analysis I review the influence of religious factors in the US House of Representatives (the House) from 1953 to 2003, considering the intersection of ethnoreligious and culture wars politics. Alignments in the House exhibit the same transition seen in the electorate: from relatively simple ethnoreligious party alliances in the 1950s, 1960s and 1970s to more complex patterns shaped by growing ethnoreligious diversity and the advent of religious restructuring. To illustrate, I employ variables most relevant to each theoretical perspective: member affiliation with *religious traditions* for the ethnoreligious approach, and *religious activity and theological orientation* for the culture wars or restructuring theory. These measures require some explanation.

Religious traditions

In order to reduce the enormous complexity of affiliations into conceptually meaningful categories, I sort legislators into religious traditions: groups of denominations and churches sharing common doctrines, practices, histories, organisational attachments and, often, ethnic roots (Steensland et al. 2000; Smidt et al. 2009). The major traditions are Evangelical Protestant, Mainline Protestant, White Catholic, Latino Catholic, Jewish, Black Protestant, Latter-day Saints and Seculars. Although I keep a few other groups (Christian Scientists, Unitarians and Eastern Orthodox) distinct for some purposes, I usually combine them as 'All Others', given their modest numbers. As some research has suggested the political distinctiveness of these traditions (Asmussen 2011; D'Antonio et al. 2013), my first approach to religious influence focuses on affiliation. For my historical review, the main problem is the difficulty of finding accurate religious information about past House members: generic directory descriptions of 'Lutheran', 'Presbyterian' or 'Baptist' do not permit confident assignments, as specific denominations in each family fall into different traditions. For more recent periods, the greater availability of information allows greater accuracy in assignments. Although ethnoreligious affiliation retains some analytic value, evidence on the mass public and political activists suggests that religious belief and behaviour are now far stronger predictors of political variables, at least within the 'older' traditions (Kellstedt and Guth 2013). Beginning with the 105th Congress (1997–99), then, I have assembled detailed portfolios of religious data on all representatives, derived from extensive searches in biographical directories, local newspapers, religious publications, member and staff interviews, congressional websites and a host of other sources (for details on methodology, see Guth 2007).

Religious activity and theological orientation

In the second part of the analysis, I use this research to add belief and behaviour measures that tap 'culture war' or religious restructuring influences in Congress.

First, I use a four-point religious activity scale: (0) no apparent religious involvement; (1) formal congregation membership, but no evidence of regular activity; (2) regular attendance at services; (3) leadership in a congregation or religious group. I have a good deal of confidence in this scale.

The second task, that of gauging the theological orientation of legislators, is however both more problematic and more crucial. After all, the 'culture wars' have been fought between the 'orthodox' on one side and religious 'progressives' and secularists on the other (Hunter 1991). Since such divisions appear among clergy, religious interest groups, political activists and the mass public, similar factions should appear in the House (Hanna 1979; Benson and Williams 1982). As these theological cleavages are most advanced in the historic white Christian traditions, rather than among ethnoreligious 'minorities' such as Black Protestants or Latino Catholics, I focus on Evangelicals, Mainline Protestants and White Catholics, classifying them as traditionalists, centrists, or modernists, on the basis of 'personal testimony' such as speeches, sermons or public statements of faith, as well as on the basis of membership in religious organisations grounded in theological stances. My approach was very cautious, but I was able to place most Evangelicals (89 per cent) and about two-thirds of the Mainline Protestants and White Catholics (69 per cent and 66 per cent respectively). The remaining members of each major tradition and most legislators from smaller traditions were unclassified.

The House 1953–1994: the challenge to ethnocultural alignments

My review of the House from 1953 to 1994 necessarily relies on historical data capturing religious affiliation, combined with some partial but tantalising hints about its influence on legislative behaviour (Grant et al. 1995). To illustrate the changing ethnoreligious alignments from 1953 to 1994, I focus on the 83rd (1953–54), 93rd (1973–74) and 103rd (1993–94) Congresses.

As Table 1 shows, religious alignments in 1953–54 reflect the broad configuration of New Deal coalitions described earlier. The Republican Party is truly 'the Mainline Protestant church in politics', as it is often described: over two thirds are from that tradition; the rest come from White Catholic, Evangelical or other backgrounds. Perhaps surprisingly, Mainline Protestants also constituted the largest ethnoreligious bloc among Democrats, a reminder of the Mainline's long dominance of national politics. Still, the historic reliance of the Democrats on ethnoreligious minorities is confirmed: their caucus includes most Catholics, Evangelicals, Jews and unaffiliated representatives.

This New Deal coalition changed over time, however, following (although lagging behind) the movement of religious groups in the electorate. The first major development was the decline of the Mainline Protestant component of the Republican Party from over two thirds in 1953 to less than half by 1993, reflecting in part dramatic losses in Mainline Protestant membership in the USA. Evangelicals declined from 21.4 per cent to only 8.7 per cent of the Democratic caucus, but rose from 6.9 per cent to 15.3 per cent of the Republican conference by 1993–94, and Catholics grew from 10.6 per cent to 22.7 per cent of the Republican conference, if all Catholics are included. In the Democratic Party, Mainline Protestants declined from 42.3 per cent to 36.5 per cent, White Catholics remained steady at about a quarter, and the percentage of Black and Latino Catholics increased. By the 1990s, White Catholics were a major element in each party, but the Democrats had a monopoly on minority Catholics. Growing numbers of Jews and Black Protestants, with a scattering of other faiths, filled the remaining Democratic ranks by 1993.

By the 1990s, then, the Republican Party was no longer the 'Mainline Church in politics', but included large contingents of Evangelical, Mainline Protestant and Catholic

Table 1.   Religious traditions in the House, 1953–1994 (per cent by Congress).

	All Members (%)			Republicans (%)			Democrats (%)		
	1953–54	1973–74	1993–94	1953–54	1973–74	1993–94	1953–54	1973–74	1993–94
Major traditions:									
Evangelical	14.2	13.3	11.4	6.9	11.4	15.3	21.4	14.9	8.7
Mainline	55.5	52.3	41.7	68.8	66.8	49.4	42.3	41.0	36.5
White Catholic	18.5	21.9	23.0	10.6	16.1	21.6	26.5	26.5	24.0
Latino Catholic	0.0	2.6	4.1	0.0	0.5	1.1	0.0	2.4	6.1
Jewish	2.3	2.7	7.3	0.5	1.0	2.8	4.1	4.0	10.3
Black Protestant	0.5	2.5	6.4	0.0	0.0	0.6	0.9	4.4	10.3
Others:									
Unitarian	2.3	1.1	1.1	3.7	0.5	0.6	0.9	2.0	1.5
Latter-day Saints	0.7	1.6	2.1	1.4	1.6	4.0	0.0	1.6	0.8
Christian Science	0.7	0.9	0.9	0.5	1.6	2.3	0.9	0.4	0.0
Orthodox	0.0	0.7	0.9	0.0	0.0	2.3	0.0	1.2	0.0
None	5.7	1.1	1.1	7.8	0.5	0.0	3.6	1.6	1.9
Totals	100%	100%	100%	100%	100%	100%	100%	100%	100%

Christians, plus a small but solid bloc of Latter-day Saints (Mormons). The Democratic Party, long the electoral home of most religious, ethnic and racial minorities, now fully exhibited that identity in its congressional corps. Mainline Protestants remained the largest Democratic bloc in 1993–94, but constituted just over a third, with combined Catholic forces close behind at about 30 per cent. Clearly, the old Mainline Protestant domination had yielded to growing religious diversity in both parties, although the House's ethno-religious composition lagged behind changes in the 'electoral bases' of each party.

Did religious affiliation influence Congressional behaviour during this period, dominated by economic policy, civil rights and foreign policy issues? Did 'culture war' politics appear during the later years, as abortion, gay rights and religious exercise became part of the national agenda? There has been little systematic analysis of these questions, but we can assemble some evidence. For example, Fenton (1960) found no differences between 'Protestants' and 'Catholics' on civil rights, foreign aid or labour issues in 1959–60, controlling for party and region (of course, Protestants and Catholics chose different parties in part because of the parties' divergent views on such issues). Rieselbach (1966) found Catholics more supportive of foreign aid, while Warner (1968) discovered that in the 89th Congress Mainline Protestants were the most conservative on social welfare and Jews were most liberal. All these studies suffered from crude affiliation measures and lacked controls for other influences. Nevertheless, the patterns found conform broadly to the outlines of New Deal party coalition politics.

A quick look at members of the three Houses under scrutiny here shows that even when we control for political party, legislators from each tradition exhibit a common ideological pattern when we use standard ratings systems, such as Americans for Democratic Action (ADA) scores (Anderson and Habel 2009). Evangelicals were the most conservative, Mainline Protestants somewhat less so, White Catholics more moderate, and Jews, Black Protestants and other religious minorities consistently the most liberal. This same pattern holds *within each party*, although naturally each Democratic contingent was more liberal than its Republican counterpart (my own data, not shown here). These findings confirm the more detailed studies by Green and Guth (1991) and Fastnow et al. (1999) on this era, both of which found substantial ideological differences between the major traditions, even after incorporating multivariate controls.

All the rating scales available for this period, however, were based on the New Deal agenda of government economic activism and foreign policy internationalism. By the 1980s some evidence suggested that religious affiliation might also influence voting on the 'new' culture war issues reaching the House agenda (D'Antonio et al. 2013). Several studies showed rather dramatic affiliation effects on abortion, gay rights and similar issues, even with rigorous controls for personal and constituency characteristics (Adams 1997; Haider-Markel 2001; Oldmixon 2005; Oldmixon and Calfano 2007). Catholics, Evangelicals and Latter-day Saints were systematically more conservative, while Jews, Mainline Protestants and most religious minorities were more liberal. At the same time, however, the influence of ethnoreligious affiliation over such issues seemed to be *declining* over time (Fastnow et al. 1999; D'Antonio et al. 2013).

Perhaps theological divisions were cutting across or even obliterating historic ethnoreligious lines. Even before Wuthnow and Hunter introduced the idea of religious restructuring in the late 1980s, Hanna (1979) had argued that Catholic members held two competing religious perspectives: one traditionalist and legalist (held by Republicans), the other progressive and communitarian (held by Democrats). Benson and Williams (1982) extended this insight to legislators generally: the influence of religious affiliation was superseded by the *type of religious belief.* They argued that conservatism was fostered by 'individualistic' religion, while liberalism was infused by 'communitarian' views. Although their terminology was different, both analyses captured new divisions among America's elites.

Religious restructuring interacted with the ongoing realignment of historic ethnoreligious traditions in complex ways. Evangelicals had always been theologically and ideologically conservative, but were now 'moving' to the conservative party, the Republican Party, and anecdotal evidence suggested that theological divisions within the Catholic and Mainline Protestant traditions influenced which Catholics and Mainline Protestants chose to run for office in each party, with traditionalists gravitating toward the Republicans and progressives toward the Democrats. At the same time, religion in the House diversified. At first this process simply meant more numerous Jewish, Black Protestant and other familiar ethnoreligious minorities, but the trend later extended to increasing denominational variety among Evangelicals and, even later, to Muslim, Hindu and Buddhist representatives (and by the second decade of the new century several members claimed no religious identification at all). With the exception of the Evangelicals, virtually all these 'new' members appeared on the Democratic side.

Religion in the House, 1997–2003: the triumph of religious restructuring?

We can investigate the complex intersection of ethnoreligious and culture war politics with our more extensive data set on House members from 1997 to 2003. First, Table 2 reveals the continuation of some historic tendencies and major changes as well. Although Evangelicals were still underrepresented in comparison with their one quarter of the national population, they had increased over the numbers reported in Table 1, with over

Table 2.   Religious traits of US House members, 1997–2003.

	$N =$	House membership (%)	Democratic proportion of group (%)	Republican proportion of group (%)
Religious tradition				
Evangelical	92	17.3	14.1	85.9
Latter-day Saints	15	4.2	20.0	80.0
Mainline	165	31.0	36.4	63.6
White Catholic	132	24.8	52.3	47.7
All others	32	6.0	40.6	59.4
Black Protestant	34	6.4	100.0	0.0
Latino Catholic	23	4.3	91.3	8.7
Jewish	32	6.0	87.5	12.5
Secular	8	1.5	100.0	0.0
Religious activity				
None known	167	31.3	61.7	38.3
Member only	79	14.8	53.2	46.8
Regular attender	119	22.3	40.3	59.7
Office/activist	168	31.5	32.7	67.3
Theology				
Modernist	40	7.5	87.5	12.5
Undetermined	222	41.7	65.8	34.2
Centrist	138	25.9	41.3	58.7
Traditionalist	133	25.0	7.5	92.5
ALL	*533*	*100.0*	*46.5*	*53.5*

17 per cent of House members from 1997 to 2003. Mainline Protestants retained about twice the proportion of their one-sixth of the population (31 per cent). Combining White and Latino Catholics produces a total reasonably in line with the national population, although the former may be slightly over-represented and the latter under-represented. Similarly, Black Protestants were somewhat fewer and Jews more numerous than 'descriptive representation' would warrant. Unaffiliated or 'secular' citizens still found few of their kind in the House, although their numbers have increased modestly since 2003 (my own data, not shown here).

The partisan location of religious groups is more interesting. As in the electorate, Evangelicals were overwhelmingly Republican, as were Latter-day Saints. Mainline Protestants were still solidly in the Republican camp, whereas White Catholics showed a slight Democratic tilt, both reflecting something of their historical allegiance rather than the current 'swing vote' status of their voters. Not surprisingly, Latino Catholics, Jews, Black Protestants and Seculars were overwhelmingly Democratic, like their mass public counterparts. Seen from the other direction, the Republican Party in the House was largely a Mainline Protestant (37 per cent), Evangelical (28 per cent) and White Catholic (22 per cent) body, while Democrats were more diverse with White Catholics (28 per cent), Mainline Protestants (24 per cent), Black Protestants (14 per cent) and Jews (13 per cent) all having substantial contingents.

Religious activity and theology differentiated the parties, much as they distinguished voters and party activists: over two-thirds of the religiously active members were Republicans, while three-fifths of those with no discernible religious involvement were Democrats. Regular attenders were solidly Republican and less faithful members Democrats. Finally, theological traditionalists were overwhelmingly Republican, while the much smaller coterie of modernists was almost as firmly Democratic. Two-thirds of those for whom we could not make a judgment (including many religious minorities) were Democrats, while centrists tended to be Republicans. Although the religious activity and theology measures must be used cautiously, it is reassuring that they exhibited the same relationship with House partisanship as they did in the mass public (Kellstedt and Guth 2013) and among party leaders (Green and Jackson 2007).

Did legislative voting vary systematically by religious affiliation, activity and belief? We analysed the record of 533 members on five standard voting scores: the DW-Nominate ideological score (Poole and Rosenthal 2007); *National Journal* scores on social, economic and foreign policy; and the party voting score of the *Congressional Quarterly*. We used the mean score for each legislator throughout his or her tenure over these six sessions, as voting has been quite consistent over this period (Poole and Rosenthal 2007). As Table 3 shows, religious traditions differed strongly on Poole and Rosenthal's standard DW-Nominate ideology score, with Evangelicals most conservative, followed closely by Latter-day Saints, and at a distance by Mainline Protestants. White Catholics fell very slightly to the liberal side, and Latino Catholics and Black Protestants much more so, while Jewish and Seculars were prominent at the liberal end. Although many scholars have assumed that the influence of religion is confined to social issues, our results belie such conclusions. The patterns on social, economic and foreign policy scales were *all* monotonously like that on general ideology, although the eta statistic was slightly higher on social issues. This finding is worth stressing: *the influence of religion is not confined to 'culture war' issues, but extends to economic and foreign policy and, indeed, to overall ideological voting.* Note that party unity scores also correlated quite strongly with ethnoreligious tradition, although at a slightly lower level than with the other measures.

Table 3. Religion and ideological orientation in the House of Representatives, 1997–2003 (means).

	DW-Nominate (liberalism)	Social issue liberalism	Economic issue liberalism	Foreign policy liberalism
All	*0.0489*	*46.17*	*47.40*	*47.41*
Religious tradition				
Evangelical	−0.3771	19.43	25.27	25.21
Latter-day Saints	−0.3599	25.56	28.32	27.51
Mainline	−0.1426	41.29	39.89	41.14
White Catholic	−0.0156	47.60	52.27	50.60
All others	−0.0137	51.32	48.84	49.33
Black Protestant	0.3322	75.01	73.15	70.21
Latino Catholic	0.3425	77.32	76.48	75.05
Jewish	0.5035	83.14	80.07	83.83
Secular	0.5511	87.22	81.69	83.74
Eta =	*0.589*	*0.638*	*0.598*	*0.589*
Theological traditionalism				
Modernist	0.3544	76.76	74.08	76.96
Not ascertained	0.1423	61.17	59.49	59.13
Centrist	−0.1050	42.86	44.73	45.30
Traditionalist	−0.4313	16.26	22.04	21.24
Eta =	*0.589*	*0.664*	*0.596*	*0.606*
Religious activity				
Unknown/none	0.1059	59.02	57.17	56.82
Membership	−0.0079	49.43	50.96	49.71
Active member	−0.0965	42.85	45.10	45.79
Office/activist	−0.1884	34.18	37.61	38.09
Eta =	*0.278*	*0.344*	*0.285*	*0.265*
Religious constituencies				
r =				
Evangelical	−0.402**	−0.507**	−0.464**	−0.425**
Latter-day Saints	−0.090*	−0.091*	−0.128**	−0.122**
Mainline Protestant	−0.350**	−0.377**	−0.357**	−0.323**
White Catholic	0.049	0.061	0.105*	0.060
Black Protestant	0.334**	0.293**	0.286**	0.318**
Latino Catholic	0.191**	0.265**	0.223**	0.210**
Jewish	0.286**	0.321**	0.314**	0.255**

Note: All variables are recoded to run so that high positive scores are most liberal or Democratic.
$*p < 0.05$; $**p < 0.01$

The 'culture war' variables were also revealing. Theology had a powerful relation with all the voting scores: modernists were most liberal, followed by those whose theology was uncertain and then by centrists, with traditionalists having the most con-servative (and Republican) scores. Once again, the relationship was strongest on social issues, but not by very much. The religious activity scale was clearly less powerful, as shown by the etas, but the patterns were consistent across the issue areas. Still, the ideological gap between 'activists' and 'non-attenders' was smaller than that for either affiliation or theology. The conservatism of the religiously active was probably an artefact of the greater religious engagement of traditionalists.

If personal religious traits of members were strongly associated with their legislative decisions, is the same true of constituency religious factors? A hoary theme of the congressional literature is the role that constituents play in legislators' calculations. To check out this possibility, we calculated the religious composition of House districts, on the basis of the 1990 Glenmary Research Centre religious census (Bradley et al. 1992). As Table 3 shows, voting bears a reasonable relationship to constituency religion. District Evangelical membership has a distinctly conservative impact on all voting scores; so, to a lesser extent, does Mainline Protestant population, followed by Latter-day Saint population. White Catholic population predicts only a modestly higher score on economic liberalism, but Black Protestant, Latino Catholic and Jewish populations are associated with liberalism across the board. Thus the religious influence of constituency parallels that of legislator affiliation.

This raises the classic issue of the relative influence of personal and constituency opinion on legislator behaviour. Do districts elect members who share their own traits and attitudes? Or do representatives defer to their constituency, even if their own traits and views differ? We cannot fully resolve this question, but Table 4 throws some light on it. We ran regressions for all five scores, including dummies for ethnoreligious tradition ('All Others' is the omitted reference category), religious activity and theology, and religious populations in legislators' districts. With the single exception of White Catholic liberalism on economics, member affiliation with the three largest traditions had no direct impact, once other religious factors were accounted for. Legislator theology was by far the best predictor, with traditionalism reducing liberalism and Democratic voting. Thus, for Evangelical, Mainline Protestant and White Catholic legislators it was *theological location* that influenced voting. On the other hand, *membership* in most minority

Table 4. Religion, ideology and partisanship in the House of Representatives, 1997–2003 (standardised regression coefficients, ordinary least squares (OLS) analysis) $N = 533$.

DW-Nominate liberalism	Social issue liberalism	Economic issue liberalism	Foreign policy liberalism	Party unity scores (Democratic)
Member faith tradition				
Evangelical	−0.013	−0.045	0.004	−0.008
Latter-day Saints	0.030	0.005	0.046	0.021
Mainline	0.034	0.061	0.036	0.037
White Catholic	0.070	0.035	0.114**	0.090
All others	—	—	—	—
Black Protestant	0.099	0.119*	0.117*	0.120*
Latino Catholic	0.171**	0.153**	0.197**	0.177**
Jewish	0.161**	0.162**	0.172**	0.150**
Secular	0.156**	0.143**	0.137**	0.147**
Belief and practice				
Theology	−0.426**	−0.422**	−0.406**	−0.454**
Activity	0.055	0.034	0.063	0.090*
District religion				
Evangelical	−0.099*	−0.212**	−0.153**	−0.139*
Latter-day Saint	−0.035	−0.050	−0.091*	−0.069
Mainline	−0.093	−0.107*	−0.118*	−0.080*
White Catholic	0.049	0.032	0.085	0.055
Black Protestant	0.211**	0.140**	0.151*	0.173**
Latino Catholic	−0.033	0.017	0.003	0.004
Jewish	0.043	0.014	0.013	−0.014
Adjusted R squared	*0.501*	*0.609*	*0.527*	*0.514*

Note: *$p < 0.05$; **$p < 0.01$.

ethnoreligious groups produced liberal and Democratic votes. Thus, both ethnoreligious affiliation and religious belief help predict behaviour in the House, as in the electorate. Constituencies influence voting primarily by electing members who share their religious orientation; most district coefficients are insignificant once member traits are included. Still, there are a few district religious effects: larger Evangelical numbers increase conservative and Republican voting on all five scores, while Black Protestant membership has the opposite effect. That these are 'core' Republican and Democratic religious constituencies, respectively, suggests that members – especially those from other traditions – pay them special attention. The only other notable constituency effect is a mild conservatising influence of district Mainline Protestant membership.

Connoisseurs of the literature on religious voting in the mass public may well experience *déjà vu*. Religious influences in the electorate have finally been reproduced with some fidelity in the House, as Evangelicals and Latter-day Saints are strongly Republican, Mainline Protestants and White Catholics have been swing groups, and religious minorities and secular voters are disproportionately Democratic supporters. Even more important, perhaps, is the fact that theological traditionalists have supported the Republicans, while modernists and secularists have supported the Democrats. The fact that representatives from these traditions and theological perspectives and from districts dominated by them are located in analogous political space in the House should not be surprising, and the fact that religious measures alone account for half or more of the variance in voting scores is impressive.

Are these real relationships, or merely 'correlations' produced by other more powerful influences? The political scientist Tom Mann (1990) alleges that in Congress 'religion has a very spurious relationship with political ideology and voting... that just explains nothing independently'. Barry Burden (2007, 113) counters that 'for many members their religious attachments are always near the surface, animating their policy views...' To address this argument, in Table 5 we added other standard variables to the regression, namely the member's party and gender and the district's party composition and socioeconomic status. Not surprisingly, district partisanship as measured by presidential vote has the largest impact on ideology and wealthier districts also produce more conservative voting. Nevertheless, theological traditionalism still has a powerful independent effect, as do Latino Catholic, Jewish and Secular identities. District religion has no direct impact, once district partisanship is taken into account. Apparently district religious influences are fully mediated by the party preferences of the faithful and their choice of representatives, a surmise reinforced by the fact that the variance explained increases only modestly from that accounted for by religious variables alone (0.621 versus 0.501).

The story for the more specialised scales is similar. For the three issue scales (social issues, foreign policy issues, economic issues) member party is the most powerful, buttressed by district partisanship, but theological traditionalism adds considerable explanatory power, as do Evangelical numbers in the district. Secular legislators are also sometimes distinct, and membership in a minority religious tradition adds a little to Democratic voting, but once again much of the influence of the religion is transmitted through partisanship – either that of the member or of the district. Women are more liberal on all three issue domains, but significantly so only on social and foreign policy. On party unity, district partisanship has the strongest impact, but theological traditionalism still pushes members away from Democratic voting, as does greater district wealth. Black Protestants, Jews and Seculars are more Democratic than other variables would predict. Once again, the gain in variance explained over the equation with religious variables alone is modest (0.522 versus 0.428).

Table 5. Religious variables, ideology and partisanship in the House of Representatives, 1997–2003 with control variables (standardised regression coefficients, OLS analysis) $N = 533$.

DW-Nominate liberalism	Social issue liberalism	Economic issue liberalism	Foreign policy liberalism	Party unity scores (Democratic)
Member Faith tradition				
Evangelical	−0.015	−0.058	−0.029	−0.001
Latter-day Saints	0.039	−0.008	−0.001	−0.014
Mainline	0.046	0.021	−0.015	0.004
White Catholic	0.047	−0.065	−0.019	−0.009
All others	—	—	—	—
Black Protestant	0.052	0.033	0.007	0.064
Latino Catholic	0.098*	0.037	0.043	0.056
Jewish	0.120*	0.025	0.005	0.002
Secular	0.103*	0.046*	0.012	0.043*
Belief and practice				
Theology	−0.308**	−0.165**	−0.094**	−0.133**
Activity	0.052	0.001	0.025	0.057*
District religion				
Evangelical	0.037	−0.132**	−0.079*	−0.087*
Latter-day Saint	0.022	−0.015	−0.039	−0.017
Mainline	−0.073	−0.018	−0.015	0.010
White Catholic	0.068	0.010	0.085**	0.026
Black Protestant	−0.018	−0.022	−0.056	−0.052
Latino Catholic	−0.049	−0.009	−0.011	−0.024
Jewish	0.012	−0.040	−0.008	−0.041
Control variables				
Party (GOP)	—	−0.508**	−0.658**	−0.664**
District party (GOP)	−0.512**	−0.248**	−0.255**	−0.212**
District income	−0.129**	0.065*	−0.041	0.003
Female MC	0.056	0.075**	0.026	0.038*
Adjusted R squared	*0.621*	*0.843*	*0.896*	*0.858*

Note: *$p < 0.05$; **$p < 0.01$.

Of course, these findings come from analysis of House members serving before 2003. We continue to assemble religious profiles for new members of Congress and will extend this study into more recent sessions. Although it takes some years before we can compile full profiles on new members, preliminary analysis suggests that the main tendencies we see in 1997–2003 have continued and intensified: Evangelicals are ever more concentrated on the Republican side, despite sporadic Democratic efforts to recruit more Evangelical candidates; ethnoreligious minorities have grown in the Democratic caucus as their share of the party's electorate rises; Mainline Protestants and White Catholics remain closely divided between the parties, with ever-clearer divisions between theologically 'traditionalist' Republicans and 'progressive' Democrats. Finally, recent elections have produced several explicitly non-religious Democratic members, paralleling the growth of 'Nones' in the national electorate.

Conclusions

This research demonstrates continuing religious influences on Congressional behaviour. We find that both the older ethnoreligious perspective, based on affiliation, and the newer restructuring thesis, stressing the impact of theological orientation, are useful in our analysis. The influence of historic ethnoreligious traditions – based on ethnicity, religious ethos and unique historical experience – still appears in the affinity of Black Protestants, Jews and Seculars for liberal Democratic policies. In the three major white religious traditions theology shows a consistently strong influence on voting: traditionalists exhibit political conservatism and Republican voting, while modernists are consistently liberal or Democratic. Apparent voting differences between the major traditions result mostly from the different sizes of theological factions within each. Thus the conservatism among Evangelicals reflects their overwhelming theological traditionalism, not some historic, regional or ethnic trait. Similarly, the 'centrist' position of White Catholics results from a close numerical balance between traditionalists and progressives, not from some inherent 'moderation' present in Catholicism. Much of the influence of religion is channelled indirectly through changes in the composition of the two legislative parties, changes tracking those in the electorate. What some observers have seen as the declining influence of religion (as measured by affiliation) is better understood as the institutionalisation of religious affiliations within party structures. Like voters, legislators are 'sorting' themselves religiously. Nevertheless, religious influences are not entirely mediated by partisanship: even when party membership and district partisanship are controlled, member theology and some ethnoreligious ties retain a direct impact.

The strong relationship that ethnoreligious and theological factors have with House voting patterns appears to contrast with the more subtle role that faith plays in the lives of European parliamentarians. Not only do religious factors appear to shape voting choices, but American representatives are far more likely to express religious reasons for those choices, participate in religious institutions and practices, and utilise religious strategies in appealing to their constituencies. Our research portfolios are full of examples. Although there is a small, but growing, number of non-religious members, representatives are still more likely than the average American to claim a religious affiliation, belong to a congregation, and actively participate in religious life.

Where do we go from here? First, political scientists studying religion and politics need to pay more attention to political elites such as members of Congress. Public officials and party leaders not only are chosen by the very electoral processes that have been so influenced by religious factors recently, but they also provide the cues that both elicit and organise religious responses to issues (Layman 2001; Leege et al. 2002). Such elite cues are not limited to abortion and gay rights, but extend to economic and foreign policy issues as well. We especially need more attention on the Senate, the subject of only a few recent articles dealing with specific 'religious' issues. Long dominated by Mainline Protestants, Catholics and Jews, the Senate has always been less representative of the national religious population than the House, but greater diversity is also appearing there. Studies of the Senate also have the analytic advantage of religious membership data that are much more easily available (and accurate) for states than for House districts (Rosenson et al. 2009; Smith et al. 2010; McTague and Pearson-Merkowitz 2011, 2013).

Beyond extending the scope of our analysis, we need to know more about religious activity among members, such as prayer and Bible study groups, 'reflection sessions' (favoured by the more liberal), and other religious engagement. Such informal networks may influence member behaviour and, perhaps, even legislative norms. For example, House prayer groups seem to be increasingly split along partisan lines, perhaps creating or reinforcing contemporary partisan animosities, while their Senate counterparts still appear somewhat more bipartisan. Indeed, the increasing influence of Evangelicals in the Republican Party and of religious minorities and secularists in the Democratic Party has been offered as a cause of growing polarisation in the House. Some argue that the lines of conflict have merely been redrawn as religious groups 'sort' themselves into the appropriate party, while other analysts claim that religious changes have actually added fuel to partisan battles (Asmussen 2011; McTague and Pearson-Merkowitz 2011). The concentration of the most theologically conservative Republican members in the most politically conservative and (often most belligerent) faction of the House party conference may be suggestive (Guth and Kellstedt 2001).

Scholars should also assess religious influence on actions other than floor votes, which increasingly follow party lines. Indeed, Burden (2007) argues that personal traits are most likely to influence decisions to introduce bills, participate in debates and undertake other preliminary legislative actions; others see such actions influenced by constituency religion as well (Highton and Rocca 2005). Here the content analysis of member interventions in the European Parliament can provide a model. Religious values may also influence choice of legislative committees or congressional caucuses, such as the House Prayer Caucus, the Values Action Team or the Republican Study Group (Guth and Kellstedt 2001). In a similar vein, there is much to learn about the way legislators relate to organised lobbies, whether the Family Research Council, the National Council of Churches, or denominational representatives (Smith et al. 2010; McTague and Pearson-Merkowitz 2011).

Finally, we should explore how members relate to constituents personally; in other words, identify their 'religious home styles' (see Fenno 1978). Our research reveals a fascinating variety of such styles. Some legislators participate vigorously in the faith dominant in their district, while others – especially members of a 'minority' tradition in their constituency – insist on the legislative irrelevance of their 'private' faith. Yet others may address such a religious gap, as some Jewish Democrats do, spending Sundays circulating among Black Baptist churches in their religiously mixed districts, hoping to solidify the vote of that important Democratic constituency.

Religion clearly matters in American politics – and we need to know much more about the myriad ways it matters to national legislators.

Funding

This research was supported by the William R. Kenan, Jr. Endowment, the Furman Advantage Program and a small grant from the Dirksen Centre for Congressional Studies.

References

Adams, G. D. 1997. "Abortion: Evidence of an Issue Evolution." *American Journal of Political Science* 41 (3): 718–737. doi:10.2307/2111673.

Anderson, S., and P. Habel. 2009. "Revisiting Adjusted ADA Scores for the U.S. Congress, 1947 to 2009." *Political Behavior* 17 (1): 83–88.

Asmussen, N. 2011. "Polarized Protestants: A Confessional Explanation for Party Polarization." Paper presented at the annual meeting of the American Political Science Association, Seattle, September 1–4.

Benson, P. L., and D. L. Williams. 1982. *Religion on Capitol Hill: Myths and Realities.* San Francisco, CA: Harper and Row.

Bradley, M. B., M. N. Green Jr, D. E. Jones, M. Lynn, and L. McNeil. 1992. *Churches and Church Membership in the United States, 1990.* Atlanta, GA: Glenmary Research Centre.

Burden, B. C. 2007. *Personal Roots of Representation.* Princeton, NJ: Princeton University Press.

Campbell, D. E., ed. 2007. *A Matter of Faith: Religion in the 2004 Presidential Election.* Washington, DC: Brookings Institution.

D'Antonio, W. V., S. A. Tuch, and J. R. Baker. 2013. *Religion, Politics and Polarization.* Lanham: Rowman & Littlefield.

Fastnow, C., J. T. Grant, and T. J. Rudolph. 1999. "Holy Roll Calls: Religious Traditions and House Voting." *Social Science Quarterly* 80 (4): 687–701.

Fenno, R. 1978. *Home Style.* Boston, MA: Little, Brown.

Fenton, J. H. 1960. *The Catholic Vote.* New Orleans, LA: Hauser.

Grant, J. T., L. A. Kellstedt, and T. J. Rudolph. 1995. "The Changing Religious Composition of the U.S. Congress." Paper presented at the annual meeting of the Society for the Scientific Study of Religion, St Louis, October 27–29.

Green, J. C., and J. L. Guth. 1991. "Religion, Representatives, and Roll Calls." *Legislative Studies Quarterly* 16 (4): 571–584. doi:10.2307/440018.

Green, J. C., and J. S. Jackson. 2007. "Faithful Divides: Party Elites and Religion." In *A Matter of Faith: Religion in the 2004 Presidential Election*, edited by D. E. Campbell, 37–62. Washington DC: Brookings Institution.

Green, J. C., J. L. Guth, and C. R. Fraser. 1991. "Apostles and Apostates? Religion and Politics among Political Activists." In *The Bible and the Ballot Box*, edited by J. L. Guth and J. C. Green, 113–136. Boulder, CO: Westview Press.

Guth, J. L. 2007. "Religion and Roll Calls." Paper presented at the annual meeting of the American Political Science Association, Chicago, August 30–September 2.

Guth, J. L., and L. A. Kellstedt. 2001. "Religion and Congress." In *In God We Trust: Religion and American Political Life*, edited by C. E. Smidt, 213–233. Grand Rapids, MI: Baker Academic.

Haider-Markel, D. P. 2001. "Morality in Congress? Legislative Voting on Gay Issues." In *The Public Clash of Private Values*, edited by C. Z. Mooney, 115–129. Chatham: Chatham House Press.

Hanna, M. 1979. *Catholics and American Politics.* Cambridge, MA: Harvard University Press.

Hansen, S. B. 2011. *Religion and Reaction.* Lanham, MD: Rowman & Littlefield.

Highton, B., and M. S. Rocca. 2005. "Beyond the Roll-call Arena: The Determinants of Position Taking in Congress." *Political Research Quarterly* 58 (2): 303–316. doi:10.1177/1065912905050900210.

Hunter, J. D. 1991. *Culture Wars.* New York: Basic Books.

Kellstedt, L. A., and J. L. Guth. 2013. "Survey Research: Religion and Electoral Behavior in the United States, 1936–2008." In *Political Science Research in Practice*, edited by A. Malici and E. S. Smith, 93–110. New York: Routledge.

Kellstedt, L. A., and J. L. Guth. 2014. "Catholic Partisanship and the Presidential Vote in 2012." *The Forum* 11 (4): 623–640.

Layman, G. C. 2001. *The Great Divide: Religious and Cultural Conflict in American Party Politics.* New York: Columbia University Press.

Leege, D. C., K. D. Wald, B. S. Krueger, and P. D. Mueller. 2002. *The Politics of Cultural Differences.* Princeton. NJ: Princeton University Press.

Mann, T. 1990. "Religion in Congress." *The Arizona Republic*, August 25.

McTague, J., and S. Pearson-Merkowitz. 2011. "Voting from the Pew: The Effect of Senators' Religious Identities on Partisan Polarization in the U.S. Senate." Paper presented at the annual meeting of the American Political Science Association, Seattle, September 1–4.

McTague, J., and S. Pearson-Merkowitz. 2013. "Thou Shalt Not Flipflop: Senators' Religious Affiliations and Issue Position Change." Paper presented at the annual meeting of the Midwest Political Science Association, Chicago, April 11–14.

Norris, P., and R. Inglehart. 2004. *Sacred and Secular.* Cambridge: Cambridge University Press.

Oldmixon, E. A. 2005. *Uncompromising Positions: God, Sex, and the U.S. House of Representatives*. Washington, DC: Georgetown University Press.

Oldmixon, E. A. 2009. "Religion and Legislative Politics." In *Handbook of Religion and American Politics*, edited by C. E. Smidt, L. A. Kellstedt, and J. L. Guth, 497–517. Oxford: Oxford University Press.

Oldmixon, E. A., and B. R. Calfano. 2007. "The Religious Dynamics of Decision Making on Gay Rights Issues in the U.S. House of Representatives, 1993–2002." *Journal for the Scientific Study of Religion* 46 (1): 55–70. doi:10.1111/j.1468-5906.2007.00340.x.

Poole, K. T., and H. Rosenthal. 2007. *Ideology and Congress*. New Brunswick, NJ: Transaction Publishers.

Rieselbach, L. N. 1966. *The Roots of Isolationism*. Indianapolis, IA: Bobbs-Merrill.

Rosenson, B. A., E. A. Oldmixon, and K. D. Wald. 2009. "U.S. Senators' Support for Israel Examined Through Sponsorship/Cosponsorship Decisions, 1993–2002: The Influence of Elite and Constituent Factors." *Foreign Policy Analysis* 5 (1): 73–91. doi:10.1111/j.1743-8594.2008.00084.x.

Smidt, C. E., L. A. Kellstedt, and J. L. Guth. 2009. "Religion in American Politics: Explanatory Theories and Associated Analytical and Measurement Issues." In *Handbook of Religion and American Politics*, edited by C. E. Smidt, L. A. Kellstedt, and J. L. Guth, 3–42. New York/Oxford: Oxford University Press.

Smith, L. E., L. R. Olson, and J. A. Fine. 2010. "Substantive Religious Representation in the U.S. Senate: Voting Alignment with the Family Research Council." *Political Research Quarterly* 63 (1): 68–82. doi:10.1177/1065912908325080.

Steensland, B., J. Z. Park, M. D. Regnerus, L. D. Robinson, W. B. Wilcox, and R. D. Woodberry. 2000. "The Measure of American Religion: Toward Improving the State of the Art." *Social Forces* 79 (1): 291–318. doi:10.1093/sf/79.1.291.

Swierenga, R. P. 2009. "Religion and American Voting Behavior, 1830s to 1930s." In *Handbook of Religion and American Politics*, edited by C. E. Smidt, L. A. Kellstedt, and J. L. Guth, 69–94. Oxford: Oxford University Press.

Toff, M. D., D. Philpott, and T. S. Shah. 2011. *God's Century: Resurgent Religion and Global Politics*. New York: W.W. Norton.

Wald, K. D., and C. Wilcox. 2006. "Getting Religion: Has Political Science Rediscovered the Faith Factor?" *American Political Science Review* 100 (4): 523–529. doi:10.1017/S0003055406062381.

Warner, J. B. 1968. "Religious Affiliation as a Factor in the Voting Records of Members of the 89th Congress." PhD diss., Boston University.

Williams, R. H., ed. 1997. *Culture Wars in American Politics*. New York: De Gruyter.

Wuthnow, R. 1988. *The Restructuring of American Religion*. Princeton, NJ: Princeton University Press.

Conclusion

Conclusion

François Foret

Institute for European Studies – CEVIPOL, Université Libre de Bruxelles (ULB), Brussels, Belgium

Seven main features

The analysis in this collection of aggregated data on the whole sample of members of the European Parliament (MEPs) has highlighted the resilience of national belongings and political spaces as the prevailing elements structuring the way to deal with religion. In this conclusion, it is worth elaborating further on the comparison between these national patterns, on their possible feedback on European politics and on the different ways they can adapt to or resist Europeanisation. The most significant national cases are referred to as illustrations of con-vergent and divergent features, and non-European countries (the USA and Israel) are used to question European specificities on these matters. Seven main points are underlined, as findings of the RelEP projects and/or possible venues for future research: (1) the general secularisation – a trend encompassing privatisation and culturalisation of religion – which has reached all European societies, to various extents and with different forms; (2) the secondarity of religion to other issues, as well as its underlying influence and its status of instrumental resource to pursue other ends; (3) the importance of the congruence or non-congruence between national and European models for articulating politics and religion in order to understand how political considerations prevail over religious adherences; (4) the fact that European integration does not alter the religious dimension of national identity but may influence the context within which this religious dimension of national identity is enunciated; (5) (a) the development of the link between religious affiliation and party affiliation at the European level, with (b) the specific role of Christian Democracy and (c) the interaction between religious representation through parties and religious advocacy through lobbies, with the exploratory hypothesis that strong religious parties may make weak religious lobbies; (6) the structure of opportunity offered for the Europeanisation of religious issues according to their status in domestic politics, with the hypothesis that the conflictualisation of religion at home opens possibilities for political entrepreneurship on religious causes at the European Parliament (EP) and encourages atheists to make themselves heard in supranational arenas; (7) the importance of the territorialisation of religion, either (a) to ensure its electoral influence through the resistance of local constituencies where religion still matters very much, or (b) to put religion on the geopolitical agenda as a result of religiously connoted relationships with neighbour countries.

(1) Secularisation, privatisation and culturalisation of religion: a common European story

Beyond national differences, it is essential to acknowledge the full reality of European secularisation, understood as the loss of social relevance of religion and the mutations of beliefs and practices. Such phenomena have been well documented by sociology of religion and contributions in this volume corroborate the fact that this is a societal trend sweeping the whole continent, with noticeable political effects. Forms and intensity vary according to the national context but converge in the same direction. The privatisation of religion marks the decline of religion as a collective authoritarian matrix for thinking and behaving, but our data show that its individualisation may lead to its comeback in the public space as expression of personal choices.

Religion is less part of the official discourse and norms and thus becomes an element of culture in free use in searches for identity, memory, recognition or power. This means that secularisation has reinforced support for the public role of religion, as a kind of symbolic public commodity. Three national cases are good examples of the fluidity of religion. In Austria, the 'return' of religion should be interpreted as a collection of 'reconfigurations' and 'interpenetrations' between the religious and the secular, defying any attempt to formulate a global logic. This is evidence of the difficulty in objectifying the actual influence of contemporary religion. It is present where it is not expected and absent where it is expected; it is visible yet impotent, or invisible yet influential, as examples provided by our data show. Religious motives are translated into secular idioms and very materialistic strategies of power may borrow the symbolic clothes of religion. Spain is also interesting regarding its very quick secularisation, driving the country from the status of a Catholic bastion to a showcase of cultural liberalisation, with possible backlash and resistances. Finally, Italy shows Catholics turning themselves from a massive majority unified into a cultural matrix into an influential and highly politicised minority, keeping alive religion as a collective reference to which all politicians have to pay tribute by showing their credentials in terms of personal faith, practice or at least lip service. These three national cases, and many others, are an invitation to consider with caution all established positions and subsequent national stereotypes and to give full attention to ongoing social and political change.

(2) Religion as secondary and instrumental political resource

Religion as an autonomous variable is no longer able to offer a political programme, to mobilise electors, to shape coalitions or to draw boundaries between parties. It is now secondary to economic, social, territorial or political parameters. Still, as underlying factors, religiosity and denominational belonging remain strong variables to predict political behaviour. They do not command but contribute to frame choices by citizens and decision-makers. Religion is also frequently used as a communicative resource to send signals and to pay tribute to historical heritages. Dutch Christian Democrats take hard stances in their electoral manifestos on ethical matters in reference to their religious values and meanwhile are very flexible as members of government coalitions to pass progressive agendas. The plasticity and availability of religion are illustrated through its use by non-religious actors. In Austria, the politicisation of Islam is carried out by far-right populists having very tenuous ties with any Christian heritage but who use majority religion as a cultural code to ostracise the 'other'. Such an instrumental reference to religion as mnesic trace and boundaries-marker is commonly seen among MEPs from all nationalities.

Such a secondary and instrumental use of religion appears as an effect of European secularisation, even if similar phenomena may have existed in a subdued way in earlier periods. In a very different context, the case of Israel illustrates that several repertoires may coexist for the political mobilisation of religion and that its main effect is not necessarily as an authoritarian sacred dictating choices but may also operate in secular fashions. In Israeli politics, religion emerges as a source of authority; as a marker of identity and nation; as a source of values. In the Knesset, only the reference to religion as a source of authority provokes a clash of opposing religious and secular MKs. The second usage of religion as a marker of identity and nation is much more consensual, which can be explained by the fact that Israel was established in great part by a secular movement drawing on a secularised version of the Biblical narrative (in the same way that Europe is, albeit to a much lesser extent, a modern yet Christian-inspired project). Regarding the last usage of religion, as a source of values, both religious and secular representatives draw on the teachings of the Bible to justify openness to the 'other' and to the interpretation of Judaism as a source of ethical principles. The ethical role of religion as reservoir of normative references and pretension to universalism is verified outside secularised Europe, including in countries hosting very religious and very secular forces.

(3) Effects of the (non-)congruence of national and European models for articulating politics and religion

The role of religion in the intertwinement between national and supranational governance and loyalty depends to a large extent on the greater or lesser congruence between the historical arrangements between religion and state in a particular country and the European pattern. The European Union (EU) as a whole and especially the EP are characterised by diversity (many denominational and philosophical groups are represented) and pluralism (the expression of diversity is strongly encouraged and actors willing to play a role in the deliberative arenas in Brussels and Strasbourg have to comply with the rules coming with the territory, for example self-restraint and interfaith coalitions). However, two main features can be underlined. On the one hand, no national model fits perfectly with the EU. It is more accurate to state that some models have more common points than others with the European political system for dealing with religion, but that these common points come generally with differences as well. This is due to the fact that the EU is the hybridisation of multiple national traditions and that it is not possible to trace back a unique national blueprint. On the other hand, the congruence between national and European models for handling religion does not mean that religion will subsequently play a positive role in favour of Europe. Its use by pro- or anti-Europe political actors is equally possible.

Three member-states can be used as relevant illustrations: Germany, the UK and Poland.

Germany is commonly presented as a multi-level governance of politics and religion offering many similarities with what happens at the European level. There is a German history of coexistence between majority denominations, and churches are given a specific role as contributors to public good and actors in social welfare. Religious non-governmental organisations (NGOs) are developed and considered as legitimate interlocutors by politicians. However, German MEPs feel a difference between religion in domestic and in European politics more than the average for their counterparts from other member-states. One reason may be that the peaceful imbrication of political and religious actors they are used to is not taken for granted at the EP and is even resented by other more secularist MEPs coming from other national traditions. Another reason is that privileged relationships with Catholic or Protestant Churches are challenged in the name of equality by other denominations, disturbing old habits and alliances.

From another perspective, the UK with its state Anglican Church and bishops sitting in the House of Lords has not seemed very compatible with a predominantly Catholic Europe. However, the openness of European institutions to lobbying has revealed itself as very hospitable to the British culture of pluralism. British MEPs are less surprised than average by the place of religion at the EP. Their interaction with religious lobbies is not significantly different from that of other nationalities, but they relate to it as 'business as usual', in London as well as in Strasbourg and Brussels. This does not mean that religion plays a major role in their loyalty to Europe. They tend to be more agnostic and atheist than representatives from other countries, reflecting the dominant trends in their society of origin. They reject the option of a specific European religious policy or of a reference to Christian heritage in treaties. The British tradition of soft law does not welcome authoritarian practices and the reification of culture in norms. Thus a national model may have aspects of both compliance and non-compliance with Europe; and in any case this has little to do with the potential Euroscepticism or Euroenthusiasm that MEPs are likely to develop.

Poland demarcates itself from other member-states regarding the intensity of religiosity claimed by Polish MEPs. However, there is no evidence of major discrepancies in political practices and principles stated by these politicians. Most Polish representatives support the separation between church and state and respect for fundamental rights. They do acknowledge a difference between national and European levels, mostly because of a less homogeneous cultural environment and a stronger secularism at the European level. Politicians who are active believers, however, duplicate the same attitudes in national and in European Parliaments. Polish MEPs define their national identity through religion and project a similar nexus onto Europe: to be European is to be Christian as to be Polish is to be Catholic. In both cases, the religious factor gives a kind of cultural superiority to national and supranational collective identity, especially regarding Islam. According to Polish representatives, when the EU is perceived as a 'secular club', this does not only harm religion, it also harms Europe, which loses this cultural superiority endowed by religion. The same symbolic logics are at work at home and in Brussels, even if political realities are different.

(4) European integration does not alter the religious dimension of national identity but may influence its context of enunciation

The EU has no direct competencies in the matter of religious regulation. The treaties stipulate that the EU respect all existing national settings and there is a large consensus to prevent any European intrusion in the complex arrangements between spiritual and profane affairs. European authorities are reluctant to touch issues likely to bring more problems than benefits, national rulers intend to protect their monopoly and religious actors are happy to continue with historical *modi operandi* and to avoid the emergence of unforeseeable new players. Are we to say, then, that European integration has no effect at all on the political uses of religion to define European identity? Case studies suggest that there is indeed no direct effect, but that the EU may function as a discursive arena where criteria of legitimacy are re-discussed and altered. Subsequently, the status of religion as identity resource in domestic politics would be indirectly impacted.

A first example is offered by the study on the Netherlands, a country where 'hard issues' such as economics or security have shifted from the national to the European level. Hence, national politics are reduced to focusing on 'soft issues' to gain back the interest of citizens and their loyalty. The appropriation of debates on materialistic matters by Europe creates space for post-materialistic controversies in domestic arenas. These post-materialistic controversies are good structures of opportunity for the re-emergence of religious influence on ethical matters.

Moreover, European integration reinforces the rule of law and the status of fundamental rights as the sacred reference against which all legitimacies are reassessed. Poland again provides a fascinating illustration. Polish Catholics intend to protect their established positions but are also aware of ongoing trends of secularisation and that any rigid resistance in the name of the authority of religion is bound to fail. So they have learned how to redefine themselves as a minority entitled to claim full protection of law against discrimination by the secularism of public action from the national state or from the EU. They develop a strategy of victimisation fully compatible with the prevailing view in Europe that the cultural majority should not exercise dictatorship and that specificities should be carefully protected. This may be a tactical move as well as an unconscious deep cultural revision; but it is still a sign that the evolution of the political and cultural environment – and European integration is a significant element in this evolution – has an impact on the way religion is expressed in political terms and with political purposes.

Another effect of European integration on the place of religion in the self-definition of Polishness is that Islam has become a substitute for communism as a scapegoat to symbolise 'otherness'. As Muslims are the favourite whipping-boys for the majority of Europeans, to adopt them in this role even if there is only a small presence of Muslims in Poland is a way to become more European. The community of hating may or may not create a community of being, but the verified effect is to change the religious material in order to define national boundaries.

In some cases, Europe may be used in attempts to redefine national identity or, more frequently, national practices rooted in deeper visions of the societal role of religion. Regarding gender issues, the European arsenal of anti-discriminatory rules may be mobilised by civil society to challenge the definition of Polish women as the 'the wombs of the nation', both images of the Polish nation and instruments of its reproduction, hence doubly sacred and necessarily different from men. In Spain, the left tries to bring pressure from Brussels and Strasbourg to bear on national politics in order to contest the established positions of the Catholic Church. These strategies deal mostly with functional concerns: the purpose is to restrict the role of religious actors, not necessarily to contest the identity and memory role of religion. The Lautsi affair has shown that supranational judges or politicians are not welcome to put in question the right for nations and states to deal with religious symbols in their own way in the framing of their collective narratives.

(5) European integration and the maintaining of religiously-related party boundaries

A hypothesis could be that European integration would endanger the established positions of religious parties rooted in historical patterns of relationships between church and state. Alternatively, the EU is sometimes presented as a 'Christian club' ruled by Christian Democracy and which reinforces the domestic prevalence of this political family. Lastly, the place given at the European level to participatory governance and the expression of civil society may raise the question of the unequal strength of religious voices in member-states, either through party representation or lobbying. Let us look at each of these topics in turn.

(a) Religious affiliation and party affiliation at the European level

As the EU respects national institutional and legal frameworks to regulate religion, it also maintains party boundaries on religious issues. At least, it does not provoke changes impacting deeply established cleavages, for example through the emergence of pan-European divides. European competencies do not cover directly issues likely to polarise throughout national and party boundaries (for example a continental referendum on abortion), and both national and supranational political actors converge to avoid Europeanisation of such matters. Here, consociationalism is a useful pattern to illustrate what happens. Consociations are systems aiming at organising diversity without reducing it. Different cultural worlds coexist in parallel and are the basis of the political system through constant negotiation and compromise. These cultural worlds are institutionalised and survive as political realities while social realities may change. The Netherlands offers a telling example of the resilience of religious or secularist identities as lines of political conflict despite the secularisation of society and the evaporation of the societal conflicts. The EU may be understood as a consociation of states, where the member-states are the cultural worlds institutionalised once for all, which themselves petrify their religious and philosophical diversity.

European integration does not significantly alter party boundaries in national politics, but these boundaries may become blurred at the EP, as political groups are not homogeneous and encompass forces with different ideological traditions. Hence, the link between denominational belonging and party affiliation seems more diffuse for Dutch MEPs than for Dutch members of the national Parliament (MPs), and this is also the case to a lesser extent for German MEPs and MPs. In other countries, the European arena may reactivate national polarisation when it is used by one side to challenge the other. This is the case of Spain, where MEPs from the left mobilise European resources to denounce the privileges of the Catholic Church and where the right defends Christian interests.

(b) The specific role of Christian Democracy

Christian Democracy represents a specific political family as a result of its core role in the history of European integration and its strong presence in many member-states. This ideological tradition has experienced a marked decline in the last 30 years and enlargements of the EU have contributed to dilute its centrality and homogeneity. Still, it has resisted as a resilient identity of the European People's Party and may even enjoy a revival through attempts to highlight its symbolic meaning. Two cases are particularly interesting. British MEPs have no Christian Democratic heritage to rely on and British Conservatives opted to join another political group at the EP. So this political family does not function as a universe of socialisation and a network of influence for British representatives, but it does not prevent them being efficient players in Brussels and Strasbourg, and they develop a very 'businesslike' relationship to religion considered as a part of civil society and a policy issue to deal with. Another case is Poland. Polish MEPs do take religion seriously but they are not inscribed in a strong Christian Democratic orthodoxy. They are very mobile between national parties and political groups at the EP. In a constantly changing party environment at home, a somehow old-fashioned and constraining label represents as much a cost as a benefit. Overall, European integration may help to maintain Christian Democracy in national politics even when its constituency is shrinking (for example the Netherlands) through its conservative effect on national systems; but it also emphasises that it is possible to do without this ideological reference successfully at the supranational level, including in efforts to promote religion.

(c) Strong religious parties, weak religious lobbies?

A last comparative question is about the various channels available for voicing religious interests, either by parties through representative democracy or by lobbies through deliberation and participatory democracy; and subsequently, the margin of influence at the European level of religious actors according to national cultures giving priority to one channel or the other.

At first sight, it could be tempting to suggest a dichotomy. In some systems, parties take charge of religious interests and make religious lobbying redundant. Dutch MEPs have relatively little contact with religious NGOs (except secularist MEPs who defend views from philosophical groups without – or with weaker – institutionalised access to decision-making). In other systems, religious views are better promoted through representation of interests. British parties keep religion at a distance but British MEPs have strong connections with religious NGOs. For some nationalities, the equation 'strong religious parties – weak religious lobbies' is verified, but for specific reasons: in Poland, considering the short history of participatory democratisation and the limited pluralism, the culture of representation of religious interests through lobbying is still burgeoning. The Polish Catholic Church matters very much, but not as a civil society actor playing the deliberative game according to Brussels rules.

Italy provides a striking example of the 'de-partyisation' of religion, of the shift of the form of religious influence from party politics to representation of interest. The breakdown of Christian Democracy as the major player has split its heritage between many formations competing to take the ownership of religion turned into a volatile ideological material. The Italian Catholic Church maintains its political role but is evolving from an institutional entity voicing its priorities through spokespersons in the party system to organisations from civil society developing networks within and outside the Italian political space. The movement *Comunione e Liberazione* is the best example of the rise of these new Christian voices. This confirms to a certain extent the equation 'strong religious parties-weak religious lobbies'. The rise of Catholic civil society dates from the decline of institutional Christian Democracy. Italian MEPs and MPs have more and more contacts with religious lobbies, but maybe still less than in other countries where representation of interest is historically the main channel for religious influence.

Overall, it is useful to cast a look at non-European countries to assess the specificity – or not – of the boundaries between party and religious affiliation in Europe. Israel is a configuration where religion is largely addressed by parties in the political space, leaving a limited place to representation of interests. Society as a whole is secularising, but some social and territorial constituencies maintain a strong salience of religion. The link between level of religiosity and political orientation on the one hand and party and religious belonging on the other hand remains strong. In short, the Israeli political world displays the same conservative bias – or a tendency to reformulate religion as an identity resource in spite of its societal loss of relevance – that can be observed in Europe, notwithstanding major differences of intensity and contexts.

In the USA, the specificity is that the combination of religious diversity with high religiosity has precluded development of 'religious' and 'secular' political parties. American parties have always been supported by coalitions of multiple ethnoreligious groups, with distinct world views, cultural preferences and negative reference groups. The logic has remained the same throughout time even if multifaith coalitions have become more and more complex since the 1980s and even if internal divisions within denominations have been reinforced between conservatives and liberals, each side rallying occasionally to a different party. In his contribution to this volume, James Guth argues that both the older ethnoreligious perspective, based on affiliation, and the newer restructuring thesis, stressing the impact of theological orientation, are useful to explain present realities. Some denominations have strong affinities with a party (Black Protestants, Jews and Seculars for the Democrats), but in the major white religious traditions, there is a gap between traditionalists voting for the Republicans and modernists voting for the Democrats. At the EP, the same double pattern may be found, with a resilient influence of denominational belonging and occasional divergences between conservatives and progressives. Again, social realities are very different but may be traversed by comparable tensions.

(6) Conflictuality of religion at home, salience at the EP

The status of religion as an issue in national politics dictates the use that MEPs can make of it at the EP. The more it is controversial, the more it may be rewarding to build political strategies on it, and the more it may also be stimulating to contest it through atheist mobilisation in Brussels and Strasbourg.

When there is a polarisation on religious topics in national politics, this means generally that religion has a strong historical position but that the evolution of society is more and more diverging from this situation; the European arena is a window of opportunity to challenge Christian prevalence. Spain offers such a scenario. There is no coherent and shared narrative framing the reconciliation of politics and religion, of the progressive and conservative sides, so the emergence of religion into contemporary politics does not take place in a stabilised and pacified context. Many politicians opt for silence to avoid clashes, but others go public at the EP by referring to European secularism to denounce the excessive influence of Spanish religious authorities. Italy offers another pattern of high conflictuality of religion in domestic politics, despite its social stronghold. Catholicism was not on the side of nation-building (notably because of the supranational interference of the Vatican and its original presence as a temporal power) or of modernity. Later, Catholicism and communism polarised Italy at the local level. Nowadays, after the demise of Christian Democracy, Catholicism has become a common reference (in the sense that most political actors defer to various contents to religion), but subsequently it may be used by everybody for everything and thus constitutes raw material for controversies such as the Lautsi affair, the selection of Italian politicians applying for European positions or ethical issues like gay rights. This domestic conflictuality means that religion is still appealing for parties as a communicative tool and that Italian MEPs have incentives to invest in this topic to support or oppose religious interests. Italians may be found among 'soldiers of God' or among embattled atheists in Brussels and Strasbourg. It is also worth noticing that the most religious Italian parties have shifted from a strong pro-European stance to a moderately pro- or anti-European one.

By contrast, in countries such as Germany where religion is positively correlated to the building of the nation-state and where the main denominations have elaborated a way to live together, there are few lines of conflict to draw on in order to build a profile of a secularist activist. Such a strategy would come with the cost of breaking the dominant consensus and would have weak benefit. Austria presents a similar logic, with a high level of approval of the existing cooperative model of religious governance and a low number of atheists among the population. When politicisation of religion occurs, it is about non-European countries (violation of religious freedom abroad) and/or non-Christian religion, in particular Islam. In her contribution to this volume, Julia Mourão Permoser argues that the religion of the Other is politicised, but the religion of the Self is not. Atheists cannot focus only on Islam, and explicit Muslim-bashing may be less directly rewarding in functionalist and rationalised deliberations at the EP than in national politics. Some Dutch MEPs are in the front row to promote fundamental rights against religious threats, reflecting the competition between secular and spiritual forces in the consociational Netherlands. Dutch Humanists find a window of opportunity to express their claims at the European level that they do not enjoy in their national closed corporatist system dominated by religious forces. But Dutch MEPs are not particularly vehement against Muslims, and are far from the violence of the domestic controversies. Finally, counter-intuitively, strongly religious or strongly secular countries are not necessarily generous providers of embattled atheist MEPs. For Polish representatives, the entry ticket for the career of anti-Catholic warrior would be very expensive. Secularisation may be progressing in Poland, but standing against religion still appears to be very complicated. Conversely, in France 'laïcité' is supposed to be universal and to concern everybody and everything, including religious actors who defer to this narrative. Some political entrepreneurs may support a more radical version aiming at totally excluding religion, but to turn atheism into a cause among others could to a certain extent be felt as a particularisation of their view. Besides, an aggressive encompassing secularism has no chance of succeeding at the EP, where many political cultures valorise the social and ethical role of religion. By contrast, British Humanists are well-structured and leading forces in the 'anti-God faction' in EU arenas. This is not a result of a high conflictuality of religious issues in the UK, but rather of the pluralist tradition allowing all visions to be expressed in a competitive process.

(7) Importance of territoriality in the resilience of religion

European integration may open national boundaries and challenge – indirectly – the monopoly of national centres on the regulation of spiritual affairs, but territoriality still matters very much for the development of interactions between politics and religion. It is visible in the context of the role of local constituencies to maintain the electoral weight of religion, as well as in geopolitics, when religion impacts neighbourhood relationships.

(a) Electoral influence and resistance of local constituencies

The survival of religion as a significant electoral variable depends largely on the way it exists on the map both regarding its intensity and its denominational distribution. Regions keeping a high level of religiosity constitute bastions where parties are incited to keep religion on the agenda as there is something to win on these issues. That is not the case when electors influenced by religious topics are disseminated all over the country. The Dutch 'Bible Belt' is a good illustration of this secondarity of religion to other belongings and cleavages, here territorial ones. Another example is Italy, where Catholicism has always relied on its positions at the local level for weight in national politics, in opposition to communism which was also retrenched in its historical strongholds. The fact that constituencies keep a certain level of religiosity (or concern for religion) obliges candidates to defer to religious values, or at least to do lip-service on relevant issues. This religious territoriality creates a path dependence likely to offer resistance for a while to secularisation, even if reform of the electoral system may quicken the evolution. More generally, the geographical concentration of a denomination that turns it into a large force able to make a decision at the ballot box is likely to impact on how candidates try or not to appeal to it. The weak representation of Muslims at the EP may be explained, among other things, by the fact that they are not dominant in regions at the scale of European constituencies.

(b) Religion to draw Europe and boundaries

Another territorial dimension of religion is the area of geopolitics. Geopolitics seems to impact on how religion is dealt with (often mobilising religion in a broader framework) rather than religion structuring geopolitics. For example, Austrian MEPs have stronger views on enlargement than their counterparts from other member-states in the context of the Turkish application to join the EU. This is a legacy of the historical conflict with the Ottoman Empire, but leads now to a focus on Islam. Meanwhile Italian MEPs clearly view Turkey as foreign to the realm of European culture defined in Christian terms. This religious territoriality is far more important than other possible geographical narratives such as the Mediterranean identity of Europe. Polish MEPs use religion to justify the adhesion of fellow Christian countries (Western Balkan countries, Ukraine, Belarus', Georgia, Armenia); this is also a way to serve national interests by creating a 'protective cushion' between Poland and Russia. Within the EU, the religious issue may also create solidarity between member-states: Polish MEPs voiced their support for Hungary when the latter was targeted by the rest of the EU over its illiberal norms inspired by a religious view of national identity. For a Catholic Polish politician, it was a strategic move to claim the right for each nation to accommodate religion freely at home without European interference.

Concluding remark

To conclude this survey of religion and politics in various configurations, it is necessary to insist once more on the importance of contextualising extensively each case study. Religion does not exist as a variable *per se*, producing deterministic effects across time and space. In each country or political system, religion influences politics (and is influenced in return) in a unique way according to history, culture, social dynamics, institutional and economic structures. Frequently, religion, culture and politics are so intertwined that it is simply impossible to distinguish one from another. Secularisation means the loss of the social grasp of religion but also its culturalisation and subjectivisation, turning it into an even more elusive and deep dimension of individual and collective identity, memory and values.

Funding

The RelEP project was funded with support from the European Commission through the Jean Monnet Chair 'Social and Cultural Dimensions of European Integration', SocEUR [529183-LLP-2012-BE-AJM-CH]. This publication reflects the views only of the author, and the Commission cannot be held responsible for any use which may be made of the information contained therein. RelEP has also benefited from the support of research grants from the Université Libre de Bruxelles and the Belgian Fonds National de la Recherche Scientifique.

Index

ADA, *see* Americans for Democratic Action
age diversity, 7
Agreement of Villa Madama, 125
ALDE, *see* Alliance of Liberals and Democrats for Europe
Alliance of Liberals and Democrats for Europe (ALDE), 77, 127
Americans for Democratic Action (ADA), 205
Austrian MEPs: brief history of, 151–153; impact of religion, 157; parliamentary questions, 159–161; policy-making, religion, 157–158; political Catholicism, 154; politics and religion, 153–156; quasi state churches, 153; religious affiliation, 155; religious belief and preferences, 158–159; secularisation, 152; survery and, 156–157

Bible Belt, 64, 66, 227
British MEPs: directives and policies, 84–88; national context, 82–84; open door policy, 78–80; religious belonging but not believing, 80–82; religious group by country, 85; religious interest groups, 78–80; religious organisations by country, 86; survey questionnaire and, 76–78; theological differences, 26

Catholic MEPs, 11
CCF, *see* Conservative Christian Fellowship
CCME, *see* Churches' Commission for Migrants in Europe
CDA, *see* Christen-Democratisch Appel
CDU, *see* Christian Democratic Party
CEC, *see* Conference of European Churches
Christen-Democratisch Appel (CDA), 61, 63–64
ChristenUnie (CU), 64
Christian Democracy, 224–225
Christian Democratic Party (CDU), 46–47, 61, 125
Christian Socialist Movement (CSM), 80
Christian Social Union (CSU), 46–47

Churches' Commission for Migrants in Europe (CCME), 31
church–state relations model: brief history, 44–45; 'regime of partial establishment,' 45; religious communities, 47; religious pluralisation, 47; secularisation, 46; social welfare system, 45–46
class politics, 20
COMECE, *see* Commission of the Bishops' Conferences of the European Community
Commission of the Bishops' Conferences of the European Community (COMECE), 114
committee memberships: Dutch MEPs, 71–72; members of the European Parliament, 8
Committee on Civil Liberties, Justice and Home Affairs, 127
Communist Party of Italy, 126
Conference of European Churches (CEC), 78
Conservative Christian Fellowship (CCF), 80
consociational democracy, 63
consociation, Dutch MEPs, 62–63
CSM, *see* Christian Socialist Movement
CSU, *see* Christian Social Union
CU, *see* ChristenUnie
'cultural Christians,' 23, 34–35
cultural liberalism, 35–36
culture war, 202, 208

Declaration of the Establishment of the State of Israel, 190, 192
democracy, consociational, 63
denominational belonging, 11
discrete cultural Christianity, 47
Dutch MEPs: beliefs of, 67; consociation, 62–63; description, 61–62; European political arena, 62; exceptionalism, 64–66; from national to European level, 66–67; pillarisation, 62–63; policy entrepreneurs and committee memberships, 71–72; religiosity, 67–68; religious and party lines, 70–71; religious lobby groups, 70; religiously divided party system, 63–64;

INDEX

UDF, *see* Union for French Democracy
ULB, *see* Université Libre de Bruxelles
UMP, *see* Union for a Popular Movement
Union for a Popular Movement (UMP), 94
Union for French Democracy (UDF), 94
Université Libre de Bruxelles (ULB), 76–77
US electoral politics, 201–202
US House of Representatives: ethnocultural alignments, challenges, 204–206; religion and ideological orientation, 208; religious activity and theological orientation, 203;
religious restructuring, triumph of, 206–211; religious traditions, 203–204; religious traits, 206; religious variables, ideology and partisanship, 209, 211

Volkspartij voor Vrijheid en Democratie (VVD), 64
VVD, *see Volkspartij voor Vrijheid en Democratie*

Zionist movement, 186–187

For Product Safety Concerns and Information please contact our EU representative GPSR@taylorandfrancis.com Taylor & Francis Verlag GmbH, Kaufingerstraße 24, 80331 München, Germany

Batch number: 08151566

Printed by Printforce, the Netherlands